WITHDRAWN

Analog
Electronic Music
Techniques

Consulting Editor: Gerald Warfield

Analog
Electronic Music
Techniques

In Tape, Electronic,
and Voltage-Controlled
Synthesizer Studios

Joel Naumann and James D. Wagoner

SCHIRMER BOOKS
A Division of Macmillan, Inc.
NEW YORK

Collier Macmillan Publishers
LONDON

Schirmer Books
A Division of Macmillan, Inc.
866 Third Avenue, New York, N.Y. 10022

Collier Macmillan Canada, Inc.

Library of Congress Catalog Card Number: 83-24809

Printed in the United States of America

printing number
1 2 3 4 5 6 7 8 9 10

Library of Congress Cataloging in Publication Data

Naumann, Joel.
    Analog electronic music techniques.

    Bibliography: p.
    Discography: p.
    Includes index.
    1. Electronic music—Instruction and study.
2. Synthesizer (Musical instrument)—Methods.   3. Musical instruments, Electronic.   I. Wagoner, James D.
II. Title.
MT723.N38   1984   789.9′9   83-24809
ISBN 0-02-873140-9

Contents

List of Figures and Patches

Foreword

For the few of us who started at the dawn of the 1950s to explore the uncharted territory of composing with sounds directly on tape (recorded by ourselves, or already existing in this form), reading this book is like viewing a series of snapshots taken on numerous trips both to known and unfamiliar destinations. The meticulously organized pages are a compendium of proven methods and approaches to utilization of the specialized electronic and mechanical resources as responsive tools to the demands of the composer's imagination. The selected compositional examples, while specifically illustrating points taken in the corresponding text, must, by all means, also be listened to as representative of the enormous literature scattered through many hundreds of recordings—a reflection of the unprecedented interest in the technological means servicing one of the most ancient of arts.

It is now only of historical interest to recall that in the early years of musique concrete in France (1946–), tape music in the United States (1951–), and electronic music in Germany (1952–), the production of what more often than not was called "Experimental Music" depended on utilization of the existing recording and engineering tools. Those were also the years when a few musically inclined engineers and technically inclined composers began to collaborate on designing specialized equipment to expand the limited potential for sound modification found in standard equipment. In France, for example, both timbral and pitch modification potential, first discovered in playing the tape at "wrong" speed, was greatly enhanced by the ingenious 12 half-step transposing mechanical device called "Phonogene" controlled by the small keyboard. I adopted a method of driving a capstan motor of an Ampex tape recorder with a combination of a sinewave oscillator and an amplifier while, in Canada, Hugh Le Cain used a DC keyboard-controlled motor to vary the speed of numerous tape loops (hear "Dripsody," listed at the end of Chapter 2). The importance of this technique has been largely overlooked in studios which depend primarily on electronic sources for synthesis. Yet it remains the only method of obtaining a complete scale of discrete steps within a total audible range from a complex, single-pitch instrument such as a gong. (Presently available digital means of achieving such a scale are very costly.) Numerous other instances of collaboration between engineering designers and composers resulted in creating tools serving the needs of composers anxious to find better solutions to processing raw materials into musically satisfying works.

It is not a purpose of this foreword to engage in reminiscences, nor is there room to propound all the questions one is tempted to ask from the position of deep personal involvement with electronic music of 32 years. Yet, how could one best summarize the present position of electronic music and its still far-from-exhausted promise for the future? Of what significance is the curious turnaround from the massive expansion of the previously untried sound resources in the late 1940s and through the early 1960s—a period of noninstrumental or *anti*-instrumental character of electronic music—to the present proliferation of digital synthesizers with conventional keyboards? Are we now concentrating on imitating conventional instruments at the expense of the ever-important search for ways by which music can be enriched through an access to the enormous body of concrete and synthesized sound materials, and through the sophisticated techniques for modification and imaginative arrangement of these materials by using the tools and the methods so thoroughly described in this book?

I recommend that the reader obtain answers to parts of these questions by first reading the excellent Introduction, and the beginning of Chapter 15, "Electronic Music Composition," which discuss the particular nature of electronic music. Specifically addressing composers, I would also like to add the well-experienced observation that it is essential to understand that one should approach the electronic gear at his or her disposal not only to execute a preconceived compositional notion, but also to set up experimental situations that are likely to produce unplanned combinations and modifications of the materials. Machines can be coaxed into improvisational modes by clever interferences with easily obtained periodicity in rhythm, in envelope control settings, random triggering, and so on. The results of such experimental sessions make it possible to assess more fully the potential of the material at hand and, at times, suggest important changes in one's original conception.

This book provides the exhaustive technical know-how. Your imagination will still be the principal guide in avoiding routine solutions and helping reach that difficult objective: to convey in sound your creative insight in the manner that would engage the interest of others and would help to sustain meaningfully that body of music which will become a permanent cultural inheritance for future generations.

Vladimir A. Ussachevsky

Preface

Throughout history, regardless of epoch, civilization, or culture, music has been regarded as an art form requiring the mastery of certain carefully defined skills. It is our belief, and the basis of this text, that the tape recorder, various electronic devices, and the voltage-controlled synthesizer are merely new musical instruments that require the learning and practice of certain skills before one is able to "perform" or "compose" effectively with them. In many ways these skills are directly analogous to those required of other musicians who learn to "synthesize" sounds by "modulating" the column of air or length of string of their acoustic musical instruments. Electronic music is but an extension of these concepts made more complex by the almost unlimited sonic resources available to it. If anything, this greater complexity requires an even greater mastery of skills than the more finitely constructed and sonically limited acoustic instruments. Yet, in practice, this seemingly obvious need is seldom realized.

All too often a school will turn its students loose in an electronic studio without any *systematic* instruction in the use of the equipment or its potential. Although any exposure is better than none, this approach is almost always frustrating and wasteful for the students, who are trying to achieve mastery of very complex instruments first hand. In this situation, any meaningful interaction with the equipment that does occur can usually be attributed to mere good fortune. It is the lack of any currently available, logical, and systematic approach to learning about electronic music instruments, techniques, and processes that has prompted us to produce this text.

Further, the electronic music composer can be said to create a new musical instrument (or ensemble of instruments) for every piece he or she composes. It is the way in which the specific components of an electronic music studio interrelate with one another that defines the sound that can be produced from them at any given moment. To leave the discovery of the nature of these relationships to blind experimentation would be about as fruitful as asking an untrained person to assemble a fifty-rank pipe organ from scratch. He might very well get sound out of his creation, but he could hardly be expected to take full advantage of the instrument's potential.

Our intent is to provide the student of electronic music with an understanding of techniques that is both fundamental and comprehensive. It was derived from courses open to students of all majors and backgrounds; so it assumes no special prior knowledge or training. Musicians with no understanding of acoustics or electronics as well as engineers unable to name the notes of a diatonic scale should be equally comfortable with the material as it is presented. Further, we believe that everyone who successfully completes the course of study outlined in this text will have the ability to effectively operate almost any analog tape, electronic, or voltage-controlled synthesizer studio with only a minimum of adjustment to any particular equipment set-up that is likely to be found. This is true principally because we have *not* attempted to discuss specific brands or models of equipment, except in those cases where the uniqueness and/or importance of a particular brand or model makes it imperative to do so. We assume that this text will be supplemented by the owner's manuals for the specific equipment available in any particular studio.

Organization

The organization of this text follows a sequence of lessons, experiments, and projects developed for electronic music classes at The Catholic University of America in Washington, D.C. and at the University of Wisconsin at Madison, Wisconsin. The course of study it outlines is suitable for a year-long course in basic analog electronic music techniques. Class sessions should be supplemented by extensive and regular "hands-on" studio experience.

. Coordinated with the description of devices and techniques are exercises and projects that not only enhance the students' understanding of the topics covered, but provide for an immediate and practical application of essential skills. The projects progress from beginning ones, in which little room is provided for the students' creative imagination, to later ones that are essentially designed by the students themselves. Since our approach is basically utilitarian, we have tried to avoid the introduction of any material before it can be experimented with and applied in the studio.

Part I, "Tape and Electronic Music Studios," deals with the equipment, techniques, and processes that, besides being complete in themselves, are a necessary prerequisite to the use of the voltage-controlled synthesizer. In doing so it accomplishes two separate goals simultaneously: it covers all of the skills and techniques of the electronic music studio up to the introduction of the concepts and applications of voltage control, and it acquaints the student with the compositional practices of the various historical schools of electronic music (musique concrète, elektronische Musik, and tape music) that existed prior to the development of the voltage-controlled synthesizer and that are still an important part of current technique.

Part II, "Voltage-Controlled Synthesizer Studios," is a systematic examination of the nature and operation of the voltage-controlled synthesizer. After an introductory chapter (Chapter 8) on the nature of the voltage-control process itself, each type of control voltage studied is first applied to one single parameter of sound: frequency. We chose this approach because it illustrates the different effects of the various control voltages in the most readily perceivable way—as a change of pitch. This method of presentation remains consistent with the deliberate layering of successively more difficult tasks and concepts that underlies the book as a whole.

Part III, "Electronic Music Composition," is devoted to the compositional concepts that most often perplex students of electronic music. By this time, the student should have enough command of, and experience in, analog electronic music techniques to benefit from such a discussion and to begin effectively "composing" in the medium. Our final chapter consists entirely of suggested composition projects that we believe will stimulate the continued growth of technical skill and musical imagination.

Some Final Thoughts

We have *not* attempted to extend our coverage of electronic music to include digital or computer synthesis. The burgeoning possibilities of this field could well fill an entire book by themselves. It *has been* our intention to develop a fundamental technique and approach to the analog studio that will enable students to progress to unsupervised creative work in analog electronic music composition. Naturally, this would lay a firm and essential foundation for later studies of digital electronic music.

Throughout this book we have stressed discipline, technique, and adherence to recognized standards. Yet, we have also tried not to strangle the student in needless pedantry. This balance is particularly evident in the system of block diagramming. It is efficient, (avoiding the need to draw or memorize special shapes and codes) and at the same time gives the student an effective, flexible shorthand that is not arbitrarily complex. It is our belief that block diagramming—in the context of analog electronic music—is needed more as a personal aid than a public notation; so we have chosen a system that is adaptable to the individual, yet, when properly used, quite meaningful.

Aside from providing a limited discography geared to the specific techniques covered in the text, we have alluded only briefly to the historical development of electronic music and the compositions produced in this medium. There are several excellent books available that do precisely this, and our suggestion is to use one of them along with this text.

The knowledge and perspective such a book can provide will acquaint the student with the infinite variety of "musics" available from the analog electronic music studio and, when he or she is proficient enough to perform or to compose in the medium, will serve as a spur to the creative imagination.

J. N. and J. D. W.

Acknowledgments

When we began writing this book, we naively expected to have it on the shelves within a year. As that year slipped past as well as another, it was the patience of Gordon T. R. Anderson, Executive Editor, and Gerald Warfield, Series Editor, that allowed us to continue our efforts. The book has greatly benefited from the technical advice of Reynold Weidenaar, who guided us through several levels of confusion and could doubtless take us even farther if we had the time. Others who have advised on specific topics include William Burns and James Stuht, and the comments of numerous students have always been instructive. As with any long-term effort, there are many who deserve recognition for their support and consideration. We hope they will accept our gratitude, which may have gone long unspoken.

J. N. and J. D. W.

Part I: Tape and Electronic Music Studios

Chapter 1
The Tape Studio

HISTORICAL BACKGROUND

The first tape composition techniques—conceived by French composer Pierre Schaeffer in 1948 as Musique Concrète—involved the manipulation and transformation of natural or environmental (noninstrumental) recorded sounds. Speaking and singing voices, animal and bird sounds, street noises, and even the shattering of glass were for the first time considered raw musical material waiting to be organized and composed in a musical context. This concept of the musical potential of *all* sounds represented an even more profound and revolutionary advancement in musical thought than the earlier dissolution of the tonal system.

Through the expansion of the available musical material to include a virtually unlimited range of sounds, the previous hierarchies of finite pitch systems and a thousand years of learned musical associations were supplemented by new possibilities of unprecedented promise and challenge. It was the introduction of a single technological advancement—the tape recorder—that made such a revision of the conception of Western music possible.

Early tape compositions were accomplished with a minimum of equipment: a microphone, a tape machine, recording tape, and splicing materials. It was the composer's imagination and technical abilities that most defined the nature of the music. Today, increasingly challenged by technological advances, the composer's most precious tools are still intellect, intuitive insight, and technical skill. The temptation to be mesmerized by special effects and easily produced sonic tricks is probably the single greatest trap for the beginning electronic music student. Though tape music does rely on technical equipment for its production, it exists solely because of human insight, and it is, in the final analysis, the creativity of the composer that will be reflected in the results.

The Recording Process

The tape studio functions in two fundamentally distinct, yet equally important capacities for the electronic music composer. First, it is a practical means for the collection, storage, and reproduction of sounds; it is capable of preserving every quality of a sound for a virtually unlimited time (assuming certain safeguards). Second, it is a collection of devices that makes it possible for the composer to manipulate and organize an infinite number of sounds in an infinite number of ways.

Essential to each of the above functions is the composer's ability to make recordings of high quality, an ability that depends on the composer's thorough understanding of the devices and techniques employed in the recording process. Since almost every electronic music composition (except for computer-generated works and some live performance

3

pieces) will require the use of the recording process at some point, the importance of good recording techniques cannot be overemphasized.

In order to understand the recording process, it is necessary to follow the progress of a sound from its source to the final recording. Although a more comprehensive discussion of the properties of sound will be given in Chapter 4, for the time being it will be enough to state that sound results from the vibration of a physical body usually, but not necessarily, in the atmosphere.

The original Edison phonograph converted vibrations in the air (sounds) directly into vibrations of a diaphragm. A needle attached to this diaphragm mechanically transmitted these vibrations to a rotating metal cylinder, cutting grooves into a thin sheet of tinfoil on its surface. These grooves were an analogous record of the vibrations of the air that had moved the diaphragm. When the needle was again placed at the beginning of the groove and the cylinder was rotated, the needle would transmit the variations in the groove back to the diaphragm, which would vibrate as it had when the sound had been recorded. The air around the diaphragm would subsequently vibrate as it had before, producing a facsimile of the original sound.

The electronic tape recording process is merely an extension of this basic concept several steps further. Sonic vibrations are converted to analogous changes in the flow of electric current. These changes are then recorded as variations in the magnetic flux of particles of metallic oxide that coat a thin strip of tape. When the tape is played back the process is reversed so that the changes in magnetic flux on the tape become changes in electric current that cause a diaphragm (this time a loudspeaker) to vibrate in the air, recreating the original sound (Figure 1.1).

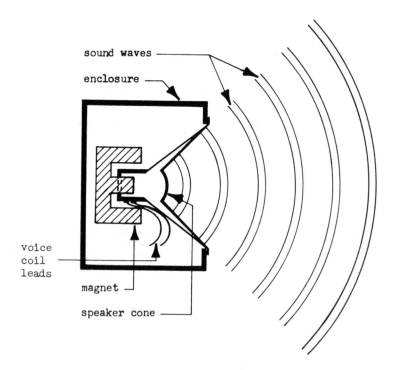

Figure 1.1   Loudspeaker Cross-Section

MICROPHONES

Electroacoustic Transducers

Both the first and last steps of the electronic tape recording process require the use of *electroacoustic transducers*, first to change physical vibrations in the air to variations in electric current and, finally, to convert variations in electric current back to physical vibrations. A transducer converts one form of energy into another. The transducer that converts sound into electric current fluctuations is a *microphone*. The transducer that converts electric current fluctuations into sound vibrations is a *loudspeaker*.

Since sound is basically vibrations in a physical medium, it is the character or pattern of these vibrations that is transformed into a synonymous electrical signal. This can be accomplished in two ways: by making direct contact with the physical body producing the vibrations, or by sensing the vibrations in the atmosphere. In the first case, the transducer used is a *contact microphone*, since it is placed in direct contact with the vibrating body producing the sound. In the second case, the transducer used is an *acoustic microphone*, since it senses vibrations in the air around the vibrating body.

Contact Microphones

Contact microphones are often used by instrumentalists who want a great deal of freedom of movement without the inconsistencies and variations in sound quality that would result if a free-standing acoustic microphone were used. There have also been many pieces composed that take advantage of the extreme sensitivity of contact microphones. Special effects, such as key slaps on woodwinds or prepared piano techniques, become quite audible when the signal is amplified by a contact microphone attached to the instrument. The contact microphone's principal drawbacks result from its usually limited frequency response and its oversensitivity to the incidental sounds made by every acoustic musical instrument (such as the sounds of the hammers striking the strings of a piano). However, many potentially interesting instrumental and noninstrumental sounds, not perceivable with acoustic microphones, can be picked up by contact microphones. (For example, try connecting a contact microphone to several different mechanical devices, such as clocks, wind-up toys, and small electric motors, and notice the effects when these sounds are amplified.)

Acoustic Microphones

Most recording involves the use of acoustic microphones, which can be classified according to their basic design characteristics as *dynamic*, *condenser*, or *ribbon*. Microphones of each type are widely available and in general use, though dynamic and condenser microphones make up the largest segment of the market and find the broadest application.

Dynamic Microphones

The *dynamic* microphone is by far the most prevalent, due largely to its economy and rugged construction. The principles behind its construction and operation are also quite simple: a flexible diaphragm, which moves in response to vibrations in the air, is connected to a coil of wire that moves in a magnetic field (Figure 1.2a). This movement creates small changes in electric current directly proportional to the vibrations. Basically, a dynamic microphone is nothing but a speaker in reverse, and in certain inexpensive intercom systems the speaker actually serves both functions.

Condenser Microphones

The *condenser* (also known as capacitor or electrostatic) microphone (Figure 1.2b) is preferred by most professional recording technicians because of its superior sensitivity to high frequencies and its faster transient response. It is designed so that a current that is passed through a very thin metal diaphragm and a parallel but stationary metal plate varies its capacitance (a measure of the opposition to change in voltage) in relation to the movement of the diaphragm. Because the foil diaphragm is extremely thin, it responds

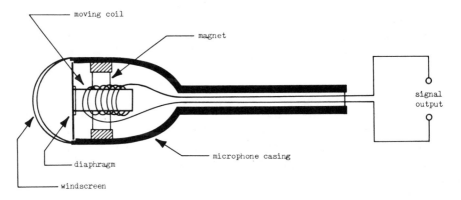

a) the Dynamic (electromagnetic) Microphone

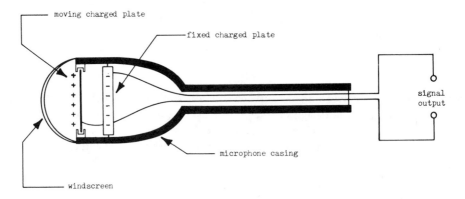

b) the Condenser (electrostatic) Microphone

Figure 1.2   Dynamic and Condenser Microphones

easily and rapidly to the full frequency and dynamic range of sounds. From the highest overtones of musical instruments to the subtleties of the human voice, a vivid presence and veracity is given to the sound. Since the purpose of any microphone is to relay the properties of the sound as faithfully as possible, the condenser microphone is deservedly popular with recording technicians. However, condenser microphones tend to be relatively expensive and also require a carefully regulated power supply (to establish the necessary capacitance) and preamplifier (external or internal—depending on the unit) for their operation.

If the mechanical principles behind the operation of a condenser microphone seem complex, it is probably useful to note that, as with many devices in the tape or electronic music studio, it is less important to understand precisely how the device works than it is to understand what it can do and how to use it effectively.

Ribbon Microphones

Ribbon microphones have diminished in popularity over recent years as the quality of less fragile dynamic and condenser microphones has improved. Basically a form of dynamic microphone, the ribbon microphone consists of a very thin ribbon of metal foil suspended in a magnetic field. When vibrating, this foil produces a small electric current just as the coil of the dynamic microphone does, except that the ribbon serves as both the diaphragm and the electrical element. Owing to this they have excellent transient response and a slight resonance that tends to subtly color the sounds picked up. This coloration, much like other forms of resonance, is said to make the sounds seem more full and "warm." Although recent improvements have made them much more rugged, while maintaining their extreme sensitivity, they are still very expensive and require a great deal of care in their handling.

Polar Patterns

An essential characteristic of any microphone, regardless of whether it is a dynamic, condenser, or ribbon design, is its directional response. The spatial area or pattern of greatest sensitivity of the microphone influences its applicability in particular recording situations. Unlike a human listener, who has the ability to direct his attention toward a desired sound and substantially block out all other sounds, a microphone cannot discriminate between the desired sound and incidental noises; nor can it redirect its attention to the location of the most interesting sounds. For these reasons, microphones have been designed so that they are sensitive to specific spatial regions or directions and insensitive to others. In effect this makes it possible to aim the microphone toward desired sounds, while limiting its response to any sounds coming from other directions. However, the microphone will still be unable to choose between wanted and unwanted sounds that lie in the same direction, since it lacks the discrimination of human perception.

Omnidirectional Polar Pattern

A microphone that is equally sensitive to sounds coming from all directions is known as *omnidirectional*. Figure 1.3 is a diagram of the polar pattern (a graph showing a microphone's sensitivity to the sounds arriving from various directions) of an omni-

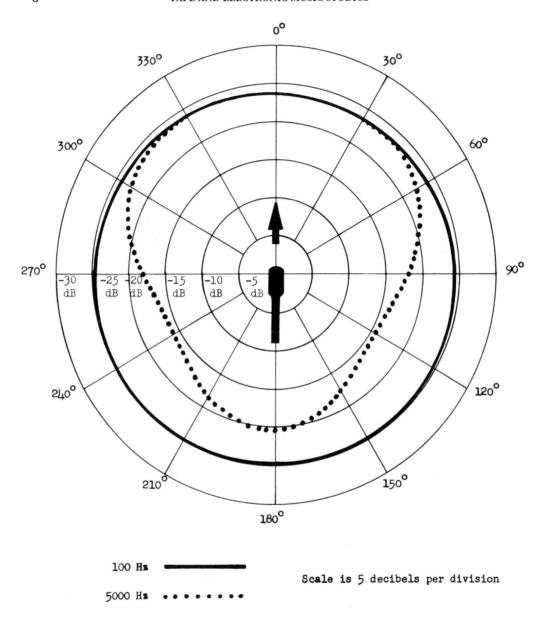

100 Hz ━━━━━━━

Scale is 5 decibels per division

5000 Hz • • • • • • • •

Figure 1.3 Polar Pattern of an Omnidirectional Microphone

directional microphone. The center of the graph is the position of the microphone, and the 0° axis is the direction in which it is pointing. Although this diagram is only two dimensional, the effects of microphone sensitivity are actually three dimensional, having vertical as well as horizontal components. As the distance from the center of the diagram becomes greater, the responsiveness of the microphone diminishes proportionally. (Note the five-decibel difference between concentric circles of the graph. The *decibel*, a measurement of the relative loudness of sounds, is discussed in Chapter 4.) The effect of the various directional patterns of microphones can be demonstrated by having someone carry a metronome in a perfect circle around the microphone as the signal is monitored over a loudspeaker. Each directional pattern should reveal its distinctive characteristics as variations in the perceived loudness of the signal.

Unidirectional Polar Pattern

The *unidirectional* (or *cardioid*—from its heart shaped pattern) microphone is most sensitive to sounds that originate from directly in front of it, as can be seen from its polar pattern (Figure 1.4). Unlike the omnidirectional microphone, which does not distin-

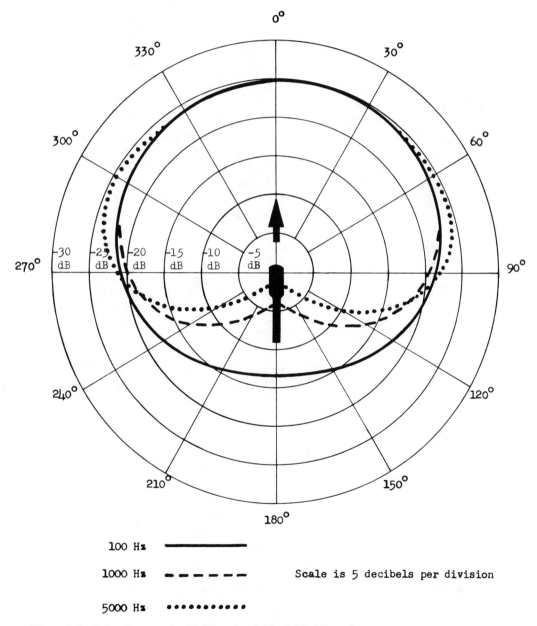

Figure 1.4 Polar Pattern of a Unidirectional (Cardoid) Microphone

guish among sounds originating from any particular direction, the unidirectional microphone clearly favors sounds originating along its 0° axis. Not only is the unidirectional microphone's sensitivity to sounds that originate off the 0° axis reduced, but the frequency response of the microphone in relation to various off-axis sources declines. In general, the unidirectional microphone will respond well to the broadest range of frequencies when the source sound is within 45 to 60 degrees of the 0° axis. Beyond this point, the high (treble) frequency response will be gradually lessened, so that sounds originating severely off the 0° axis will appear dull or muddy. This effect is known as *off-axis coloration*, because of the distorted, or colored, frequency response characteristics in these areas of its polar pattern.

Another peculiarity of many unidirectional microphones is known as the *proximity effect*. Basically, this is an increase in the low (bass) frequency response as the microphone is moved closer to the sound source (Figure 1.5). Although this can be beneficial in some cases, since it increases the apparent depth or warmth of a source sound, the effect may be quite inconsistent and oversensitive to very small changes in the distance between the microphone and the source. Sudden shifts in the bass response caused by even small changes in the distance from the sound source to the microphone (typical when recording an acoustic instrument) can become quite noticeable. In general, this effect will only be significant at distances of two feet (61 cm) or less, and many high-quality unidirectional microphones have built-in bass "roll-off" filters to compensate for the effect when it is undesirable. The omnidirectional microphone usually suffers neither from off-axis coloration nor the proximity effect, making it a viable substitute for the unidirectional microphone in some cases.

Bidirectional Polar Pattern

The polar pattern of a *bidirectional* microphone (Figure 1.6) shows two areas of maximum sensitivity, one directly in front of the microphone, along the 0° axis, and one

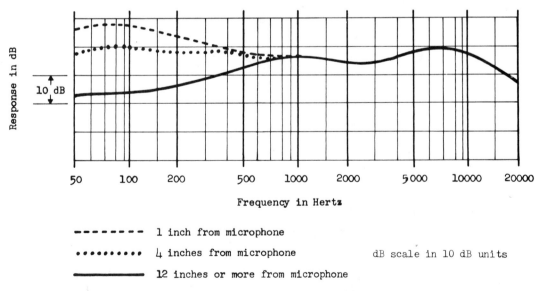

– – – – – – – 1 inch from microphone

• • • • • • • • • 4 inches from microphone   dB scale in 10 dB units

—————— 12 inches or more from microphone

Figure 1.5 Proximity Effect in a Unidirectional (Cardoid) Microphone

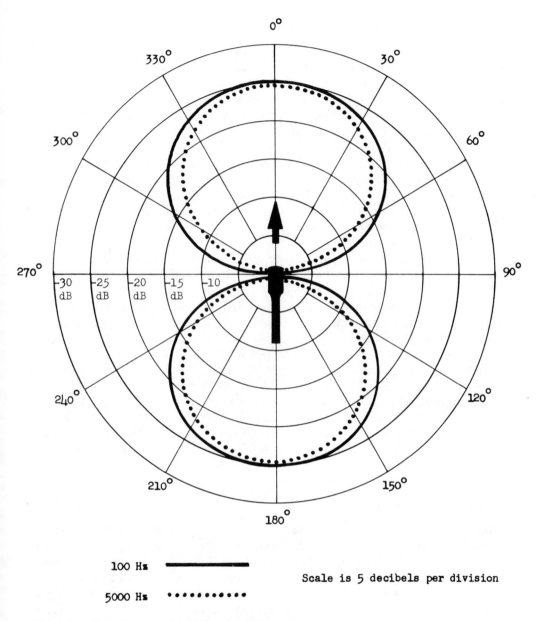

Figure 1.6 Polar Pattern of a Bidirectional Microphone

directly behind the microphone, along the 180° axis. This design is of limited utility in most recording situations, but it can be used quite effectively for recording two separate sound sources simultaneously, such as musical duets or across-the-table conversations. In some cases, where incidental noise is not significant, the rear sensitivity of the bidirectional microphone can be used to pick up room ambience and reverberation. Some bidirectional polar patterns are created by combining, in the same unit, two unidirectional polar patterns facing in opposite directions, making them susceptible to the proximity effect and off-axis coloration.

Microphone Selection

Selection of a microphone particularly suited to a specific recording situation or desired effect is a complex process relying, as often as not, on subjective judgments. However, from the various descriptions of microphone types and polar patterns already given, it is easy to see that some performance characteristics would be better suited to some situations than would others. When the source sound is moving—for instance, an actor on a stage—an omnidirectional microphone would be most useful, since it is less dependent upon the direction of the source sound than a unidirectional or bidirectional microphone. On the other hand, if the source sound is stationary and there are other, unwanted sound sources present in the recording environment (audience noise at a lecture, for instance), a unidirectional microphone would produce the most favorable ratio of desired to undesired sonic material. In some cases, microphones are designed so that the directional pattern can be changed to fit any of the standard polar patterns merely by flipping a switch.

Another characteristic of microphone design is *impedance*, the resistance of the microphone circuit to the flow of alternating current (measured in ohms, represented by the symbol "Z"). Virtually all professional-quality microphones are low-impedance (less than 600 ohms), because this allows the use of very long microphone cables without the high-frequency signal loss that would result from the use of high-impedance microphones over long cable lengths. High-impedance microphones (several thousand ohms or more) will lose the high frequency content of the signal over relatively short cable lengths. However, this effect can be avoided by inserting an impedance transformer in the line (usually no more than 10 feet from the microphone).

Microphones should generally be acquired in pairs, initially, since accurate stereophonic recording would normally require the microphones to have the same characteristics. A pair of condenser microphones with multiple-directional-pattern capabilities and relatively flat frequency response would be a wise first investment, finances permitting.

Recording Environment

The characteristics of a sound are greatly influenced by the environment in which the sound is produced. Thus, singing in the shower is substantially different from singing in a closet, though each space might be the same size. Essentially, the two rooms would normally have different ambient characteristics, that is to say, greater or lesser degrees of sound absorption and reflection. This acoustic effect will be discussed more fully in Chapter 4. For now it is enough to realize that the size, shape, and furnishings of a room will affect the characteristics of a sound produced in that environment and that these effects will be picked up by a microphone placed in the environment (Figure 1.7). Some of these effects can be limited or accentuated by simple physical alterations, such as drawing the curtains and adding carpeting to a room that is too reverberant ("live"), or removing the carpeting and opening the curtains in a room that is too muffled ("dead"). Electronic music composers have often made effective use of unusual acoustic environments to produce special effects, for example, recording in a highly reverberant, concrete stairwell in order to take advantage of the smooth overlapping of sounds caused by extreme reverberation. Thus, it is less pertinent to speak of "good" or "bad" recording environments than it is to consider the appropriateness of the environment to specific goals.

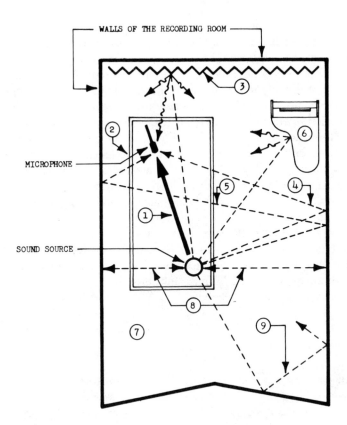

WALLS OF THE RECORDING ROOM

MICROPHONE

SOUND SOURCE

① The distance between the microphone and the sound source will largely determine how many reflections (echoes) of the sound source will be picked up by the microphone. The farther apart they are, the more sound reflections will be picked up; the closer they are, the fewer.

② A sound-absorbing floor covering, such as a rug, will minimise sound reflections from the floor.

③ Drapes absorb sound and will greatly reduce sound reflection from the walls.

④ Single reflections of the sound source from hard wall surfaces will arrive at the microphone later than the direct sound.

⑤ Multiple reflections of the sound source from hard wall surfaces will arrive at the microphone even later than single reflections.

⑥ Furniture in the room will diffuse sound reflections.

⑦ The ceiling will also produce sound reflections, depending upon the material of which it is made.

⑧ Parallel walls will produce multiple or repeating reflections of the sound source (echoes).

⑨ Non-parallel walls will diffuse sound reflections and will prevent multiple or repeating sound reflections (echoes).

Figure 1.7   Effects of the Recording Environment

Microphone Placement

Often the placement of the microphone will have a substantial effect on the nature of the recorded sound, as was noted earlier with the proximity effect. Close microphone placement will result in a much more intimate, less reverberant sound, since the source sound will be much louder than any of its reflections. It will also reduce sensitivity to extraneous sounds or noises, especially if a unidirectional microphone is used (though, again, the proximity effect should be considered). When a microphone is placed very close to the mouth of a speaker or singer, it is advisable to shield the microphone with a windscreen in order to eliminate the thuds and pops caused by plosives (explosive consonants—such as p, t, k, or b). But close microphone placement would not be appropriate in all or even most cases. A number of incidental sounds, such as that of fingers moving across the strings of a guitar from position to position, are masked by distance and room reverberation. Large sound sources, such as orchestras, choirs, or locomotives, require a certain distance for the various distinct component sounds they produce to meld into a single, characteristic sound. Generally, one should experiment with several microphone types and placements to arrive at the most desirable sound. Always bear in mind that the microphone's physical distance from the source sound determines not only the intensity of the sound, but also its clarity, frequency characteristics, and degree of isolation.

MIXERS

In the tape studio, one of the most essential processes is the combination of one sound with another, or with many others, to produce a new, composite sound. This process, known as *additive synthesis*, is made possible by the use of a mixer. Basically, a mixer combines several input signals together to form one, composite output signal. This process can have two results: (1) a single, more complex output in which the various input signals have lost their individual identities while creating a new sound (more or less analogous to the blending of paints); or (2) a texture with various individual components occurring simultaneously but distinctively (as with conventional orchestration).

Signal Regulation

Most mixers provide a separate volume level control for each individual input signal, so that the controls exercised over one signal do not affect any of the others. This ability to isolate and regulate each individual input signal is a very important aspect of the mixer's operation. Since some of the signals are stronger than others, they could adversely affect each other were it not for the mixer's valvelike action, which keeps all of the signals flowing in only one direction. As an analogy, imagine two water pipes (A and B) that join to form a single pipe (C) (Figure 1.8). If the water pressure in pipe A is stronger than that in pipe B, the water of pipe A will flow not only into pipe C, but will also force back the flow of pipe B. The mixer acts as a directional control on each input, channeling it through the system, joining it with other signals, but keeping the signal flow in the same direction at all times. For this reason, "Y" connectors and nonregulated multiples (several jacks linked together) should not be used as mixers, but solely as signal dividers. It is possible to lose or distort the signal or even to damage electronic equipment by

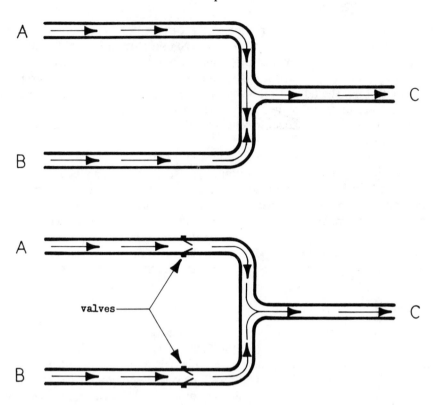

Figure 1.8 Signal Flow

causing signal flows to be impeded or reversed, so the use of a mixer is both a sensible and an efficient safeguard.

Impedance Matching

Another vital function of the mixer is to ensure that each input's impedance is matched to that of the others in order for them to function together. If one input signal to a mixer has a low impedance and another has a high impedance, they cannot be combined together and applied to the same circuit. For this reason, most quality mixers allow for inputs of various impedances that are subsequently matched to the single impedance of the mixer circuit by means of independent impedance transformers for each input. This is another vital function that simple multiple jacks or "Y" connectors cannot provide.

Naturally, the degree of sophistication and versatility of a mixer is reflected in its cost, and many of the features provided on complex mixers are superfluous to most electronic music mixer applications, duplicating the functions of other equipment found in the tape studio. It is best, therefore, to consider the particular situation and its technical demands and to attempt to fit the specifications of a mixer to those needs.

Active and Passive Mixers

The circuitry of a mixer can always be classified as either *active* or *passive*. A *passive mixer* combines two or more input signals without amplifying them. It can be a very simple device that merely regulates the direction of the current flow (providing the valvelike action previously described), or it can be a more complex arrangement allowing for the independent regulation of individual input and output signal levels. If the latter is the case, it is important to note that a passive mixer regulates relative signal strength by *resisting* (attenuating) the flow of the signal, not by amplifying one signal in relation to another. A passive mixer is, by its very nature, incapable of amplifying any signal and will reduce the level of any signal presented to it, to some degree, due to the inherent resistance of its circuitry.

An *active mixer* performs all the functions of a passive mixer but with the added ability to amplify individual input and output signals, allowing for a much broader range of relative signal levels. One input might be quite strong to begin with, requiring little or no amplification, but a weaker signal would have to be amplified in order to balance the stronger one. More important, any signal can be amplified to a greater degree than the other signals present in order to give that specific sound more prominence. All active mixers require a power source of some kind—batteries or line-current—but this is a minor inconvenience in comparison to the advantages they provide.

Mixer Formats

The simplest form of mixer is a circuit that combines two signals together to form one composite signal, often described as 2-in/1-out (or 2 × 1) in order to show the number of incoming and outgoing signals. In most cases, this type of mixer has independent level controls—either rotary potentiometers ("pots") or vertical potentiometers ("faders")—for each input as well as for the composite output signal. They control the level of the signal by resisting its flow to some degree, much as a faucet resists the flow of water.

Simple signal mixers that merely regulate relative signal levels and assign the signals to various outputs are found in most electronic music studios. A typical monophonic mixer would be 4-in/1-out (4 × 1), that is, four input signals combined to form one output signal. A stereo mixer with six inputs would usually be either 6-in/2-out (6 × 2) or 3+3-in/2-out (3+3 × 2) (Figure 1.9). In the former case, any of the six input signals could be assigned to either of the two output channels. In the latter case, three inputs would be inherently assigned to one output channel, and the other three would be assigned to the other output channel. Obviously, the 6-in/2-out (6 × 2) arrangement offers a greater degree of versatility than the 3+3-in/2-out (3+3 × 2).

Often, mixers that allow for switchable output channel assignment also allow for variable signal routing controls called "pan-pots." *Panning* is a recording term that evolved from the visual term *panorama*, meaning an unlimited view in all directions. In motion pictures, to *pan* means to move the camera to get a panoramic effect. When stereophonic recording became popular, the movement of a sound from one channel (or speaker) to another was said to be panoramic, since it gave a sense of spaciousness. Therefore, to move a signal from one channel (speaker) to another by degrees is to *pan* the sound. Pan-pots (panoramic potentiometers) allow a signal to be assigned partially to one output channel and partially to the other, creating the aural effect that the sound originates from neither speaker alone but from the space in between them (Figure 1.10). As the sound becomes louder in one channel, it is decreased in the other channel proportionally, so that when the pan-pot is centered, the sound is balanced in both channels and centered between both speakers.

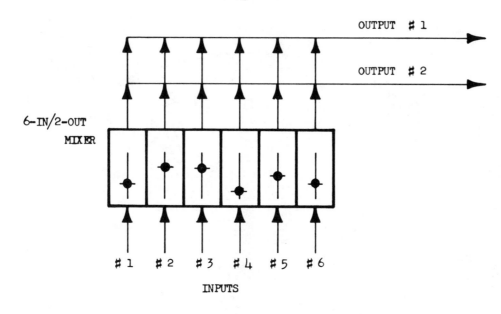

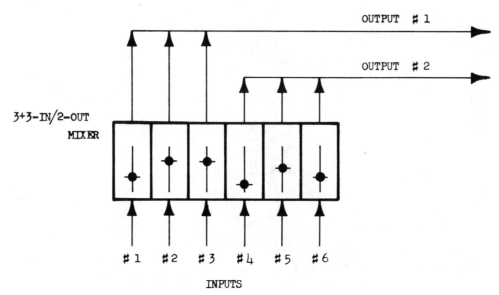

Figure 1.9   Mixer Formats

Channel assignment capabilities of even simple mixers can become quite complex. It is not at all uncommon to find 5+5-in/2-out mixers capable of summing the output channels to form a 10-in/1-out circuit. Even more flexible is the *matrix mixer*. This variant of the simple mixer allows any of its input signals to be assigned to any of its output channels and offers individual amplitude pots for each possible assignment. A 4-in/4-out matrix mixer (Figure 1.11) would therefore offer four channel assignment pots (small circles in the figure) for each signal input and, in some cases, individual pots for the control of each output channel level.

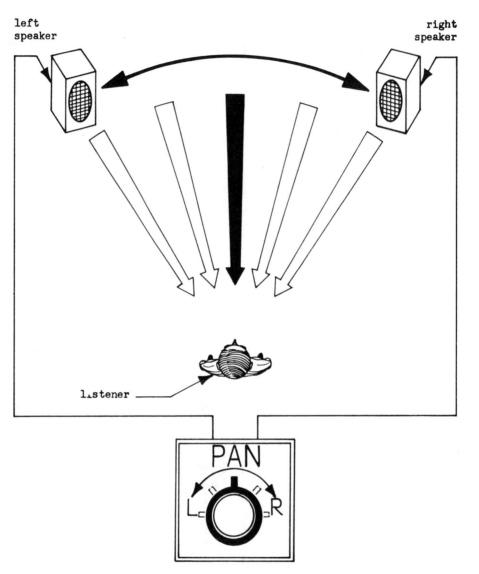

Figure 1.10   The Effects of a "Pan-Pot"

VU Meters

Many simple signal mixers have *VU meters* for each output channel. A VU meter (Figure 1.12) indicates relative signal strength (sound level) and is calibrated in decibels (dB) from −20 dB to +3 dB or as much as +10 dB (decibels will be discussed in Chapter 4). A second demarcation, parallel to the decibel scale, is set out from 0 to 100% so that the 100% mark coincides with the 0 dB mark. The percentage scale is used in radio broadcasting to indicate the amount of signal modulation taking place. Any signal consistently stronger than the 0 dB mark (into the red colored region of most VU meters) has a good chance of being distorted by the circuitry of the mixer, but occasional momentary signal peaks over the 0 dB mark are usually tolerable.

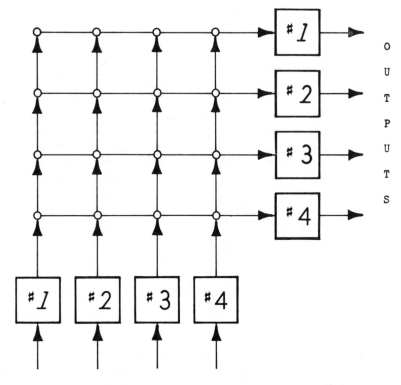

Figure 1.11   4-In/4-Out Martrix Mixer

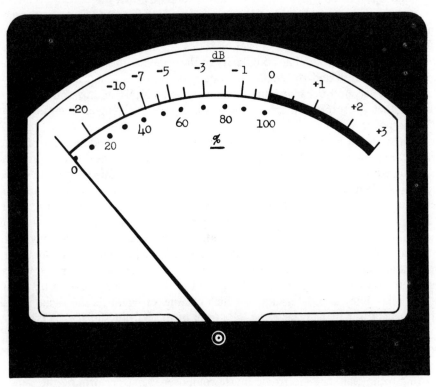

Figure 1.12   VU Meter

19

VU meters have progressed somewhat in recent years from the simple rotary needle to variously colored, sequential, fluorescent or light-emitting-diode (LED) displays. Though these flashy meters might seem more complex or sophisticated, they work in much the same manner as their more humble predecessors. Many VU meters, both mechanical and light emitting, now offer the option of selecting a *peak reading* or *peak hold* mode of operation. In either case, the meter shows the usually rapid fluctuations of the peak (maximum) loudness (response time is about 10 milliseconds) of the incoming signal, rather than the *average level* (with a response time of about 300 milliseconds) it would normally show. In the *peak hold* mode the meter holds the level of the loudest peak readings for a short time before releasing. It is quite normal for the peak VU level to remain consistently above the 0 dB mark. As long as the average signal level is at about 0 dB, there should be no distortion of the signal, since electronic circuits are generally designed to accommodate peaks much higher than their continuous signal tolerance. There are no hard-and-fast rules in judging signal strength, however, because VU meters are often calibrated differently, at the discretion of the manufacturer. This measurement is most useful when viewed as relative to particular equipment and recording situations.

Complex Mixers

The development of audio signal mixers has been greatly influenced by the commercial recording industry, especially by the growth of multitrack recording. The typical multitrack recording studio has a mixer capable of handling from 16 to 48 input signals assigned to from 4 to 24 output channels. Redundant input modules (Figure 1.13) controlling signal level, signal equalization, pre- and post-mix monitoring, echo (reverb) send, and channel assignment are linked together *ad infinitum* and routed into an output signal control section. It is not unusual for each input and output to have its own VU meter, adding to the impressive cluster of knobs and faders an almost carnival array of lights and moving objects. The complexity of these devices has become so extreme that many are now controlled by small, integrated computers that aid in the processing of individual signals and the matrixing of as many as 56 inputs to any combination of an equal number of outputs. Such technological wonders are an extravagance that few electronic music studios need or can afford.

In the modern recording studio, the mixer serves such a wide variety of functions beyond the simple combining of input signals that it is sometimes the sole piece of signal processing equipment to be found. The signal path through this processing network is rigidly controlled by the design of the system (Figure 1.14). A signal, usually from a microphone (but conceivably from a "line" source, such as a tape machine), enters one of the input modules, and its incoming level is set. It is then passed through an equalization section that amplifies or attenuates specific areas of the frequency content of the signal (usually in high, mid, and low ranges). Next, it can be sent to an external reverberation or other signal processing device. The remaining controls determine whether the signal is being monitored (listened to) before (pre-mix) or after (post-mix) the final mix. They also determine to which channel or channels the signal is assigned and (as usually set by a linear fader) the level of the output signal strength.

The electronic music studio has generally evolved toward a different type of mixer design, one that calls for separate signal-processing devices external to the mixer, providing the greatest possible system flexibility. Unlike the commercial recording technician, the electronic music composer is not performing the same set of

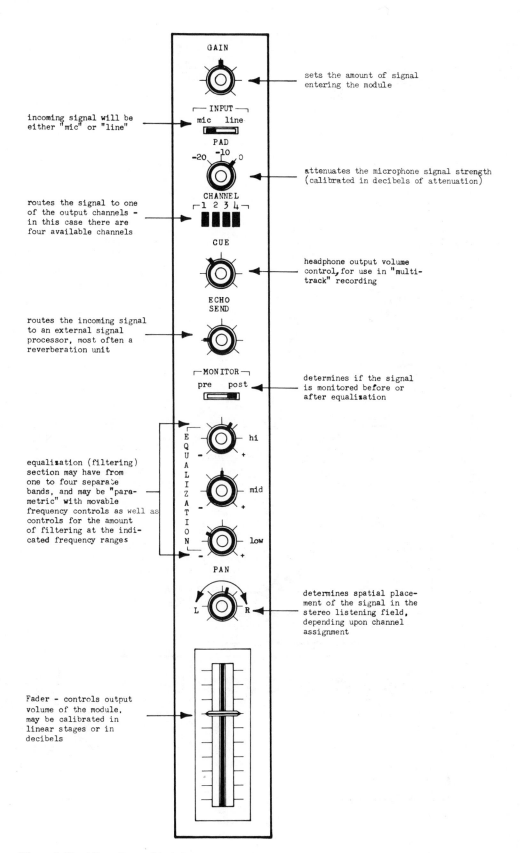

GAIN

sets the amount of signal
entering the module

incoming signal will be
either "mic" or "line"

┌─ INPUT ─┐
mic   line

PAD
-20 -10   0

attenuates the microphone signal strength
(calibrated in decibels of attenuation)

routes the signal to one
of the output channels −
in this case there are
four available channels

CHANNEL
┌─ 1 2 3 4 ─┐

CUE

headphone output volume
control, for use in "multitrack" recording

routes the incoming signal
to an external signal
processor, most often a
reverberation unit

ECHO
SEND

┌─ MONITOR ─┐
pre   post

determines if the signal
is monitored before or
after equalization

equalization (filtering)
section may have from
one to four separate
bands, and may be "para-
metric" with movable
frequency controls as well as
controls for the amount
of filtering at the indi-
cated frequency ranges

E
Q
U
A
L
I
Z
A
T
I
O
N

hi

mid

low

PAN

L   R

determines spatial place-
ment of the signal in the
stereo listening field,
depending upon channel
assignment

Fader − controls output
volume of the module,
may be calibrated in
linear stages or in
decibels

Figure 1.13   Mixer Input Module

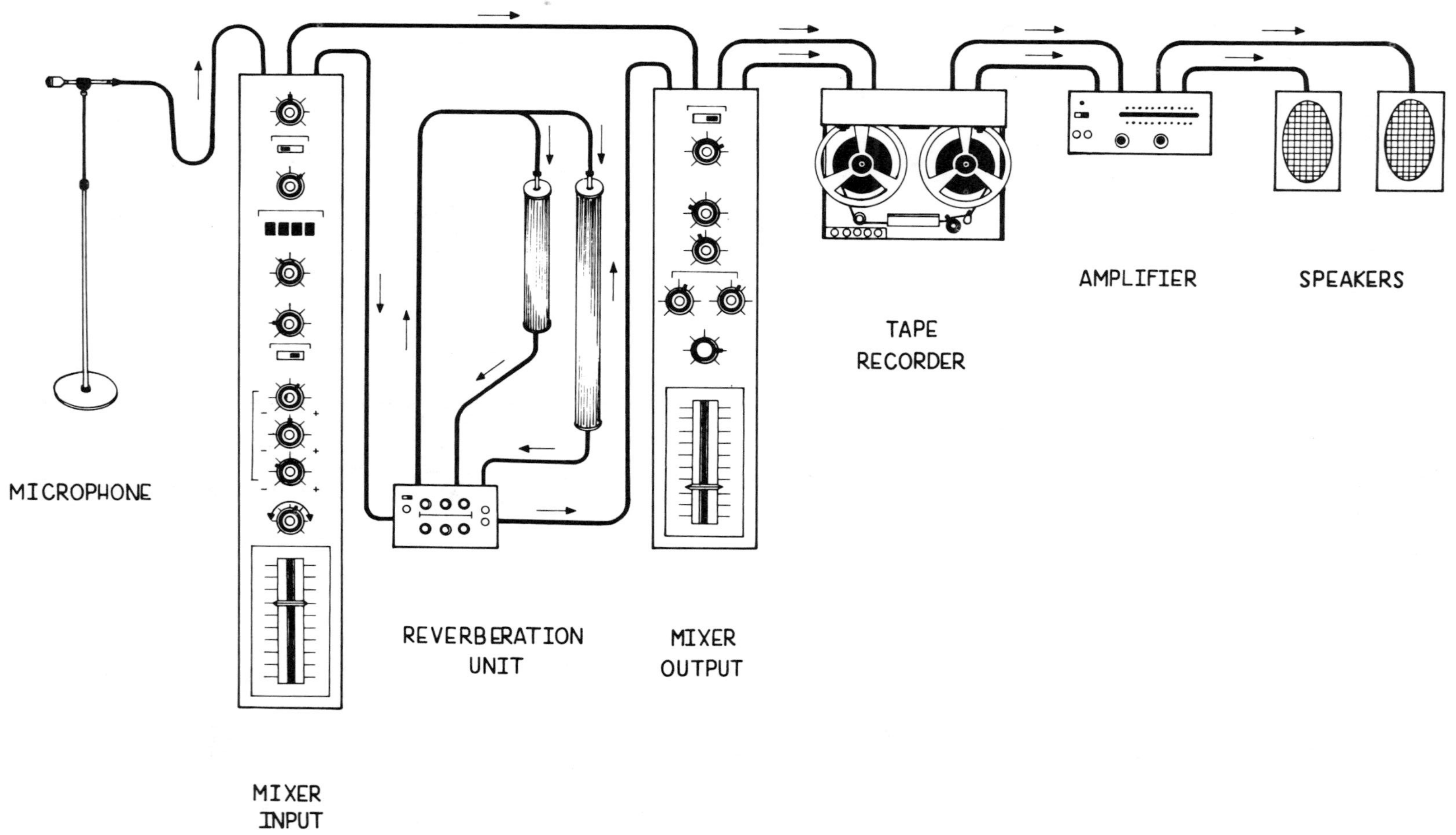

SPEAKERS

AMPLIFIER

TAPE
RECORDER

MIXER
OUTPUT

REVERBERATION
UNIT

MIXER
INPUT

MICROPHONE

Figure 1.14 Signal Path

22

tasks in the same operational system on a consistent basis. Therefore, the flexibility—not the compactness—of the system is the optimum concern. Another significant consideration is that simpler mixers often result in a clearer sound, because the signal does not have to go through the many separate stages and amplifiers typical of a large mixer, each of which may cause the signal to lose some of its original frequency or amplitude characteristics.

Even the simplest mixer has the capacity to perform several invaluable functions for the composer. Not only does the mixer set the loudness of the final sound, it balances the individual input signals, often producing a sum quite different from the nature of its component parts. In the case of stereophonic panning, the mixer gives the composer the ability to create a kind of spatial counterpoint, literally moving the apparent source of the sound from place to place and juxtaposing this movement with the movement of other sounds. The mixer can be used at every stage of the compositional process from the creation of the original sonic events to the control of the balance of individual elements and their spatial locations. For many electronic music composers, a high–quality mixer is the most important tool in the electronic music studio.

TAPE RECORDERS

Magnetic tape recorders are the most fundamental pieces of equipment in any electronic music studio. Through the tape recording process, electronic music is recorded, manipulated, stored, and retrieved, regardless of whether it originated from the tape studio, a synthesizer, or a computer. In its capacity to transform, transpose, modulate, and organize sonic events, the tape recorder is a resourceful compositional tool that demands careful consideration and technical expertise in its use. A poorly executed tape composition can haunt a composer more fiercely than any specter.

In general, a tape recorder's operation can be considered in terms of two primary functions: mechanical and electronic. The mechanical system, known as the *tape transport*, moves the magnetic tape past the head assembly, which either encodes (records) or decodes (plays back) the tape in accordance with the *electronic system*. The magnetic tape acts as the storage medium for the information transmitted by the electronic system.

Magnetic Recording Tape

Magnetic recording tape consists of a plastic backing material, either *acetate* (rarely found these days) or *polyester*, coated with an emulsion of microscopic particles of metal or various metal oxides. When the tape is subjected to a magnetic field, such as the one produced by the record head of a tape machine, the polarity of the particles in the coating is aligned according to the changes in polarity of the magnetic field (Figure 1.15). When the encoded tape passes over the playback head of a tape machine, the recorded magnetic polarity changes are converted to electric signals, then to sound. The quality of the tape backing and coating, therefore, directly affects the quality of the recorded information. Less expensive, acetate backings will break cleanly when too much stress is put on them. Polyester backings, which have become the predominant medium, are more durable, but excess stress will cause them to stretch. The reason recording tape is so fragile is that it is extremely thin, the three most prevalent thicknesses being 0.5 mil (a mil is one

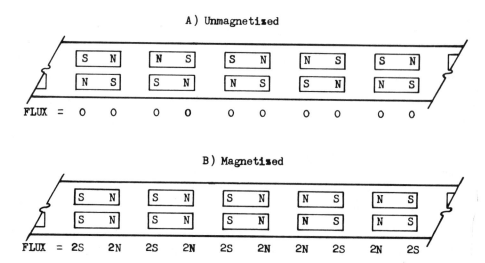

Figure 1.15   Particle Alignment and Magnetic Flux on Recording Tape

one-thousandth of an inch), 1.0 mil and 1.5 mil. As one might expect, a tape recorder reel can hold three times as much of the 0.5-mil tape as the 1.5-mil tape, making the former somewhat more economical. However, 0.5-mil tape is seldom, if ever, used for professional recording; it is much too fragile, and it is so thin that strong signals are often transferred from one layer of the tape to any adjacent layer of the tape (an effect known as *print-through*).

The width of magnetic recording tape varies from $\frac{1}{8}$ inch, for cassette tape recorders, to 2 inches for professional, multitrack tape recorders. The most common tape width is $\frac{1}{4}$ inch, though well equipped studios will often have a tape machine that takes $\frac{1}{2}$ inch tape.

There is continual progress being made in the development of new tape coatings, especially in the development of tapes for high-equality cassette recorders. The result of this research and development has been a proliferation of "low noise," "high output," "super" tapes with coatings of ferric oxide, chromium dioxide, or metal. The improvement in the signal-to-noise ratio, dynamic range, and frequency response of such special tapes is quite audible, but some of these tapes are quite expensive. Use medium-quality tape for experiments and exercises, reserving the finest quality tape for compositional efforts.

Transport System

In considering the *transport system* of a tape recorder, the first objective is to follow the *tape path* from the *supply* reel to the *take-up reel* (Figure 1.16). (We will not be considering cassette or cartridge tape recorders, since they are impractical for editing.) *Tape reels* come in many sizes, but the standard studio sizes are 7 inches and $10\frac{1}{2}$ inches in outside diameter and either $2\frac{1}{4}$ inches or $4\frac{1}{2}$ inches at the hub (the central part of the tape reel, around which the tape is actually wound). The larger of these sizes—$10\frac{1}{2}$ inches outer diameter, $4\frac{1}{2}$ inches hub diameter—is known as an NAB reel, since it is the standard size of the U.S. National Association of Broadcasters (NAB). In order to keep the tension on the tape equal throughout the movement of the tape from one reel to the other, use two reels of the same hub size at all times. Some 7-inch reels are made with the

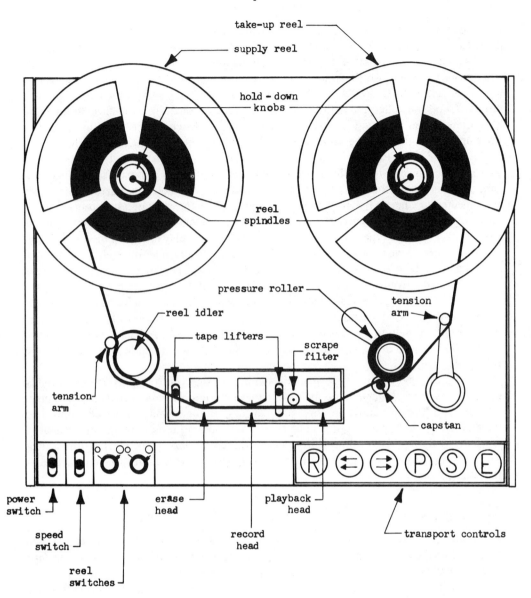

take-up reel
supply reel
hold - down
knobs
reel
spindles
pressure roller
tension
arm
reel idler
tape lifters
scrape
filter
tension
arm
capstan
power
switch
erase
head
playback
head
speed
switch
record
head
transport controls
reel
switches

Figure 1.16 The Tape Transport

larger NAB-size inner hub and are consequently compatible with the $10\frac{1}{2}$-inch NAB reels. In any case, when a tape machine has provisions for different reel sizes, it is the diameter of the hub that is important, not the overall size of the reel. Once the *supply reel* is placed on the *supply spindle*, the tape from it is fed past a *tape guide* and spring-loaded *tension arm* to the *head assembly*. The head assembly houses (in the order in which the tape passes over them) an erase head, a record head, and a playback head. Some machines position a *photoelectric sensor* in the head assembly so that, if the tape breaks or runs off the supply reel, a beam of light signals the reel motors to shut off. Other machines use a mechanical switch attached to one of the tension arms to sense when the tape breaks or goes slack.

On each side of the head assembly there are usually *tape lifters*. Constructed of glass or metal, the tape lifters move the tape away from the sensitive erase, record, and playback heads in the fast-forward or rewind modes (in order to avoid unnecessary friction against the heads that would cause excessive wear) but recede to allow the tape to make contact with the heads in the record or playback modes. In some cases, the tape lifters can be controlled manually, allowing the tape to touch or come close to touching the heads in the fast modes of operation in order to listen for *cues* on the tape. But constant use of this feature will significantly increase the wear on the tape heads.

After the head assembly, the tape passes between the capstan and the *pressure* (or *pinch*) *roller*. The capstan is chiefly responsible for maintaining a constant and consistent tape speed as it pulls the tape from the supply to the take-up reel. This narrow metal shaft is connected to a heavy flywheel and a well-regulated motor. The pressure roller, moved away from the capstan when the machine is in a fast mode or when the transport is turned off, keeps the tape firmly against the capstan in the play or record modes. Finally, the tape moves past another tension arm/tape guide to the take-up reel.

The initial tape guide sometimes takes the form of an *idler*, that is, a shaft connected to a free-moving flywheel. This helps to ensure a consistent tape speed. To hold the tape against this idler, a spring-loaded tension arm is used, which also helps to eliminate *tape flutter* (small but rapid variations in the tape speed caused by friction). Professional tape machines often include a *scrape filter* between the record and playback heads to smooth out any fluctuations in the tape speed caused by the friction of the tape as it is pulled past the heads.

A professional-quality tape machine with this type of transport system usually incorporates three independent motors in its operation: supply reel (rewind) motor, take-up reel (fast-forward) motor, and capstan motor. Constant speed control is maintained by the capstan motor. The supply and take-up motors maintain a balanced tension on the tape by pulling it in opposite directions, except in the fast-forward or rewind modes, when one motor is allowed to run without the counterbalancing action of the other.

Mechanical Controls

There are three basic operational modes for the tape transport. The play and record functions of the tape recorder actually involve the same mechanical process: the tape lifters are allowed to recede, leaving the tape in contact with the heads; the pressure roller makes contact with the rotating capstan to move the tape; and both reel motors are engaged to maintain the proper tape tension. The fast-forward mode disengages the pressure roller from the capstan and releases the supply reel, giving the take-up reel motor free rein. In the rewind mode the same set-up is used, except that it is the take-up reel that is released and the supply reel motor that pulls the tape.

Many tape recorders also include *pause* and/or *edit* controls. The pause control disengages the pressure roller from the capstan, leaving the tape in place against the heads. This mode of operation is particularly useful when editing, since the reels can be turned slowly by hand in order to locate a desired sound on the tape. The edit function disengages the take-up reel motor but allows the rest of the mechanics to work as if in the play or record mode. As its name implies, this feature is very useful in editing, since, after passing the playback head, any unwanted tape is allowed to spill out freely until a desired sound is located. (The terms "pause" and "edit" are often used interchangeably by equipment manufacturers.)

Maintaining a consistent tape speed is the most critical function of a tape transport. Most professional tape recorders will offer one or more of the following tape speeds: $7\frac{1}{2}$ ips (inches per second) (19 cm/s), 15 ips (38 cm/s), and 30 ips (76 cm/s). Variation in tape speed, easily perceivable to even the untrained ear, are known as *wow and flutter* and should never exceed 0.1%. The faster the tape speed, the less apparent wow and flutter and tape *dropout* (caused by minute flaws in the tape coating) become. Faster tape speeds also increase the frequency response and dynamic range of a recording by raising the point at which the tape becomes saturated with information. When this point is reached, called the *saturation/distortion level* of the tape, all the magnetic particles on the tape are being used to their fullest potential, and any further signal will result in distortion of the sound. The value of higher tape speeds lies in the fact that the more tape that passes the record or playback head at any given moment, the greater the amount of information that can be accurately transmitted. Thus, twice the tape speed means that there are twice as many magnetic particles available to store the same amount of signal information. In general, the much more economical tape speed of $7\frac{1}{2}$ ips is adequate for experiments and exercises, but 15 ips or 30 ips, if available, should be used for actual composition. This distinction is not minor, since 30 ips devours tape four times as quickly as $7\frac{1}{2}$ ips. Of course, another advantage of the faster tape speeds is that they allow much more room on the tape for editing. It is much easier to cut a 30-inch piece of tape into 0.1–second segments than it is to do the same with a $7\frac{1}{2}$-inch piece.

Track Configuration

Track configuration (Figure 1.17) is a function of the head design of the tape machine. The first tape machines recorded signal information on a single track extending for most of the width of the tape (0.238 inches). This arrangement, still popular in many European tape studios, is known as *full-track monophonic* (Figure 1.17a), since only one channel of recorded information can be contained on a track that, for all practical purposes, covers the full width of the tape. Soon after the advent of the first full-track machines, *half-track monophonic* heads were designed (Figure 1.17b), allowing a single channel of information to be contained on less than half the width of the tape (0.082 inches). When that track of the tape had been used from one end of the tape to the other, the tape could be turned over and the other portion used. Economic considerations made this arrangement quite popular. However, it is impossible to splice and edit either of the two tracks without adversely affecting the other.

With the advent of stereophonic recording, both tracks of the half-track configuration were used simultaneously, one for each of the two channels (Figure 1.17c). *Half-track stereo* is still the standard format for master tapes (including record masters), since maximum fidelity and editorial flexibility are maintained.

Recording machines designed primarily for home use often sacrifice some recording quality for the greater economy offered by *quarter-track stereo* formats (Figure 1.17d) using a track width of 0.043 inches. As with half-track mono, this system does not allow for uninhibited splicing and editing, since one of the stereo pairs of tracks is recorded in the opposite direction of the other. It is important to note that tape machines with different track configurations, particularly quarter-track and half-track formats, are incompatible. Tapes recorded on a machine of one track configuration cannot be played back on another machine of a different track configuration without serious signal loss. For this reason it is important that recorded tapes have their track configuration clearly labeled.

For many years, professional recording machines using tape of widths of from $\frac{1}{2}$-inch to 2 inches have been designed to record and play on from 4 to 48 simultaneous tracks. Four-track (Figure 1.17e) and eight-track (Figure 1.17f) tape machines using half-inch tape have become quite standard in electronic music studios.

A fairly recent development has been the popularization of the quarter-track, four-channel* tape machine that uses quarter-inch tape (often referred to as "quadra-phonic"). Since these machines are relatively inexpensive, the possibilities of multitrack recording have been made available to even the smallest studio. However, the reduced width of the recording track of these machines limits the recording quality.

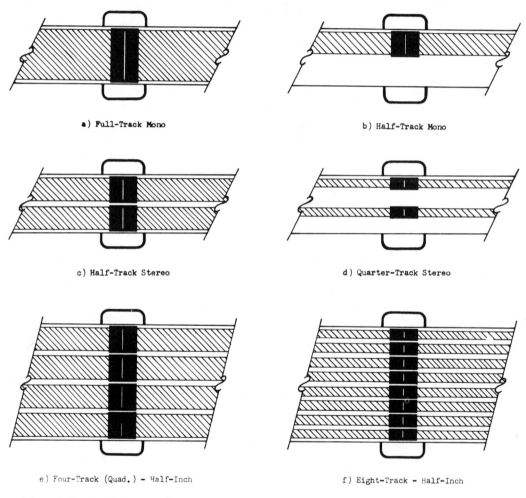

a) Full-Track Mono

b) Half-Track Mono

c) Half-Track Stereo

d) Quarter-Track Stereo

e) Four-Track (Quad.) - Half-Inch

f) Eight-Track - Half-Inch

Figure 1.17   Track Configurations

---

* The usual distinction between "channels" and "tracks" is that tape machines have head configurations designed to produce a certain number of *channels* of simultaneously recorded information resulting in a comparable or related number of *tracks* on the tape.

Electronic System

The electronic system of a tape recorder can best be understood by following the signal path through the recording and playback processes (Figure 1.18). Most tape machines accept both microphone and line inputs, the primary distinction being the differences in the impedance and amplitude of the two types of signals.

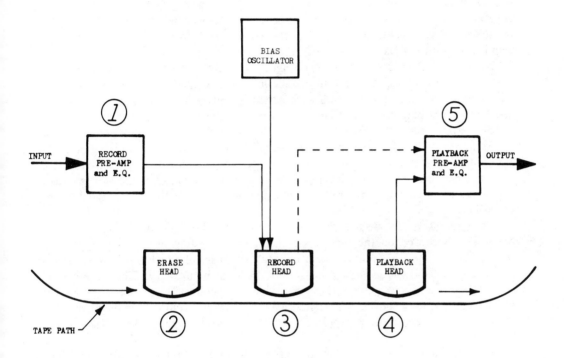

① The signal to be recorded enters the system.
Pre-recording frequency equalization takes place here.
The recording level is set.
The signal is assigned to the desired channel or channels.

② Any pre-recorded signal on the tape is erased.

③ The signal is mixed with a BIAS current and recorded onto the tape.
The signal may be monitored here as it is being recorded (dashed line).

④ The signal can be monitored as it appears on the tape,
already recorded, at the playback head.

⑤ The playback level of the signal is set.
Post-recording (playback) frequency equalization takes place here.
The recorded signal leaves the system.

Figure 1.18 The Electronic Signal Path in a Tape Recorder in the Record Mode

Before the signal can be sent to the record head for transmission to the tape, it must be pre-amplified, equalized, and biased. The operator sets the level of signal amplification with the record level controls, using the VU meters to monitor the signal to be recorded ("input" or "source"). It is very important to find an optimum recording level. If the recorded signal is too weak, it will not mask the inherent noise (*tape hiss*) produced by the recording process itself, but, if it is too strong, it will oversaturate the tape, causing signal distortion.

Signal *equalization* attempts to compensate for discrepancies in the tape machine's frequency response that take place in both the record and the playback modes. Most tape machine equalization systems boost low frequencies at the playback head to make up for low-frequency loss induced by the recording process and boost high frequencies at the record head to make up for high-frequency loss usually encountered at the playback head. High-frequency equalization has the added advantage of reducing the incidence of tape hiss during playback, since tape hiss is made up of high-frequency noise.

Before the tape reaches the record head to be encoded with the audio signal, the *erase head* removes any previously recorded signal from the tape by applying a high-amplitude, high-frequency erase current, effectively randomizing the polarity of the tape's magnetic particles. This current is supplied to the erase head by the *bias oscillator*, which also plays an important role in the actual recording of the audio signal at the record head.

The *recording head* translates the frequency of the audio signal into magnetic pulses that can be recorded on the tape. Essentially, the recording head is nothing but a carefully constructed and refined electromagnet, the poles of which form an extremely narrow gap (called the *head-gap*) at the front of the head (Figure 1.19). The narrower the gap is (it is commonly about 0.00025 inches wide!), the greater the frequency range that can be recorded, since shorter, higher frequency wavelengths (pulses) can be transmitted to the tape—just as a sharply pointed pencil can produce more detail than a fat, dull-pointed one.

Since magnetic tape does not respond effectively to the extremes of signal amplitude (either very strong or very weak), resulting in either distortion or nonretention of the signal, the audio signal to be recorded is mixed at the record head with a very high-frequency (100,000 to 200,000 Hz) *bias current* that is supplied by the *bias oscillator*. The bias current acts to ensure a more linear (even) response of the tape to the frequency of the signal being recorded. The amplitude of the bias current is optimized for a particular tape formulation and can usually be adjusted for different types of tape by a technician. The high frequency of the bias current makes it inaudible.*

After it has been magnetically encoded with the signal by the record head, the tape moves across the playback head, where it can be monitored by the playback amplifier. The playback head works very much like the record head in reverse; the magnetic pulses encoded on the tape create alternations in the current flowing through the playback head, which are subsequently amplified and equalized by the playback amplifier. There are, however, significant differences in desirable characteristics of the record and playback heads that make them only superficially interchangeable.

Nevertheless, most professional tape machines allow the record head to serve in a limited way as a playback head. The purpose of this option is to defeat the inherent time

---

* For more detailed information about the role of the bias current in the recording process see Woram's *The Recording Studio Handbook* or Runstein's *Modern Recording Techniques*.

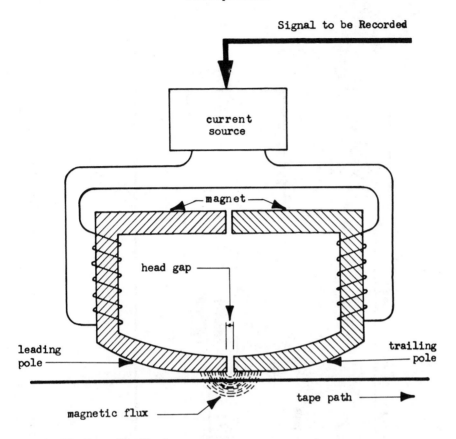

Figure 1.19 The Recording Head

delay between the record and playback heads (caused by the distance the tape must travel between them) so as to allow existing information already recorded on one track of the tape to be synchronized with new information being recorded on a separate track (Figure 1.20). This special capability, called *sel-sync* (for selective-synchronization), *simul-sync* (for simultaneous-synchronization), or *sel-rep* (for selective-reproduction), forms the basis for most of the success of multitrack recording, since it allows each instrumental or vocal part to be added to the tape independently of any other part, at any time.

Regardless of whether the record or playback head is monitored, the signal passes through the playback equalizer and playback amplifier before arriving at the tape machine's outputs. Though some inexpensive tape machines do not have output level controls, professional ones do. And, since professional machines allow the VU meters to be switched to monitor either the source (input) or recorded signal, it is important not to confuse the recording level with that of the output signal level when switching the VU meters between the two modes. It is the record (or the input/source) level reading that indicates the signal strength actually going onto the tape.

Recording machine VU meters function exactly as do those of mixers and with just as much variation in their calibration. Generally, when a signal pushes momentarily over the 0 dB mark into the red zone, the recording quality will still be good. Some VU meters can be switched between "peak-reading" and "average-reading" modes. As

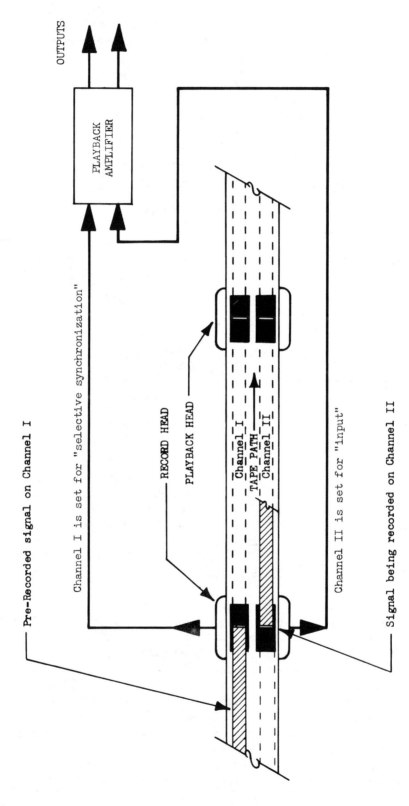

Figure 1.20 Selective-Synchronization: Pre-recorded signal on Channel I is monitored at the same time as signal being recorded on Channel II. Note: Playback heads are not used.

32

noted before, a peak-reading meter shows the almost instantaneous peaks of the signal level (response time is about 10 milliseconds). The average-reading meter responds to changes in signal level much more slowly (response time is about 300 milliseconds), showing more general or average indications of the signal level. Magnetic tape, and most electronic equipment, can accommodate stronger instantaneous peaks (transients) than sustained levels, so an average-reading VU meter would give a conservative measure of the recording quality. A peak-reading meter would help the operator to get the widest possible dynamic range and signal-to-noise ratio that a particular tape formulation would allow. However, there would also be a greater risk of distortion if the average signal level was inadvertently allowed to become too strong.

Maintenance

In order to function properly, all of the tape heads must be correctly aligned. If they do not meet the tape on the same vertical, horizontal, and tangential planes, some or all of the signal information will be lost (Figure 1.21). Specific head alignment procedures are usually included in the tape machine's owner's manual and should be performed regularly.

It is normal for small amounts of the tape coating to accumulate on the tape guides, capstan, and head surfaces. Periodically, this accumulation should be removed with a recommended solvent, such as isopropyl alcohol, in order to prevent signal loss at the heads or increased friction between the tape and the transport and head surfaces. After

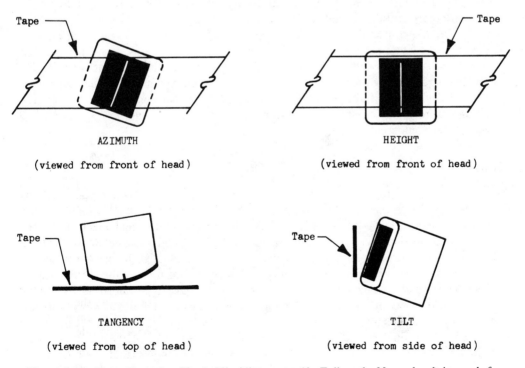

Figure 1.21 Tape Recorder Head Mis-Alignment. (A Full-track Mono head is used for illustration)

several hours of use, it is also possible for a small magnetic charge to build up on tape heads and various metal surfaces that make contact with the tape, causing a loss of high-frequency response. The magnetic charge is easily neutralized by a demagnetizer.

There are a number of technical calibrations—pertaining to bias and equalization, among other things—that must be occasionally checked and adjusted. Technical guides and test tapes are commercially available to those who feel competent to perform such tasks, but most operators would do well to consult a skilled, professional technician for such services. Calibration checks and adjustments for tape machines, mixers, and noise reduction units, are usually performed weekly in studios receiving a great deal of use. Commercial recording studios are usually re-calibrated before each recording session. The object, in all cases, is to ensure that all studio components handle the signal in exactly the same way, reducing the chances of signal loss or distortion.

AUXILIARY EQUIPMENT

Noise Reduction

The unavoidable and eternal struggle in the recording process is against unwanted noise introduced by the electronic system and the tape medium itself. Since multitrack recording and subsequent multiple overdubbing have become standard practices, the effects of tape noise have become all the more evident. Over the years, a number of noise reduction devices have been created that have met with varying degrees of success. The most successful have been the Dolby and the *dbx* systems, which have been developed from different combinations of somewhat less sophisticated devices.

It can be assumed that every tape recorder and every magnetic tape will have an inherent noise level, regardless of the technical improvements made to them. So long as the desired signal information is significantly stronger than the inherent noise level—without oversaturating the tape—the unwanted noise will be masked by the signal to be recorded. However, if the signal (particularly if it contains many low frequencies) becomes softer, the unwanted noise—usually in the form of tape hiss or hum—will become more apparent.

Compressors

The most obvious means of masking the unwanted noise is to make certain that the desired signal is always louder than the noise. This can be accomplished by raising the recording level of the signal, as long as the louder parts of the signal do not exceed the saturation/distortion level of the tape. Of course, this could be avoided by reducing the signal level during loud passages while maintaining a fairly high signal level during the softer passages. Not long ago this process of physically turning up the recording level of soft signals and turning down the recording level of loud signals (known as "riding the gain") was the sole form of noise reduction available. Aside from the obvious problems created by sudden changes in the loudness of the signal that might surprise the recording technician, the final recording would often lose a good deal of its dynamic range. Although there are now electronic devices, known as *compressors*, that "ride the gain" automatically, and with remarkable precision, recordings made using them still suffer from a significant reduction in the dynamic range of the recorded material (Figure 1.22).

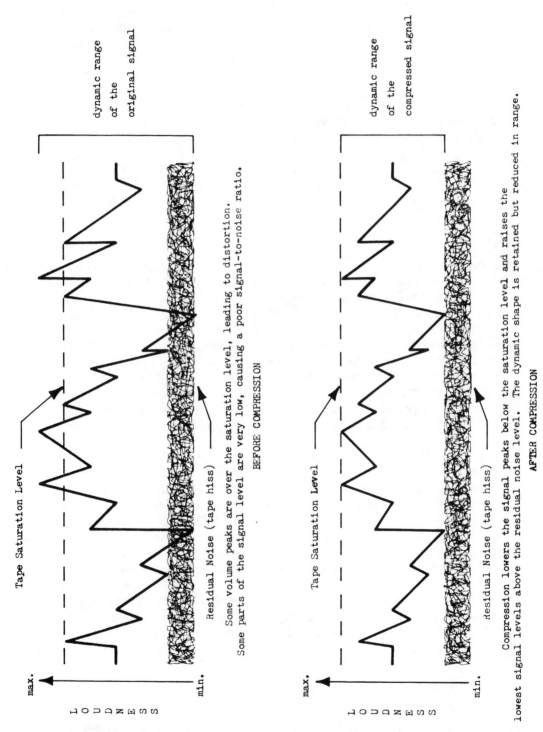

Figure 1.22　The Audio Compressor

35

This effect may not be all that noticeable with some sounds (such as the speaking voice), but many sounds derive a great deal of their musical interest from their wide dynamic variation.

Expanders

When a compressor acts on a signal before it is recorded, it reduces the dynamic level of the loud sections by the same proportion that it increases the dynamic level of the soft sections. By reversing this compression process (i.e., *expanding*) by the same ratio when the tape is played back, the compressed signal can be restored to its original dynamic range. And, most significantly, the residual noise level is reduced in the process, often becoming an insignificant or even inaudible percentage of the total sound. The combination of a compressor and an expander is often called a *compander* (Figure 1.23).

dbx

The *dbx* noise reduction system is a sophisticated compressor/expander with a matched compression/expansion ratio of 2:1. If a signal entering the compression side of the device (encoder) *before* being recorded has a dynamic range of 100 dB, it is compressed to a dynamic range of 50 dB (Figure 1.24). After being recorded at the 50 dB dynamic range—well within the capacities of most tape machines and magnetic tapes—the tape is played back through the expansion side of the device (decoder), returning the signal to its original, 100 dB dynamic range, thereby effectively doubling the saturation/distortion level of the tape and the signal-to-noise ratio of the tape machine. Note that signal compression takes place *before* the signal is recorded by the tape machine and that signal expansion takes place *after* the signal is played back by the tape machine. Since the problems of tape hiss and saturation/distortion are only introduced by the tape machine itself, a compression/expansion device such as the *dbx* system avoids these problems entirely. With the compression/expansion occurring at precisely the same ratio, and the signal acted upon almost instantaneously, the effects of the *dbx* process are unnoticeable to most listeners—except, of course, for the almost total absence of noise and distortion. Compression/expansion in the *dbx* system occurs evenly across the full frequency range of the signal. There is, however, a pre-emphasis of high frequencies during the encoding (recording) process and a complementary de-emphasis during the decoding (playback) process in order to further mask the effects of tape hiss.

Since the encoding/decoding processes of the *dbx* system are exactly matched to each other, the *dbx* system is incompatible with all other noise reduction systems. Any recording encoded by a *dbx* device must be decoded by a similar *dbx* device, because both the dynamic range and the frequency content have been substantially altered. Likewise, the *dbx* system cannot reduce the noise on tapes that have not been initially encoded by this process.

Dolby B

The Dolby noise reduction system (actually three different systems: Dolby A, B, and C) was the first to have a significant impact on the signal-to-noise ratio without producing audible, unacceptable side effects. Indeed, the astonishing success of the cassette tape format has been largely due to the adoption of the Dolby B process as a standard

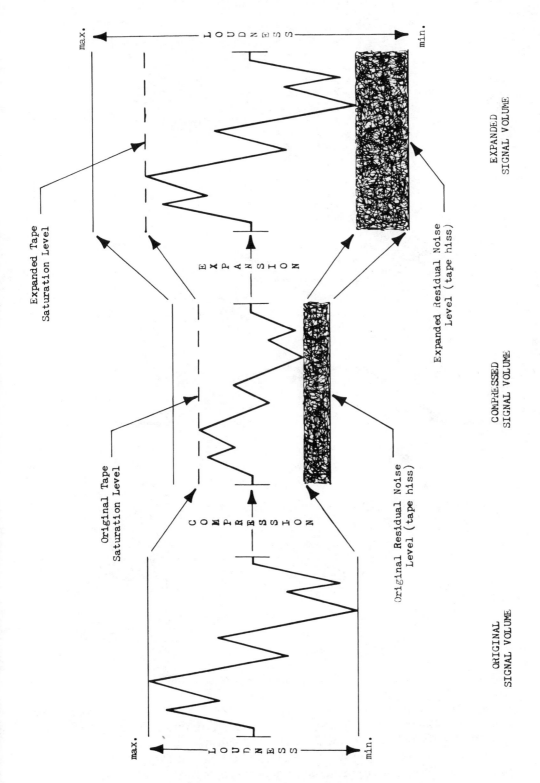

Figure 1.23 The Audio Compressor/Expander (Compander)

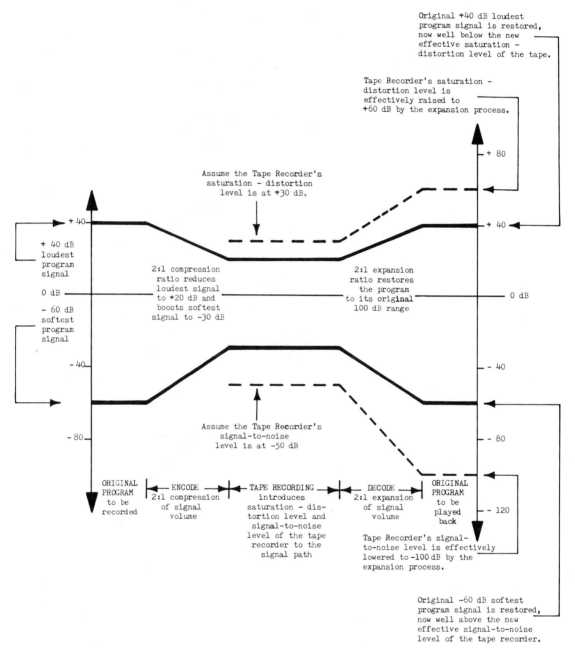

Figure 1.24 The DBX Noise Reduction (Compander) System

throughout the hardware and software industries. Aside from this single, formidable market, the Dolby B and C (consumer) and Dolby A (professional) systems have generally been supplanted by the more effective *dbx* system.

Dolby B, unlike the *dbx* system, does not affect the full frequency and amplitude range of the signal. Instead, the response of only one, high-frequency band is modified whenever the signal level falls below a certain point (Figure 1.25). High-level (loud)

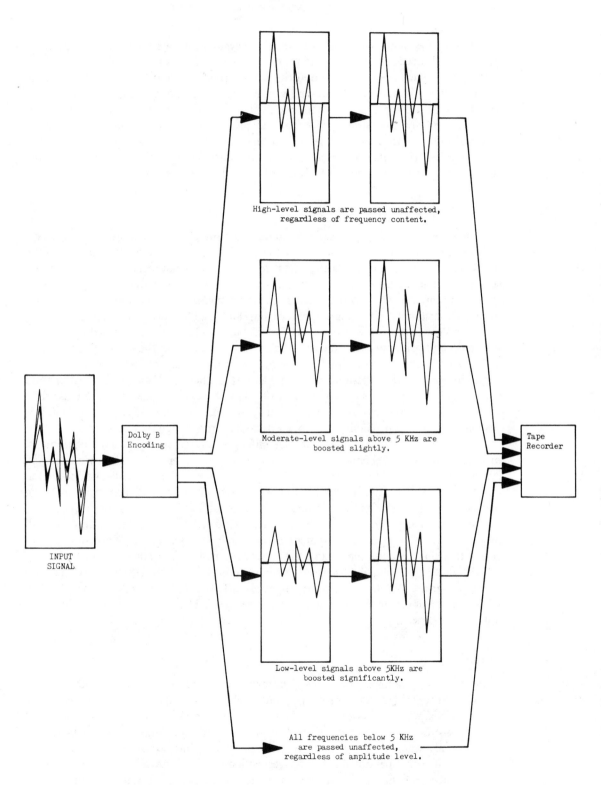

Figure 1.25 The Dolby B Encoding Process

signals of all frequencies are passed through the system without effect—the theory being that they will mask any noise without help. However, frequencies above 5 KHz (5000 cycles per second) are boosted proportionally for medium- and low-level signals. Only signals below a certain amplitude and above a certain frequency are affected.

When the Dolby B encoded tape is decoded (Figure 1.26), the process is reversed. The medium- and low-level signals that had their high-frequency content boosted are returned to their original levels. In the process, the extraneous high frequencies (noise) introduced in the tape recording process are also reduced, usually improving the signal-to-noise ratio by about 10 dB in the high-frequency range.

Dolby A

The Dolby A noise reduction process is somewhat more complex. Although it works on a compression/expansion principle similar to that of the *dbx* system, it does not act on the full signal as a unit, but splits the signal into four frequency bands that are acted on separately. The justification for this quadrupled complication is that each of these four frequency bands has its own particular noise problems that, theoretically, should be dealt with separately. The first frequency band (80 Hz and below) is associated with hum and rumble noises; the second band (80 Hz to 3 KHz) includes broadband noise, crosstalk, and print-through; the third band (3 to 9 KHz) and the fourth band (9 KHz and above) focus on high-frequency tape hiss. During average orchestral music, band 1 would be compressed occasionally; band 2 almost all the time; band 3, fairly often; and band 4, quite rarely. This system offers a 10 dB improvement in the signal-to-noise ratio over the total frequency range of the signal, in contrast to the effect of the Dolby B system, which improves only the upper frequency range signal-to-noise ratio.

All Dolby systems require complementary encoding and decoding equipment, making them totally incompatible with each other. In either case, just as with the *dbx* system, an unencoded tape cannot be improved and an encoded tape must be decoded to be of use (tapes encoded by the Dolby B process can be played back without being decoded, but the high-frequency content of the signal may be quite out of proportion to the total frequency spectrum of the original sound). Although most studios can still locate Dolby B processing equipment if absolutely necessary, very few studios have access to Dolby A equipment, and the success of Dolby C is not yet known.

All of the previously discussed systems required two processes—encoding and decoding—to be effective. However, there are a few techniques that can be useful in limiting noise or distortion (though never as effective as Dolby or *dbx*) through the use of only one process.

Limiting

A *limiter* works by allowing only a certain, maximum signal level to pass through it. This cutoff or threshold level is manually controllable and is usually set just below the saturation/distortion level of the tape. In this way, the signal level can be increased until even the softest sounds mask the residual noise of the tape (Figure 1.27). Limiting is effective only when used *before* the recording is made, but no subsequent decoding is necessary. Its principal drawback is the restriction it places on the dynamic range of the signal, since any signal that is louder than the threshold setting is "clipped" or suppressed, causing some degree of signal distortion.

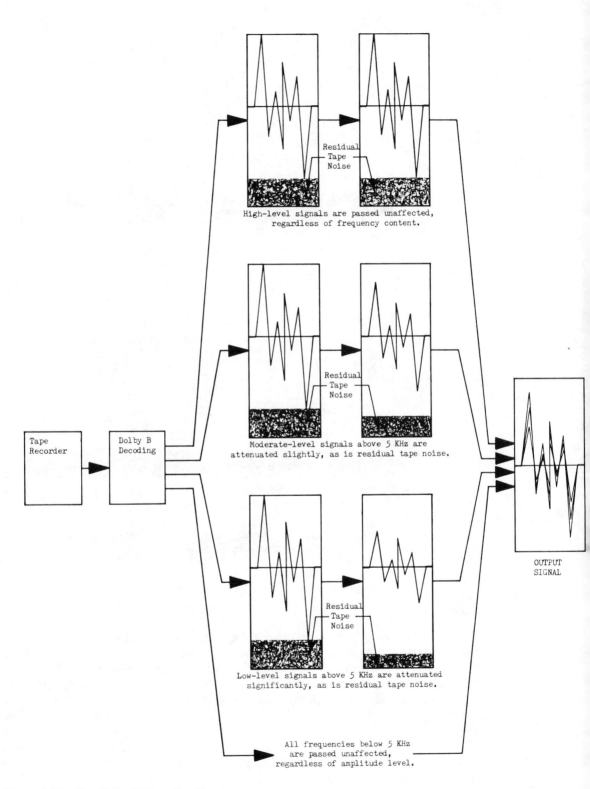

Figure 1.26 The Dolby B Decoding Process

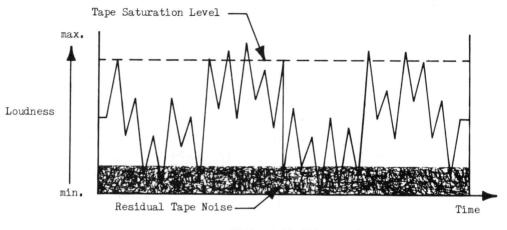

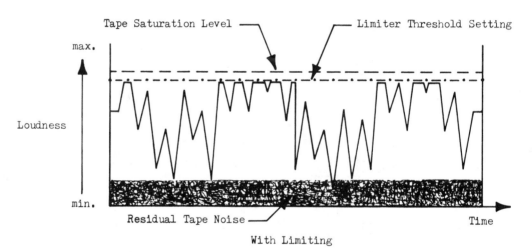

Figure 1.27   The Audio Signal Limiter. Overall signal level is increased to mask noise but may result in "clipping" of loudest portions of signal.

Noise Gates

A *noise gate* allows only those signals exceeding a preset, minimum amplitude level to pass through. In this way, low-level signals, such as tape noise, are never let through the circuit except when they will be masked by other, stronger signals. Figure 1.28 shows the effect of a noise gate on the sound of a snare drum and a piano. Notice that the effect of the noise gate on the snare drum beats is relatively negligible (although all of the noise is eliminated), but the effect of the gating action is detrimental to the piano tones. Since the switching of most noise gates is very abrupt and can be annoying—especially at the end of an expected long amplitude decay (such as that of a piano tone)—noise gates should be used only for rather percussive and quickly decaying sounds. It can be inserted in the audio signal path either before or after a recording is made. Noise gates and limiters are often used together to control both minimum and maximum signal levels.

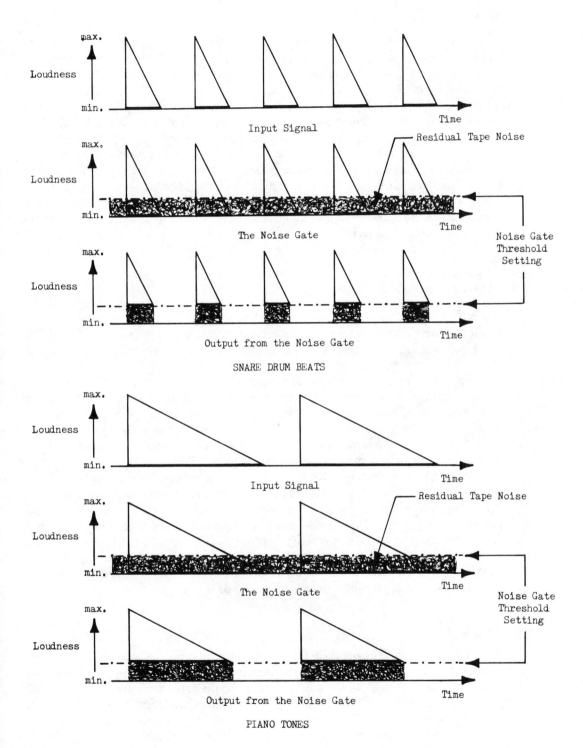

Figure 1.28 The Noise Gate

43

High-Pass Systems

One of the most effective methods of eliminating high-frequency tape hiss has been to simply remove all of the high-frequency signal content (e.g., turning down the treble control on a pre-amp). Of course, this method also eliminates all the desirable high frequencies that give brilliance to sounds. There are a few single-ended devices, for insertion in the playback system only, that reduce noise by selectively removing high frequencies altogether. The basic principle is that if there is already a lot of high-frequency content in a signal, it is passed through the device unaffected (high-*pass*), since it will mask any high-frequency noise that is present. However, if there is no high-frequency content in the signal, then there is no need to pass any high frequencies through the device at all, since the only audible result would be high-frequency tape hiss. Though the end results are far less impressive than those of Dolby or *dbx* noise reduction, these devices are still of significant use because of their ability to "clean up" previously recorded material.

Equalizers

Equalization is playing an ever more prominent role in both the recording and the playback processes. An *equalizer* is a filter or a set of filters (frequency-dependent amplifiers—see Chapter 6) used to emphasize or attenuate certain portions of a signal's frequency content. The balance of various regions in a signal's frequency spectrum greatly affects the way in which the resultant sound is perceived.

In a very limited sense, the tone controls of a home stereo system act as an equalizer. They function not only as a means of satisfying the esthetic demands of the listener, but also as a means of compensating for the acoustical properties of the listening environment. If the room is heavily furnished and draped, the high-frequency content of the signal can be boosted to compensate for the normal high-frequency loss in such a setting. Various other environmental effects can be compensated for likewise.

The playback system in a recording studio is often equalized according to very precise measurements of the monitoring room's acoustics in order to ensure a perfectly "flat" (consistent) frequency response over the total frequency range. Recording equalization is largely an esthetic and subjective concern. Very few professional recording technicians equalize an initial recording, because they like to get a feel for the relatively unaffected sound before attempting to modify it. Only in the final "mix-down" does the equalizer play a significant role. The technical concepts, designs, and functions of equalizers will be discussed in detail in Chapter 6.

Amplifiers

Although all amplifiers perform essentially the same function—to increase the strength of a signal—there are two distinct types used in audio equipment: pre-amplifiers and power amplifiers. *Pre-amplifiers* (a misnomer, since they are themselves amplifiers) are found in the electronics of tape machines, active mixers, active equalizers, receivers, and virtually every other signal processing device. They are generally designed to very exacting standards, since they amplify extremely weak signals, such as those produced by magnetic tape heads or magnetic phonograph pick-ups. If the signal is distorted at this stage, the distortion will only be further exaggerated by the power amplifier.

Pre-amps must also be very responsive to a wide frequency range, because if some frequencies are lost at this early stage in the signal path, they cannot be retrieved in later stages. The amplitude output level of any pre-amplifier is known as *line level* in most studios, the level at which the signal may be sent to the studio's power amplifiers.

The following is a list of terms and qualities normally used in assessing the quality of a pre-amplifier:

Frequency Response: generally 20–20,000 Hz is desirable, though 30–18,000 Hz is acceptable. (Usually measured ±1 dB)

Distortion: often measured in two ways, as a nominal level above 1 KHz, which seldom exceeds 0.05%, and as Total Harmonic Distortion (THD), which should never exceed 1.0%.

Input and Output Impedance: vary with the purpose of the pre-amplifier.

The function of the *power amplifier* is to take the still relatively weak signal of the pre-amplifier and raise it to a level sufficient to drive loudspeakers. Although its frequency response and distortion characteristics are important, they are somewhat less critical than those of the pre-amplifier simply because they will not be exaggerated by further amplification. However, as a general guideline, look for similar characteristics in the amplifier as in the pre-amplifier.

The importance of the output wattage (a watt is a measure of power) of a power amplifier is greatly overemphasized, except for those few who regularly play their music in football stadiums. Fifty watts RMS (root mean square—a standard scale of power measurement) per channel is usually powerful enough to reach the pain threshold (see Chapter 4) of the listener if the monitoring room is of average size (about 150 square feet—14 m^2). Larger rooms absorb more sound energy than smaller ones and, therefore, require more powerful amplifiers to drive larger, more efficient speakers. A point can be made for having excess "headroom" in the amplifier's power rating, since it allows the amplifier to respond more efficiently to instantaneous peaks of energy, especially in the upper frequency range. But, it would be very rare indeed to have use for an amplifier of more than 200 watts RMS per channel. Many people, when constructing their own home stereo system, get carried away in spending inordinate amounts of money for excessively powerful amplifiers, believing this to be a measure of the quality of their system. This is simply not the case—much more care and money should be given to the purchase of the highest possible quality pre-amplifier.

Reproducers

The ideal speaker creates a sound exactly analogous to the characteristics of the signal applied to it, with the least possible energy loss and distortion. This hypothetical speaker would, therefore, be very sensitive and efficient. Most speakers will tend, because of their design limitations, to color the frequency characteristics of signals applied to them. This is due to resonant peaks (see Chapter 4) that are formed by the construction of the speaker enclosure and various other physical variables. Electronic music is best suited to "dry" speakers with a relatively even or "flat" frequency response. No particular speaker design completely fulfills this function, and none is specifically incapable of fulfilling it. Therefore, speaker selection must be made by carefully auditioning various speaker systems. As noted earlier, many electronic music and recording studios use some form of equalization to compensate for speaker frequency coloration in relation to the monitoring room's acoustics.

Headphones

Advancements in headphone design have made them quite sensitive and accurate. They can be extremely useful in the recording studio, since a performer can listen to a prerecorded track and play along with it as he or she is being recorded on another track—without the sound of the prerecorded track being picked up by the microphone. Other than the specifications already discussed for loudspeakers, headphones can be evaluated in terms of their weight, comfort, degree of soundproofing (as desired), and durability.

Patch Panels

A tape studio is nothing more than an assemblage of machines and devices linked together by a kind of nervous system of wires. In order to make connections between various pieces of equipment quickly and efficiently, most studios route all of the input and output wires of every piece of equipment in the studio into a central *patch panel*, which resembles an old-fashioned telephone switchboard and operates in the same way.

Patch panels (also called patch bays) may be organized in a number of ways. The input jacks (receptacles for patch cord plugs) may be on one side, with all of the output jacks on the other side (Figure 1.29), or output jacks may be directly above the inputs. These jacks can then be interconnected by using relatively short "patch cords"—wires with plugs on both ends made to fit into the receptacles. In this way, a variety of system-wide interconnections can be made efficiently from a central location. Figure 1.30 shows a typical "patch": oscillators to mixer inputs, mixer outputs to tape recorder inputs, tape recorder outputs to amplifier inputs, and amplifier outputs to speakers (amplifiers are wired directly to speakers in most studios).

A BASIC TAPE STUDIO

In building a tape studio, there are a few (actually very few) essential pieces of equipment:

Two microphones
A simple, 4-in/2-out (4 × 2) or 2+2-in/2-out (2+2 × 2) mixer
One four-track, four-channel, quarter-inch tape machine
One half-track stereo, quarter-inch tape machine
One stereo power amplifier (pre-amp optional)
Two loudspeakers
Various cables, wires, reels, and splicing equipment

Even this is not the bare minimum needed to begin working with tape composition, but it represents a flexible basic studio capable of producing compositions of sophistication and quality.

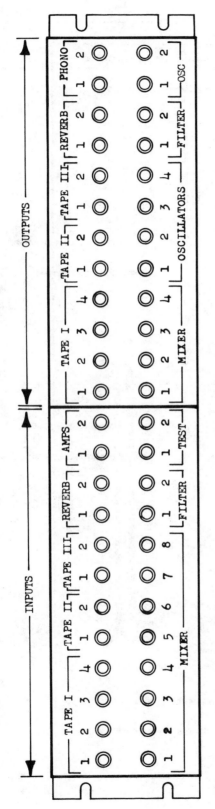

Figure 1.29 A Double Rank Patch Bay

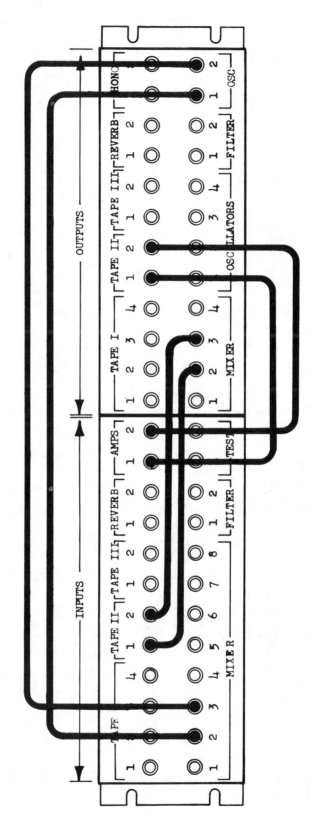

Figure 1.30 A Typical Patch

SOURCES OF UNWANTED NOISE

The following is a list of problems often encountered in the electronic music studio. The student should be familiar with all of them and know how to avoid them.

Tape Hiss: a characteristic of the tape medium; can be reduced by using "low-noise," "high-output" tape formulations and a variety of noise-reduction devices.

Electronic System Noise: noise introduced by the electronic circuits of the machines and devices involved.

Tape Saturation/Distortion: distortion of the signal caused by overloading the tape with too strong a signal.

Hum: caused by improperly matched grounding between equipment or a defective power supply.

Mechanical Vibrations (flutter): causes the heads to lose perfect contact with the recording tape if strong enough vibrations are present. Can be caused by dirty capstan, tape guides, or idlers.

Wow: caused by changes in the tape speed due to a defective speed control or physical drag on the tape, often from reel flanges.

Cross-Talk: caused by head misalignment, so that one or more of the tape channels crosses its assigned track on the recording head or playback head to appear on another, adjacent track.

Tape Drop-Out: signal loss caused by flaws in the tape coating, many of which can be removed by playing a tape through before recording on it.

Print-Through: the transfer of a recorded signal from one layer of tape to an adjacent layer, usually due to recording at too high a level, particularly on thin (less than 1 mil) tape. The negative effects of print-through can be minimized by storing recorded tape with the tail end out, causing the print-through to occur after the actual recorded sound and to be masked by it.

STANDARD PRACTICES

Since tape compositions are often produced using a variety of equipment (sometimes with quite dissimilar calibrations), and performance situations usually vary considerably from the circumstances under which the tape compositions were created, it has become increasingly obvious that certain procedures should be standardized in order to ensure uniform results of high quality. Although strict standards for the production and storage of electronic music tapes have yet to be developed, there are several generally observed practices that will help ensure the proper use and care of tape compositions.

Labeling: all tape boxes and reels should be labeled with the following information:
 Subject or title
 Composer or owner and current address
 Tape speed
 Track configuration
 Number of channels

Use of noise-reduction devices (*dbx*/Dolby)
Tail-out or head-out tape winding
Timing of each composition

Calibration Tones: at the beginning of the tape, about 10 to 20 seconds of a 1 KHz calibration tone should be recorded and isolated by leader tape. Many composers favor A-440 Hz, so that pitch problems can be easily detected and corrected. The volume of this tone should match the level of the loudest continuous sound of the composition, usually set to 0 dB on the VU meters. This enables others playing the tape to determine the correct playback level.

Tape Storage: tapes should always be stored "tail-out" (the last of the tape toward the outer edge of the reel) to minimize the effects of print-through; standing on their edges (to prevent reel warping); and in a cool, moderately dry place.

Chapter 2

Simple Tape Manipulations

THE RECORDING PROCESS

The techniques associated with composition in the tape studio encompass a broad range of interactions among and applications of various equipment, but the most essential skill for a composer of tape music is the ability to make very high-quality tape recordings. Since, to some extent, a composer of tape music not only conceives but actually executes his music in the studio (often producing the only "performance" of the piece himself), the audience's perception of the results will depend to a great extent on his own technical abilities. If a composer is unable to make a good recording with very little noise or distortion, he is automatically limited to the use of noisy, distorted sounds in his compositions. Although it is quite possible that such sounds might be used interestingly and to the composer's advantage, such limitations would seem to be rather arbitrary. Compositional decisions should be made through the exercise of discipline and technical skill, not by the lack of them.

The first consideration in making a good recording is the choice of appropriate equipment. In the most basic sense this can be limited to the selection of a microphone, a tape machine, and recording tape. Each of these items places a limitation on the recording quality that cannot be overcome by subsequent processing or reproduction equipment.

Equipment Connections

The physical connection between the tape machine and the microphone can usually be made directly. A standard, balanced microphone cable consists of two leads surrounded by a grounded shield (Figure 2.1). Most professional microphones will use either XLR (Figure 2.2a) or DIN (Figure 2.2b) plugs and jacks, although many commonly available recording machines use phone plugs (Figure 2.2e) at their microphone inputs. Several other commonly available plugs are also shown in Figure 2.2. Since most tape machines that have phone jacks at the microphone inputs are designed for use with high-impedance microphones, and most professional microphones are low-impedance, these machines will usually require the use of an impedance transformer so that the impedances of the tape machine and microphones will be compatible. Many of these transformers are designed to fit directly in-line, between the microphone cable and the tape machine input jacks, simultaneously adapting the microphone's XLR connector to the tape machine's phone-plug jack (Figure 2.3). In the recording studio this may be handled by a mixer with internal impedance matching capabilities. However, in considering the basic recording process, all that is of immediate importance is the basic

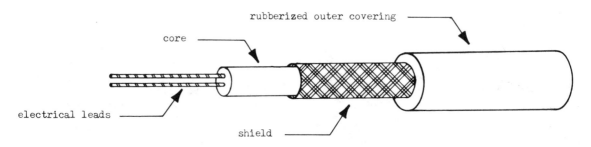

Figure 2.1 Balanced Microphone Cable

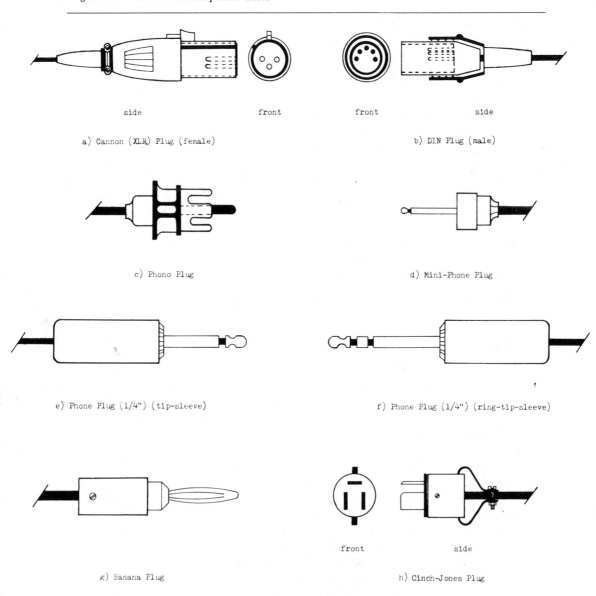

side   front   front   side

a) Cannon (XLR) Plug (female)   b) DIN Plug (male)

c) Phono Plug   d) Mini-Phone Plug

e) Phone Plug (1/4") (tip-sleeve)   f) Phone Plug (1/4") (ring-tip-sleeve)

front   side

g) Banana Plug   h) Cinch-Jones Plug

Figure 2.2 Common Connectors (not to same scale).

52

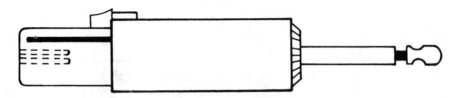

Figure 2.3   Impedance Transformer-Adaptor

recording signal path (Figure 2.4) and the basic playback or monitoring signal path (Figure 2.5).

EDITING AND SPLICING

Magnetic tape itself is nothing but a storage medium—as paper is to the printed word. As the tape passes the active recording head of a tape machine, it is imprinted with a magnetic message representing the sound event being recorded. Therefore, specific portions of the tape contain specific messages that have meaning not only in themselves, but also in the context of preceding and succeeding events. The most obvious way to control the succession of sound events on the tape would be to record them in the desired order. However, this is often impractical, cumbersome, and noisy, so the usual practice is to record the sound events in the most convenient or "natural" order, then rearrange the sounds by cutting and reconnecting (editing and splicing) the tape. Thus, the desired sequence of sound events can be constructed after the actual recording has been completed.

A *splice* is nothing but the joining together of two pieces of recording tape. In order to ensure that the tape ends can be joined securely and accurately, and held fast for extended periods of time, special adhesive splicing tapes and mechanical splicing aids have been developed. The simplest, most practical, and most effective splicing process requires an aluminum splicing block to hold the recording tape, a single-edged razor blade to cut it, and specially formulated splicing tape to join it.

The Splicing Block

The splicing block (Figure 2.6), often mounted on top of the tape machine's head assembly cover, is usually a rectangular piece of aluminum (to avoid magnetization of the block) with a concave groove along its length—into which the recording tape will fit securely—and two fine slots across its width to guide the razor's cutting edge across the tape, either perpendicularly or at an angle. The diagonal cut will result in a more secure splice, since the joint occurs more gradually and is longer.

Cutting and Splicing

The process for splicing two pieces of recording tape together is quite simple and can be done quickly with only a little practice:

- Place the first tape firmly in the splicing block and trim the end with a single-edged razor blade, using one of the cutting slots as a guide. Slide the tape away from the cutting slot.

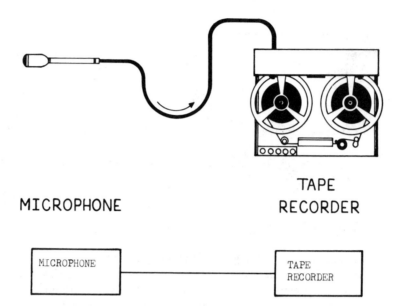

MICROPHONE   TAPE
RECORDER

Figure 2.4   The Recording Signal Path and its Block Diagram

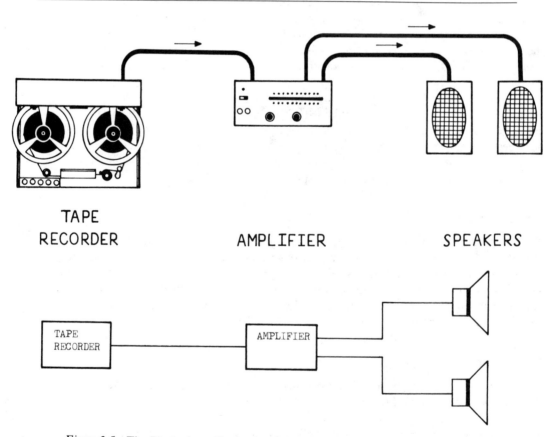

TAPE
RECORDER   AMPLIFIER   SPEAKERS

Figure 2.5   The Playback or Monitoring Signal Path and its Block Diagram

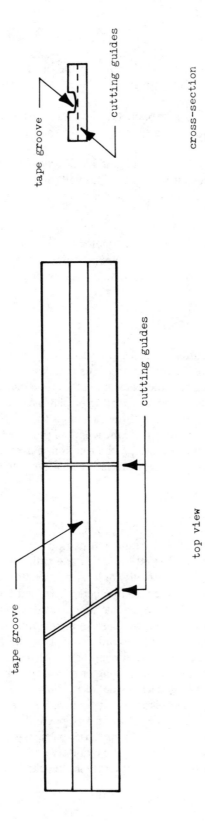

tape groove

cutting guides

cross-section

cutting guides

top view

tape groove

Figure 2.6 The Splicing Block

- Place the second tape firmly in the splicing block from the other direction, and cut its free end similarly.
- Move both of the cut tape ends to the center of the block (but out of the way of the cutting slots) and carefully butt them together. The ends should meet perfectly, without gaps or overlaps.
- Press a piece of splicing tape approximately $\frac{3}{4}$-inch (2 cm) long firmly over the joint, making sure that no portion of the splicing tape overhangs the edges of the recording tape.
- Remove the recording tape from the splicing block groove by lifting it from *both* ends simultaneously with a gentle outward pull. This will cause the tape to "pop" out of the groove, avoiding damage to the edges of the tape.

Splicing is just one part of the editing process. It is interesting to note that the term "edit" was borrowed from publishing terminology and generally means to rearrange, delete, or insert. When editing a recorded tape, the purpose is almost always to reorder the recorded sound events, remove unwanted sounds or noise, or insert additional material.

Tape Length and Time

The length of a piece of tape directly corresponds to a period of time. In the most general sense, this means that the greater the length of the tape, the longer the period of time it represents. However, to determine the exact amount of time that a specific length of tape will take to pass across a fixed point (a recording or playback head), one must take into account the speed at which the tape will be traveling. To determine the duration of a length of tape moving at a set speed, divide the length of the tape by the speed at which it is moving. Note that if the speed doubles, the duration halves and vice versa. Careful editing gives the composer an extremely precise control over the temporal elements of a composition.

Editing Sequence

A typical editing sequence involves locating and marking the separate sound events on the tape, cutting the tape at the desired locations, and splicing the chosen events back together in the desired order. The difficulty of locating specific sound events on the tape varies depending on the type of tape machine being used and the nature of the sounds themselves. It is essential that the tape be able to move freely while in contact with the active playback head and that the reel spindles can be manipulated with some freedom. To locate the exact beginning or end of a sound, the tape machine is put in the playback (or edit) mode, and, with one hand on each reel, the tape is moved back and forth across the playback head. When the precise beginning or end of the sound is found, a mark is made on the back (the visible or uncoated side) of the tape at the center of the playback head using a grease pencil, china marker, or felt-tip pen. Some people prefer to mark the tape with a thumbnail scrape, in order to avoid any possibility of leaving any marking residue on the heads or tape transport. In any case, particular care should be taken to keep the marking off of either the head or the oxide side of the tape. The marking can then be aligned with the cutting slot on the splicing block. In the event that the tape machine heads are inaccessible (an unfortunate circumstance that should be taken into account when purchasing equipment), a cueing mark can be made on the tape machine at a more convenient location, such as at the end of the head assembly cover. A corresponding mark is then made on the splicing block so that the distance from the cueing mark on the splicing block to the desired cutting slot is the same as the distance from the cueing mark on the tape machine to the center of the playback head (Figure 2.7).

In general, it is easier to locate sudden changes in the loudness of a recorded sound than it is to locate the beginning or end of a gradual change in the loudness of a sound. If the tape is moved too slowly across the playback head, no sound will result at all. For these reasons it is often advisable to increase the playback volume as high as possible when editing, but remember to return the playback level to a more moderate setting when normal playback is resumed.

Although splicing and editing might initially seem awkward and imprecise, repeated practice will reveal subtleties of manipulation and listening that will improve the accuracy of the process. A few cautions should be restated and noted:

- Avoid contacting the coated side of the tape with grease pencils, china markers, or felt-tip pens. Touching the coated side of the tape with the fingers is unavoidable when editing, but such contact should be kept to a minimum, since it leaves skin oils on the tape.
- Keep splicing equipment clean—free from dust, oil, or liquids of any kind.
- Demagnetize all razor blades before using them. If they become magnetized, a sharp "pop" will occur at the location of every cut made with them when the tape is played back. A sharp tap of a razor blade on a hard surface will eliminate weak magnetization.
- Never use anything but audio splicing tape to connect pieces of recording tape. The adhesives of other kinds of tapes will "bleed" onto surrounding surfaces, removing tape coatings, attracting dust particles, and sticking to neighboring layers of the tape.

PROJECT NO. 1: HAIKU EDITING

This project is designed to provide practice in basic tape recording and editing skills. As with most such projects, three distinct stages or tasks make up the overall production process:

Planning: including 1) a statement of a project goal, 2) a description or list of the materials and equipment required, and 3) an outline of production steps.

Production: the enactment of the plan: performing the actual production steps.

Assessment: a critical review of the outcome of the project: the attainment of the project goals, the aptness of the production plans, the efficiency of the production process, and the quality of the results.

The following is an example of the planning stage and some guidelines for the assessment of a simple Haiku recording and editing project.

58

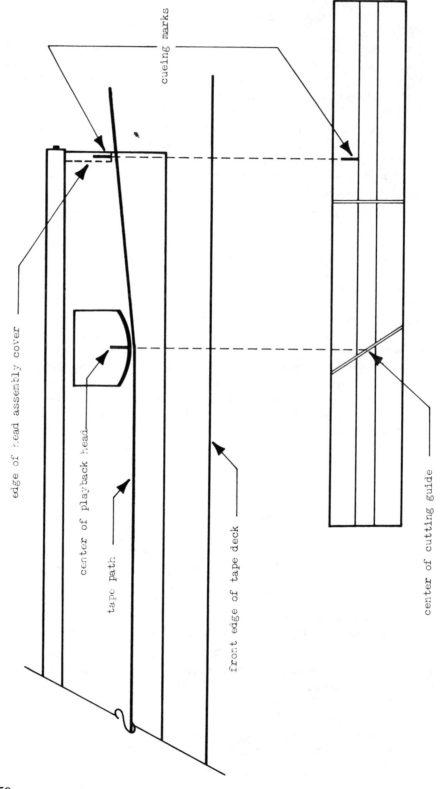

cueing marks

edge of head assembly cover

center of playback head

tape path

front edge of tape deck

center of cutting guide

Figure 2.7 Cueing Marks on Tape Head Assembly and Splicing Block

Production Plan

A. Project Goal: restructure a recording of the following Haiku:

White lightning struck
And where it harshly tickled
Now jagged lilacs grow.

by editing the tape to read:

Jagged lightning harshly struck
And where it tickled
Now white lilacs grow.

B. Equipment Needs and Connections (see Figure 2.8):
   1. Microphone.
   2. Tape machine. (A mixer and noise reduction equipment may be used, but are not essential.)
   3. Splicing block, razor blade, splicing tape, and marker.
   4. Amplifier and speakers.
C. Production Steps:
   1. Set the tape machine to its fastest speed, and record about 15 seconds of a 1000 Hz calibration tone, setting the level at 0 dB on the tape machine's VU meter. Isolate this tone with leader tape on each end by cutting and splicing. (This tone may later be used to set the optimum playback level, since no sound on the tape should exceed this level for more than a fraction of a second.)
   2. Set the tape machine recording level while rehearsing the reading of the original Haiku. Pay particular attention to the distance of the microphone from the reader. If the microphone is too close, breath pops from explosive consonants will result. If the microphone is too distant, excessive environmental noise will be introduced, and the recording will have a lifeless quality to it. The reader should speak clearly and rhythmically, slightly isolating each word—otherwise, precise editing will be difficult or impossible.
   3. Record the Haiku at the fastest speed of the tape machine. This will allow the maximum room for editing the tape.
   4. Play back the recording of the Haiku, listening for the factors described in step 2 above and for any extraneous sounds or noises. If the recording is good, proceed. If it is not, repeat steps 2 and 3. Although more wasteful of tape, it might be wise to save all recording attempts or "takes," since successive attempts might prove to be less adequate than earlier ones.
   5. It may be advisable to make a "dub" (copy) of the original recording. This is to ensure that, if an error is made in the editing, the entire recording process need not be repeated. In making the dub use the set-up shown in Figure 2.9. The calibration tone on the original tape can be used to set the recording level of the second tape machine to its 0 dB mark.
   6. Isolate the beginning and end of the recording with leader tape. Absolute precision is not necessary at this point, but special care should be taken to avoid cutting away opening or closing sound material.
   7. Locate and remove the word "White" from the tape by cutting at the beginning of the *W* sound and just before the *l* sound of "lightning." This preserves not only the word "White" but the natural silence that follows it. Set this piece of

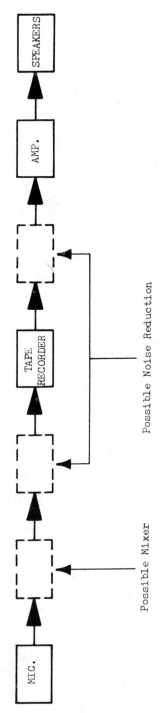

Possible Mixer   Possible Noise Reduction

Figure 2.8 Project No. 1: Patching Diagram

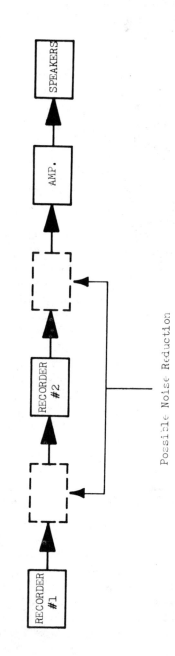

Possible Noise Reduction

Figure 2.9 Project No. 1: Dubbing Patch

tape aside, carefully labeling what it is and noting which end is the beginning. Join "lightning" to the opening silence with a temporary splice.

8. Locate and remove the word "jagged" from the tape by cutting at the beginning of the *j* sound and just before the *l* sound of "lilacs." Set this piece of tape aside and label it.

9. Permanently splice "White" into the space previously occupied by "jagged."

10. Rewind the tape to the beginning, remove the temporary splice, and permanently splice "jagged" into the space previously occupied by "White."

11. Locate and remove the word "harshly" by cutting at the beginning of the *h* sound (note: soft consonants are often difficult to hear when editing) and just before the *t* sound of "tickled." Set "harshly" aside and label it. Close up the tape with a permanent splice.

12. Locate "struck" and cut the tape just before the *s* sound. Insert "harshly" between "lightning" and "struck," and join with permanent splices.

A valid technical assessment of this project can be made by considering the following:

Recording quality:

- signal-to-noise ratio (recording level too low?)
- distortion through tape saturation (recording level too high?)
- microphone distortion or noises (pops, handling noises, etc.?)

Splicing quality:

- splicing noises (pops and clicks)
- splicing accuracy (particularly at the opening consonants of spliced words)
- splicing cuts, abutments, alignments, and bonding

A more general assessment of the completion of the project would be to consider its effectiveness in terms of the skills acquired by the participants, including the design and execution of a thorough production plan, tape recording techniques, and a certain dexterity at splicing.

As with all the projects presented in this book, students are encouraged to improvise similar or related exercises and to develop their own production steps for their execution. In any studio project, careful planning, efficient and precise execution, and critical assessment are all essential elements.

SPEED TRANSPOSITION

When a tape recording is played back at a speed faster than that at which it was recorded there are two basic, related results: the information on the tape is accelerated (in musical terms, the tempo gets faster) and the frequency (pitch) of the recorded sound is higher. The opposite is true of a recording played at a speed slower than that at which it was recorded.

Transposition by Fixed Increments

Because of natural acoustic laws (discussed more fully in Chapter 4), when the playback speed of a tape is changed by a factor of two—one-half the original speed or twice the original speed—the resulting frequency change is one octave. If a tape is played at half its recorded speed, the pitch of the recorded material will sound one octave lower, and the sound events will occur half as fast. If a tape is played at twice the speed at which it was recorded, the pitch of the recorded material will sound one octave higher, and the sound events will occur twice as fast. This process can be repeated many times, each time producing a similar result. For example, if we were to record the tone A-220 Hz for 16 seconds on a tape moving at $7\frac{1}{2}$ ips and subsequently play the tape back at 15 ips, the tone would sound as A-440 Hz and last only 8 seconds. By recording this new tone with another tape machine onto a tape moving at $7\frac{1}{2}$ ips, then playing this second recording back at 15 ips, the tone would sound as A-880 Hz and have a duration of only 4 seconds. This process could be continued indefinitely, the only limitation being the progressive loss of signal quality unavoidable with multiple rerecordings of the material, except with extremely high-quality recording equipment or the use of noise reduction devices. (An interesting exercise would be to plan the production steps necessary to reduce the frequency of a sustained tone by two octaves. What is the ultimate limitation to lowering the pitch?) In the early development of tape music, transposition by fixed increments in this manner was one of the few means available for the transformation of sounds, and it is still one of the basic techniques of tape manipulation.

Oscillator Speed Control

Most professional tape recorders use either a servo-controlled hysteresis synchronous motor or a DC servo motor to control the speed of the capstan. The hysteresis synchronous motor maintains an almost perfectly constant capstan speed through the regulation of the frequency (usually 50 to 60 Hz in the U.S.) of the line current. The frequency of the line current maintains the speed of the motor independent of the slight variations in voltage that are common in most community power systems.

Often a provision is made for overriding the control of the line-current frequency through the use of an internal oscillator that controls the power to the capstan motor. The range of this control is seldom more than $\pm7\%$. Since the speed of the capstan motor changes in direct proportion to changes in the frequency of the control oscillator, variations in the speed of the tape are easily produced over a continuous range. Even when a tape machine does not have a variable speed control built into the unit, there is often some provision made for overriding the internal, fixed-speed, control oscillator by an accessory external oscillator.

The speed of a capstan driven by a DC servo motor is analyzed by a microprocessor and compared with the frequency of an extremely precise oscillator. Any difference that is detected between the speed and the frequency of the oscillator is rapidly corrected. Variable speed operation almost always requires an external variable oscillator as a substitute for the internal oscillator, but the range of control may be as great as $+100\%$ and -50%, producing a total variation of ±1 octave.

There are several advantages to variable speed control for both recording and playback. When a recording is made on a tape machine that runs slightly slower than the speed at which it is supposed to operate, and the resultant tape is played back on a machine that runs at perfect speed, the tape will sound as if it is moving too fast; the speed of the recorded sound events will be slightly accelerated, and the frequencies (pitches) of the sounds will be slightly higher. Usually this effect is so slight as to be imperceptible. But, in critical situations where exact frequencies, rhythms, and synchronization between two tape machines are essential, such speed discrepancy could produce annoying or disastrous results.

Variable Speed Transposition

Rising pitch and acceleration of sound events can be accomplished in either of two ways:

1. The speed of the recording machine can be gradually *decreased* as the sounds are being recorded.
2. The speed of the playback machine can be gradually *increased* as the tape is played back.

The first of these two techniques is preferable in most cases, since it produces an exact and permanent record of the degree and velocity of the speed change. The second provides no such permanent result, unless a subsequent recording is made of the altered playback (introducing an extra production step into the process and adding, in most cases, about 3 dB of unwanted noise in the form of tape hiss).

Falling pitch and a deceleration of sound events can be produced in precisely the opposite ways:

1. The speed of the recording machine can be gradually *increased* as the sound events are being recorded.
2. The speed of the playback machine can be gradually *decreased* as the tape is played back.

For the same reasons, the first technique is preferable.

OVERDUBBING

Overdubbing is the process by which new material and prerecorded material are combined into a new recording. The simplest version of this process (sometimes called "sound-on-sound") requires a mixer and two tape machines, one to play the prerecorded tape and one to record the mixture of the prerecorded and new material (Figure 2.10). Some older stereo tape machines are equipped with a simple internal "sound-on-sound" mixer, making it possible to do overdubbing between the two channels of the same machine, and avoiding the need for an external mixer and a second tape machine.

By repeating this process several times, a number of new sounds can be added to existing material. The drawbacks of this technique are that one has little control over the balance between the sound events occurring in successive recordings (none after the recording is made, since all the sounds are on the same track), and each rerecording causes a progressive loss of signal fidelity and the further addition of undesirable noise.

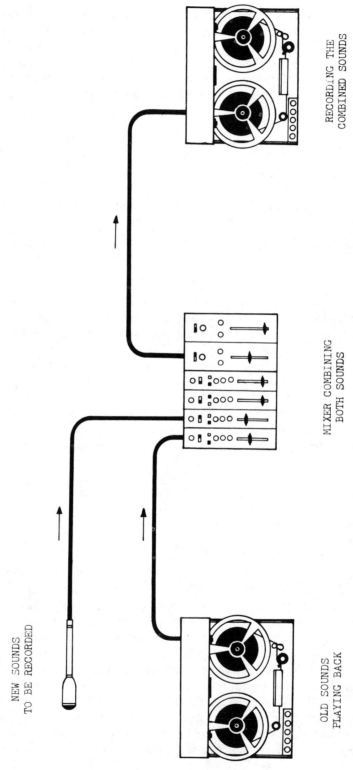

RECORDING THE
COMBINED SOUNDS

MIXER COMBINING
BOTH SOUNDS

NEW SOUNDS
TO BE RECORDED

OLD SOUNDS
PLAYING BACK

Figure 2.10 Overdubbing

SIMULTANEOUS SYNCHRONIZATION

Often referred to as *Sel-Sync* (for selective synchronization) or *Sel-Rep* (for selective reproduction), and popularly known as "sound-with-sound," simultaneous synchronization (*Simul-Sync*) allows the playback and record functions of a multitrack tape machine to occur simultaneously on separate tracks. Normally, if a tape with material recorded on one track was played back while new material to be synchronized with it was being recorded on another track, a noticeable time delay would exist between the two tracks because of the distance between the recording and playback heads on the tape machine (Figure 2.11). The length of this delay can be computed precisely by dividing the distance between the centers of the two heads by the tape speed. With most tape machines, the delay will range from about 0.3 to 0.5 seconds at $7\frac{1}{2}$ ips or from about 0.15 to 0.25 seconds at 15 ips. However, tape machines equipped with simultaneous synchronization capabilities allow the recording head to also serve as a playback head. Therefore, the new material is recorded at the same time—*the same place on the tape*—as the prerecorded material that is being played back (Figure 2.12). Further, since the different sounds are recorded on separate tracks, in contrast to the "sound-on-sound" method where all the sounds are mixed together on a single track, the playback levels of each track can be adjusted independently.

The obvious advantages of being able to add new sounds to pre-existing recorded material, in perfect synchronization with prerecorded tracks, yet without affecting them in any way, have led to the development of multitrack tape machines capable of recording up to 64 separate tracks. Even the common eight- or four-track tape machine is made many times more versatile through the use of simultaneous synchronization. Not only can each of the tracks be used to record a different instrument, voice, or type of sound, but each track can be recorded at a different time, and even in a different place from any other track, yet in perfect synchronization with tracks that have been recorded earlier.

In a more sophisticated adaptation of the previously discussed overdubbing process, this time using simul-sync capabilities in a process called "dubbing down," two or three synchronous tracks of a four-track tape machine might be played back, mixed, and rerecorded onto the fourth track of the same machine, thereby making room for three new, separate tracks of material (Figure 2.13). The fourth track would, of course, be a second-generation recording with the balance of its component parts permanently set, but the capability of the tape machine would be expanded to seven channels (eight, if an external sound source was mixed in with the three prerecorded tracks as they were being recorded onto the fourth track). With the improved performance characteristics of modern tape machines and the use of noise reduction equipment, three or four overdubbings of this type should not prove to be too damaging to the final sound quality. Because many electronic sounds are constructed from the simultaneous combination of several independent sounds, the ability to record a large number of different sound events simultaneously can be very advantageous—if not absolutely essential—to the electronic music composer.

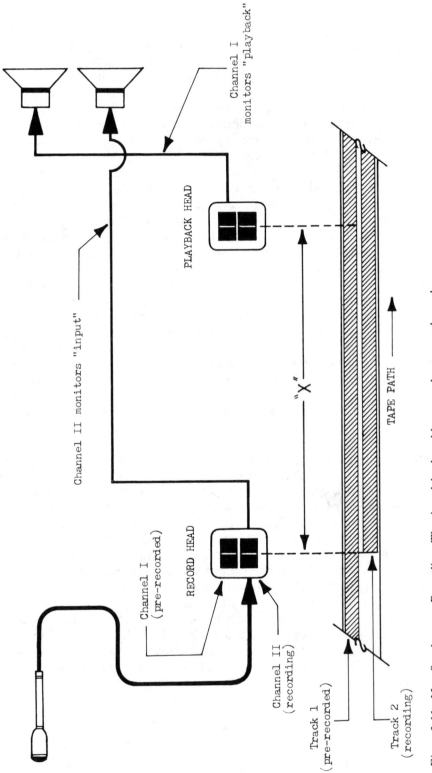

Figure 2.11 Non-Synchronous Recording. The time delay heard between the two tracks as they are monitored will be equal to the distance ("X") between the center of the record head and the center of the playback head divided by the speed of the tape.

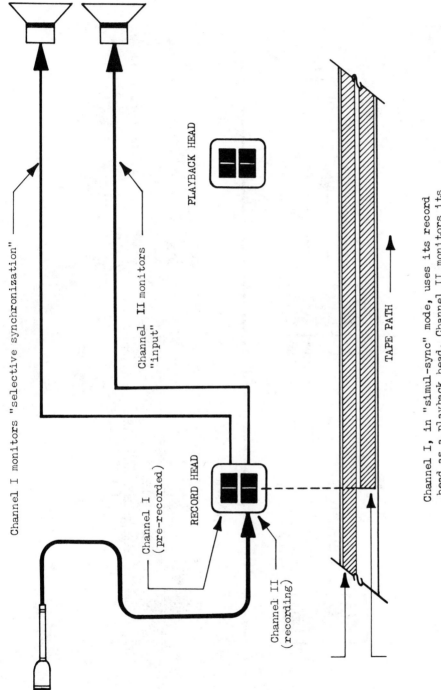

Channel I monitors "selective synchronization"

Channel II monitors "input"

Channel I (pre-recorded)

RECORD HEAD

Channel II (recording)

PLAYBACK HEAD

TAPE PATH

Channel I, in "simul-sync" mode, uses its record head as a playback head, Channel II monitors its record head on "input". There is no time delay heard between the sounds on the two channels.

Figure 2.12 Synchronous Recording: Channel I, in "simul-sync" mode, uses its record head as a playback head, Channel II monitors its record head on "input". There is no time delay heard between the sounds on the two channels. Note: Playback head is not used.

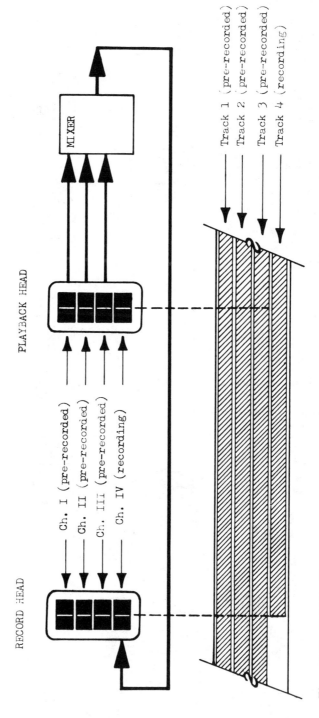

Figure 2.13 Dubbing Down

68

LISTENING EXAMPLES

Berio, Luciano

Thema (Omaggio a Joyce)
Turnabout 34177
Philips 836–897

Boucourechliev, Andre

Text II
BAM LD–971

Ferrari, Luc

Presque Rien No. 1
DGG 2543004

Gaburo, Kenneth

Exit Music II: Fat Millie's Lament
Nonesuch H–71199

LeCaine, Hugh

Dripsody
Folkways FM 3436

Mimaroglu, Ilhan

Le Tombeau d'Edgar Poe
Bowery Bum
Turnabout TV–34004S

Penderecki, Krzysztof

Psalmus
Philips 6740–001

Schaeffer, Pierre

Etude aux chemins de fer
Ducretet-Thomson DUC–8
Philips 6521–021

Takemitsu, Toru

Vocalism Ai
Water Music
RCA VICS–1334

Ussachevsky, Vladimir

Sonic Contours
Desto 6466

Xenakis, Iannis

Concrete P–H II
Nonesuch 71246

Chapter 3

Extended Tape Manipulations

REVERSE PLAYING

There are many sounds that we have grown quite accustomed to over the course of our lives that most people could not have imagined just a hundred years ago—certainly not before the invention of the phonograph. One of the simplest of these sounds is that of a spoken word played backwards. Try as we might, most words—even quite simple words—would be impossible for us to vocalize backwards.

This is a simplistic example at best, but the point is that sounds are inherently different when reversed. It is important to realize that this is not merely a retrograde succession of individual sound events, but a complete reversal of the shape of each sound and all of its components. The customary set of attack characteristics that our brains use to distinguish one type of sound from another doesn't occur until the end of each sound component, and even then backwards, creating a great deal of mental confusion as the brain attempts to classify the sound. Because there are many instances in which a reversed sound might be effective in the context of an electronic music composition, several methods have been developed to produce such sounds easily.

Reel Inversion

If we record a sound on a monophonic tape machine, then exchange the take-up and supply reels with each other, the sound when played back will be backwards. This is not possible on all tape machines because of the limitations posed by some track configurations. In these instances, when the supply and tape-up reels are exchanged, they also invert the tape tracks. What was originally on channel *A* of a half-track/stereo tape machine would then be heard on channel *B* backwards (Figure 3.1). A quarter-track/ stereo playback system could not be used for this effect at all since the playback head is designed so that the inversion of the tape will not give access to the original two tracks, but, instead, to a second pair of unrelated tracks (Figure 3.2). The two original tracks will not even make contact with the active portion of the playback head. Full-track/ mono, half-track/stereo and quarter-track/four-channel tape machines are all capable of producing reversed sounds by the reel inversion method.

Reverse Tape Threading

Another technique that produces reversed sounds, and which will work with *any* track configuration, requires the use of a tape machine that has three separate motors: one for

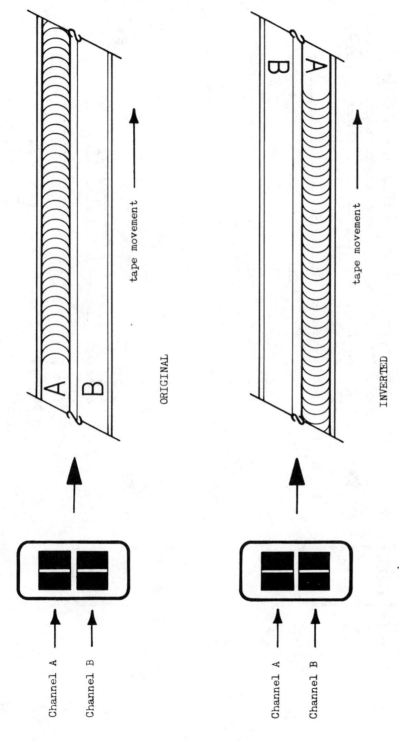

Figure 3.1 Reel Inversion ($\frac{1}{2}$-track stereo)

71

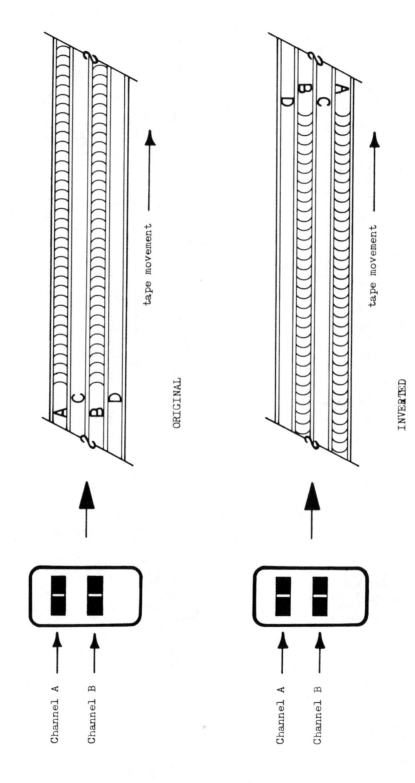

Figure 3.2 Reel Inversion ($\frac{1}{4}$-track stereo)

the take-up spindle, one for the supply spindle, and one for the capstan. Machines of this type usually regulate the tension on the tape by keeping both the take-up and supply motors engaged when in the play or record modes. The equilibrium maintained by the two reel motors pulling the tape in opposite directions is then counteracted by the operation of the capstan motor to make the tape travel forward or backward across the heads. If the capstan pulls the tape toward the take-up reel (as in normal operation), that motor takes up the slack and maintains a constant tape tension. If, on the other hand, the tape is threaded around the *backs* of the capstan and pressure roller (Figure 3.3), the tape will be sent toward the supply reel by the capstan. In such a balanced-tension system, the *supply reel* motor will now act to take up the slack in the tape, so the tape will move backwards from the take-up to the supply reel, causing previously recorded sounds to be played backwards. (Note that it is not possible to record during this reverse playing operation because the sounds recorded would immediately be removed from the tape by the erase head.)

This technique is very useful, especially for multiple-channel recordings, since the track positions against the heads are not changed as they are with the reel inversion technique. Sounds recorded initially on channel *A* are played back on channel *A*, eliminating the possibility of confusion that might easily result from the use of four or more tracks in the reel inversion process. However, there are many tape machines that either do not used a balanced-tension, three-motor design or make it physically impossible to reverse-thread the tape around the capstan and pressure roller. Obviously, these machines would not be capable of playing in reverse by this method, and the reel inversion technique would be the only option available.

Even when technical considerations make the reverse-threading method practical, extreme care is advisable. It is very easy to stretch or entangle the tape by handling it carelessly. The fast-forward and rewind controls should never be used. Not only will they have a tendency to pinch the tape, thereby stretching or breaking it, but the excessive friction and wear on the tape is harmful.

TAPE LOOPS

One of the first used and most common tape manipulation techniques was the tape loop, and it has proven to be a technique of enduring value to the electronic music composer. A tape loop is formed simply by splicing the two ends of a piece of tape together, creating an endless loop. In most cases, the piece of tape has had a sound or a group of sounds recorded on it before being made into a loop, though it is quite possible to record on an already assembled loop. Limitations on the length of the tape loop depend on certain physical considerations. It can be no shorter than the circumfrence of the tape machine head assembly, but it can be as long as there are tape guides and supports to keep it taut. Maintaining tension on the tape is important, since the tape must make consistent contact with the tape machine heads in order to maintain good fidelity. For the same reason, the friction produced by the tape supports and guides that are needed should be kept to a minimum, otherwise the tape will flutter and drag.

Although there are many special devices that various tape studios have custom built for maintaining tape-loop tension, a wide variety of means can be improvised from unrelated common objects normally found in the tape studio. Microphone stands, empty

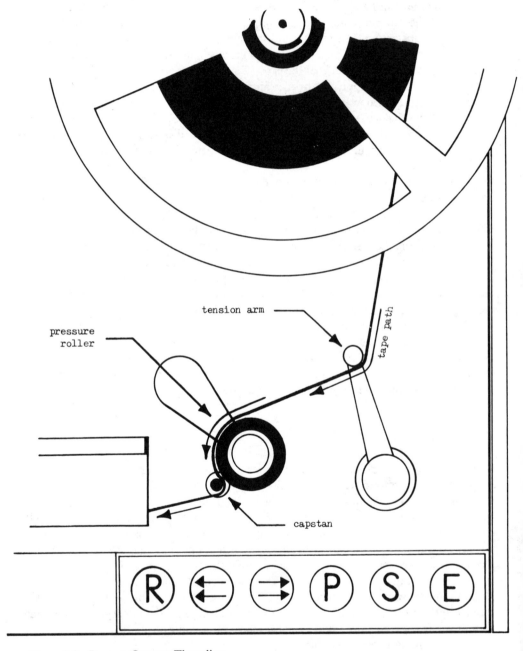

Figure 3.3 Reverse Capstan Threading

tape reels, music stands, and hand-held pencils can be used with long tape loops (Figure 3.4). Heavy, smooth-surfaced cylindrical objects, such as jars or cans, can be used with short tape loops (Figure 3.5).

Tape Loop Applications

A resourceful composer can find many uses for tape loops. The basic ostinato effect created by the continuous repetition of the sounds recorded on the loop can be gradually modified by changing its speed, amplitude or timbre. Loops of long length may be juxtaposed with other loops of shorter lengths so that many levels of repetition and periodic change occur over an extended length of time. Several small loops of only slightly different lengths can also create extremely complex, continually changing relationships among the sounds recorded on them. Although it is difficult to eliminate the disturbing effect of the instant change of sonic quality at the location of the tape loop's splice, it is sometimes possible to make very steady sounds infinitely long with no perceptible interruptions. When there is a sequence of separate events on the tape loop, it is usually possible to mask the necessary splice by placing it at the point of attack of one of the events. Of course, tape loops may also be played either forwards or backwards, and the simultaneous combination of several different tape loops going in either direction can be quite effective.

TAPE ECHO AND DELAY TECHNIQUES

Because most high-quality tape machines have individual heads for the erase, record, and playback functions, and these heads must be physically separated by some distance, an interesting tape manipulation technique becomes available. If a sound is recorded by the recording head and monitored by the playback head, a short delay will occur between the time the sound was recorded and the time the sound is played back, because of the physical distance the tape must travel between the two heads. The distance between the recording and playback heads varies from machine to machine and could be anywhere from 1 to 3 inches. Depending on the speed of the tape, the delay time produced might be anywhere from 0.1 to 1.5 seconds. In any case, the length of time will be too great (more than 20 milliseconds) and too regular in its occurrence to be perceived as reverberation (see Chapter 6). For this reason this effect is called *tape echo*.

Double Channel Echo

The simplest tape echo effect is produced by recording a signal on one channel of a stereo tape machine and sending the monitored signal from the playback head of that channel to the recording head of the second channel. A single echo will occur when the playback head of the second channel is also monitored (Figure 3.6). The delay time of the echo can be exactly determined by dividing the distance between the recording and playback heads—measured head-gap to head-gap—by the tape speed.

Single Channel Echo

All other tape echo effects require the use of a mixer. By mixing the signal monitored from the playback head with the signal input to the record head, a whole series of echoes

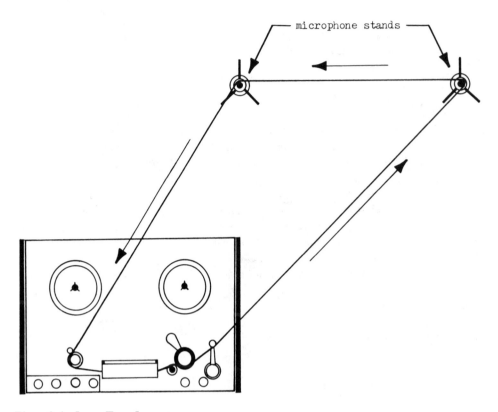

Figure 3.4 Long Tape Loops

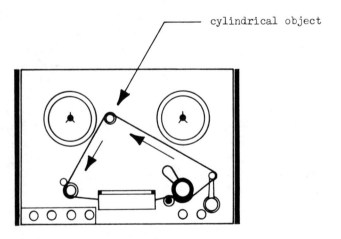

Figure 3.5 Short Tape Loops

76

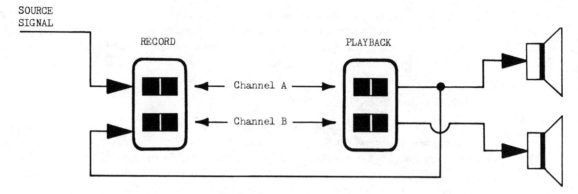

Figure 3.6   Double Channel Echo

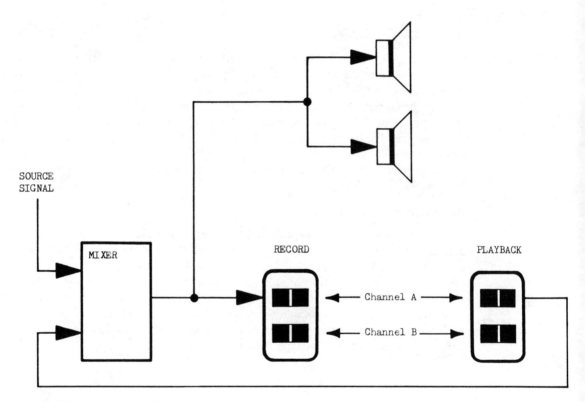

Figure 3.7   Single Channel Echo

can be initiated using only a single channel of a tape machine (Figure 3.7). Care must be exercised, in using such a patch, to prevent the build-up of too much feedback, an effect that will become very recognizable with only one occurrence.

Multiple Channel Echoes

An even more intricate series of echoes is produced when the output of the playback head of one channel is monitored while it is also sent to the recording head of another channel, which then returns the signal from its playback head to the input mix (Figure 3.8). If this same process is applied to a four-channel tape machine, the results can become very complex, particularly if the sound source is continually changing in character (Figure 3.9).

Echo-Feedback Regulation

In each of the above cases the number and amplitude of the echoes produced is determined by the various input/output gain settings of the mixer. If the gain of the returned signal is too low there will be no echo at all. As the gain of the returned signal increases, the number and amplitude of the echoes produced also increase until the echoes eventually become stronger than the source sound itself and saturate the tape with feedback.

Speed Change Effects

Since the length of the delay time is in part related to the speed of the tape, a wide variety of effects can be produced by making speed changes while the tape machine is running. For example, by using the patching system shown in Figure 3.7 and controlling the speed of the tape machine with a variable speed control, gradual changes in the length of time between the echoes can be made without affecting the pitch or duration of the source sounds. On the other hand, by playing back the tape just made, now at a steady speed and without any added echo effects, the pitch and duration of the original sounds will change radically while the length of time between the echoes remains constant.

Multiple Mixed Echoes

Several tape machines may be patched together to produce even more diverse echo effects, especially if the machines are running at different speeds and have different distances between their recording and playback heads. The arrangement in Figure 3.10 illustrates the use of specific brands of tape machines with various tape speeds and recording/playback head distances. Most studios will have several tape machines with their own characteristics available for similar effects. In situations where several tape machines are used, it is often more practical to set up a simple tape loop for each machine than to use a separate reel of tape for each machine.

Extended Tape Delay Systems

Extended delay times may be produced by threading a single reel of tape from the supply reel of one tape machine to the take-up reel of another tape machine, in effect making the distance between the record head (that of the first machine) and the playback head (that of the second machine) variable over much longer distances (Figure 3.11). If the tape speed is $7\frac{1}{2}$ ips, the delay time will be 1.6 seconds for each foot of separation (or 5.26 seconds per meter) between the recording head and the playback head. As with long tape loops (which could also be used with extended delay systems) it is important to maintain a consistent tension on the tape so that it is in constant contact with the heads. It is usually best to use the capstan of the take-up machine alone, since there may be a small speed discrepancy between the two machines. If the tape is threaded through the

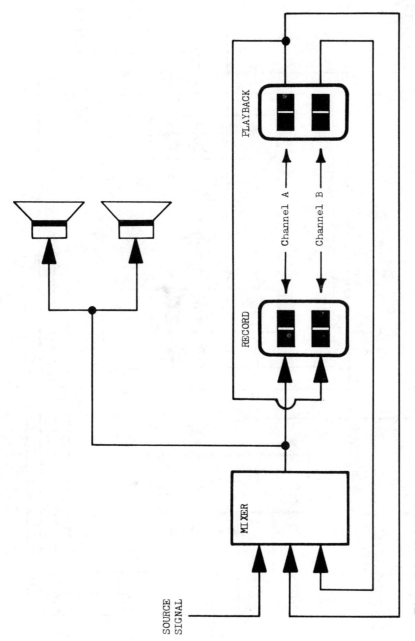

Figure 3.8 Multiple Channel Echo (2 channel)

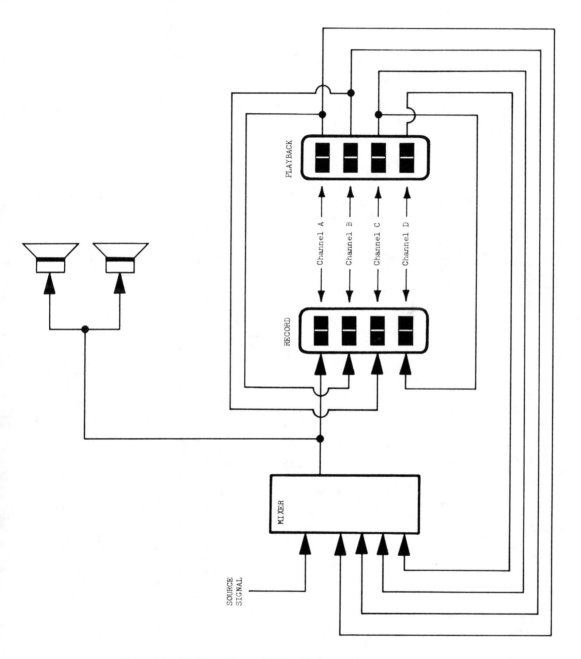

Figure 3.9   Multiple Channel Echo (4 channel)

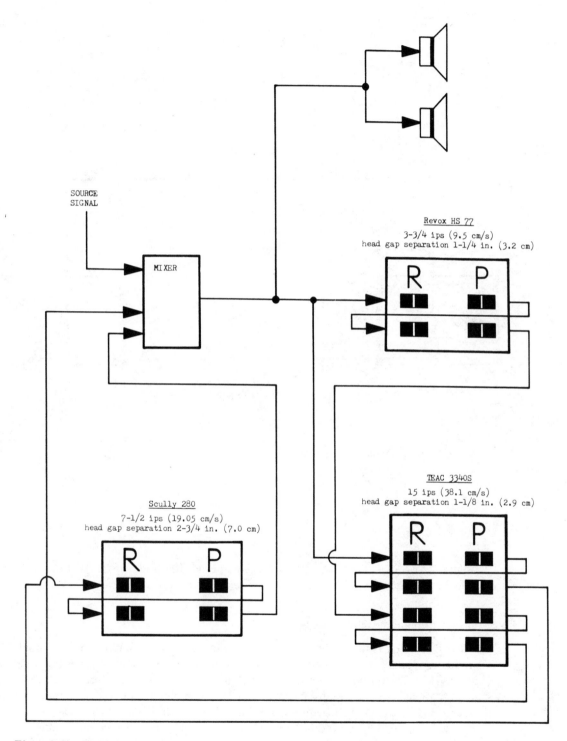

Figure 3.10　Multiple Mixed Echoes

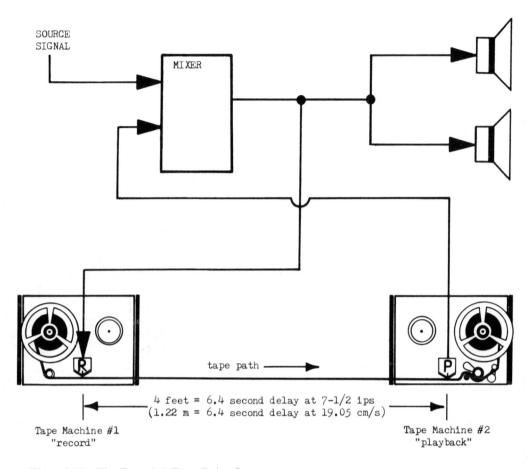

Figure 3.11   The Extended Tape Delay System

capstans of two machines of slightly differing speeds, the faster of the two machines should be used for the take-up reel.

Multiple Extended Delay Effects

Another possibility is to introduce one or more additional tape machines into the single extended tape path, producing a mixture of several delay time lengths of the same sound (Figure 3.12). The outputs of any of these machines could be routed to any of the other machines, mixed together (as in Figure 3.12), or any combination of both. In addition to these effects, the individual machines might be patched to produce echoes between their own heads (Figure 3.13). An infinite number of possible echo/delay combinations can thus be used to transform rather conventional sounds into complex montages of multiple attacks, changing amplitudes, tone colors, and densities.

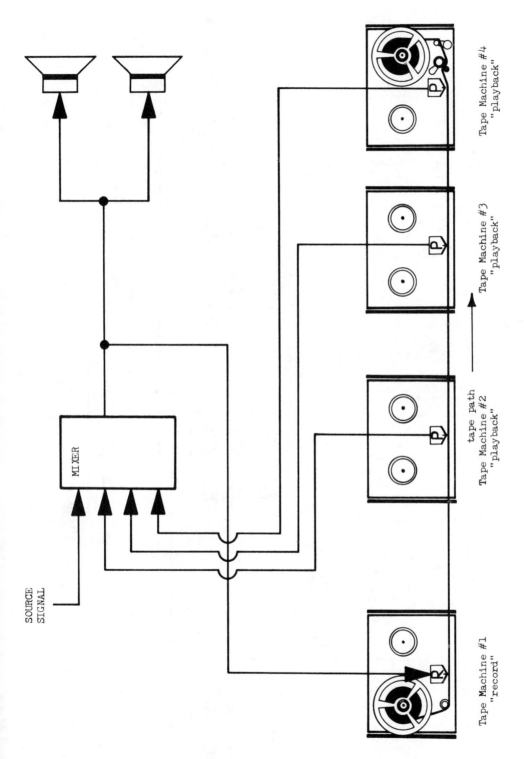

Figure 3.12 Multiple Playback Head Effects (1)

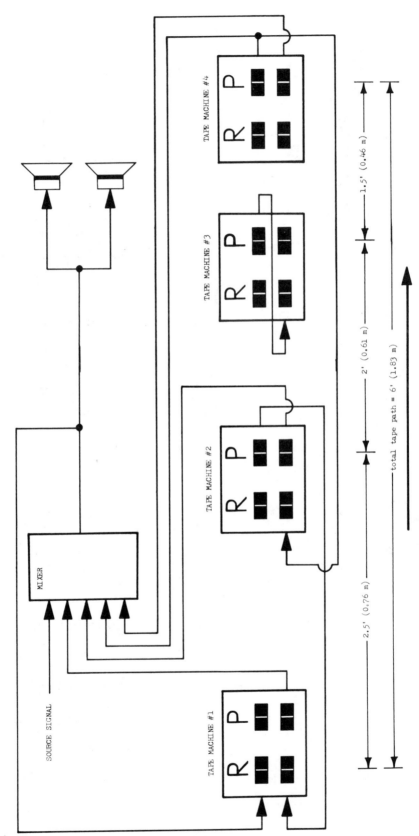

Figure 3.13 Multiple Playback Head Effects (2)

TAPE MACHINE SYNCHRONIZATION

Trial and Error

Particularly when mixing sounds from separate tape machines together for a single dub, it is often necessary to develop some means of synchronizing two or more tape machines. The most basic of these procedures, requiring no special equipment, relies on a trial-and-error process. First, each of the tapes is marked with a grease pencil at its beginning. These marks are then set back from the playback heads of their respective machines some common distance—from 8 to 10 inches—in order to allow the machines to reach a steady speed before the sounds cross the playback heads. This reference point could be some physical object on each machine or a grease pencil mark on the machine itself. Starting the tape machines simultaneously, time the succession of events and note if one tape lags behind the other(s); a second attempt can be made to correct any error. The tape that was lagging behind may be set a little closer to its playback head, or the tape that was ahead may be set further back. Once the new position is marked for future reference, the tapes can be played and checked again. If discrepancies still exist, the procedure must be repeated until the tapes are coordinated. This can be a time-consuming and frustrating process, particularly if the speed of one tape machine is slower or faster than that of the other(s) or if the speed of one of the machines is inconsistent.

Shared Speed Control

When this last problem is the case, it is often effective to vary the speed of one of the tape machines. It may also be possible to control the speed of several tape machines from a single external speed control. However, particular care must be taken to ensure that all of the tape machines are compatible with the same control unit and that the speed control device is capable of regulating more than one tape machine simultaneously. Use of a shared speed control will not eliminate the necessity of the trial-and-error process, but it may simplify it to some degree.

Pulse-code Systems

Probably the surest way to synchronize several tape machines is by using a pulse-code system. This process requires some fairly sophisticated special equipment that records a 60 cps pulse-code on the tapes as they are recording the desired sound sources, then compares and synchronizes the pulses when the machines play back the tapes. This synchronization method is very useful because of its high degree of accuracy, but its expense may prohibit its availability in most tape studios.

PROJECT NO. 2: MANIPULATED CYMBAL SOUNDS

Purpose of Project

This project is intended to give students the opportunity to exercise their tape manipulation skills in a relevant compositional form. Though it could hardly be considered an esthetically complete piece of music, the project has been designed to relate a wide variety of tape manipulation techniques to standard compositional practices and to instill basic disciplines, such as organized planning and production processes, into the students' approach to the tape studio. Experienced electronic music composers, usually faced with limited actual studio time, generally plan out their production steps in as much detail as possible. They realize from experience that the studio should be used for what the studio alone can provide, the *means* to produce the piece the composer has in mind.

We recommend that large classes be broken into studio groups of from two to five students, so that every student will have the opportunity to refine the skills necessary to produce this project and tape music in general. It is assumed that these groups will have access to the studio outside of class times. Approximately 8 to 10 hours of studio time should be required to complete the production of this project if, as we suggest, the source-sound tape and the edited first 30 seconds of channel A are produced by the instructor during class time as a demonstration of the methods and techniques employed in the production process for this project.

In most cases, it will be most practical to record one set of source sounds, separating them from one another by leader tape, and have each studio group make its own dub from this master copy. Not only does this give a common basis for the assessment of the completed projects, but it does away with the need to obtain a performer to play the source sounds for each studio group. All of the timings and tape lengths that will be used in the description of this project assume a final tape speed of 15 ips. If noise reduction devices are available, they should be used in every appropriate step of the production process.

Source Sounds

The four sounds shown in Figure 3.14 form the basic sonic material of this project; all are performed on a single suspended cymbal. The instructor may substitute other source sounds, or have each studio group make its own sounds, as long as the four sounds are clearly differentiated from one another.

Production Plans

The complete production plans for this project, which should be finished by each studio group *before* the actual studio work begins, include 1) a graphic score illustrating the successive events of both channels and their relative amplitudes (provided here as Figure 3.15), 2) written descriptions of the first 15 sound events of channel A and the first 17 sound events of channel B (given below), and 3) a detailed outline of the production steps necessary to produce the first 30 seconds of channels A and B. The production steps for the first five sound events of channel A are given as an example below. A careful examination of the graphic score (Figure 3.15) should reveal why only the first 30 seconds of each channel need actually be produced. The final result should be a correctly synchronized, two-channel, stereo tape, recorded at 15 ips, lasting exactly 60 seconds.

The following sound events correspond numerically to those in the graphic score (Figure 3.15).

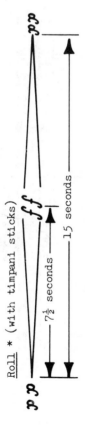
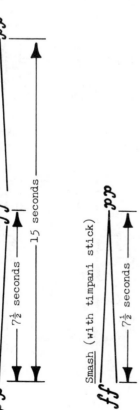
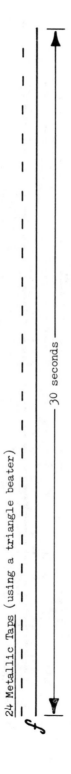
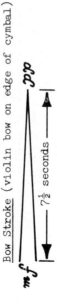

Roll * (with timpani sticks)

Smash (with timpani stick)

24 Metallic Taps (using a triangle beater)

Bow Stroke (violin bow on edge of cymbal)

Figure 3.14 Source Sound Diagram for Project No. 2. *Drum stick strokes are heard for the first half of this source sound. The second half is a gradual decay.

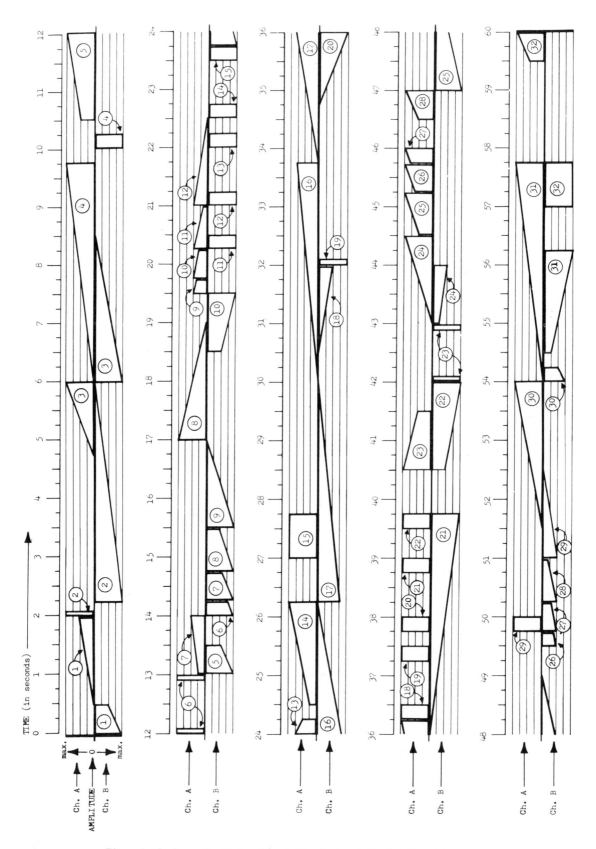

Figure 3.15 Score for Project No. 2 (Manipulated Cymbal Sounds).

Channel A (0–30 seconds)

1. Bow stroke, backwards, 2 octaves higher, 1.5 seconds.
2. 1 metallic tap, 3 octaves higher, reduced to 0.1 second.
3. 4 metallic taps, 2 octaves higher, lasting 1.25 seconds; crescendo from *pp* to *ff*.
4. Smash, backwards, starting about one-half octave above original pitch and descending to original pitch; 3.75 seconds; crescendo from *pp* to *ff*.
5. Smash, backwards, 2 octaves higher, reduced to 1.5 seconds.
6. 1 metallic tap, 3 octaves higher, reduced to 0.1 second.
7. Bow stroke, backwards, 1 octave higher, lasting 1.0 second.
8. Several metallic taps, 4 octaves higher, lasting 2.0 seconds; record as many times as needed (or use a tape loop); decrescendo from *ff* to *pp*.
9. Bow stroke, 2 octaves higher, reduced to 0.25 second.
10. Repeat #9, reduced to 0.5 second.
11. Repeat #9, reduced to 0.75 second.
12. Repeat #9, reduced to 1.5 seconds.
13. Repeat #9, exactly.
14. Roll, 2 octaves higher, reduced to 1.75 seconds, rising in pitch.
15. Several metallic taps, 4 octaves higher, lasting 0.75 second.

Channel B (0–30 seconds)

1. 1 metallic tap, original pitch, reduced to 0.5 second.
2. Smash, 1 octave higher, lasting 3.75 seconds, descending in pitch.
3. 1 metallic tap, 1 octave lower, with a lot of "double channel echo," lasting 2.5 seconds.
4. 1 metallic tap, 2 octaves lower, reduced to 0.25 second.
5. 1 metallic tap, original pitch, reduced to 0.5 second.
6. 1 metallic tap, 1 octave lower, reduced to 0.25 second.
7. Repeat #6, reduced to 0.5 second.
8. Repeat #6, reduced to 0.75 second.
9. Repeat #6, reduced to 1.5 seconds.
10. Roll, 2 octaves higher, reduced to 1.0 second.
11. 1 metallic tap, 2 octaves lower, reduced to 0.25 second.
12. 1 metallic tap, original pitch, reduced to 0.25 second.
13. 1 metallic tap, 2 octaves lower, reduced to 0.25 second.
14. 1 metallic tap, 1 octave lower, reduced to 0.25 second.
15. 1 metallic tap, original pitch, reduced to 0.25 second.
16. 1 metallic tap, 1 octave lower, with a lot of "single channel echo," lasting 2.5 seconds.
17. Bow stroke, 1 octave higher, lasting 3.75 seconds, ascending in pitch.

Production Step Outline

It is important that the production step outline be completed *before* actual production work in the studio begins. Otherwise, studio work will usually prove to be inefficient, resulting in mistakes and false starts. The production step outline should aim for the maximum efficiency and speed of execution. Our practice has been to treat the production step outline as equal in importance to, or even more important than, the actual finished product itself. The production step outline may be tailored to accommodate specific equipment, but it should follow the comprehensive form illustrated below (showing the first five sound events of channel *A*). The instructor should continue the production step outline for all of the sounds on channel *A* (0–30 seconds), and the students should then devise a similar production step outline for channel *B* (0–30 seconds).

Channel A, 0″–30″ (Production Steps)

ALL SOUNDS ARE RECORDED AND PLAYED ON CHANNEL *A* ONLY!

$$\begin{aligned}
\text{T.M.} &= \text{tape machine} \\
\text{Master} &= \text{final tape (to be played at 15 ips)} \\
\text{spare tape} &= \text{a reel of tape to be used for the intermediate stages of the} \\
& \quad \text{indicated transformation—it may be used many times over.}
\end{aligned}$$

Note: All sounds and silences are recorded for a greater duration than their final edited length to ensure sufficient length of each event when edited to its final duration.

Silence #1
0.0″–0.5″

Silence
1. Record on Master on T.M. #1 @ 15 ips, w/input @ "0", 2.0 sec.

Sound #1
0.5″–2.0″

Bow stroke, backwards, 2 octaves higher, 1.5 seconds.
⌐1. Play original backwards on T.M. #1 @ 15 ips.
└2. Record on spare tape on T.M. #2 @ $7\frac{1}{2}$ ips.
⌐3. Play spare tape on T.M. #2 @ 15 ips. (=1 − *8va**).
└4. Record on Master on T.M. #1 @ $7\frac{1}{2}$ ips (=2 − *8va* when played at final speed).

Sound #2
2.0″–2.1″

1 metallic tap, 3 octaves higher, reduced to 0.1 second.
⌐1. Play original on T.M. #2 @ 15 ips.
└2. Record on spare tape on T.M. #1 @ $7\frac{1}{2}$ ips.
⌐3. Play spare tape on T.M. #1 @ 15 ips (=1 − *8va*).
└4. Record on spare tape on T.M. #2 @ $7\frac{1}{2}$ ips.
⌐5. Play spare tape on T.M. #2 @ 15 ips (=2 − *8va*).
└6. Record on Master on T.M. #1 @ $7\frac{1}{2}$ ips (=3 − *8va* when played at final speed).

Silence #2
2.1″–4.75″

Silence
1. See Sound #3, step 3.

Sound #3
4.75″–6.0″

4 metallic taps, 2 octaves higher, lasting 1.25 seconds; crescendo from pp to ff.
⌐1. Play original on T.M. #1 @ 15 ips, making crescendo.
└2. Record on spare tape on T.M. #2 @ $7\frac{1}{2}$ ips.

---

* The notation for one octave is 1 − *8va.*

    3.   *Record Silence #2* (4.0″) on Master on T.M. #1 @ 15 ips.

    ⌐4.   Play spare tape on T.M. #2 @ 15 ips (=1 − *8va*).

    └5.   Record on Master on T.M. #1 @ 7½ ips (=2 − *8va* when played at final speed).

Sound #4
6.0″–9.75″

Smash, backwards, starting about one-half octave above original pitch and descending to original pitch; 3.75 seconds; crescendo from pp *to* ff.

    ⌐1.   Play original backwards, on T.M. #2 @ 15 ips, using speed control, starting at 150% of nominal speed and going to 100% of nominal speed in about 3.75 seconds.

    └2.   Record on Master on T.M. #1 @ 15 ips.

Silence #3
9.75″–10.5″

Silence

    1.   See Sound #5, step 3.

Sound #5
10.5″–12.0″

Smash, backwards, 2 octaves higher, reduced to 1.5 seconds.

    ⌐1.   Play original backwards, on T.M. #1 @ 15 ips.

    └2.   Record on spare tape on T.M. #2 @ 7½ ips.

    3.   Record *Silence #3* (2.0″) on Master on T.M. #1 @ 15 ips.

    ⌐4.   Play spare tape on T.M. #2 @ 15 ips (=1 − *8va*).

    └5.   Record on Master on T.M. #1 @ 7½ ips (=2 − *8va* when played back at final speed).

CONTINUE PRODUCTION STEPS IN A SIMILAR MANNER

Production Suggestions

The first step of the production process will be to make a dub of the source sounds, separated from one another by leader tape. Since these sounds will form the basis of every sound event in the score, it is very important to obtain low noise and distortion levels.

Many of the production steps will require the tape machines to be patched together in different ways, so students would do well to develop among themselves a consistent system of patch changing from one machine to the other. Much time can be saved and much confusion can be avoided if these procedures are agreed upon and made clear from the outset.

In general, it is advisable to produce all of the silences and sound events in their given order on the tape, making all of the speed changes and dynamic shapes before attempting to edit the sounds down to their proper lengths. An excellent safety measure is to produce silences about twice their needed lengths (they should be recorded tape, with the recording level set at "0", not leader tape, in order to get a consistent background tape sound). Sound events should be produced to exceed their needed lengths whenever possible. There is nothing more frustrating than finding that the sound event one has produced is a fraction of a second too short. The only recourse in such situations is to begin the production of the sound all over again. If some blank (unrecorded) tape is left between each of the sound events, it will be easier to locate the individual sounds during the editing process.

Because the sound events of this project must be so precisely timed, it is more practical to measure the lengths of tape than it is to try to time them with a stopwatch. It is a simple process to convert units of time into lengths of tape.

Combining Channels *A* and *B*

When the first 30 seconds of channel *A* have been completed and edited (by the instructor during class time) and the studio groups have each completed and edited the first 30 seconds of channel *B*, the two channels should be synchronized and combined on a separate tape. This tape will have no splices in it. The second half of the project (30″–60″) can then be constructed simply by synchronizing the first 30 seconds of channel *A* with the first 30 seconds of channel *B* played backwards—a careful examination of the score (Figure 3.15) will show why this is the case. When the dub for the second 30 seconds is made, the channels are simply inverted to complete the process. The two halves of the tape, 0″–30″ and 30″–60″, are subsequently joined with a single splice in the middle to form the completed project.

Project Assessment

Several considerations should be taken into account in assessing the quality of the projects produced. Naturally, all of the sound events should occur as described, at the proper speed transposition, in the correct direction, and following the dynamic contour indicated on the score. But timing accuracy might prove to be one of the most critical means of assessment. The overall timing of the completed project should fall within 0.2 seconds of the desired 60 seconds if reliable equipment is being used, and the events on channel *A* should interract with those on channel *B* exactly as they appear on the score. There are several places in the score where proper synchronization—or the lack of it—becomes quite obvious: e.g., at 6, 21, 30, 39.75, 40.5, 49.75, 54, and 57.75 seconds, to name just a few. Finally, the timing of the individual sound events should be precise, but if the overall tape length is correct and the synchronization of the channels is accurate, this is almost a foregone conclusion.

Another important characteristic of the project production is the overall recording quality. Noise levels should be kept as low as possible, but this has to be assessed in relation to the quality of the recording equipment used and the availability of any noise reduction equipment. Signal distortion levels should be negligible regardless of the equipment used, since this characteristic is easily avoided with even the lowest quality tape machines. In general, the relationship between the levels of the individual sound events should be consistent with their graphic representation in the score. Although this quality is difficult to define precisely, gross variations in the continuity of the signal levels are usually easily perceivable. Naturally, there should be no noise resulting from splices.

Finally, the quality of the production process and its planning should be assessed. Students should be encouraged to realize this project and all studio projects as quickly and efficiently as possible. The key to this is a carefully thought out, detailed production plan, as was illustrated for the first five sound events of channel *A*. This kind of detailed advance planning can save many hours of precious studio time and will go a long way toward making the studio experience enjoyable and productive.

LISTENING EXAMPLES

Cage, John	*Fontana Mix*
	Turnabout TV–34046S
	Williams Mix
	Avakian JC–1
Henry, Pierre	*Vocalise*
	Ducretet-Thomson DUC–9
	Variations on Door and a Sigh
	Philips 836–898DSY
Kotonski, Wlodzimiez	*Microstructures*
	Philips 6740–001
Lucier, Alvin	*I Am Sitting in a Room*
	Source Record No. 3 in
	Source: Music of the Avant Garde, 4, No. 1
	1971
Luening, Otto	*Fantasy in Space*
	Folkways FX–6160
	Desto 6466
	Low Speed
	Desto 6466
Luening, Otto and	*Incantation*
Vladimir Ussachevsky	Desto 6466
Reich, Steve	*Come Out*
	Odyssey 32 16 0160
	It's Gonna Rain
	Columbia MS–7265
Schaeffer, Pierre	*Etude aux piano II*
	Variations sur une flute mexicaine
	Ducretet-Thomson DUC–8
	Etude violette
	Philips 6521–021
Stockhausen, Karlheinz	*Solo*
	DGG 137–005
Ussachevsky, Vladimir	*Of Wood and Brass*
	CRI S–227
	Transposition, Reverberation Experiment,
	Composition
	Folkways FX–6160
	A Piece for Tape Recorder
	Finnadar QD 9010 0798
	CRI–112
Xenakis, Iannis	*Bohor I*
	Diamorphoses II
	Nonesuch 71246

Chapter 4

Basic Acoustics

PHYSICAL SYSTEMS OF SOUND

Perhaps the simplest definition of sound might be "That which is heard." Implicit within this statement is a recognition of the two fundamental qualities of sound: 1) its quantifiable, physical nature, and 2) its subjective, psycho-physiological nature. More precisely, sound is the perception of pressure waves in the air (or any other elastic medium) that emanate from a vibrating body.

Although the physical properties of sound are governed by predictable, universal physical laws, the perception of sound is dependent on a number of variable neurological and psychological processes, some of which are only partially understood and perhaps ultimately unpredictable. The very act of observing a psychological sensation interferes with the normal psychological process. As an example, observe your own breathing for a few moments. Try to determine its speed, its depth, and its rhythm. Can you be certain that your breathing has remained the same under your observation as it was before you became conscious of it, or has it been affected by your very attention? The latter is probably the case, and similar, though infinitely more complex problems exist in observing the perception of sound. For these reasons this discussion will begin with the definite, physical properties of sound and only later proceed to the more ambiguous properties of the perception of sound.

In a physical sense, sound is a form of mechanical energy governed by a chain of systems. These systems are:

sound source ➤ *transmitting medium* ➤ *sound receptor.*

The source emits the energy, the medium transmits the energy, and the receptor is affected by the energy. In musical terms, the source might be a musical instrument, the transmitting medium would be the air, and the receptor would be the ears of the listener. That which is emitted, transmitted, and received is energy in the form of sound waves—alternating compressions and rarefactions of air molecules.

Sound Source

A closer look at these systems reveals their components. The sound source consists of three, interrelated elements: the energy source (the player of the instrument), the vibrating element (part of the instrument), and the resonator (the body of the instrument). Each of these components helps to determine the nature of the sound. The amount of energy used to excite the sound-source system, the speed and complexity of the vibrations produced in the vibrating element, and the degree to which these vibrations are reinforced by the resonator establish the fundamental characteristics of the sound.

Transmitting Medium

The transmitting medium limits the characteristics of the sound that can be transmitted. A bell ringing in a vacuum makes no sound, because there is no medium (air) to transmit the bell's vibrations. A bell ringing under water sounds vastly different than it would in the open air because of the different properties of the two mediums. Air itself is by no means a perfectly efficient transmitting medium, since many of the vibrations of the sound source are quickly lost because of friction between the molecules that make up the air.

Another element relating to the transmitting medium is the environment in which the sound is propagated. Physical boundaries that reflect or absorb the sound waves will affect the characteristics of the sounds produced in that environment.

Sound Receptor

The sound receptor can generally be divided into the following components: a transducer, a processor, and a storage medium. If the receptor is a human being, these components are represented by the eardrum (transducer), the inner ear and parts of the nervous system (processor), and the various centers of the brain (storage medium). If the receptor is an electromechanical system, the three components could be compared to a microphone (transducer), an electrical system (processor), and magnetic tape (storage medium). In either case, the various components of the receptive system affect the characteristics of the sound as a result of their own physical limitations. A partially deaf person or an inefficient microphone is incapable of receiving the complete energy or characteristics of the sound being transmitted. Likewise, imperfections in the processing circuitry of the electronic network or in the human nervous system will alter or distort the information to be stored or interpreted.

SIMPLE WAVE MOTION

Pendulum Motion

The physical characteristics of a sound can be described in terms of the wave motion the sound produces in the transmitting medium. Since our atmosphere is an essential part of our existence and it has certain predictable qualities, it has become the normative medium for describing the various characteristics of sound. For the moment, however, let us take a more visible and simple example of motion—the pendulum. First, hang a pendulum (a weight on a string will suffice) from some free-standing, motionless body (such as a table edge or the top of a door frame). Unless disturbed by some outside force, the pendulum will maintain perfect equilibrium with its surroundings; that is, it will be motionless. However, if one pulls the pendulum out to one side, it will have potential energy. The force of gravity will now tend to restore the pendulum to its lowest point—the point of equilibrium. If the pendulum is released after it has been pulled out to one side, the potential energy will become kinetic energy as the pendulum begins to move.

Once released, the pendulum will swing back to its point of rest, but it will not stop when this point is reached. Instead, it will continue to move in the same direction, past the point of rest, to a point equally as far from the point of rest as it was when it started its movement. If there were no friction, this movement from the point of release to the opposite point and back again could continue forever. However, since friction is a part of our physical system, the length of the pendulum's swing will gradually become shorter, until eventually the pendulum is once again at rest. The forces that have been acting on the pendulum are described by Newton's third principle of motion: for every action there is an equal and opposite reaction. The characteristics of the pendulum's motion— its consistent, measured swinging back and forth across the point of equilibrium—are described by the terms *periodic motion* or *simple harmonic motion*.

Periodic Motion

Periodic motion is characterized by a recurrence of the same or similar events within a specific unit of time. The swinging of our pendulum is periodic because the pendulum crosses the point of equilibrium in equal intervals of time. Even as the distance traveled by the pendulum decreases due to friction, the length of time it takes the pendulum to return to its point of equilibrium remains the same.

Imagine for a moment that we are looking at the moving pendulum from above (Figure 4.1). If we pull the pendulum back to point $+A$ from its point of equilibrium (point E in the diagram), and assume that it takes the pendulum one second to move from point $+A$ back to point E, we know that it will also take one second for it to move from point E to point $-A$, from $-A$ back to E, from E back to $+A$, and so on. This type of motion, from $+A$ through E to $-A$ and back, etc., is described as *simple harmonic motion*.

Sinusoidal Motion

A closer examination of the movement of the pendulum over time (six seconds in Figure 4.2) reveals that the distance traveled from each equal fraction of a second to the next is not the same. This is because the pendulum slows down as it approaches the extremes of its swing (points $+A$ and $-A$) and speeds up as it approaches the middle of its swing (point E). In Figure 4.2, the curved line with the large dots represents the path of the pendulum over small divisions of time. This shape (much like an "S" on its side) is the result of *sinusoidal motion* (because this particular type of repetitive motion from $+A$ to $-A$ can be represented by a trigonometric function called a *sine wave*). It is a plot of the continuous motion of the object in time and shows not only the instantaneous displacement of the object from the point of equilibrium but its speed of movement at any given moment in time. Sinusoidal motion is the simplest form of periodic, simple harmonic motion. There are many examples of it that can be found in physical phenomena besides that of the pendulum, including the up and down motion of a spring, the oscillations of disturbed molecules in the air, the motion of water molecules in the ocean, and, most important to this study, the vibrations producing sound waves.

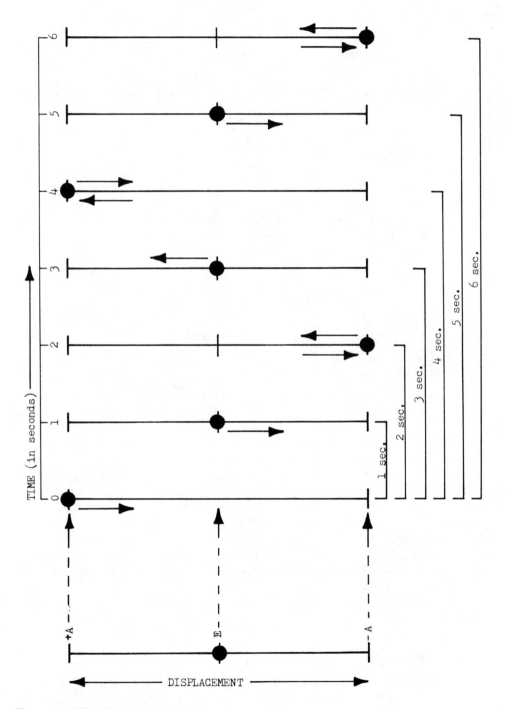

Figure 4.1   The Motion of a Pendulum

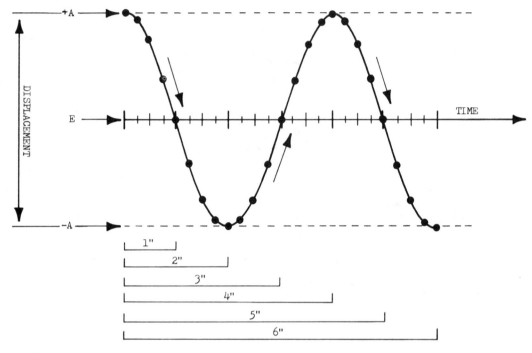

Figure 4.2 The Displacement Waveform of the Pendulum

Waveform Terms

There are several terms that are used to describe the characteristics of sine waves (Figure 4.3). The *period* is the length of time it takes for the wave to go through one complete *cycle*, that is, from its point of equilibrium (zero displacement in the figure) to +*A*, back through the zero point to −*A*, and back again to the zero point. In our pendulum example (Figure 4.2), the period was four seconds, so there were 0.25 *cycles per second* (cps). The number of cycles per second is called the *frequency* of a waveform. Frequency is expressed in either cps or, the equivalent, Hertz, abbreviated as Hz (named for the German physicist Heinrich Hertz); one cycle per second equals one Hertz.

The distance from the outermost excursion (positive or negative) of a sine wave (Figure 4.3) to its zero (equilibrium) line is called the *displacement* or *amplitude* of the waveform. Amplitude is a relative measurement of waveform displacement and is, in terms of sound, an indication of the loudness of the sound; the louder the sound, the greater the waveform displacement. Frequency and amplitude characteristics can easily be demonstrated in the studio, both aurally and visually, with an oscillator, an amplifier, and an oscilloscope.

Waveform Measurement

The period of a waveform can be measured between any repeating point of the waveform. The period, when measured from the positive-going crossing of the equilibrium line to the positive-going return to the equilibrium line is called the *sine*. When it is measured from positive crest (maximum displacement above the zero line, +*A*) to positive crest, this wave is called the *cosine*. As the cycle of the waveform

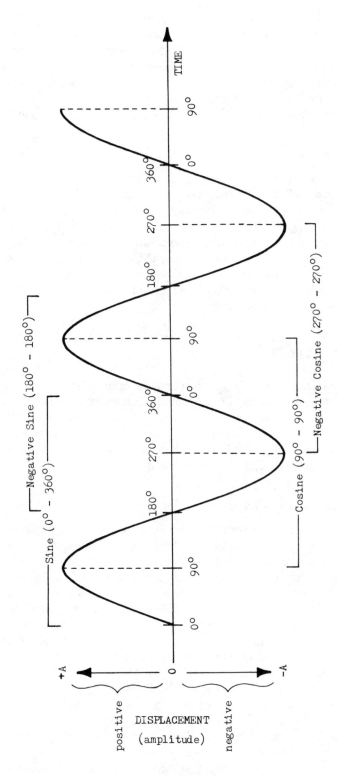

Figure 4.3 Displacement Waveform Designations

99

progresses, it is said to be in different phases relative to an abstract "point" in time (Figure 4.3). Note that any complete cycle always travels through a total of 360°. The *sine* wave is measured from the 0° to the 360° (positive-going equilibrium crossing) portions of the wave, and the *cosine* wave is measured from the 90° to 450° (360° + 90°) or maximum positive displacement points of the wave. The *negative sine* is similarly measured from 180° to 180° (negative-going equilibrium crossings) and the *negative cosine* is measured from 270° to 270° or maximum negative displacement points.

Waveform Phase

Phase is the position of the waveform in time. If there are two sine waves of equal frequency occurring at precisely the same time, they are said to be *in phase* with each other. If one sine wave (of the same frequency) lags behind the other by one-fourth of the length of the cycle (Figure 4.4), the two waves are said to be 90° *out of phase*. Similarly, a lag of one-half wavelength would put the waves out of phase by 180°; a lag of two-thirds wavelength would put them 240° out of phase, and so on. Although every waveform can be said to have a particular phase, this characteristic of a waveform is only significant (and audible) in relation to some other concurrent waveform or some arbitrary standard of time used for phase measurement.

WAVE PROPAGATION

In order to consider the way in which sound waves are transmitted in the air, it is necessary to understand that air is not a "solid" medium but, instead, is made up of an infinite number of individual molecules. These small particles of matter respond to the vibration of other bodies (such as a musical instrument) by vibrating in a like manner. It is this vibration that is transmitted as sound energy. The movement—or *displacement*—of the individual air molecules is actually very slight.

Equilibrium, Rarefaction, Compression

Imagine that there is a bass drum in a completely silent, stable environment (Figure 4.5a). The air molecules surrounding the bass drum head are in *equilibrium*, equally spaced and (for the sake of argument) motionless. If the drum head is struck from the right it will stretch back (to the left) from the blow, and it will, in the process, "pull" the adjacent air molecules (those to the right) with it. These air molecules become separated from each other, forming a partial vacuum (*rarefaction*) that other, more distant (further to the right) air molecules try to fill (Figure 4.5b). At the same time, the drum head has reacted to its initial movement after the impact of the blow and (just as with the swinging of the pendulum) has reached its maximum displacement in one direction. Now it moves in the opposite direction, passing its point of equilibrium and causing the adjacent air molecules (to the right) to compress against each other (Figure 4.5c). These molecules bump into others (*compression*) still further to the right, causing their motion to be transmitted outward from the source of the vibration. The waves of compression and rarefaction that are produced by the vibrating drum head are pushed out in every direction from the source and are an exact duplication of all the characteristics of the vibrations of the sound source. Figure 4.5 illustrates the effects of vibration in the air in

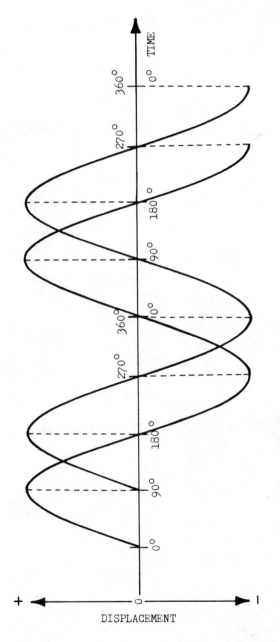

Figure 4.4 Waveform Phase Relationships

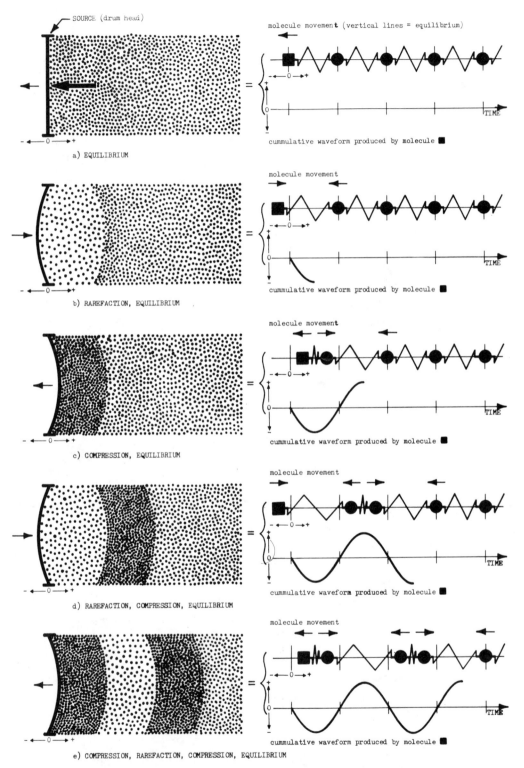

Figure 4.5 Waveform Propagation in the Open Air. Note: All stages of the diagram are shown at the instant *after* maximum molecule displacement. The squared molecule symbol is immediately next to the vibrating drum head. The arrow to the left of the drum head shows the direction of the forthcoming movement.

three ways. First, the effects of the drum head on the air molecules adjacent to it (in this case, only to the right, though similar, opposite reactions would also take place to its left) are shown as waves of compression and rarefaction in the transmitting medium (air). Second, a mass/spring model (several equal masses, each representing an individual air molecule, are connected by springs representing the changing forces between the molecules) shows the effects of the bass drum disturbance on just a single string of air molecules. Third, a displacement curve shows the continuous or accumulated motion, in time, of just one of these particles—in this case the one closest to the drum head.

Uniform Waveform Propagation

Eventually, due to the effects of friction and inelasticity, the vibrations of the drum head will diminish, and it will displace fewer and fewer air molecules until it finally comes to rest. As a result, the compressions and rarefactions produced in the air will become less extreme, and the sound will gradually become softer until it subsides into silence. Notice that both the drum head and the individual air molecules (see the mass/spring model of Figure 4.5) move only slightly from their initial points of equilibrium and ultimately come to rest there. It is the energy, in the form of waves of rarefactions and compressions called sound waves, that has been transmitted—often over great distances. Yet, the frequency, spectral, amplitude, and phasing characteristics of that initial vibration (of the drum head in our example) will be preserved even in the most distant resulting sound wave. This property, known as *uniform waveform propagation*, is fundamental to the consistent recognition of sounds; if it were not so, our world would be an aural chaos in which sounds would change form across the distances they travel to reach our ears, becoming completely unrecognizable in the process.

In terms of the properties of periodic motion previously discussed, frequency relates to the speed at which the sound source (in this case the drum head) vibrates: the faster the vibrations, the closer the compressions and rarefactions produced in the air and the higher the frequency of the sound. (A bass drum head actually vibrates at several frequencies simultaneously, but the principles are the same nonetheless.) The amplitude of the vibrations is a function of the strength of the impact on the drum head—the greater the force of the impact, the greater the displacement of the head and the more forceful the compression and rarefaction of the air molecules. In no way does the amplitude of the wave influence the frequency of the wave; nor does the frequency (which is determined by the size, density, and elasticity of the source) affect the amplitude of the wave.

RESONANT SYSTEMS

In the previous example, the bass drum head was struck and a set of vibrations began that were transmitted through the air to (it may be assumed) the ears of some listener. Although the drum head did not vibrate at one particular frequency but at several frequencies, all of the vibrations were at fairly low frequencies. If we had wished to create a sound of higher frequencies, we would have had to change the size of the drum; a smaller drum would produce higher frequencies because it would vibrate faster than a larger one. The physical dimensions of the different sized instruments would produce and reinforce vibrations of different frequencies. The characteristics of physical systems—both acoustic and electronic—by which certain frequencies are reinforced in preference to others is called *resonance*.

In one sense, resonance is the tendency of one body to vibrate at the same frequency as another body. The body of a violin (shown in cross-section in Figure 4.6) and the sounding board of a piano are each *resonators*; they vibrate—resonate—almost equally well across the full range of frequencies created by the strings of the instruments. When a string of either instrument is made to vibrate—by plucking, striking, or bowing it—the vibrations of the string are transferred to the body of the instrument by the bridge (the support over which the string crosses before being secured). The violin body or the piano sounding board then begins to vibrate sympathetically (at the same frequency) with the string. These *sympathetic vibrations* reinforce the sound produced by the string by converting the energy that the string (with its small surface area) would otherwise dissipate through friction into vibrations across the full surface of the resonator, where the vibrations can be more efficiently transferred to the air by the resonator's larger surface area. In essence, the resonator functions as a natural amplifier for the source of the vibrations.

The Helmholtz Resonator

Not all bodies resonate equally well across a broad range of frequencies. Some are limited to one *resonance frequency*. Take, for example, a narrow-necked bottle. If one blows across the top of the bottle, the air within the bottle will begin to vibrate at one specific frequency, which is the resonance frequency of the volume of air in the bottle. The German physicist Hermann von Helmholtz (1821–1894) observed that the narrow neck of the bottle constricted the flow of air so that, when excited by a cross current of air blown across its top, the "plug" of air contained in the neck would move up and down in the neck, alternately compressing and decompressing the air in the bottle, thus producing a tone. By changing the volume of air contained in the bottle (i.e., the size of the bottle or the usable air space within it), the resonance frequency would be changed (von Helmholtz 1863).

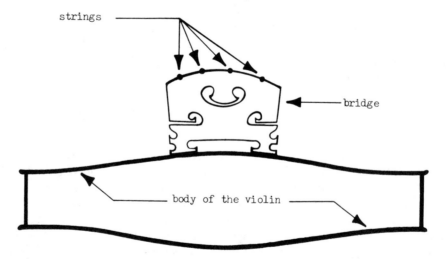

Figure 4.6 Cross-Section of a Violin Body

Wind Instruments

All wind instruments operate on the same principles as the Helmholtz resonator. A *column of air* defined primarily by the length of the instrument vibrates at a frequency inversely proportional to the length and diameter of the column—the shorter and narrower the column of air (the less its volume), the higher the frequency at which the column will resonate. The holes in the body of a wind instrument allow the player to instantly change the length of the column of air (thereby the volume of air) contained in the instrument, thus changing the frequency of the tone produced (Figure 4.7).

COMPLEX PERIODIC WAVEFORMS

The previous discussion assumed that the tones produced by the flute and other wind instruments are "pure" (a *pure tone* consists of only one frequency, i.e., a sine wave), but there are actually no traditional, acoustic musical instruments that produce pure tones. Even the relatively pure sounding tone of the flute is far from simple. In fact, almost all naturally occurring sounds are *complex*; that is, they are created from a variety of simpler component sounds that, when simultaneously combined, give these complex sounds their distinctive "colors" or "timbres."

Acoustic Musical Instruments

Many factors contribute to the complexity of a sound. For now, consideration will be limited to what, for lack of a better word, might be called "musical" sound—that is, *complex*, sustained tones, with a single fundamental frequency (perceivable as a single steady pitch), created by acoustic (as distinguished from electronic) musical instruments. There are two principal physical systems that determine the complexity of tones produced by acoustic musical instruments: the nature of the source of vibration, and the peculiarities of the shape and composition of the resonator.

Acoustic musical instruments may be grouped according to their vibrating elements as: *chordophones* (string instruments, such as the piano or violin), *aerophones* (wind instruments, such as the flute or the trumpet), *idiophones* (instruments that are struck and vibrate as a unit, such as the xylophone), and *membranophones* (instruments that have stretched skins as the principal vibrating element, such as the drum). (Although not a part of our current discussion, electronic musical instruments are classified according to this system as *electrophones*.) An understanding of the characteristics of the vibrating element of a given musical instrument is essential for determining the qualities of the sound that it produces. Although the instrument's resonance system may modify the characteristics of the vibrations as they are conveyed to the transmitting medium, it cannot of itself create sound where no vibration already exists.

Harmonic Series

First consider the actions of a vibrating string that might be part of virtually any chordophone. If a string is fixed (stopped) at both ends and set into motion, the full length of the string will vibrate (Figure 4.8a). The number of times per second that the full length of the string vibrates is the *fundamental frequency* of the tone produced. If the

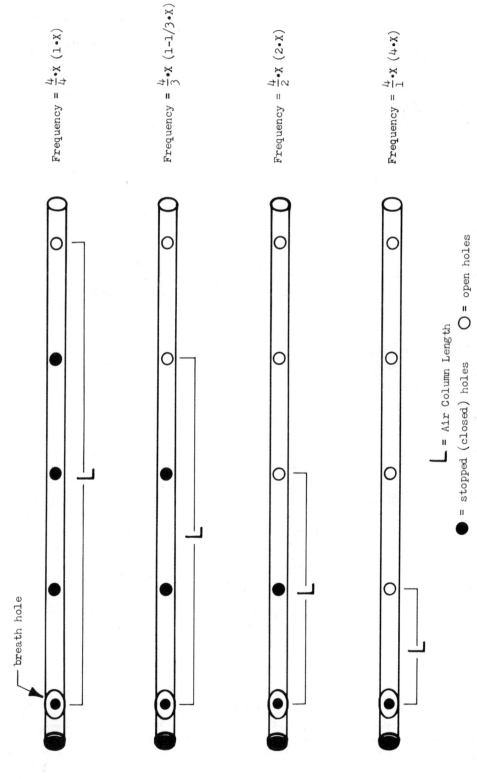

Figure 4.7 Producing Different Frequencies (pitches) on a flute by Changing the Length of the Air Column

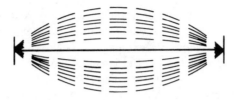

a) A string stopped at both ends vibrating
at its fundamental frequency
(Harmonic #1)

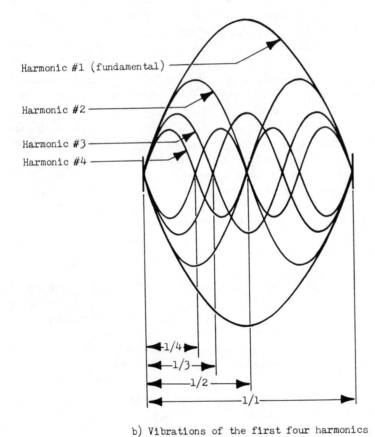

b) Vibrations of the first four harmonics
of a stopped string.
(The subdivisions of the vibrating length of
the string continue, at least theoretically, through infinity, i.e. $\frac{1}{\infty}$.)

Figure 4.8   The Subdivisions in a Vibrating String. Note: The vertical dimension (displacement) is exaggerated in Figure 4.8b, to show the relationships among the harmonics more clearly.

string vibrated only at this frequency, it would produce a pure tone (a single sine wave), but this is not the case. Strings actually vibrate in integral (integers are whole numbers—1, 2, 3, 4, etc.) divisions of their lengths. That is, a string will not only vibrate across its full length ($\frac{1}{1}$), producing the fundamental frequency of its vibrations, but it will also vibrate at $\frac{1}{2}, \frac{1}{3}, \frac{1}{4}, \frac{1}{5}, \ldots$ its length. These subdivisions of the string's vibrating length (Figure 4.8b) produce tones called *harmonics* or *overtones*,* of gradually lessening amplitude, that contribute greatly to the overall sound and its "timbre," not as individually perceivable tones but as a complex mixture of tones.

Just as with the column of air in a flute, the shorter the vibrating length of these subdivisions of the string, the higher the frequencies produced. Therefore, the frequency of the second harmonic, which results from the string vibrating over half of its length (thus twice as fast), is twice that of the first, or fundamental harmonic. Likewise, the vibrating length of $\frac{1}{3}$ of the full length of the string produces a harmonic of three times the frequency of the fundamental. *The frequency of any harmonic is the reciprocal of the vibrating (wave) length of that harmonic multiplied by the fundamental frequency* (Figure 4.9). This progression of frequencies—*all whole-number multiples of the fundamental frequency*—is known as the *harmonic series*. Though the intensities of the harmonics may vary, their progression (in whole-number multiples of the fundamental frequency) upward from the fundamental is unerring in musical sounds produced by all chordophones and aerophones, and most membranophones that have a specific fundamental frequency. It should be noted, however, that not all instruments produce every harmonic in the series.

The differences in the characteristics of many idiophones (especially bells) are much too complex for this discussion. Very simply, their *spectra* (the relationship of the overtones that are present to the fundamental, including their frequencies, their amplitudes, and their phasings) are described as *inharmonic*; that is, they do not follow the harmonic series and are not whole-number multiples of the fundamental frequency. The overtone components of inharmonic spectra are usually called *partials* in order to avoid their confusion with harmonics and the harmonic series.

Octaves

Although we have yet to relate frequency (a physical reality) to pitch (a somewhat contrived, subjective perception), it may be useful to illustrate the harmonic series in terms of the pitch relationships produced by it (Figure 4.10). Note that doubling the frequency of the first harmonic or fundamental (110 Hz, A in our example) results in a tone an octave higher (220 Hz, a), the second harmonic. The next higher octave does not occur until 440 Hz (a'), the fourth harmonic, which is twice the frequency of the previous octave (220 Hz). The doubling of the reference frequency will always produce a tone an octave higher. Thus, the next octaves on A are at 880 Hz (2 × 440 Hz, a''), the eighth harmonic, and 1760 Hz (2 × 880 Hz, a'''), the sixteenth harmonic. This type of relationship, in which the change of one fixed increment (one octave) corresponds to some other change (frequency) by a fixed ratio (2:1 in this case), is known as a logarithmic progression. Figure 4.11 shows a graph of the relationship of octaves to frequency change. The line curves because the actual *amount* of frequency change

---

* If these terms are properly applied, the first *harmonic* is the fundamental frequency itself, but the first *overtone* is the first tone *above* the fundamental (the *second* harmonic).

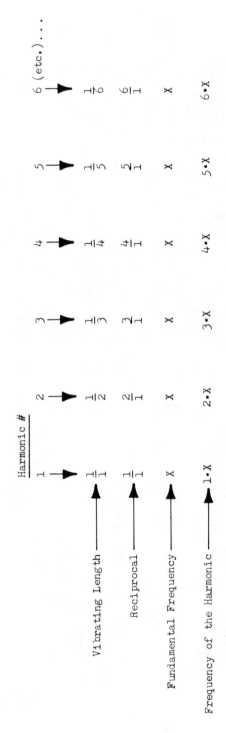

Figure 4.9 The Relationship between Vibrating Length and the Frequency of the Harmonics Produced

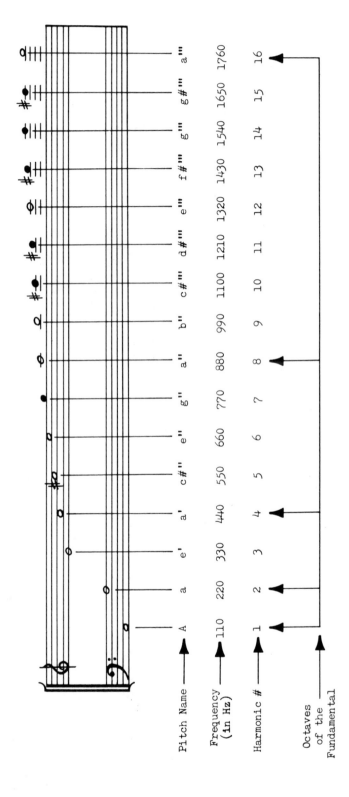

Figure 4.10 The Harmonic Series on A-110 Hz (solid notes are not correctly tuned in equal temperament)

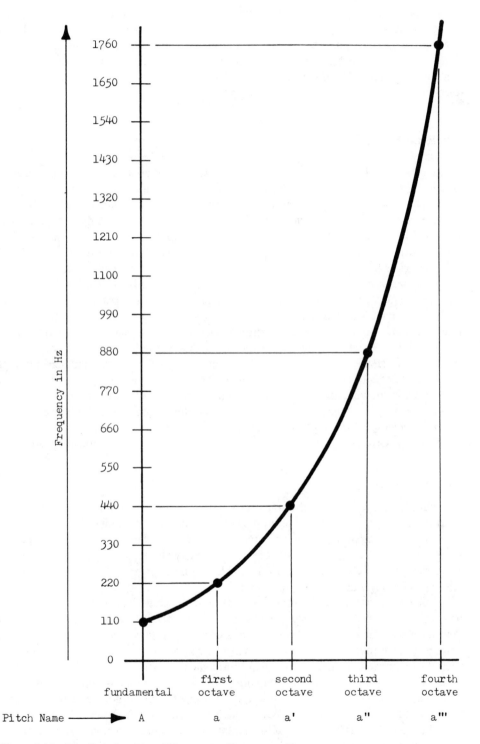

Figure 4.11 The Relationship of Octaves to Frequency Change

doubles for each successive change of only one octave. From A, 110 Hz to a, 220 Hz is an octave consisting of only 110 Hz difference, yet from a″, 880 Hz to a‴, 1760 Hz the octave comprises an 880 Hz change. This phenomenon continues *ad infinitum*, so each higher octave becomes progressively larger in the frequency change it encompasses— 1760 Hz, 3520 Hz, 7040 Hz, 14,080 Hz . . . . yet, we *perceive* the differences between all adjacent octaves to be equal in terms of pitch.

FOURIER'S THEOREM

It has been established that periodic vibrations of strings and air columns result in complex sounds made up of harmonics that follow a fixed series of frequency relationships, but there are more profound observations that can be drawn from the characteristics of complex, periodic motion. Foremost is Fourier's Theorem, a principle that has had an important impact on all branches of physics—especially the physics of sound—since it was first proposed in the early nineteenth century by the French mathematician Jean Baptiste Fourier. The theorem states that *any periodic vibration (or waveform), no matter how complex, is equal to the sum of a series of simple vibrations (pure sinusoids), called components, whose frequencies are harmonically related.*

An essential condition of the theorem is that the waveform is periodic (repetitive) in time and that the period of the complex waveform is equal to the period of the fundamental frequency. The implications of this principle are twofold: first, by analyzing the shape and frequency of a complex waveform, we can determine the characteristics of its components; and second, we can predict the shape of a complex waveform by knowing the relationships among and characteristics of its components. Put another way, complex sounds can be broken down into their simpler components (*Fourier Analysis*), and simple sinusoids may be combined to form complex, periodic waveforms (*Fourier Synthesis*). In both cases the results are mathematically predictable.

Sawtooth Waveform

The complex waveform resulting from a bowed string (spectral content is in part determined by *how* the string is set into motion—plucking, striking or bowing—and the place on the string where contact is made) may be idealized as a *sawtooth waveform* (Figure 4.12a). The sawtooth waveform is also one of the most frequently encountered waveforms produced by electronic means. (Three others, the triangle, the square and the pulse waveforms, will be discussed below.)

A *sawtooth waveform* is the sum of *all* harmonics, each with an amplitude of $1/n$ times the amplitude of the fundamental (in which n is the number of the harmonic) and with all even-numbered harmonics shifted 180° out of phase. Figure 4.12c shows the first six harmonics (unsummed) starting at the half cycle of a sawtooth waveform. Notice that when the beginning of the first harmonic (fundamental) is positive-going, the beginning of the second harmonic is negative-going. In fact, when all of the odd-numbered harmonics cross the node (point of equilibrium or "0" amplitude) in a positive-going direction, all the even-numbered harmonics cross the node in a negative-going direc- tion—180° out of phase with the fundamental and the other odd-numbered harmonics. Also, each successive harmonic has a smaller amplitude ($\frac{1}{n}$, i.e., $\frac{1}{1}, \frac{1}{2}, \frac{1}{3}, \frac{1}{4}, \frac{1}{5}, \frac{1}{6}, \ldots$).

The waveform shown in Figure 4.12b is the sum of the first six harmonics shown in

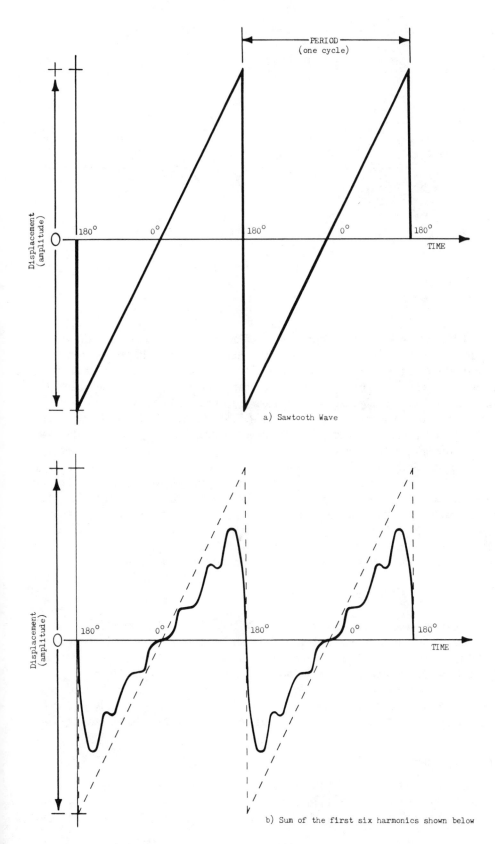

a) Sawtooth Wave

b) Sum of the first six harmonics shown below

Figure 4.12 The Harmonic Structure of a Sawtooth Wave

113

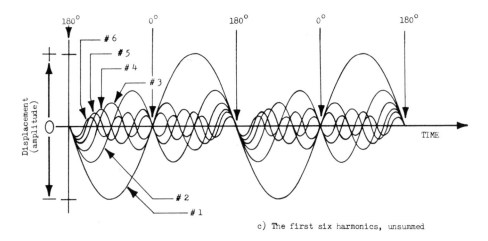

c) The first six harmonics, unsummed

Fig. 4.12 Con't.

Figure 4.12c. When all of the harmonics have a negative displacement, as at the start of the graph, their sum is at its greatest negative value. When every harmonic crosses the equilibrium line at the same time, regardless of direction (every half-cycle), there is zero total displacement. As more and more of the harmonics are added to this shape, the result will more closely approximate the sharply defined sawtooth waveform in Figure 4.12a (represented by a dashed line in Figure 4.12b). Figure 4.13 shows the shape and graphic spectrum analysis (a graph of frequency, amplitude, and phase) of the sine, sawtooth, triangle, and square waveforms at a fundamental (first harmonic) frequency of 100 Hz. Particularly notable in the shape and spectrum analysis of the sawtooth waveform (Figure 4.13-IIa and IIb) is the relative prominence of the fundamental component, which determines the basic frequency of the total, complex waveform. The fundamental frequency is also reinforced by the coincidence of the upper harmonics over the period of the fundamental (as was shown in Figure 4.12c). (Remember that every even-numbered harmonic has a phase shift of 180° and is, therefore, negative in value—shown in the spectrum analysis as a downward-going vertical line.)

Triangle Waveform

The shape of the *triangle waveform* (Figure 4.13-IIIa) more closely resembles that of its fundamental sine wave component because a larger percentage of the total energy of the waveform is invested in the first few components. A triangle waveform has a spectrum (Figure 4.13-IIIb) containing only the odd-numbered harmonics (numbers 1, 3, 5, 7, etc.), whose amplitudes are each in the ratio of $1/n^2$. (For example, the third harmonic—the second actual component—would have an amplitude of only $1/3^2$ or 1/9 that of the fundamental.) Further, every other component is shifted 180° out of phase.

Square Waveform

The *square waveform* (Figure 4.13-IVa) consists of all odd-numbered harmonics, in phase with each other, having amplitude ratios of $1/n$. As one might expect, the spectrum analysis of the square waveform (Figure 4.13-IVb) reveals that the upper harmonic

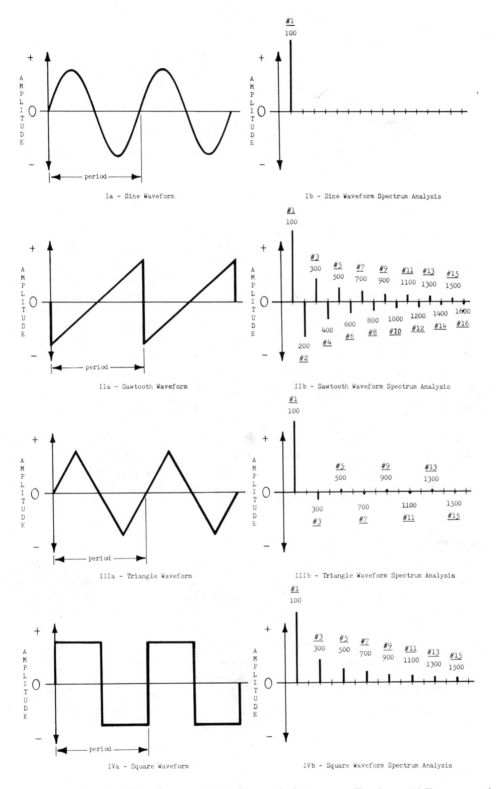

Figure 4.13 Standard Waveforms and their Harmonic Spectra at a Fundamental Frequency of 100 Hz.

115

components make up a much greater part of the total energy of the waveform than was true of the triangle wave. The square wave has a *duty cycle* of $1/n$; that is, it is positive (above the equilibrium line) for one half of its total period. This is an important distinction, because there are other waveforms—called *pulse waves*—that resemble the rectangular shape of the square wave but have different duty cycles. (Actually, the square wave is only one particular type of pulse wave.) Figures 4.14-Ia and Ib show the same square wave of Figure 4.13-IV in order to easily compare it with the various pulse waves of Figures 4.14-II, III, and IV.

Pulse Waveforms

Figure 4.14-IIa shows a pulse wave (sometimes called a rectangular wave) with a duty cycle of $\frac{1}{3}$—in other words, positive over $\frac{1}{3}$ of its duration. Figure 4.14-IIb shows an approximate spectrum analysis of this waveform, illustrating the relative change in harmonic content and distribution that has taken place (compare this illustration to that of the square wave in Figure 4.14-Ib). Notice that this waveform has every third harmonic missing from its spectrum. As was the case with the square wave, any harmonic which is a whole-number multiple of the reciprocal of the duty cycle is missing from the harmonic spectrum. (For example, the reciprocal of $\frac{1}{3}$ is 3, so every third harmonic is absent in the pulse wave with a duty cycle of $\frac{1}{3}$.) As the duty cycle of the pulse wave becomes smaller (Figures 4.14-III and IV), the number of upper harmonic components that are actually present in the waveform becomes greater. Therefore, the sounds produced would be perceived as getting "richer" (having a greater number of higher frequency components).

The harmonic content of all of the basic waveforms (sine, sawtooth, triangle, and square/pulse) may be easily demonstrated in the studio, both aurally and visually, by the use of a lowpass filter (with a resonance control) and an oscilloscope—refer to Chapter 6. A complete understanding of complex waveforms and their frequency/amplitude characteristics is essential to later work in electronic music.

Subtractive and Additive Synthesis

Sine, triangle, square, pulse, and sawtooth waveforms are only the basic building blocks of many complex timbral contructions. In a process known as *subtractive synthesis*, various harmonics may be removed by filtering (see Chapter 6) to change the frequency spectrum (timbre) of complex waveforms. Carried to the extreme, any complex sound can be filtered to remove upper harmonics and partials so that its fundamental sine wave component is all that remains. *Additive synthesis* involves the construction of complex spectra by adding various sine tones together, tones that may or may not be harmonically related, depending on the spectra desired. Each of these synthesis processes will be more fully discussed in later chapters, but they have been mentioned here to illustrate the practical applications of Fourier's theorem and their importance in the development of electronic music.

NOISE

In electronic music, the most complex sound possible is noise, of which there are two basic kinds: "white noise" and "pink noise." *White noise* is defined as random

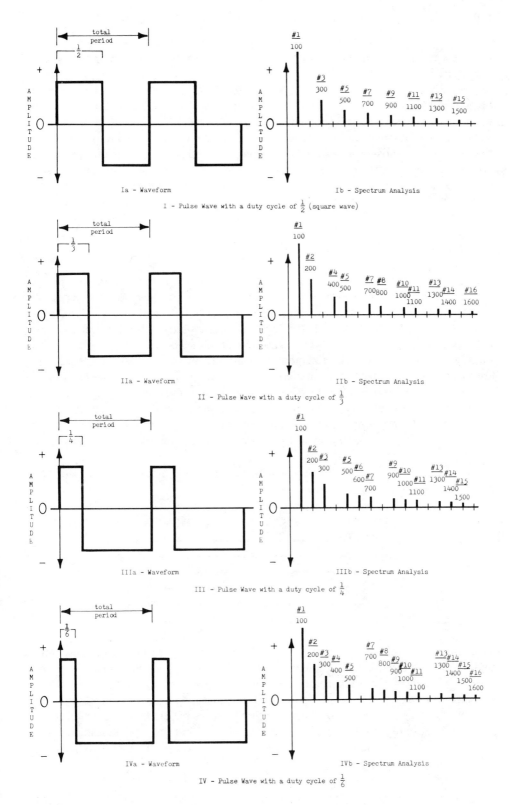

Ia – Waveform

Ib – Spectrum Analysis

I – Pulse Wave with a duty cycle of $\frac{1}{2}$ (square wave)

IIa – Waveform

IIb – Spectrum Analysis

II – Pulse Wave with a duty cycle of $\frac{1}{3}$

IIIa – Waveform

IIIb – Spectrum Analysis

III – Pulse Wave with a duty cycle of $\frac{1}{4}$

IVa – Waveform

IVb – Spectrum Analysis

IV – Pulse Wave with a duty cycle of $\frac{1}{6}$

Figure 4.14 Pulse Waveforms and their Harmonic Spectra

117

occurrences of all frequencies so that the sound energy contained in every equal *bandwidth* is the same (e.g., the same total sound energy is contained between 100 Hz and 200 Hz as is contained between 1000 Hz and 1100 Hz—the bandwidth in this case being 100 Hz). *Pink noise* is defined as random occurrences of all frequencies so that every *octave* possesses equal sound energy (e.g., the octave 100 Hz–200 Hz contains the same sound energy as the octave 1000 Hz–2000 Hz). From these definitions we can see that white noise tends to emphasize high frequencies while pink noise tends to emphasize low frequencies (Figure 4.15). Like all other complex sounds, noise, of any coloration, can be created by adding many thousands of sine waves together, and it can also be filtered to form less complex sounds.

AURAL PERCEPTION OF SOUND

Up to this point, we have limited our observations almost entirely to those aspects of acoustics that are mathematically quantifiable. The principles outlined have been objective and often absolute. Yet, recalling our initial definition of sound—"That which is heard"—we must now complete the equation by examining the properties of sound as they are *perceived*. At this point the quantifiable absolutes become few, not because the physical (or psycho-physical) principles to quantify them do not exist, but because they are so complex that many of them are not yet accurately discernible. The basis for the complexity of perceptual mechanisms and the difficulties they present lies at the source of all perception—the human brain—the most complex and mystifying information processor that we know of. To date, little is understood (in comparison to what remains to be known) of its functioning, even about how it handles such an omnipresent stimulus as sound.

For every objective criterion ascribed to sound, there is a corresponding subjective attribute describing how it is perceived:

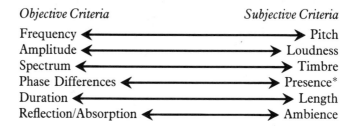

Objective Criteria		*Subjective Criteria*
Frequency	⟷	Pitch
Amplitude	⟷	Loudness
Spectrum	⟷	Timbre
Phase Differences	⟷	Presence*
Duration	⟷	Length
Reflection/Absorption	⟷	Ambience

Frequency is, within limits, described as pitch, amplitude as loudness, spectrum as timbre, phasing differences as presence, duration as length, and reflection/absorption as ambience. Each of these characteristics is intricately related to the others so that an awesome number of sounds with differing frequencies, spectra, phasings, and spatial locations (such as those made by a full symphony orchestra) can be heard simultaneously, yet remain individually identifiable—a task well beyond the capabilities of the most sophisticated analytical machines yet devised, but one that is second nature to the human auditory network.

---

* As this term is used here, it means the characteristic that distinguishes the sound made by several instruments from the sound that would be made by only a single instrument playing the same material. Other synonyms might be "texture" or "chorus effect."

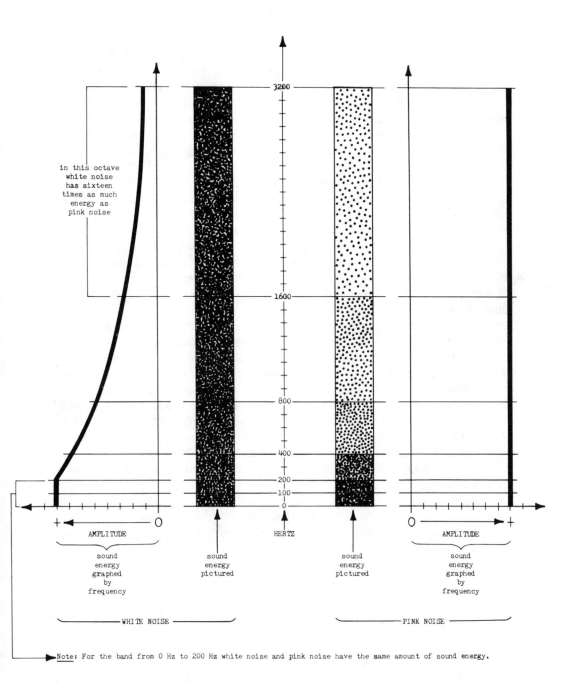

in this octave
white noise
has sixteen
times as much
energy as
pink noise

3200

1600

800

400

200
100
0

+ ◄───── O
AMPLITUDE

O ─────► +
AMPLITUDE

sound
energy
graphed
by
frequency

sound
energy
pictured

HERTZ

sound
energy
pictured

sound
energy
graphed
by
frequency

───── WHITE NOISE ─────

───── PINK NOISE ─────

Note: For the band from 0 Hz to 200 Hz white noise and pink noise have the same amount of sound energy.

Figure 4.15   Comparison of the Relative Sound Energy Levels of White and Pink Noise

PITCH

The Human Ear

In order to firmly grasp the concept of pitch perception—which is essentially a relative ranking of frequencies as "high," "low," or some degree of one or the other—one must first examine the human auditory mechanism (Figure 4.16). The outer ear acts like a funnel, focusing air pressure waves (sound waves) on the eardrum. By means of an articulated series of bones, the vibrations of the eardrum are transmitted to a membrane at the entrance (oval window) to the *cochlea* (wound up like a snail's shell as it appears in the ear—Figure 4.16a, and stretched out in a simplified illustration—Figure 4.16b). The cochlea, filled with an incompressible liquid (*perilymph*), is divided longitudinally into two chambers by the *basilar membrane*, which holds the actual auditory nerve and its corresponding nerve endings. Running from the broad base to the narrow apex (*helicotrema*) at the far end of the cochlea, the basilar membrane gradually narrows and becomes less flexible from the base toward the apex.

When the membrane at the oval window is set into vibration, it causes the perilymph fluid to oscillate, creating waves that move across the surface of the basilar membrane. About 30,000 hair cells (*cilia*) on the surface of the basilar membrane act as receptors, responding to the movement of the perilymph fluid and transmitting information about the vibrations to the neurons in contact with them. Specific places on the basilar membrane vibrate sympathetically with specific bands of frequencies presented to them because of the gradual stiffening and narrowing of the membrane. Further, these *resonance regions* of the basilar membrane are arranged logarithmically, from low-frequency regions at the base of the membrane to high-frequency regions at the apex of the membrane, so that a change of one octave (a doubling or halving) in the frequency of a tone results in the shifting of the resonance region excited by a fairly consistent distance of 3.5 to 4 millimeters (von Bekesy 1960). Whether the octave is from 100 Hz to 200 Hz or from 3200 Hz to 6400 Hz, the distance between the related resonance regions will remain roughly constant (Figure 4.17). Note that the most important frequency range for music (roughly from 20 Hz to 4000 Hz) covers approximately three-fourths of the length of the entire membrane.

Once the basilar membrane has been set into motion, the neurons, excited by the movement of the hair cells on the membrane, begin to fire impulses to the brain. The time distribution, rate of firing, and localization of the impulses determine much of what is perceived about the sound.

Pitch Perception

The ear's degree of sensitivity to changes in pitch (*frequency resolution*) varies greatly from one person to another, but there are overall limits to the ability to perceive pitch change. When the difference in frequency between two tones becomes too small, both tones are perceived as being at the same pitch. This minimum perceivable difference between two tones is remarkably small for most people. A gradual, smooth change of only 0.5% (only 10 Hz at 2000 Hz) is perceivable across most of the musical frequency spectrum (Zwicker, Flottorp, and Stevens 1957). Sudden changes in frequency are detected with even finer resolution. However, frequency resolution is somewhat dependent on frequency range, so changes in frequencies become increasingly difficult to perceive

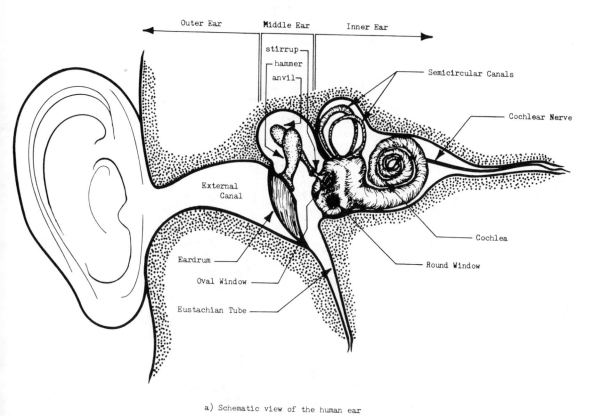

a) Schematic view of the human ear

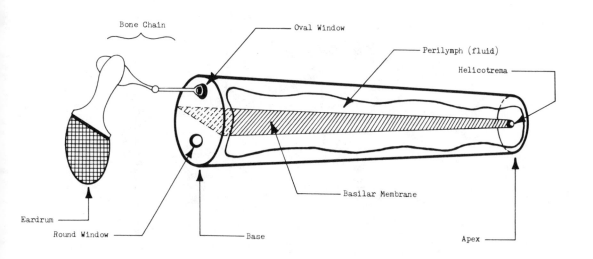

b) Simplified view of the Cochlea stretched out

Figure 4.16 The Human Auditory Mechanism

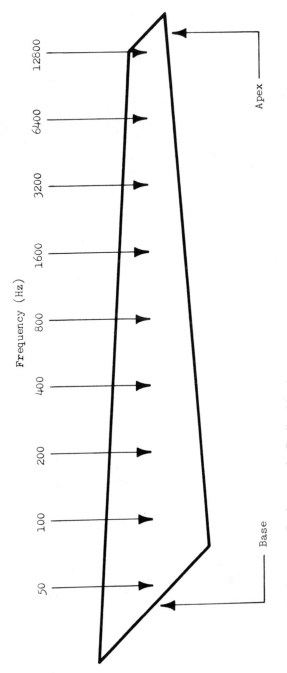

Figure 4.17 Resonance Regions on the Basilar Membrane

below about 1000 Hz (at 100 Hz, frequency resolution is only about 3%) (Roederer 1975).

BEATS

Constructive/Destructive Interference

When two pure (sine wave) tones of equal frequency and precisely the same phase occur simultaneously, their amplitudes are summed together, creating an increase in loudness (Figure 4.18a). This is known as *constructive interference*. However, if these same tones have even a slightly different phasing, the amplitudes of the waveforms will tend to cancel each other out at some point in their combined periods. If the phase difference is 180°, and the amplitudes of the two tones are equal, the opposing amplitudes of the waveforms will completely counteract each other, and there will be no sound at all (Figure 4.18b). This is called *destructive interference*. Of course, neither of these cases is likely to occur precisely in conventional, acoustic circumstances, but phasing interference is a useful technique in the electronic music studio and will be discussed in more detail in later chapters.

Beats

A far more noticeable and common phenomenon takes place when two tones occurring simultaneously are of slightly different frequencies. For example, if a tone with the frequency of 100 Hz is heard simultaneously with a tone with the frequency of 101 Hz, the result will be a composite sound (still perceived as a single tone) that gradually changes amplitude—from a maximum level to total silence—at the rate of one cycle per second (1 Hz), the difference between the two frequencies. This *differential waveform* is the result of the periodic, gradually changing constructive and destructive interference between the two tones. In our example, once every second the two waveform displacements are precisely opposed to each other, causing total destructive interference, therefore, silence. Exactly one half second after this point of total silence the displacements of the two waveforms are exactly complementary, causing a maximum constructive interference that results in the maximum amplitude. One will hear this as a periodic pulsation in the amplitude of the combined sound. Because of the lack of absolute precision in the tuning of any two musical instruments, this phenomenon, known as *first-order beats*, is common in almost all musical situations.

Frequency Discrimination

If the frequency of the 101 Hz tone is gradually increased, while that of the 100 Hz tone remains the same, the frequency of the beats (the *beat frequency*) will also increase. Eventually, the frequencies will become far enough apart to be perceived as two separate tones, exciting two separate regions on the basilar membrane. The minimum frequency distance between two tones necessary for them to begin to be perceived separately is known as the *frequency discrimination limit*. However, even beyond this limit, a certain "coarseness" will persist in the composite sound until a still larger frequency distance between the two tones, called the *critical band*, is passed, when the two tones will finally

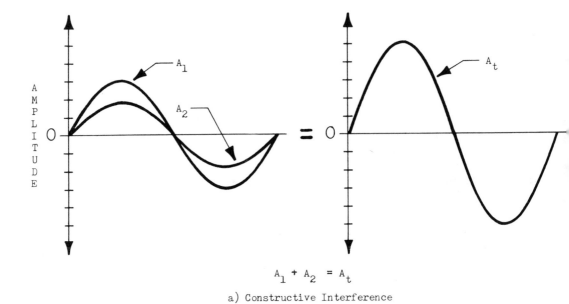

$$A_1 + A_2 = A_t$$

a) Constructive Interference

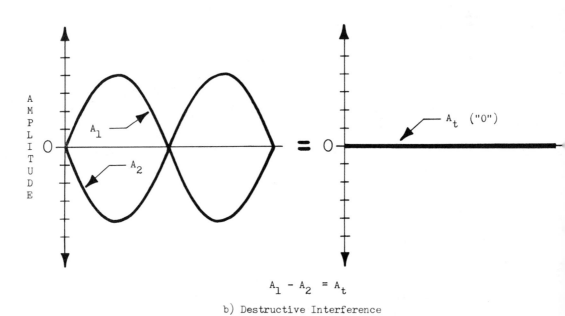

$$A_1 - A_2 = A_t$$

b) Destructive Interference

Figure 4.18 Constructive and Destructive Interference

be perceived as distinctly separate and pure, and we are actually aware of a pitch space, or void, between them (Roederer 1975).

The transition from the perception of beats, through "coarseness," to the perception of two pure, distinct tones is quite gradual, but both the frequency discrimination limit and the critical bandwidth can be measured subjectively. As was found in measurements of frequency resolution, these perceptual capabilities are severely diminished toward the lower end of the frequency spectrum. Below about 500 Hz, the critical bandwidth exceeds 20% of the frequency of the lower of the two tones (an interval of a minor third), and below about 100 Hz even the frequency discrimination limit exceeds that same amount. Generally speaking, although we can perceive very small frequency changes occurring in a single pure tone, the frequency difference between two simultaneous pure tones must be relatively large for the two tones to be heard clearly as separate entities.

COMBINATION TONES

Primary Difference Tone

If we take our two tones of the previous example, one (f_2) starting at 100 Hz and gradually rising in pitch over the other (f_1), which is held constant at 100 Hz, a number of audible effects will occur (assuming the tones are of sufficient intensity). As f_2 rises beyond the critical bandwidth we will hear an extremely low-frequency tone begin to rise in pitch, in perfect step with the rising f_2. The frequency of this tone, called the *primary difference tone*, is equal to the difference (in Hz) between f_2 and f_1. For very small differences in frequency between f_2 and f_1, the difference "tone" (which would not be perceived as a tone at all, but as first-order beats) is synonomous with the beat frequency. Only when the frequency difference between f_2 and f_1 exceeds about 20 Hz (the approximate low threshold for the perception of a pitched tone) does it sound as a separate tone. When f_2 is $1\frac{1}{2}$ times f_1, the difference frequency will sound one octave below f_1 (e.g., if $f_2 = 150$ Hz and $f_1 = 100$ Hz, the difference tone would be 50 Hz, an octave below the 100 Hz tone). This effect has long been used by organ builders to give the impression of having even lower sounding pipes than are actually present. When f_2 equals twice the frequency of f_1 (e.g., $f_2 = 200$ Hz and $f_1 = 100$ Hz in our example), the difference tone has the same frequency as f_1 (200 Hz − 100 Hz = 100 Hz). If f_2 continues to rise above twice the value of f_1 (200 Hz, in this case), the primary difference tone will rise above f_1 proportionally (Figure 4.19). The phenomena of beats, beat frequency, and combination tones can be aurally and visually demonstrated in the studio using two oscillators and an oscilloscope.

Other Combination Tones

There are three other *first-order combination tones* (the overall designation of these types of phenomena—so called because they arise directly from the combination of two primary tones), all shown in Figure 4.19, two of which are also difference tones and are easily perceivable even at relatively low volume levels. Each of these difference tones decreases in frequency as f_2 rises. The frequency of the first of these tones is equal to $f_1 - f_2$, and it decreases in frequency at the same rate that the primary difference tone, $f_2 - f_1$, rises. The frequency of the second of these tones is equal to $3 \cdot f_1 - 2 \cdot f_2$, and it decreases in

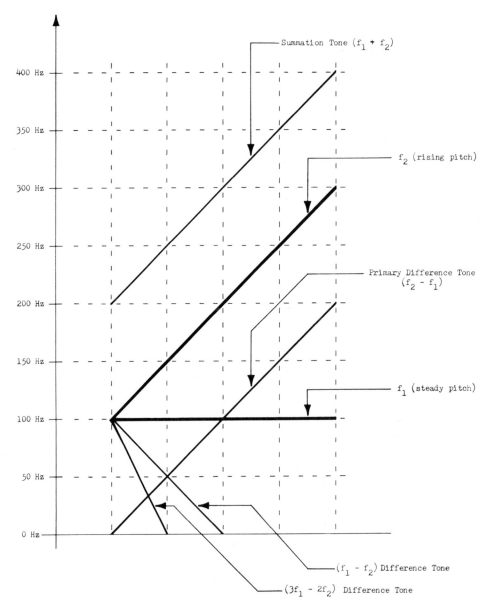

Figure 4.19 First-Order Combination Tones

frequency twice as fast as the first. Also shown in Figure 4.19 is another first-order combination tone, the *summation tone* $(f_1 + f_2)$, but its production in the studio is difficult, since it is easily masked by the other first-order combination tones.

In the above examples, the two primary tones were assumed to be pure (sine waves). In cases where other waveforms (triangle, sawtooth, pulse, or square) or sounds (e.g., a human voice) are used, first-order combination tones would also be generated between all the combinations of the upper harmonics that are present. Furthermore, first-order combination tones of sufficient amplitude will interact among themselves and with the two primary tones, in a manner analogous to the interaction of f_1 and f_2 above, to create a large complex of *second-order combination tones* which, though of lesser amplitude, can often be heard.

Aural Harmonics

Curiously, combination tones are not present in the actual, original sounds, nor, therefore, in the vibrations of the eardrum or of the oval window of the cochlea. Yet, they do correspond to activated regions of the basilar membrane and are, thus, thought to be the result of "nonlinear" distortion of the sounds occurring in the cochlea. In fact, this distortion effect can even cause several tones to be heard when only one, extremely intense pitch is sounded. These additional tones, called *aural harmonics*, occur at integral multiples of the source frequency ($2 \cdot f$, $3 \cdot f$, $4 \cdot f$, etc.), and are perceived as members of the harmonic series built on the single, intense tone (Roederer 1975).

LOUDNESS

In the physical sense, loudness is usually referred to as intensity—the amount of acoustical energy transmitted to the ear in a specified length of time. The range of sensitivity of the human ear to loudness varies greatly among different people due to such considerations as age, disease, working environment, and listening habits. These last two variables are newer to the human condition; before this century of high technology and 100-watt amplifiers, the average person's acoustical environment comprised few sounds louder than the clatter of horses' hooves and the tolling of church bells, with the notable exception of the sounds of cannon fire and gunshots.

Limits of Hearing

There are two basic limitations to human perception of loudness, both of which are to some extent dependent on the frequency of the sound heard. The first of these is known as the *threshold of hearing*—the minimum intensity necessary for a given sound to be heard. The second is the upper limit of sound intensity, often called the *threshold of pain*, beyond which actual physiological pain is experienced and physical damage to the ear can result. Generally, the range between these two extremes is greatest for a tone of about 1000 Hz, at which frequency the ratio of the threshold of pain to the threshold of hearing would be about one trillion to one (Roederer 1975). Admittedly, the intensity range of normal musical interest is smaller, being only about ten million to one!

Perception of Changes in Intensity

As was the case with the perception of pitch, there is a certain minimal degree of change in the intensity of a sound that must occur to be perceived by the human ear, which is much less sensitive to gradations of loudness than it is to gradations of pitch. Interestingly, it seems that this minimal necessary degree of change is roughly proportional to the intensity of the given sound. *The greater the initial intensity of a sound, the larger a change in intensity must be in order for it to be perceived.* (This is known as Weber's Law—so named for the German physicist who performed the experiments leading to its development.) For this reason, intensity is described on a logarithmic scale.

The degree of intensity is measured in units called *decibels* (dB) and is usually found by measuring the *Sound Pressure Level* (SPL), which is determined by the following equation:

$$SPL = 20 \cdot \text{Log} \frac{\Delta p}{\Delta p_0}$$

The Sound Pressure Level is equal to twenty times the logarithm of the ratio of the average pressure variation (Δp) to a reference pressure variation (Δp_0).

The minimum change in SPL (intensity) that can be detected by most people ranges from 0.2 to 0.4 dB within the range of pitch and loudness usually encountered in music (Roederer 1975). In more practical terms, a change of ± 3 dB (on a VU meter, for example) results in a change in intensity by a factor of 2. Thus, a sound at -3 dB is twice as intense as a sound at -6 dB and only half as intense as a sound at 0 dB. The logarithmic nature of our response to changes in intensity becomes even more apparent if we compare two sounds, one at 0 dB and the other at -15 dB. We will find that the intensity of the first sound is 32 times greater than the second!

Equal Loudness Curves

The sensitivity of the ear to changes in the intensity of a sound is highly dependent on the frequency of the sound. Figure 4.20 shows a set of *equal loudness curves* illustrating the relative loudness of various frequencies as perceived by the average human ear (Fletcher and Munson 1933). Notice that the threshold of hearing is much higher for low frequencies than it is for midrange or high frequencies, so low frequencies must be louder than midrange or high frequencies before they can be perceived. For example, a 100 Hz tone must be almost 40 dB louder than a 1000 Hz tone to reach the threshold of hearing. This phenomenon also accounts, in part, for the tendency of low-frequency sounds to diminish in intensity faster than high-frequency sounds.

When two tones of the same frequency and intensity are heard at the same time, one might expect that the perceived loudness of the total sound would double, yet, in fact, it is increased by a factor of only about 1.3 times that of a single tone. It would actually take ten tones of the same frequency and intensity to double the perceived loudness! However, two tones separated by a frequency interval greater than the critical bandwidth (about a minor third in most cases) will be perceived to have a greater combined loudness than two tones of the same intensity that are tuned to the same frequency. This phenomenon has long been exploited by composers in many types of music. Indeed, for much of the history of music composition for the organ, "doubling" (adding ranks of pipes at different octaves) was the only means of dynamic variation available to the organist (other than the natural variation evidenced by the equal loudness curves, Figure 4.20).

Masking

A related phenomenon is that of *masking*. When one sound is present, a second sound must *exceed* the intensity level of the first sound by a certain amount in order to be heard separately. The degree of intensity, or the "masking level," that must be reached or exceeded is highly dependent on the various characteristics outlined above. The higher

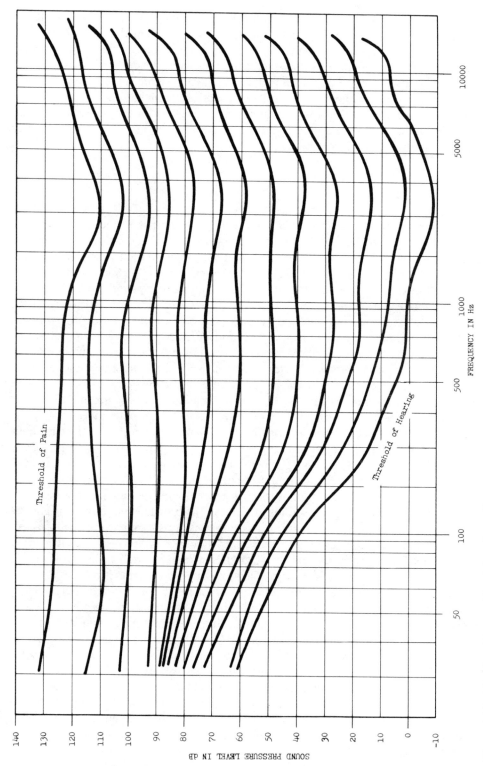

Figure 4.20 Fletcher-Munson Equal Loudness Curves

129

the frequencies of any two sounds and the smaller the frequency interval between them, the greater the difference in their intensities must be for each of the tones to be heard distinctly. In general, it is the lower of the two frequencies that is the masking sound and the higher of the two frequencies that is masked. The overall loudness of the two sounds is also important, since the greater the loudness of the masking sound, the greater the increase in intensity required of the masked sound to overcome the masking effect. Finally, the duration of the sounds would also have an effect on the perception of their relative loudness. It becomes progressively more difficult to perceive the two sounds separately as their durations are reduced.

TIMBRE

The physical parameter most closely associated with the perception of timbre (the "color" of a sound) is the spectrum (harmonic or inharmonic) of the sound. However, the physiological and psychological systems that contribute to the perception of timbre are so complex that we can only speculate as to the actual perceptual processes involved. Therefore, for convenience, let us define timbre simply as *the spectral characteristics of a sound that distinguish it from other sounds*. These characteristics may be either variant (transient) in nature, that is, changing over a period of time, or invariant (static) in nature, that is, remaining constant over a period of time, or a combination of both.

Unlike pitch and loudness, there are no known minimum degrees of timbre that can be perceived (except for the special case of a pure sine wave, the simplest sound possible, which would necessarily have the minimum spectral characteristics possible). Although there must be some minimal degree of timbral variation necessary for one to sense a change in the "color" of a sound, this quantity has not been determined due to the extraordinary complexity of such a measurement. Therefore, almost all of the characteristics encompassed by the term "timbre" are merely relative, not to some physically definable limitations but, in more general and subjective terms, to the previous experiences of the listener. This is illustrated by the kinds of descriptions people generally give of the timbres of sounds that are new to their experience. A musician will almost always describe such new sounds in terms of the instrumental timbres he already knows; for example, in Western cultures, comparisons of new sounds to known subjective qualities, such as "clarinet-like," "reedy," or "flute-like" would be typical. The brain stores information about the timbral characteristics of known sounds against which it can compare those of new sounds. In this way, an "unmeaningful" sound is related to known experiences and is thereby made "meaningful." If the new sound is heard often enough, it will receive its own meaningful label, and it may subsequently be used as a point of comparison for other new sounds. For example, when electronic music synthesizers were first developed, it was common to hear people describe the new sounds produced by them as variants of the sounds made by instruments they were already familiar with (e.g., "string-like" or "trumpet-like"), and most of the sounds made by different types of synthesizers seemed indistinguishable from one another. As more listening experience was acquired with the various models and designs of synthesizers, people began to discern the subtle characteristics (caused by differences in their design or construction) that distinguished a sound created on one synthesizer from a similar sound created on a different synthesizer. Thus, one began to find more experienced listeners identifying electronically synthesized musical sounds or pieces as "Moog-like," "ARP-like," or "Buchla-like."

Envelope

As noted earlier, timbral characteristics may be either static or transient in nature, and most sounds (*all* naturally occurring sounds) are actually a combination of both. The attack and decay (beginning and ending) portions of a sound are obviously transient in nature, and the more or less steady portion in between is relatively static. The human psychological network derives the greatest meaning from *changes* in stimuli. Static timbres are difficult to label, difficult to distinguish, and, therefore, less meaningful to human perception than are transient timbres. Although the attack characteristics of a sound may comprise only a small fraction of the length (in time) of the entire sound, they carry a great deal of the information needed by the brain for the comparison and identification of the sound. A simple experiment that would illustrate this point would be to record a single tone from a piano (or a trombone, or a violin, etc.) and then to edit out the attack portion of the sound, producing a sound that may be quite difficult to identify. Figure 4.21 shows simplified envelopes or "dynamic shapes in time" for the first harmonic or partial of a clarinet tone and a cymbal crash. Higher harmonics or partials of the same fundamentals will have markedly different envelopes than the envelope of the fundamental, accounting for the great complexity of timbral formations.

Timbre Discrimination

Among the most complex auditory perceptions made by the brain is the distinction between simultaneously occurring sounds of different timbres. A chord of five different

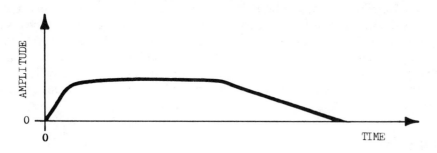

a) the envelope of the fundamental of a clarinet tone

b) the envelope of the fundamental of a cymbal crash

Figure 4.21 Envelopes

pitches played by a woodwind quintet (flute, oboe, clarinet, horn, and bassoon) is not only perceived as a composite sound, identifiable as an entity in itself, but is simultaneously perceived as five separate sounds that can be individually identified by differences in timbre as well as by differences in pitch.

The subtleties of timbral discrimination are, to some degree, the very essence of musical interest. Without this ability to react to sounds at complex levels of meaning, music would have to remain extremely facile, perhaps even monophonic, in order to be comprehensible to the listener. The course of Western music over the centuries has been toward ever-increasing complexities of timbre, indicative of a continuing refinement of human perception that has occurred due to the accumulation of *cultural* experiences passed on to successive generations of listeners.

AMBIENCE

Sound Absorption

Sound waves, especially at higher frequencies, are most effectively absorbed by porous, semi-flexible materials such as thick cloth, spun fiberglass, or loose cotton batting. These kinds of materials absorb the energy of the sound waves, converting it into heat (at very low temperature levels, due to the relatively low energy content of the sound waves themselves). Many recording studios have heavy drapes or movable panels made of such materials, which are used specifically to reduce sound reflection (refer to Figure 1.7). Some acoustic environments have been designed to *completely* absorb the sound waves that occur within them. These *anechoic* rooms, used for exact physical measurements of sound characteristics, allow virtually no reflections off their surfaces. A listener within such an environment would perceive sounds as "dull" and "lifeless," since they would lack the dynamic and spatial complexity we have become used to in our natural listening environments, which contain a variety of surfaces with different absorption/reflection characteristics.

Sound Reflection

In a typical concert hall, the sound coming from a single instrument on the stage travels out in all directions and is reflected, to some degree, off every surface it encounters. The sound travels with greatest intensity directly to the listener, because this is the shortest path between the source and the listener; the sound would, therefore, lose the least energy to the transmitting medium (air). However, an infinite number of reflections of the sound from the various surfaces of the concert hall also reach the listener, but at somewhat lower intensities and at slight time delays, since the reflected sounds must travel greater distances than the direct sound. Because the reflected sounds (in a typical concert hall) have been significantly absorbed by the semi-reflective surfaces of the hall, the listener perceives only one sound source (that on the stage), but the sound he hears has an increased breadth and depth due to the slightly delayed reflections of lesser amplitude that are also perceived. Because of their later arrival, these reflected sounds are, to a greater or lesser degree, out of phase with the direct sound, causing a good deal of complex constructive and destructive interference that is perceived as "liveliness" in the sound.

Reverberation and Echo

As long as the reflected sound arrives within about 20 milliseconds (ms.) of the arrival of the direct sound (or another reflection of the sound) the listener will perceive only one, elongated sound. This effect is called *reverberation*. However, if the reflected sound arrives more than about 20 ms. after the direct sound, the reflection will be perceived not as an integrated elongation of the direct sound, but as a separate iteration (reattack or *echo*) of the sound. *Reverberation time* (the "elongation" time of the sound) is defined as the time it takes for the intensity of a sound to diminish from its original level to a level of one-millionth the intensity of the original level. This is equivalent to a change of 60 dB. Acousticians and musicians generally agree that the ideal reverberation time of most large concert halls is about 1.5 to 2.0 seconds. (See Figure 6.19.)

Directional Discrimination

If only a little of the energy of the reflected sound (whether it is perceived as an echo or as reverberation) is absorbed, the ears can easily become confused as to which sound (the direct or the reflected) is the actual sound source. This is quite common in very large rooms, such as cathedrals, where the sound of a choir or an organ may seem to come from no single place in particular but from several different directions at once. The ears depend on subtle differences in phasing and intensity (both the result of the increased distances reflected sounds must travel) to determine the true direction of the source of a sound. If very little of the total energy of a sound is transmitted in the direct waves, the auditory system can easily become confused about the direction of the sound source.

The human auditory system uses two different processes to determine the direction from which a sound originates. Low frequencies (up to about 1000 Hz) are localized by means of the very small differences between the time a sound arrives at one ear and the time it arrives at the other. This is possible because the wavelengths of sounds below about 1500 Hz are much larger than the distance separating the ears of the listener.* Once the wavelength becomes smaller than the distance between the listener's ears (i.e., the frequency becomes higher), this phase difference information cannot be accurately determined. At this point another discrimination process begins to take over that takes differences in intensity into account. The large wavelengths of low-frequency sounds arrive at the ears slightly out of phase, but at the same intensity. High-frequency sounds arrive at the ears at significantly different intensities but with irrelevant phase differences (since the wavelengths are shorter than the distance between the ears). Ironically, the frequency range to which the ears are most sensitive, roughly 2000–4000 Hz, is the range that is least effectively served by either of the localization processes. However, most sounds contain a good deal of high-frequency information in their spectra that contributes to the effectiveness of the localization process. An interesting, "uncorrected" flaw in the low-frequency localization process is that pure tones originating from directly behind or in front of the listener are indistinguishable from one another, since the phase difference (none, as far as the ears are concerned) would be the same in either case.

---

* The formula for computing the wavelength for a given frequency is $X = \frac{v}{f}$, where X is the length of the wave, v is the transmitting velocity in the given medium (1130 feet/second in air) and f is the frequency of the sound. Thus, for a sound at a frequency of 100 Hz the wavelength would be more than one foot— $X = \frac{1130'/\text{sec}}{100 \text{ Hz}} = 1.13$ feet/cycle.

Chapter 5

Electronic Signal Sources

ELECTRONIC SOUND SYNTHESIS

Although one often hears a composer speak of producing or manipulating a particular sound in the electronic music studio, this is a somewhat misleading use of terminology. Except in an initial recording of acoustic sounds, the electronic music composer creates his or her compositions by producing and manipulating *electronic signals*, not actual sounds. These signals have certain properties—frequency, amplitude, spectral complexity, etc.—that are analogous to the physical properties of sound discussed in Chapter 4, but, until the signal is sent through a transducer (loudspeaker), no sound actually exists.

This would be a trifling semantic distinction were it not for the fact that electronic signals behave in several respects quite differently from sounds. Electronic signals are created, combined, and transformed by various *absolute* means (that is, they are subject entirely to the objective laws of physics) in an almost completely closed environment (the electronic circuit). There are *no* subjective qualities to an electronic signal; its effects on other signals and the effects of other signals on it are absolutely predictable when enough information is known about each signal. There are no perceptual or acoustic variables until the signal is converted into sound by a transducer. In this and the following two chapters we will examine the electronic devices that initiate, modify (an additive or subtractive process), or modulate (an interactive process) electronic signals. We will also discuss the objective and subjective properties of the sounds ultimately produced by these signals.

As in any compositional process, the composer of electronic music is concerned with the *creation, manipulation, and organization of sound events in time*. The first of these activities, creation of the various sounds from which the composition will be developed, is known as *sound synthesis* and involves the translation of an imagined sound into a set of quantifiable physical parameters—frequency, spectrum, transient characteristics, amplitude, length, etc.—that can be produced with the available electronic equipment. Synthesis is an interactive process in which each of three principal activities (imagination, analysis, and execution) affect each other, causing a constant reevaluation of the imagined sound and the practical means by which to realize it.

The electronic music composer must learn to perceive the complex relationships of the physical properties of a desired sound and must also understand the variety of modifying and modulating processes that can be applied to a basic signal or combination of signals in order to produce an intended final sound. Further, if the electronically created sounds are to hold a listener's attention and interest as effectively as the sounds of acoustic musical instruments (which are naturally quite complex), they usually must be nearly as subtle as natural sounds. For this reason, the first part of the compositional process—synthesis of the sounds to be worked with—occupies a substantially greater proportion of the electronic music composer's time and interest than it does for the composer working exclusively with readily available acoustic sounds. Later operations—manipulation of the various sound events in relation to each other, and the overall shaping and organization of the composition—are tasks involving skills familiar to most composers in any medium (horizontal and vertical structuring, development of a formal shape, etc.).

The only *required* element for the production of a synthesized final sound is the signal source itself. The electronic devices that function primarily as signal sources include oscillators, harmonic generators, and noise generators. It should be noted that the initial signal source is usually the primary determinant of the qualities of the final synthesized sound made from it. Therefore, signal generating equipment must be fully understood before progressing to the operation of modifying and modulating devices that may be used to alter the source signal.

OSCILLATORS

Oscillation is, literally, any regular back-and-forth motion. The pendulum described in Chapter 4 would be an oscillator and so would the bowed string of the violin and the vibrating column of air in an organ pipe or flute. An oscillator is, therefore, any device capable of producing and sustaining periodic variations in some medium, whether the medium is a string, the atmosphere, or electric current. Since an oscillator produces periodic variations in its medium, its actions are subject to all of the principles and laws of periodic motion previously described.

Essentially, an electronic oscillator produces periodic variations in the flow of an electric current. The resulting *alternating current* (AC) behaves exactly like the ideal acoustic waveforms (sine, triangle, sawtooth, pulse/square) previously described. Further, an electronic oscillator can produce frequencies so low (often 0.1 Hz or lower) as to be imperceptible except as gradual changes in other events affected by it, and so high (well beyond 20,000 Hz) as to exceed human perception.

Contemporary electronic music studios usually have several oscillators available, either as independent units or as components of a voltage-controlled synthesizer. (The voltage-control aspects of oscillators will be discussed in Chapters 9, 10, and 11.) These oscillators may produce only one waveform, such as the sine wave or square wave, or they may offer a complete variety of waveforms—such as sine, triangle, sawtooth, pulse, and square waveforms—that are individually selectable or available simultaneously via separate outputs for each waveform.

Early electronic music studios often had large banks of a dozen or more independent or phase-locked oscillators that could be used in combination to create complex harmonic or inharmonic spectra. The additive synthesis made possible by banks of oscillators is still very useful in obtaining extremely well-defined or unusual spectral qualities, as will be demonstrated by the project at the end of this chapter.

Controls and Functions

The oscillators shown in Figure 5.1 are idealized versions of typical oscillators available in most current electronic music studios. Note that the control potentiometers may be either rotating (pots) or sliding (faders) without affecting the basic operational principles of the device.

The *frequency* of the oscillator is usually determined by a combination of two

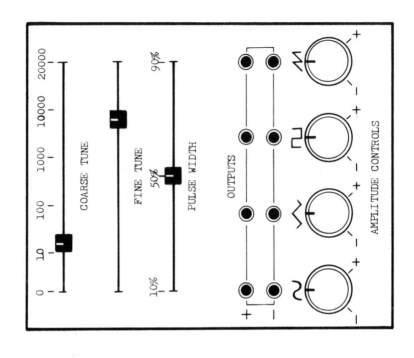

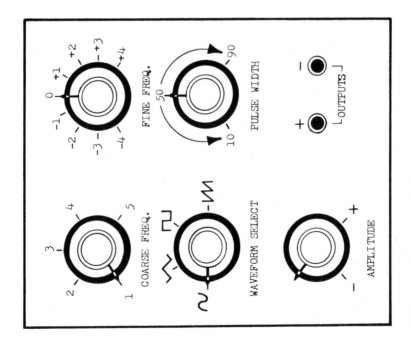

Figure 5.1 Electronic Oscillators

separate controls: a coarse tuning control that sets the general frequency range being used (this is often calibrated in discrete steps such as X·1, X·10, X·100, X·1000, etc.), and a fine-tuning control that allows the selection of frequencies within a much narrower but continuously variable frequency span. Many oscillator modules of voltage-controlled synthesizers have an additional switch that sets the oscillator in either an "audio" frequency range (roughly 20–20,000 Hz) or a "sub-audio" or "low" frequency range (roughly 0.01–100 Hz). Partially for this reason, the primary frequency setting controls are often calibrated only in arbitrary units, rather than in an exact frequency scale. Except for extremely well-calibrated test oscillators, which have highly accurate and finely marked frequency verniers, few oscillators provide anything even approaching an exact frequency readout. To determine the precise frequency that the oscillator is producing, the output must be fed into a *frequency counter*, which will indicate—usually on a digital display—the exact frequency of the oscillator output, often to within 0.01 Hz.

Waveform selection is usually accomplished through the use of either a single selection switch or individual output for each waveform (sine, triangle, sawtooth or "ramp," pulse/square). In most cases, if a selection switch is used, only one waveform can be accessed at a time (a distinct disadvantage in many instances). Some oscillators, especially those that derive the various waveforms they offer by filtering out the undersired harmonics of a more complex waveform (usually a sawtooth wave), also provide the user with mixtures, or hybrids, of the standard waveforms. Although this feature can be very useful, it is generally an indication of a less sophisticated oscillator that probably will not be able to produce the precise waveforms that are often necessary for many kinds of electronic sound synthesis.

Output *amplitude* controls are usually available and may sometimes be offered for each individual waveform output (where there are multiple waveform outputs). However, there are a few oscillators, usually modules of a voltage-controlled synthesizer, that do not offer any means of setting the output amplitude. These units almost always incorporate input attenuators at any module to which one would be likely to send the oscillator's signal output (the Serge modular and ARP 2500 and 2600 synthesizers are examples).

Pulse-width controls allow the user to vary the harmonic content of the pulse–wave output (only) by changing the ratio (duty cycle) of the positive-going* and negative-going portions of the waveform (see Chapter 4). The usual range of this control varies continuously from 10% positive/90% negative to 90% positive/10% negative, with the square wave (50% positive/50% negative) falling in the center of this range. Not all pulse wave oscillators offer a pulse-width control; in which case, the output will always be a square wave.

Although the phasing of a waveform can be very important to accurate additive synthesis, most oscillators do not provide any easy means of *phase-locking* their waveform outputs with those of other oscillators. The exceptions are oscillator modules within a voltage-controlled synthesizer or an oscillator bank, which are often—but not always—phase-locked within the system itself (but not with other oscillator banks or with other synthesizers, even of the same brand or model). These units will sometimes have dual

---

* Owing to the circuitry used in many oscillators (particularly those found in voltage-controlled synthesizers) the sawtooth (ramp) and pulse waveforms are often positive-going only. In such cases, the pulse is either "on" or "off" instead of positive or negative. The significance of this will be further explored in Part II.

outputs for the same waveform—one "positive" and one "negative" or "inverted" (the two outputs are simply 180° out of phase with each other).

The *output jacks* of oscillators may be designed to accept any of a wide variety of plugs, depending on the integration of the oscillator in the overall system (voltage-controlled synthesizer, oscillator bank, etc.) and the manufacturer's particular design. Phone plug jacks, phono plug jacks, banana plug jacks, and screw terminals are all found, the first three usually for synthesizers and the last two usually for test equipment.

Functional Parameters

Oscillators vary widely in their design parameters and tolerances. An oscillator used for calibrations and test measurements will usually be built to much more exacting standards (and at much greater expense) than an oscillator intended for use as a signal source in an electronic music studio. However, since the human ear is sensitive to very small variations in frequency and, to a lesser extent, variations in the amplitude and spectral content of steady-state tones, there are certain characteristics that should be carefully considered in assessing any oscillator intended for use in an electronic music studio.

Frequency stability is probably the most important factor to consider in judging the quality of any oscillator. A frequency shift of only 0.5% in a tone of 2000 Hz is easily detected by the human ear (Zwicker, Flottorp, and Stevens 1957). The amount of frequency change ("drift") occuring in an oscillator set to a specific frequency is measured in relation to the time it takes the change to occur. The faster the frequency drift occurs, the more noticeable it will be.

Although *spectral stability* is very rarely a problem, certain anomalies in the waveform shape (observable on an oscilloscope as notches in the peaks of sine or triangle waves or as distorted corners of pulse and square waves) that remain constant will affect the use of the waveform as a sub-audio control signal (discussed in Part II). Yet, these slight waveform imperfections are usually imperceptible and of little consequence when the oscillator is operated in its audio frequency range (above about 20 Hz). Gross variations from the standard waveform shapes should be avoided, not only to maintain standard spectral content but, also, to ensure overall oscillator quality. Inaccurate waveforms are often indications of a generally careless approach to oscillator design and construction.

Amplitude stability is seldom a problem with most solid-state circuitry oscillators, since the human ear is much less sensitive to variations in loudness than it is to changes in frequency. However, imperfections in the amplitude control potentiometers of an oscillator can cause wide variations in amplitude (and can interject unwanted noises) that will be quite noticeable.

Many compromises are usually made in the design of oscillators for electronic music applications, often in the interest of economic competitiveness. The variety of optional features and expanded capabilities of many top-of-the-line oscillators may not be needed for most studio applications, but the fundamental design parameters described above must always be considered. As pointed out in the discussion of amplitude stability, the quality of seemingly insignificant components—such as potentiometers—can affect the quality of the whole instrument. All controls and jacks should function smoothly and should be well-constructed, since they will directly affect one's ability to set the device accurately. Further, the controls (especially fine-frequency tuning controls) must be sensitive to extremely small variations in their settings. If the controls are too coarse, the flexibility and applicability of the instrument will be severely limited.

HARMONIC GENERATORS

A number of special instruments have been developed by various studios in an effort to make additive synthesis more precise and practical. One of the most useful of these devices is the harmonic generator, which usually consists of a bank of phase-locked oscillators preset to the harmonic series and ganged together so that one control changes the frequency settings of the whole bank while maintaining the harmonic series relationship among the component oscillators. For the most part, many of the controls of the harmonic generator will be the same as those usually found on individual oscillators (in multiples, however). There are also harmonic generators that function as a single unit and offer only one overall frequency control for the several individual harmonics, each of which have separate amplitude and phasing controls and output jacks. These harmonic generators simply access or "tap" the individual harmonics of a single complex waveform (usually a sawtooth wave) produced by a single oscillator.

NOISE GENERATORS

The noise generator (or random signal generator) found as a component of most synthesizers produces continuous bursts of random frequencies at random amplitudes across the entire audio spectrum (about 20 Hz to 20 KHz) in a close approximation of theoretical "white noise" (which would consist of all frequencies, $0-\infty$ Hz, at equal amplitudes, a physical impossibility). Many noise generators also offer a separate output for "pink noise" (possessing equal sound energy across each octave), which is created by passing white noise through a low-pass filter with a cut-off slope of -3 dB per octave (see Chapter 6). Some units that have a built-in filter of this type provide a potentiometer to vary the slope of the filter continuously, producing noise colorations ranging from "white" to "pink" and, occasionally "red" (which suppresses the amplitude exponentially with respect to increases in frequency, further emphasizing the low end of the frequency spectrum). Although other colorful terminology is often applied to variants of noise ("blue," "azure," etc.), these terms have no literal definition as do the designations "white," "pink," and "red."

PROJECT NO. 3: FOURIER SYNTHESIS

In this project, we will attempt to synthesize each of the three basic complex waveforms—the triangle, sawtooth, and square waves—by summing together (mixing) the sine-wave outputs of several oscillators. The purpose is two-fold: 1) to gain experience working carefully with oscillators, mixing, and test equipment in a precisely controlled exercise with appreciable results and 2) to gain a fuller understanding of Fourier synthesis and the structure of the various common harmonic waveform spectra. As with all of the projects in this book, it is essential that this project begin with careful planning and progress with comprehensive record-keeping. All tape machine and mixer settings and all patchings should be so well documented that the results could be duplicated by someone else without further explanation. At the completion of the project, it might prove interesting to tape record the final results of all the students or student groups and compare them with each other and with the actual, corresponding outputs from a complex waveform oscillator.

In order to offer a sample procedure, we will first examine the equipment needs for this project as a whole, then set up an example of a production step outline for synthesizing a triangle wave, and, finally, offer some guidelines for assessing the results. We recommend that the instructor follow this sample procedure in illustrating the entire process for the class. After having noted the process involved in producing the triangle wave, the students should set up their own production routines independently and produce the sawtooth and square waveforms using the waveform descriptions given in Chapter 4 as a starting point.

Equipment Required

The following equipment is needed to successfully complete this project:

- *Oscillators*: six or more sine-wave oscillators, preferably phase-locked (if phase-locked oscillators are not available, the project is still a beneficial exercise, but the possibility of achieving a precise and predictable result is extremely small). It would also be helpful if the oscillators used offer both positive and negative outputs.
- *Frequency Counter*: this may be of any type, so long as it is capable of resolution to at least 0.1 Hz.
- *Oscilloscope*: an oscilloscope is almost essential to monitor the progress of this project. A dual-trace oscilloscope would be particularly useful, but not necessary.
- *VU Meter*: a standard VU meter to be used for all level settings; it could be a part of the mixer or of a tape machine. The percentage scale (0 VU = 100%) will be especially useful in this project. (The LED displays often found on mixers will *not* work for this project since they read in discrete stages and are not capable of indicating subtle differences in signal strength.)
- *Voltage Polarity Inverter*: if the oscillators used are not equipped with positive and negative outputs, other modules of a voltage-controlled synthesizer often employ some sort of phase-shift capability (for example, the "voltage processor" section of the ARP 2600 synthesizer and the directly opposed outputs of the Moog 902 voltage-controlled amplifier).

Procedure

Synthesize a 100 Hz triangle wave, according to Fourier's Theorem, by summing together the first six (or more) harmonic components as provided by sine-wave oscillators.

    Definition of a triangle wave: *A triangle wave contains only odd-numbered harmonics, with amplitudes in the ratio of $1/n^2$, and with every other component 180° out of phase.*

Component Chart

Construct a chart showing necessary component frequencies, phases, and amplitudes; the oscillator from which each component is obtained; and the mixer input number and setting for each component. Also, provide room for notes and information about various potentiometer settings and production details (Figure 5.2).

COMPONENT NUMBER	HARMONIC NUMBER	FREQUENCY (in Hz)	PHASING	AMPLITUDE (in %)	OSCILLATOR	MIXER INPUT	NOTES
One	One (Fund.)	100	+	100 (1/1)	a	1	
Two	Three	300	–	11.11 (1/9)	b	2	
Three	Five	500	+	4.0 (1/25)	c	3	
Four	seven	700	–	2.1 (1/49)	d	4	
Five	Nine	900	+	1.2 (1/81)	e	5	
Six	Eleven	1100	–	0.8 (1/121)	f	6	

Figure 5.2 Component Chart for Fourier Synthesis of a 100 Hz Triangle Wave. Note: A triangle wave is composed of only odd-numbered harmonics whose amplitudes are determined by the ratio $1/n^2$; every other component is shifted 180° out of phase.

141

Production Process

Connect the output of the oscillator producing the fundamental frequency (100 Hz) to the frequency counter. Although this entire project can be performed without ever listening to a single sound, it might be advisable to listen at every step of the process, if only to verify that patching connections are correct. If so desired, take the output of each oscillator to a multiple that splits the signal into two or more identical outputs. Patch one output to an amplifier and another to the frequency counter. Keep in mind throughout this project that most frequency counters can safely accept only one signal at a time! Make certain that the range setting of the frequency counter is correctly set. If there is no response at first, check the input gain to the frequency counter to make certain that it is high enough. Once a reading is gotten, adjust the frequency controls of the oscillator until the proper frequency is obtained. All frequencies, particularly that of the fundamental, should be set as precisely as possible, otherwise the waveform components will slip in and out of tune with each other.

Once the proper frequency is found, note the settings on the oscillator. Then, disconnect the output of the oscillator from the frequency counter (and amplifier), and connect it to the first input of a mixer (preferably one having a VU meter of its own; otherwise, connect the output of the mixer to a tape machine having a VU meter). Set the input gain of the mixer so that the VU meter reads 0 dB or 100% and note the mixer input setting. Once these level settings are begun, do not readjust the output gain of the mixer or the input gain of the tape machine (if one is being used), since this will throw off all previous settings.

Follow the same procedures for the second sine-wave component, this time using the negative output of the oscillator or inverting the waveform by taking the oscillator output through a voltage inverter before patching it to the mixer's second input. Adjust the frequency of this component to 300 Hz. Before attempting to set the second mixer input's amplitude, be sure to disconnect the first input. The amplitude of this second component should be only $\frac{1}{9}$ (11.11%) that of the fundamental, a reading which will be fairly difficult to discern on the VU meter.

Follow the same procedure for each of the remaining components according to the parameters shown on the Component Chart (Figure 5.2). Be careful to connect only one signal at a time to the frequency counter and to disconnect all previous inputs to the mixer before trying to set the amplitude of each new component. It is expected that the finer amplitude settings of the higher harmonic components will be mostly guesswork, since the majority of VU meters are not as finely calibrated as this project would require under ideal conditions. This does not negate the value of the exercise, however. (If available, a VTVM—vacuum tube volt meter—will generally allow for more accurate adjustment of the components' amplitude levels.)

Assessment

When each of the components has been individually set to its proper frequency, amplitude, and phase, reconnect all of the oscillators to their respective mixer inputs and patch the output of the mixer to both an amplifier/speaker system and to an oscilloscope. Note the audible qualities of the timbre of the synthesized "waveform" and its shape on the oscilloscope. Is the audible result a single sound or several sounds occurring simultaneously? Does the waveform remain steady on the oscilloscope, or does it periodically change shape? If there is a change, does it change slowly? Rapidly? Can you hear any change take place? What are the variables inherent in this project that introduce a high probability of error? How does the sound of the synthesized waveform compare with that of a triangle wave output from an oscillator set at the same frequency? What are the differences? How are they alike? Could this experiment be performed perfectly? If so, how?

At this point, the students should set up procedures and component charts for the additive synthesis of the square and sawtooth waveforms. Try using more components if more oscillators and greater mixing capability are available. What would be the benefit of having as many components as possible? Would there be any drawbacks to having a great many components? As noted before, it might be interesting for students to record their results on a tape machine and compare them to those of other individuals or groups.

LISTENING EXAMPLES

Messiaen, Olivier   *Fêtes des belles eaux*
                                           Erato LDE–3202

Stockhausen, Karlheinz   *Momente*
                                           Nonesuch H–71157
                                           Wergo 60024

Chapter 6
Electronic Signal Modifiers

SIGNAL PROCESSING

Once an electronic signal has been produced, whether by a microphone, a tape machine, or an oscillator, it can be used in several ways. The signal may simply be fed directly to an amplifier and a transducer to produce a sound, or it may be processed in one or more of a number of ways by other electronic or electro-mechanical devices so as to change any of its characteristics (frequency, spectrum, amplitude, etc.) and, hence, the sound it will produce. For our purposes, we have divided these signal processing devices into two basic types: *signal modifiers* and *signal modulators*. Essentially, the difference between the two processes or types of effects is that a signal modifier merely adds to or subtracts from some characteristic of the original signal, imposing its effect upon the signal, but a signal modulator interacts with the original signal to produce a new output that is often a drastic transformation of the original input. Signal modulators will be discussed in Chapter 7.

For the most part, signal modifying devices fall into four categories: filters, reverberation/delay systems, automatic switching devices, and recording machines. The last of these has already been discussed at some length, and the others have been alluded to briefly. However, the diversity, complexity, and importance of these devices makes a careful and thorough understanding of them essential for the electronic music composer.

FILTERS

Passive Filters

A filter is a *frequency-selective attenuator or amplifier*. It acts much as any other amplitude or level control except that it affects the amplitude of only a specific range or band of frequencies. In its simplest form, a filter can only *remove* certain frequencies from a signal, because it has a *passive* electronic circuit. A *passive filter* requires no power source, since it is strictly an attenuator of the amplitude of specified portions of the signal. Consequently, the signal is always weakened to some extent as it passes through the circuit. Passive filters are flexible in that they are relatively simple to design and build, they are relatively inexpensive, and they can be quite portable (since they require no power source for their operation). Their principal drawbacks include an unavoidable amount of signal loss and the inability to boost the amplitude of specific portions of the signal's frequency spectrum above the rest.

Active Filters

An *active filter* has the ability not only to attenuate the amplitude of selected bands of frequencies, as does the passive filter, but, since it incorporates an amplifier, it can also boost the amplitude of selected areas of the signal's frequency spectrum. With the increasing sophistication of integrated circuits, the cost of a good-quality active filter is becoming competitive with that of less versatile passive filters.

Regardless of the sophistication of the circuitry employed, filters are not usually designed to amplify or attenuate just a single frequency of a given input signal. Rather, discrete ranges or bands of frequencies are usually acted upon. There are two basic types of filter circuits: *Low-Pass*, which attenuate high frequencies (pass only low frequencies), and *High-Pass*, which attenuate low frequencies (pass only high frequencies). Don't be confused by what is passed and what is attenuated! Obviously, "low" and "high" are general terms that distinguish only the *kind* of effect the filter will have, not the specific range of frequencies it will affect. A high-pass filter may be set to pass everything above about 20 Hz or a low-pass filter may be set to pass everything beneath 20,000 Hz; in both cases, the entire audible frequency spectrum will remain unaffected. Simple high-pass or low-pass filters (particularly passive ones) are often called *shelving filters*. All other kinds of filters (band-pass, band-reject, etc.) result from the different ways in which these two filters may be combined.

Cut-off Frequency

The point in the frequency spectrum at which a high- or low-pass filter begins to act on the input signal (technically, the point at which the output signal level has already been reduced by 3 dB) is called the *cut-off frequency* (f_c). For instance, 20 Hz was the cut-off frequency of the high-pass filter in the above example, and 20,000 Hz was the cut-off frequency of the low-pass filter. Depending on the design of the filter, the cut-off frequency may be either preset or variable; obviously, the latter is much more flexible.

Although the filter begins to act on the input signal at the cut-off frequency, the resulting effect is not a sudden "cut-off," as the term would seem to imply, but rather a gradually increasing attenuation. The degree of attenuation, usually calculated in decibels per octave, is called the filter's *slope*. Figure 6.1 shows the response curve of a low-pass filter with its cut-off frequency set at 100 Hz (the point at which the output amplitude of the filter has already fallen by 3 dB) and an attenuation slope of 6 dB/octave. Note that the response curve closely approximates a straight line shortly after the cut-off frequency is passed. Since the effect of the filter is not abrupt at the cut-off frequency, the portion of the input signal that is above 100 Hz (in this example) would pass through to some degree. But remember that a dB scale is logarithmic and that a change of ±3 dB affects the intensity of the signal by a factor of 2. Thus, a signal at −3 dB is only half as intense as a signal at 0 dB. At the point at which the signal has been attenuated by six decibels, it is only one-fourth as strong. Because the typical attenuation slope for active filters used in electronic music studios is about 24 dB/octave (providing an amplitude ratio of 256:1 within the frequency span of only an octave!), a high degree of frequency resolution is possible. Figure 6.2 shows the response curve of a high-pass filter with its cut-off (f_c) frequency set at 200 Hz and an attenuation slope of 6 dB/octave.

Most active filters have a variable cut-off frequency adjustment, often consisting of

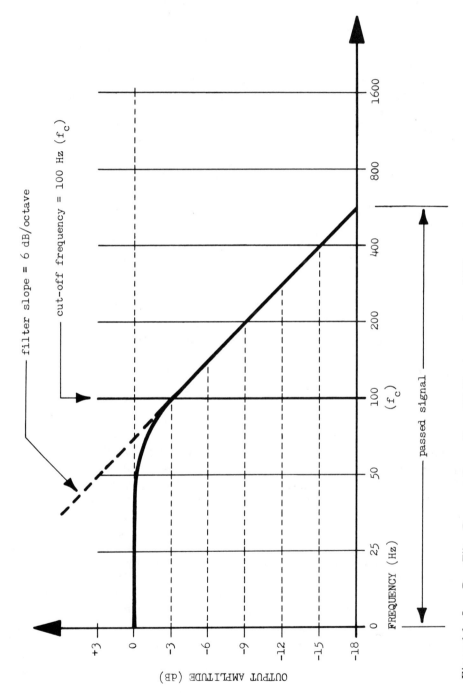

Figure 6.1 Low-Pass Filter Response Curve (f_c = 100 Hz; Attenuation = 6dB/octave.)

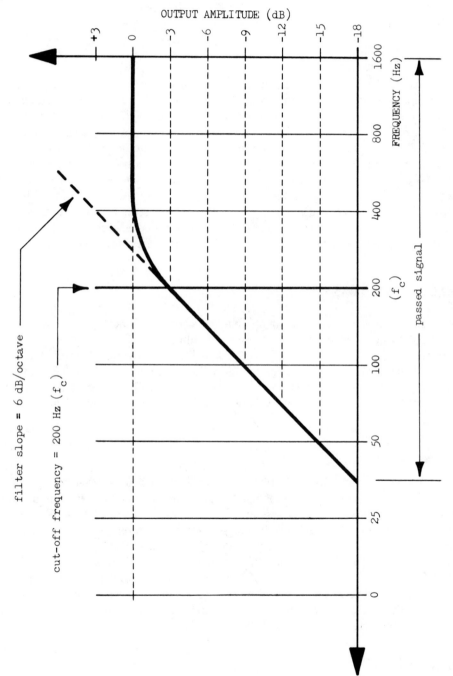

Figure 6.2 High-Pass Filter Response Curve (f_c = 200 Hz; Attenuation = 6 dB/octave).

coarse and *fine* control pots or faders, similar to those used on oscillators. A fairly typical cut-off frequency range would be from 20 Hz to 20 KHz (approximately the entire audio frequency range), but some filters built specifically for electronic music applications have a frequency range as wide as 1 Hz to 40 KHz.

Filter Resonance

The attenuation slope of a filter is most often an unalterable function of its design. However, many active low-pass filters and even some high-pass filters designed for electronic music applications incorporate a variable *resonance* control (sometimes referred to as a Q or *regeneration* control), which makes the attenuation from f_c far more abrupt. Figure 6.3 illustrates this effect. The resulting resonant (amplitude) peak is produced by *feedback* at the cut-off frequency, and is analogous to the feedback effects that can be produced with a tape machine and a mixer or by a microphone being too close to the speaker it feeds. In the example given (Figure 6.3), the attenuation slope of the filter is effectively increased from 6 dB/octave to 9 dB/octave once the resonant peak at the cut-off frequency is passed. If the level of feedback is increased enough, the filter will, in fact, act as an oscillator, producing a pure sine tone at the cut-off frequency.

COMPOUND FILTERS

Different filter combinations, made up of high- and low-pass components, can be used to modify an input signal in very particular ways. The filters may act on the signal one after the other (in "series"), at the same time (in "parallel"), or as a group of several filters at once (filter banks). Many high-pass and low-pass filters (particularly when they are parts of a voltage-controlled synthesizer) come as a unit and often have a third component, called a *filter coupler*, which allows the two filters to be used independently or in combination.

Band-Pass Filters

If a high-pass filter and a low-pass filter are connected in *series* so that the f_c of the high-pass filter is lower than the f_c of the low-pass filter, a *band-pass* filter is formed (Figure 6.4). Essentially, the high-pass filter removes the frequencies *below* its cut-off frequency; then its output is fed into the low-pass filter, which removes the frequencies *above* its cut-off frequency. (Actually, the order of the filter sequence does not matter, but most band-pass filters route the output of the high-pass filter to the input of the low-pass filter.) What remains is a band of frequencies that each of the filters has allowed to pass. The geometric mean between the two cut-off frequencies is called the *center frequency* of the passed band, and the frequency range between the two cut-off frequencies (measured in Hz) is called the *bandwidth*.

Band-Reject Filter

On the other hand, if a high-pass filter and a low-pass filter are connected in *parallel*, and the f_c of the high-pass filter is higher than the f_c of the low-pass filter, a *band-reject* filter is formed (Figure 6.5). In this mode of operation, the input signal is split, sent through

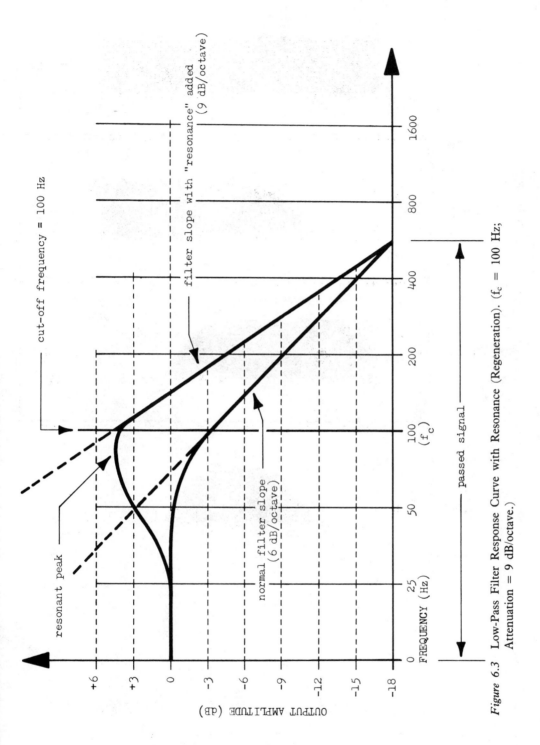

Figure 6.3 Low-Pass Filter Response Curve with Resonance (Regeneration). (f_c = 100 Hz; Attenuation = 9 dB/octave.)

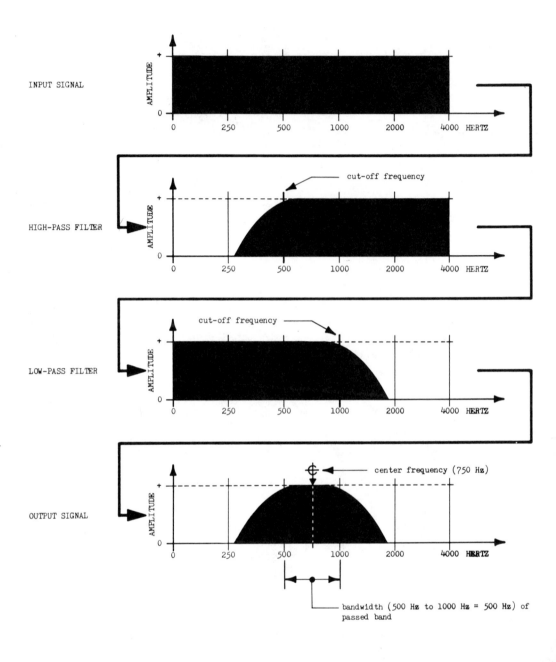

INPUT SIGNAL

HIGH-PASS FILTER

LOW-PASS FILTER

OUTPUT SIGNAL

cut-off frequency

cut-off frequency

center frequency (750 Hz)

bandwidth (500 Hz to 1000 Hz = 500 Hz) of passed band

BLOCK DIAGRAM

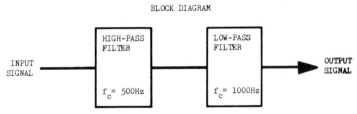

INPUT
SIGNAL

HIGH-PASS
FILTER

$f_c = 500Hz$

LOW-PASS
FILTER

$f_c = 1000Hz$

OUTPUT
SIGNAL

Figure 6.4 Band-Pass Filter

150

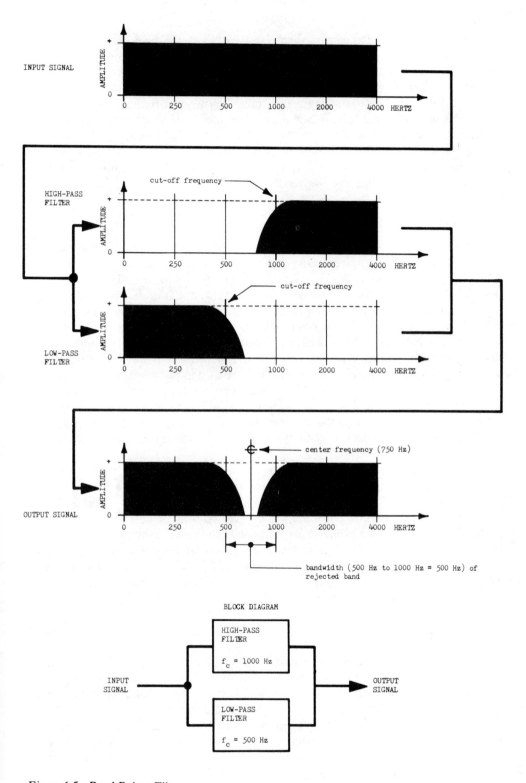

Figure 6.5 Band-Reject Filter

151

each of the filters simultaneously, then re-mixed before the final output. Each filter must act on the signal separately; if either of the filters were fed the output of the other (as in the series configuration for the band-pass filter), *all* of the signal would be filtered out. However, when each of the filters acts separately but simultaneously on the total signal, and the resulting outputs are then mixed, a band of frequencies between the cut-off frequencies of the high-pass and low-pass filters will be eliminated (though the gradual effect of the cut-off slopes of the two filters must still be taken into account). As with the band-pass filter, the geometric mean between the two cut-off frequencies is called the *center frequency* and the frequency range between the two cut-off frequencies (measured in Hz) is called the *bandwidth*.

Cut-off Frequency Relationships

It is important to emphasize that in order to get the desired effect from either a band-pass or a band-reject filter, the respective cut-off frequencies of the high- and low-pass components must be set to interact properly. Figure 6.6a illustrates the correct cut-off frequency relationship for a band-pass filter; that is, the cut-off frequencies of the high-pass and low-pass filters *must* overlap. Figure 6.6b shows what happens if the cut-off frequencies do not overlap—no signal is passed at all! Note, however, that the somewhat gradual cut-off slopes of each of the filters make it possible to set both filters to the same cut-off frequency and still pass a narrow band of frequencies (Figure 6.7) focused around the common f_c. When the filters are used in this manner, they form what is known as a "peak" or "peaking" filter which is used in the design of various kinds of equalizers. If the cut-off frequencies were gradually spread apart from this common cut-off point, lowering the f_c of the low-pass filter and raising the f_c of the high-pass filter, the amplitude of the passed band would gradually diminish, and eventually be eliminated.

In using the band-reject filter, it is important to remember that the cut-off frequencies of the high- and low-pass filters *should not* overlap if a clearly defined frequency notch (band of rejected frequencies) is desired (Figure 6.8a). If the high- and low-pass cut-off frequencies do overlap, there will be little or no effect on the signal (Figure 6.8b), except for a probable *amplification* of the band of sound between the two cut-off frequencies! Since the high-pass and low-pass component filters act on the signal independently of one another in the band-reject mode, the entire signal will be passed when the signals from each of the filters are mixed before the final output. However, there is an important exception to this rule.

Phase Shift Effect

Because of the phase-shifting characteristics of filters, a particularly sharp (steep-sloped) definition of the rejected band can be produced when the high- and low-pass cut-off frequencies overlap by about two octaves. Generally, in a band-reject filter with attenuation slopes of 24 dB/octave, the high-pass and low-pass components will each introduce a phase shift of approximately 90° per octave as their cut-off frequencies progress away from the center frequency of the rejected band. The phase shift of the low-pass filter will be negative (perceived as "lag time" on an oscilloscope), and the phase shift of the high-pass filter will be positive (perceived as "lead time" on an oscilloscope). Therefore, if the cut-off frequency of the low-pass filter is set at about

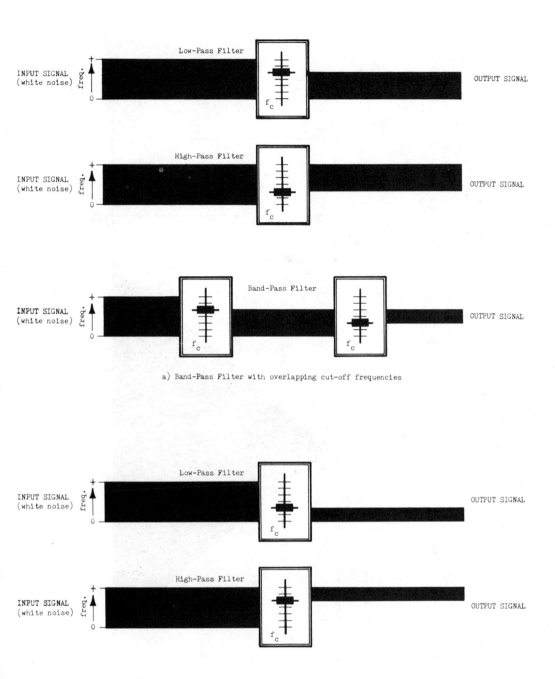

a) Band-Pass Filter with overlapping cut-off frequencies

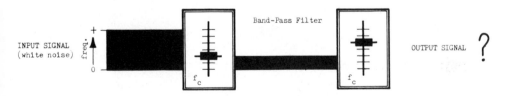

b) Band-Pass Filter with non-overlapping cut-off frequencies

Figure 6.6   Cut-off Frequencies in the Band-Pass Filter

153

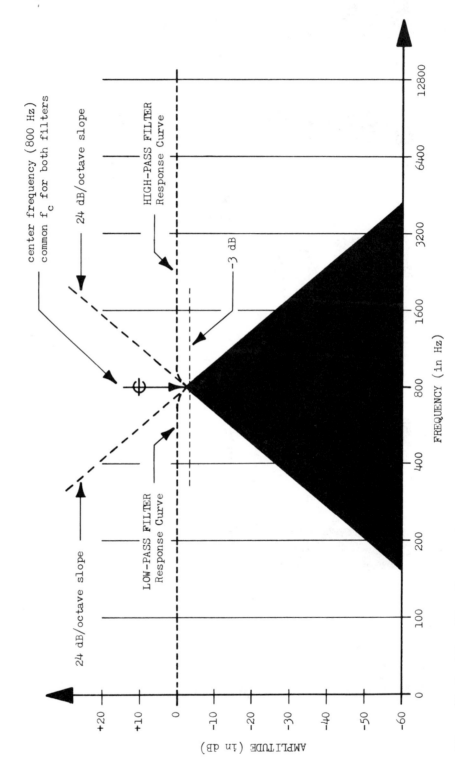

Figure 6.7 Band-Pass Filter Response Curve with High and Low Cut-off Frequencies in Common (800 Hz)

154

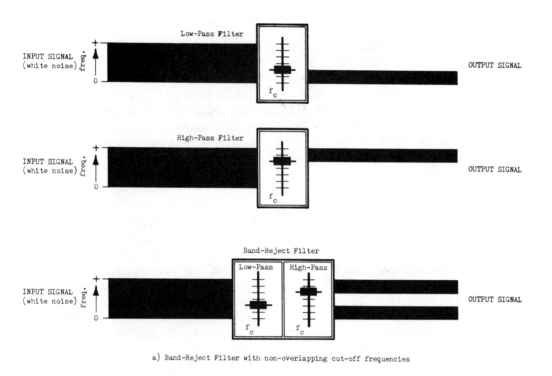

a) Band-Reject Filter with non-overlapping cut-off frequencies

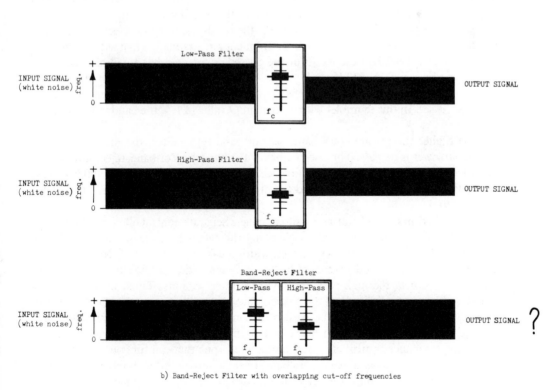

b) Band-Reject Filter with overlapping cut-off frequencies

Figure 6.8   Cut-off Frequencies in the Band-Reject Filter

155

twice the center frequency of the rejected band (one octave higher) and the cut-off frequency of the high-pass filter is set at about half the center frequency of the rejected band (one octave lower), the total phase difference between the output signals of the two component filters will be 180° ($-90°$ plus $+90°$), and the center frequency will be almost entirely canceled out (Figure 6.9). The extremely sharp attenuation slopes this phase difference causes makes the focus of the rejected notch highly discriminate. This effect is often employed in filtering out the 50 or 60 cps hum of an unbalanced alternating current (AC) circuit (all too often encountered in electronic music studios).

Q

Another important characteristic of band-pass and band-reject filters is determined by the ratio of the center frequency of the passed or rejected band to the bandwidth (center frequency/bandwidth). This quantity is known as the Q of the filter and is related to the resonance phenomenon described earlier. For example, if a band-pass or band-reject filter has a center frequency of 120 Hz and a bandwidth of 60 Hz it will have a Q value of 2 (Q = 120 Hz/60 Hz = 2). This ratio becomes particularly useful in determining the actual span of frequencies covered by a band-pass or band-reject filter. For example, a band-pass or band-reject filter with a center frequency of 300 Hz and a bandwidth of one octave around its center frequency results in a passed or rejected band between 200 Hz and 400 Hz. The bandwidth is 200 Hz, so the Q value is 1.5 (Q = 300/200 = 1.5). But the same band-pass or band-reject filter with a center frequency of 1200 Hz must have a bandwidth of 800 Hz to result in a passed or rejected band of an octave around its center frequency (1600 Hz $-$ 800 Hz = 800 Hz). Notice that the Q value of this filter is also 1.5 (Q = 1200/800 = 1.5). Thus, if the Q value of the band-pass or band-reject filter remains constant (in this case 1.5) but the center frequency is gradually changed (in this case from 300 Hz to 1200 Hz) the width of the passed or rejected band will also gradually change (in this case from 200 Hz to 800 Hz). The result is a passed or rejected band that always has the same relationship to the center frequency, no matter where the center frequency is set. In this example, with a constant Q value of 1.5, the bandwidth is always one octave.

The higher the Q value of a band-pass or band-reject filter, the more selective it is—the narrower is its passed or rejected band. If a band-pass or band-reject filter with a center frequency of 1200 Hz has a bandwidth of only 400 Hz (1000 Hz to 1400 Hz) its Q value is 3. If the bandwidth is reduced to only 300 Hz (1050 Hz to 1350 Hz) its Q value increases to 4.

Many band-pass and band-reject filters have a separate control allowing the user to vary the Q value of the filter without changing the center frequency. This can also be accomplished by merely changing the bandwidth (changing both cut-off frequencies) of the filter, or by increasing the resonant feedback (regeneration) at the cut-off frequencies (Figure 6.3) of *both* the high-pass and low-pass filter sections. Thus, in the case of a band-pass filter, the amplitude of the passed band is actually increased as the bandwidth is narrowed (Figure 6.10). In the case of a band-reject filter, an increased Q value obtained in this way results in an increased attenuation of the rejected band. For this reason, the resonance control of a multimode filter—one that can function as a high- or low-pass filter as well as a band-pass/band-reject filter—is often referred to as a Q control. (A variable Q control is also often incorporated as a component of parametric equalizers.)

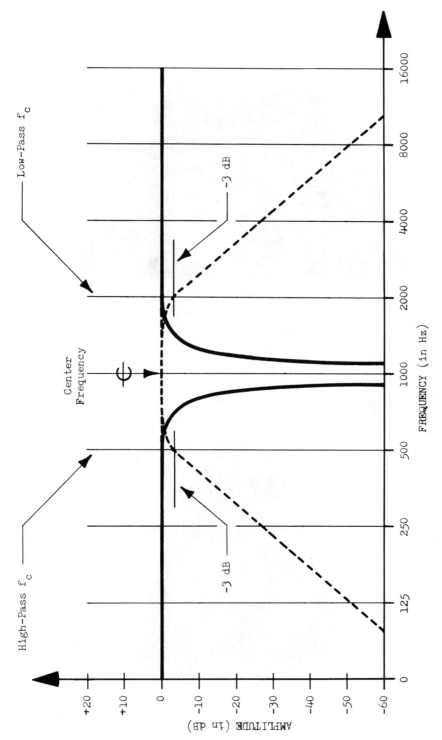

Figure 6.9 Band-Reject filter response with filter slopes of 24 dB/Octave. High-Pass f_c = 500 Hz; Low-Pass f_c = 2000 Hz; Center Frequency = 1000 Hz; High-Pass phase shift = +90°; Low-Pass phase shift = −90°; Total phase shift at 1000 Hz = 180°.

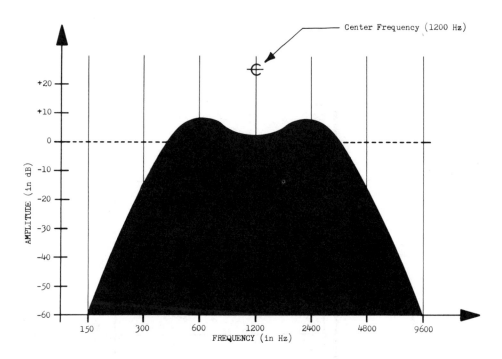

a) Band-Pass filter with low "Q" setting

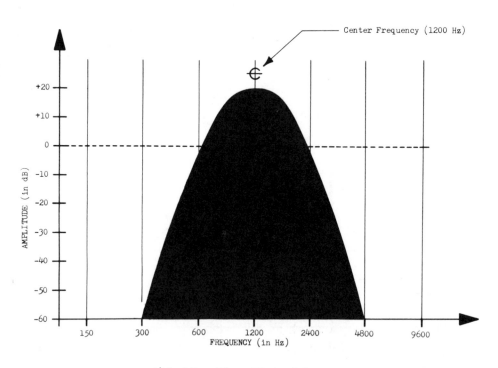

b) Band-Pass filter with high "Q" setting

Figure 6.10 The effect of Variable *Q* in a Band-Pass Filter

158

In contrast to Figure 6.10, the response curves of a band-pass filter for which the amplitude is increased while the Q value remains constant encompass a much broader range of passed frequencies (Figure 6.11). Because the attenuation slopes are much more gradual, the effect of the filter in this case is more subtle, avoiding the "ringing" quality (caused by the resonance or feedback) that often accompanies high Q settings. Either of these characteristics can be desirable in particular situations, and their uses will be discussed later in this chapter.

Filter Banks

High-pass, low-pass, band-pass and band-reject filters are often combined in various ways to form *filter banks*. A typical filter bank (such as the Moog 907-A Fixed Filter Bank shown in Figure 6.12) will have several band-pass filters ("peaking" filters), each with a fixed bandwidth and center frequency. The Moog 907-A module employs eight band-pass filters with center frequencies of 250 Hz, 350 Hz, 500 Hz, 700 Hz, 1000 Hz, 1400 Hz, 2000 Hz, and 2800 Hz. Notice that these settings follow two overlapping, four-octave ranges (250 Hz, 500 Hz, 1000 Hz, 2000 Hz and 350 Hz, 700 Hz, 1400 Hz, 2800 Hz). Thus, the filter can be set to emphasize the harmonic or inharmonic characteristics of a given input signal depending on how the input signal's frequency components relate to the fixed center frequencies of the eight bands. Like most fixed filter banks, the Moog 907-A also has a high-pass filter and a low-pass filter that act on the frequencies above and below those affected by the band-pass filters. Although the Moog 907-A module is an active filter bank, it functions primarily as an attenuator rather than as an amplifier (the potentiometers shown in Figure 6.12 are all volume control pots). The active circuitry is used to improve the attenuation slopes of the filters (in this case to 24 dB per octave), to reduce signal loss, and to improve output noise levels (in this case to −65 dB). Figure 6.13 is a graphic representation of the effect of a fixed filter bank.

Graphic Equalizers

Most electronic music studios have access to at least one fixed filter bank, whether it is part of a synthesizer (as with the Moog 907-A), a separately assembled group of individual band-pass filters, or a graphic equalizer. A *graphic equalizer* is an *active* fixed filter bank and, as such, can amplify as well as attenuate selected frequency bands. Although it is possible for a "graphic" equalizer to have rotary potentiometers (pots), it is much more usual for them to have individual vertical sliders (faders) for each frequency band. These sliders are arranged in a single horizontal row so that the amount of attenuation or amplification applied to each frequency band becomes a part of an overall visual representation of the equalizing taking place over the total frequency spectrum (Figure 6.14). Graphic equalizers commonly contain from 6 to 36 individual frequency bands, 24 being something of a norm for a studio instrument. The center frequencies of the bands (which usually overlap to some degree) are most often fixed at frequency intervals of one-third, one-half, or one octave. Equalizers with many bands at narrow frequency intervals usually employ extremely steep attenuation slopes allowing a great deal of selectivity. Those with fewer frequency bands at wider frequency intervals generally use more gentle attenuation slopes.

Figure 6.15 shows the response curve for a single, typical component filter of a

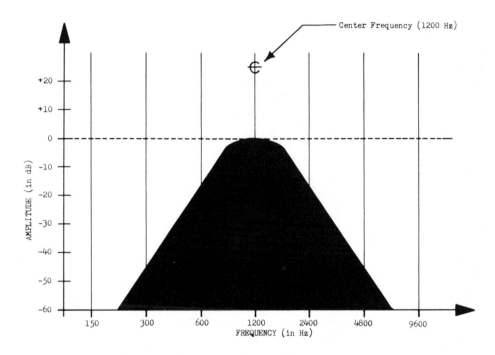

a) Band-Pass filter with low amplitude setting

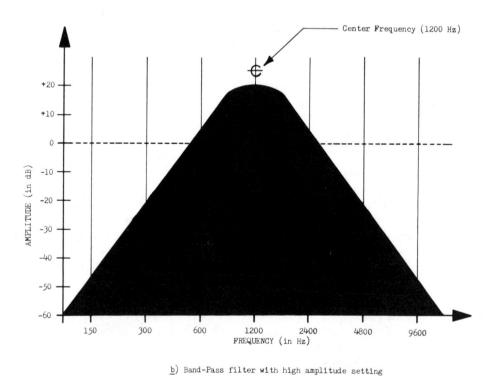

b) Band-Pass filter with high amplitude setting

Figure 6.11 The Effect of Variable Amplitude and Constant Q in a Band-Pass Filter

160

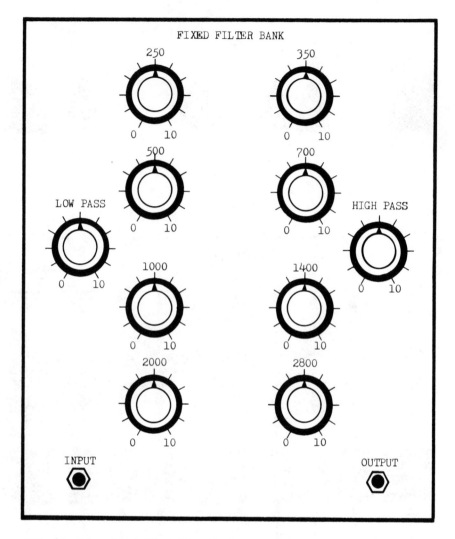

Figure 6.12 The Moog 907-A Fixed Filter Bank

one-third octave equalizer. Notice that the attenuation slope for such a narrow-band filter is very steep, reaching 120 dB/octave in this illustration. The response curves for an equalizer made up of twenty-five of these filters, covering a range of center frequencies from 63 Hz to 16 KHz, are shown in Figure 6.16. Notice that at the zero-attenuation setting indicated in Figure 6.16 a "plateau" extends evenly across the full audible frequency spectrum, so the incoming signal is passed virtually unchanged. From this point, any of the individual filter bands can be set to boost or to attenuate a specific region of the frequency spectrum of the input signal. Instruments of this type, containing many filter bands with very steep attenuation slopes, are also known as *spectrum shapers*. With such exacting equipment, the spectral characteristics of any sound can be shaped to fit very particular needs, including the elimination of hiss or hum, the emphasis or de-emphasis of particular resonant characteristics (*formants*) of a sound, and the adjustment of room acoustics.

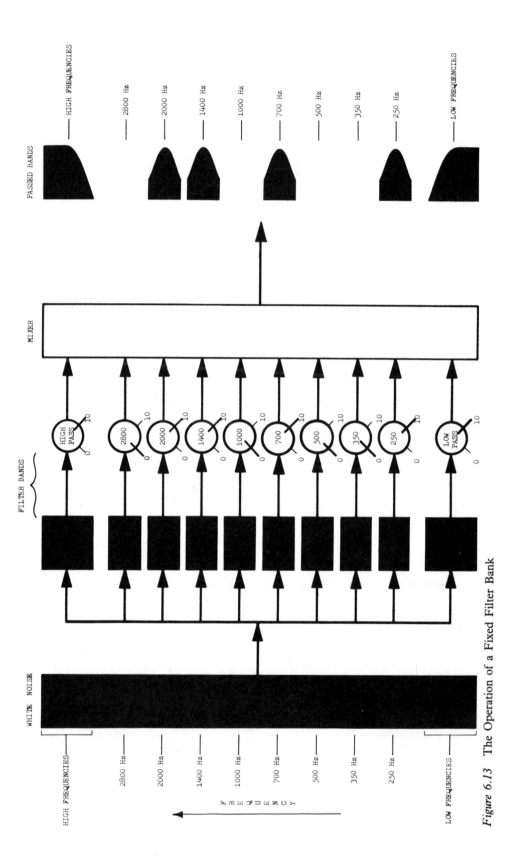

Figure 6.13 The Operation of a Fixed Filter Bank

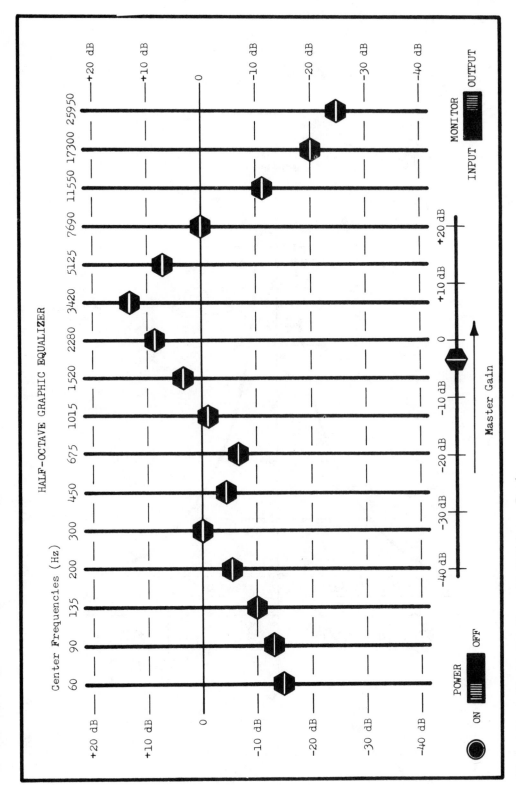

Figure 6.14 A Graphic Equalizer with Half-Octave Bands

163

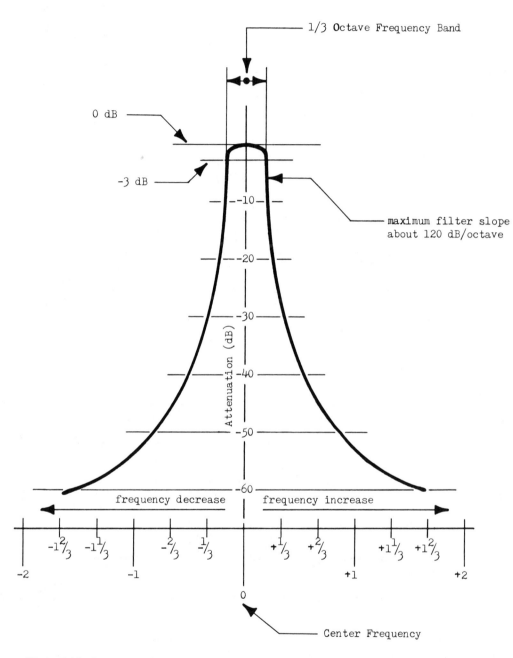

Figure 6.15 The Response Curve for One Band of a Third-Octave Filter

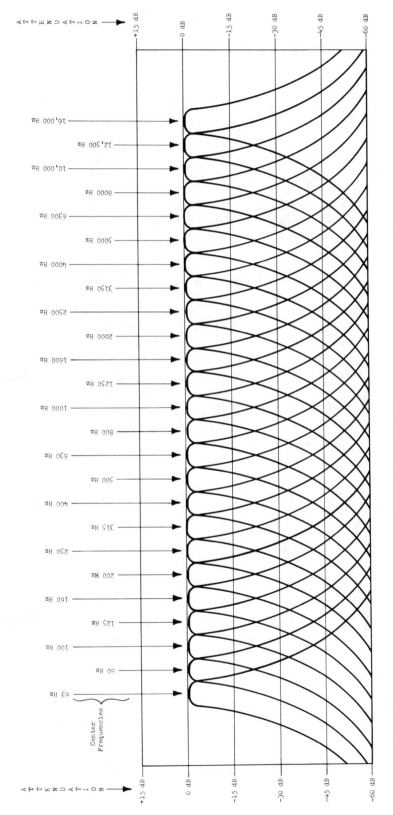

Figure 6.16 The Response Curves for a 25-Band One-Third Octave Equalizer

Parametric Equalizers

A *parametric equalizer* can be designed and defined in several ways. It is usually a bank of active, band-pass filters that have continuously variable center frequencies (*not* fixed, as with a fixed filter bank or a graphic equalizer) and overlapping frequency ranges. Some control over the Q value or bandwidth is usually provided, either by fixed increments or by a continuously variable adjustment, and the amount of amplification or attenuation is usually continuously variable. Many parametric equalizers are designed so that the bandwidth, center frequency, and amplitude controls of each band are completely independent of one another and of the controls for the other bands, a characteristic that makes the instrument very flexible. Otherwise, if the various controls within each band are interdependent, the adjustment of any one of them will affect all the others in a practically unpredictable manner.

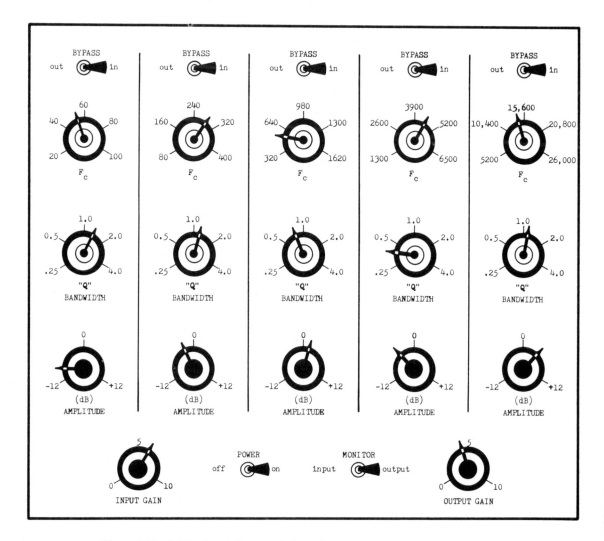

Figure 6.17   A Five-Band Parametric Equalizer

A parametric equalizer may be composed of any number of individual band-pass filters, but three to six bands are typical. Figure 6.17 shows the faceplate of a possible, five-band parametric equalizer. The principal advantage of a parametric equalizer over a graphic equalizer is the increased flexibility that the parametric equalizer offers in varying the center frequencies and bandwidths of its filters. However, the graphic equalizer will usually have a greater number of individual filter bands and generally steeper attenuation slopes with which to shape a signal more discretely.

Multimode Filters

Many synthesizers employ what has come to be called a *multimode filter*, which consists of a high-pass filter and a low-pass filter that can function independently of one another or can be combined to function as a band-pass or a band-reject filter, sometimes providing separate signal outputs from each filter combination simultaneously (Figure 6.18). Because of the voltage-controlled aspects of these modules (which will be discussed in Chapter 13), their controls are generally not precisely calibrated, but their ability to act an input signal in a variety of ways at the same time makes them useful in many electronic music studio applications.

FILTER APPLICATIONS

The function of a filter is to reshape the spectral characteristics of an input signal either by suppressing (attenuating) or emphasizing (amplifying) parts of its frequency spectrum. A filter may be used to attenuate or even eliminate an unwanted sound, such as high-frequency tape hiss or low-frequency grounding hum. As the primary means of *subtractive synthesis*, a filter may be used to remove or attenuate certain portions of a signal's frequency spectrum, thereby giving it a new timbral identity. By emphasizing certain bands of frequencies, new *formants* can be created in the signal, again redefining the timbral nature of the resultant sound. Finally, a filter or a group of filters may be used to alleviate flaws in the acoustics of the recording or listening environment, providing more balanced or desired response characteristics across the full audible frequency range.

Signal Suppression

The suppression or removal of unwanted portions of an input signal is the most basic function of a filter. By setting a band-reject filter with steep attenuation slopes to an extremely narrow bandwidth or notch, a small band of frequencies can be completely eliminated from a signal without affecting the frequencies above or below the rejected band to any noticeable degree. Unwanted high-frequency noise, such as tape hiss, can be eliminated simply be sending the signal through a low-pass filter with an f_c slightly lower than the frequency of the hiss. However, care must be taken so that the desired upper components (harmonics or partials) of signals are not eliminated along with the noise. It should also be noted that a signal completely lacking in high-frequency components, which tend to be the most complex parts of a sound, has a tendency to sound lifeless and unreal.

Subtractive synthesis can range from a subtle reshaping of the frequency spectrum

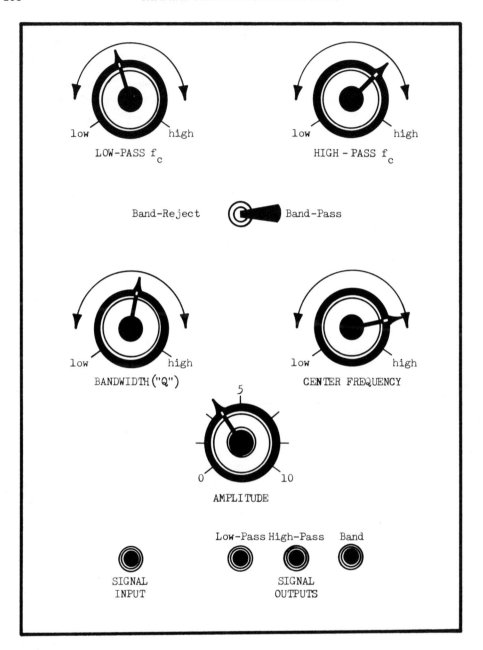

Figure 6.18   The Multimode Filter

of a sound to a radical excision of entire portions of a sound. An oscilloscope will show how the characteristics of a complex waveform, such as a sawtooth wave, are changed as the lower harmonics are progressively removed by a high-pass filter or the higher harmonics are gradually removed by a low-pass filter. A band-pass filter can have an even more dramatic effect on a signal, as may be heard and seen (on an oscilloscope) when a white noise source signal is gradually eliminated except for an extremely narrow band of frequencies in a particular frequency range. The narrow focus of the band will tend to make the remaining noise actually sound pitched, and can be narrowed enough to produce an almost pure tone (sine wave). In fact, if a sine tone with the same frequency as the center frequency of the passed band is mixed with the white noise signal and filtered along with it, the result will be a rich, "chorus-like" sound.

Formant Processing

The spectra of most acoustic musical instruments and of the human voice (particularly vowel sounds) tend to emphasize distinct frequency regions that largely define the timbral characteristics of the sounds produced. These regions are known as *formants*. An active band-pass filter, filter bank, or an equalizer can synthesize these formants in sounds that would otherwise have no particular regions of frequency emphasis (such as electronically produced waveforms), or they can suppress the formants of sounds that do have them, significantly altering the character of the sounds. Formant synthesis is one of the primary purposes of several recently developed devices, such as the *vocoder* (see Chapter 12).

Equalization

Equalization is one of the most omnipresent uses of filters in the electronic music or recording studio. The crossover network of a speaker system is actually an equalizer circuit that correctly matches the response of high-, mid-, and low-range speakers to the frequency characteristics of the signals presented to them. Tape machines employ equalizer circuitry in both their recording and playback electronics to compensate for the frequency-response characteristics of the recording and playback heads and the tape formulation being used. Equalization has become an essential part of the recording process, particularly in the recording studio, where the acoustics of the recording and monitoring environments are often completely controlled by careful, multiband equalizer systems. In most cases, the purpose of this type of equalization is to ensure a completely "flat" frequency response across the entire audible frequency spectrum, and to compensate for any deficiency in the recording/listening environment. The third-octave equalizer is particularly effective in adjusting the acoustics of a recording or playback environment, but the use of a *spectrum analyzer* and a calibrated pink noise source is required to determine which regions of the frequency spectrum need to be amplified or attenuated to obtain a perfectly flat response. The human ear is rarely sensitive enough to detect the small discrepancies that may exist but which can significantly alter the qualities of the sounds being recorded or reproduced.

FILTER EXPERIMENTS AND EXERCISES

1. Using a 500 Hz sawtooth wave as an input signal to a low-pass filter with a cut-off frequency (f_c) of 500 Hz, gradually increase the amount of resonance (Q) of the filter. What is the effect? Why?
2. Using the same 500 Hz sawtooth wave as an input signal to a band-pass filter with a high Q value, gradually move the center frequency of the passed band upward from 500 Hz. What is the effect? How does this effect relate to Fourier's Theorem?

3. Set the high-pass cut-off frequency of a band-pass/band-reject filter to 500 Hz and the low-pass cut-off frequency to 2000 Hz. What is the center frequency of the band? Using a 1000 Hz sine wave as an input signal, switch from the band-pass setting to the band-reject setting. What is the effect? Repeat this experiment using a 1000 Hz sawtooth waveform as the input signal. What is the difference between the filter's effect on the sine and sawtooth waveforms? Why?

4. Adjust a third-octave filter bank or equalizer so that every second filter band is set for complete attenuation. Using a sawtooth wave as a signal input, gradually change the frequency of the sawtooth signal over a span of one octave. What is the effect? Try the experiment with every third and then with every fourth filter band set for full attenuation. What is the effect? Repeat this experiment, this time setting the various filter bands for maximum amplification.

5. Use a radio program as an input signal to each of these filters: low-pass, high-pass, band-pass, band-reject. Change the cut-off frequencies, amplitude and Q settings (where available), noting the different effects produced. At what point does the program material become unrecognizable?

6. Repeat experiment #5 using a microphone and speaking and singing voices as the signal input.

7. Mix a pure tone (sine wave) with an extremely narrow band of white noise centered on the same frequency as the sine wave to produce the chorus-like effect mentioned earlier. How narrow must the bandwidth of the white noise be to produce this effect?

8. Use a band-pass filter, a multi-band equalizer, or a fixed filter bank to locate formants in steady-state instrumental or vocal tones. How do these formants change when the pitch of the input signal is changed? When their amplitude is changed? What is the effect on the normal timbre of the source sounds when the formants are emphasized or de-emphasized?

9. As an extension of experiment #8, if a third-octave equalizer, a spectrum shaper, or a band-pass filter with steep cut-off slopes is available, attempt to locate individual harmonics or partials that are contained in a variety of instrumental and acoustic sounds. (Filters with regeneration—Q—capability will make this experiment easier.) Do any of the sound sources have spectra that are similar to the basic waveforms discussed in Chapter 4?

REVERBERATION/DELAY DEVICES

The primary use of reverberation/delay devices is to add a more complex acoustical ambience to an otherwise nonreverberant sound. Since reverberation in a natural environment is the result of the fractional time delays produced by sound waves being reflected off different surfaces at varying distances from the listener, the electronic synthesis of reverberation relies principally on the mixing of a source signal with several, minutely delayed reiterations of itself. This can be accomplished in a number of ways:

- Physical Delay
- Analog Delay
- Digital Delay

Each of these systems has its adherents and detractors, just as different concert halls are both praised and criticized for their natural or unnatural ambient characteristics. No system can be called ideal, nor can any system be labeled totally unacceptable. The usefulness of any device must, in the final analysis, depend on the end for which it is being used and on a certain degree of subjective personal evaluation and taste.

Echo, Reverberation, and Delay Time

Several terms are commonly used to describe the qualities or characteristics of any reverberation/delay system. *Delay* itself denotes the amount of time that transpires between hearing an initial (direct) sound and hearing a repetition of that sound. Technically, a delay of more than about 20 milliseconds (depending on the nature of the initial sound) will be perceived as a separately identifiable repetition (*echo*) of the initial sound, and a delay of less than about 20 milliseconds will be perceived more as an elongation (*reverberation*) of the initial sound. Note that this is the same time relationship that applied to the distinction between audio and sub-audio waveforms described earlier.

Decay Time

A single sound may generate both echoes and reverberations, as shown in Figure 6.19. Another important parameter in reverberation/delay systems is the *decay time* of the reverberations or echoes that are produced. In a general sense, this term is synonymous with *reverberation time* — the amount of time it takes for a signal to diminish in amplitude to a level that is one-millionth of its original intensity (a change of −60 dB). This definition is the same regardless of the intensity of the original sound. Thus, if an initial sound has an intensity of only −20 dB, its decay or reverberation time will be the time it takes the sound to diminish in amplitude to −80 dB. In the illustration of Figure 6.19, the decay time is 2.5 seconds. This is a somewhat longer decay time than that favored by most musicians and acousticians for concert halls. A decay time of from 1.5 to 2.0 seconds is most generally favored, depending on the intended use of the hall. Note that the sound (as reverberation) is still present after this decay time has elapsed, but at amplitude levels below the −60 dB decrease in intensity. For a more detailed examination of the characteristics of reverberation and echo, see "ambience" in Chapter 4.

Physical Delay Systems

The earliest used and perhaps most realistic means of adding reverberation or echo to a source signal is based on the manipulation of a live or reproduced sound in an actual physical environment. Special rooms (echo chambers) may be constructed to permit the control of delay and decay times by actually changing the size and shape of the room itself, but a tiled washroom, a concrete stairwell, or similar hard-surfaced enclosures have often been adapted to serve the same purpose at much less expense. In any of these cases, a live or recorded sound source (if recorded, the sound source is then a loudspeaker) is positioned at one location in the space, and a microphone or a group of microphones is positioned at another location or at several locations. When the original sound is recorded along with the reflections of it picked up by the microphone(s), the result is a naturally complex and random reverberation whose delay and decay times can

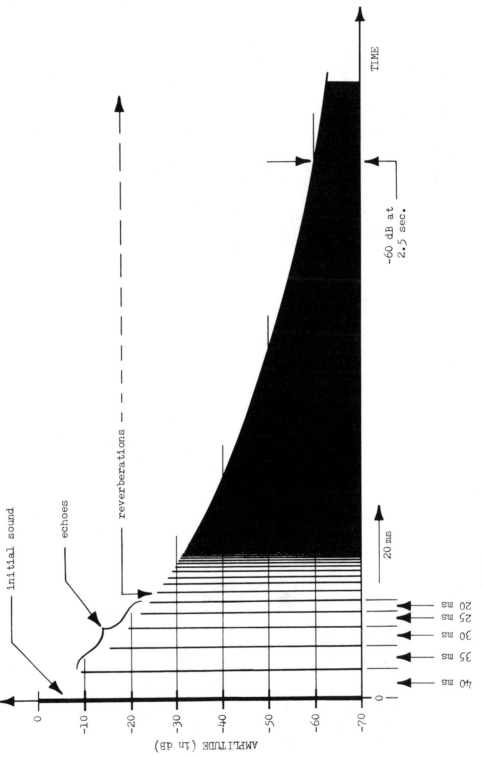

Figure 6.19 Echo and Reverberation

172

be controlled by moving dampers (acoustically absorbent panels) within the space or by repositioning the sound source or the microphone(s). The primary advantage of this reverberation method is that it is entirely acoustic and, therefore, both naturally complex and random. However, few studios can afford the space and the expense necessary for a real echo chamber, and washrooms and stairwells tend to be placed under somewhat conflicting demands.

Plate Reverbs

A number of devices have been developed that, in essence, replace the ideal acoustically reverberant environment with a synthetic but similar model. Many professional recording studios and some well-equipped electronic music studios use a *plate reverb*, which consists of a rectangular metal plate that is suspended within a wooden cabinet (Figure 6.20). A "driver" element, which functions like a small loudspeaker, transmits the sound to be reverberated to the plate and one (mono) or two (stereo) asymmetrically placed contact microphones act as pickups. When the plate is set in motion by the driver element, its vibrations reflect off the edges of the plate much like sound waves in the air would reflect off of walls. Owing to the asymmetrical placement of the contact microphones, a complex, random set of delayed vibrations reaches the pickups. The pickup closest to the driver element receives vibrations slightly sooner than does the more distant pickup, increasing the overall complexity and density of the signal available at the final output, which is usually a mixture of the signals from the two pickups. The decay time produced can be varied by moving a "damper plate" (covered with acoustic absorbing material) closer to the vibrating plate to reduce the decay time and farther from the plate to lengthen it. In this way, the decay time can usually be adjusted over a range of about one to four seconds. In any plate reverb system, the resulting signal output contains none of the original (unreverberated) signal. If a combination of the original and reverberated signals is desired, as it usually is, an external mixer must be used.

In general, plate reverb systems produce relatively realistic effects. However, they are usually very heavy and bulky, very delicate, and quite sensitive to extraneous disturbances. They also require careful calibration. An adaptation of the metal plate reverb system is the gold foil reverb plate, such as the EMT 240, which is somewhat more portable (weighing only about 130 pounds) and much less sensitive to extraneous noise and vibration. The EMT 240 produces an unusually realistic reverberation effect, because the initial reflection of the source signal is delayed longer, while the later reverberations are much more dense. Either system is relatively expensive in comparison to most other artificial reverberation systems currently available.

Spring Reverbs

The reverberation device found most often in electronic music studios, either as an independent unit or as a module in a voltage-controlled synthesizer, is the *spring reverb*. Although the quality, controllable characteristics, and prices of spring reverberation devices vary considerably, the principles behind their design and operation remain relatively constant. A driver element creates vibrations at one end of a suspended spring, which often contains several sections made up of different wire sizes and coil densities, that are transmitted to a pickup attached at the opposite end. The signal arriving at the

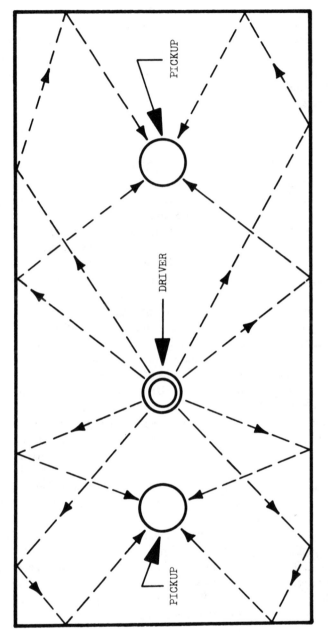

Figure 6.20   Wave Reflections in a Reverberation Plate

pickup is delayed by the relatively slow transmitting medium of the metal spring. Since the vibrations reflect off the ends of the spring as well as off of every joint of the spring (where a spring section of one size and coil density is connected to a section of differing size and density) a fairly complex vibration pattern is set up. Figure 6.21 shows some of the reflections produced by a spring reverb using a single spring consisting of only two sections.

Most spring reverb systems tend to have a metallic sound quality (often called

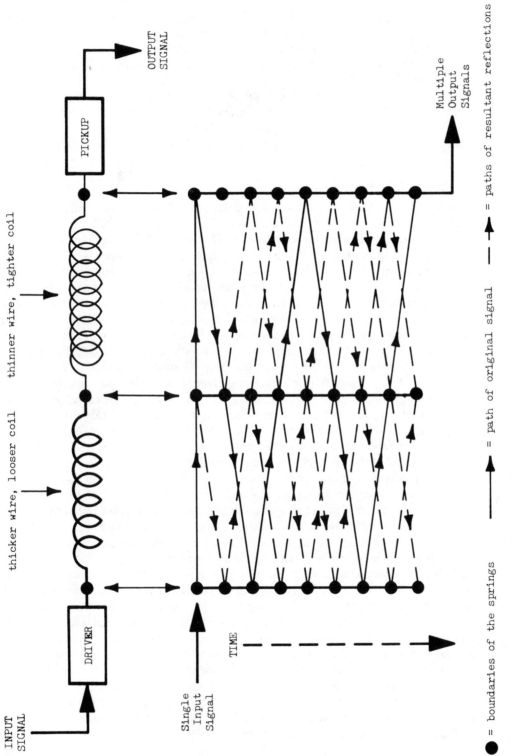

Figure 6.21 Reflections Produced in a Two-Section Reverberation Spring

"twangy" or "springy") that compares unfavorably with the more natural sound of other reverberation systems. However, some units have been carefully designed to overcome these problems by using two or more isolated springs of differing lengths and coil densities, electronic damping circuits, and very precise equalization circuitry. The springs work independently of each other and have different reverberant characteristics, because of their different lengths and coil densities, so their mixed output can be very complex and can maintain a high reverberation density. Electronic damping circuits allow the user to vary the decay time, usually from about 2 to 4.5 seconds. The equalization circuits reduce formant peaks produced by the spring's frequency response.

Magnetic Tape/Disc Delay

As described in Chapter 3, it is possible to delay a signal by using an ordinary magnetic tape machine. However, the characteristics of the echoes produced with most tape machines are not adequate for a realistic reverberation effect. The fixed delay time, determined by the distance between the recording and playback heads, is usually too long to be convincing as reverberation—and the density of the reiterations is comparatively low. This effect can be substantially improved with the use of a mixer to feed back the delays from the playback head to the recording head (forming a feedback loop), but even then the overall effect is not very realistic and is, as well, difficult to control. However, a few tape reverberation/delay devices have been specially designed (usually by individual studios) to create fairly convincing reverberation effects using magnetic mediums (magnetic tape in the form of tape loops or oxide-coated discs). Figure 6.22 shows such a *magnetic tape delay* system, using a tape loop and six heads—one erase head, one recording head, and four playback heads. The playback heads are movable; they can be positioned at various distances from the recording head and from each other, thereby producing several different delay times. The signal to be delayed passes from the record head onto the tape, which then moves past each of the playback heads in turn. The outputs from all of the playback heads are then mixed together with the direct (source) signal to produce an initial (direct) sound and a first-level series of four different reiterations. To increase the complexity and density of the delays or reverberations produced, the outputs of any or all of the four playback heads can also be fed back to the recording head, through the device's own "feedback" mixer, to produce a wide variety of multilevel reverberation/delay effects. Thus, the number and amplitude of the reverberations can be controlled by varying the amount of feedback from each of the playback heads, much as was done in earlier tape machine experiments (Chapter 3). The density (spacing) of the reverberations can be controlled not only by the spacing of the playback heads but also by changing the speed of the tape—the faster the speed of the tape, the greater the density of the reverberations produced. The signal path of the tape reverberation/delay device in Figure 6.22 is shown in Figure 6.23. A variation of the general system described above uses an oxide-coated disc (similar to a small phonograph record) in the place of the tape loop, but the operational principles are the same.

The primary drawbacks of the magnetic tape or disc reverberation/delay systems are the same as those encountered with any tape recording: the quality of the signal and its reiterations is dependent on the mechanical and electronic specifications of the tape machine as well as the characteristics of the tape itself. As with all multiple rerecordings of a sound, the signal quality of the recording diminishes with each successive reiteration, so high-frequency signal loss is a particularly noticeable side effect. The tape loop or oxide-coated disc must also be replaced fairly often, since it deteriorates quickly.

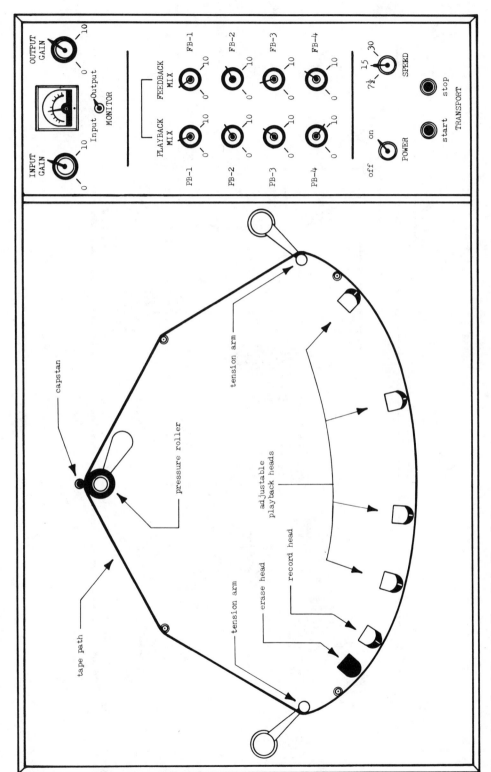

Figure 6.22 An Adjustable Tape Delay/Reverb System

177

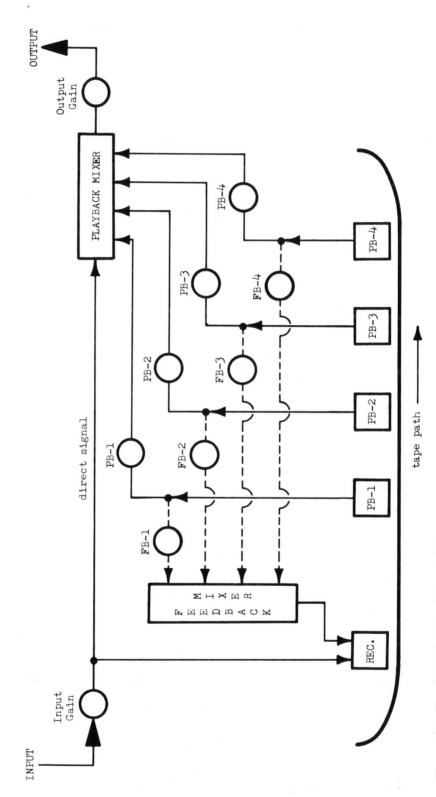

Figure 6.23 The Signal Path for Figure 6.22

Digital Reverberation/Delay

A more recent type of reverberation/delay system that has become increasingly popular in analog electronic music studios and professional recording studios is the *digital reverberation/delay* unit. Without venturing too far into the design and functioning of digital systems, the operation of a digital reverberation/delay unit can be compared to that of a long series of sequentially routed switches (Figure 6.24). The signal passes through all the switches that happen to be connected together and is delayed for a fraction of a second at each switch until it is finally diverted at one of the switches. Each switch may add as little as 1 or 2 ms. of delay time, and the total number of switches may be as many as 800. Of course, these are electronic, not mechanical switches, so there are none of the drawbacks usually associated with purely mechanical systems—no sensitivity to extraneous noise, no heavy or immovable parts, no mechanical components to malfunction, and very little or no maintenance required. Since each delay circuit can produce only one specified delay time, several delay circuits must be combined to get a good reverberation density. Each individual delay circuit functions much as the playback head in a tape reverberation/delay system, producing a single delayed signal that can then be mixed with the delayed signals produced by any or all of the other delay circuits at the output and can also, if desired, be fed back into the delay network for recycling. A complex set of delay times, ranging from widely spaced echoes to very dense reverberant fields, can thus be produced if the spacing of the initial delay times are set properly.

Digital reverberation/delay systems are relatively economical, lightweight, and easy to operate. However, their very precision tends to work to their disadvantage, since natural reverberation is usually entirely random. Unless several, nonrepetitive delay circuits are combined, the effect produced can be an all too regular "fluttering" of signal reiterations rather than a complex, reverberant decay. Better digital reverberation systems avoid the use of delay time sequences such as 2 ms., 4 ms., 8 ms., 16 ms., etc., where the delay times produced by later stages in the delay sequence are simple (whole number) multiples of earlier delay times. Such reinforcement of one delay time by another would be heard as periodic pulsations in the output signal, or, for very short delay times, as a band-pass filter tuned to octaves: 2 ms. = 500 Hz, 4 ms. = 250 Hz, 8 ms. = 125 Hz, 16 ms. = 62.5 Hz, etc., especially evident with source material with wideband frequency content. The use of nonrepetitive delay time sequences such as 2 ms., 3.5 ms., 9 ms., 15 ms., etc., avoids this problem and produces a more random reverberant field. Because of the technical complexity involved, most digital reverberation/delay devices do not operate on the portions of an input signal above about 8 KHz. This is not too significant, because the energy of higher frequencies, with their short wavelengths, is usually dissipated very quickly in a natural acoustic reverberation environment. There are as yet no standard specifications for digital reverberation/delay systems, so specific brands and models will vary widely in their realism and versatility.

REVERBERATION/DELAY APPLICATIONS

Stereo Reverberation

Of course, the principal application of reverberation/delay systems is to synthetically produce or enhance the effects of a given ambient environment. This effect is most

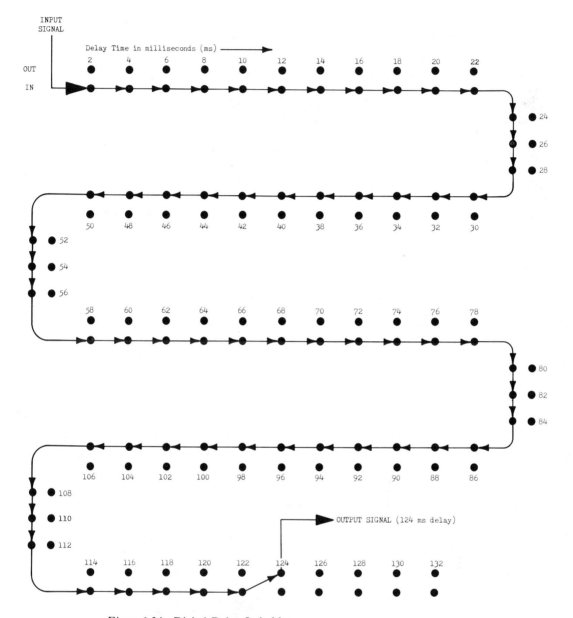

Figure 6.24 Digital Delay Switching

convincingly accomplished with *stereo reverberation*. Since the effect of natural reverberation is to surround the sound source (and the listener) with a diffuse envelope of sound, a sense of spatial dimension is also needed in the artificial simulation of reverberation. A monophonic reverberation unit will be unable to provide this spatial information. Figure 6.25 shows the signal path of a typical stereo reverberation set-up. In a high-quality stereo reverberation system, the phase relationships between the two speakers will be constantly changing so that the ears will hear a diffuse envelope or field of reverberant sound, rather than a static field of reverberation isolated to the right, left, or center

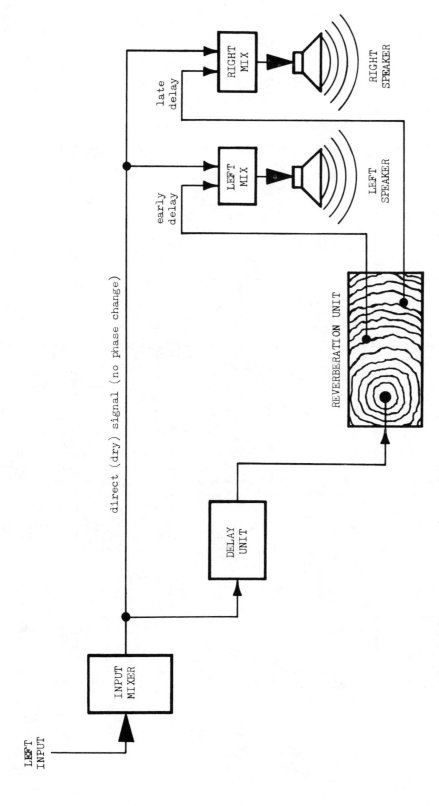

Figure 6.25 The Signal Path of One Channel of a Stereo Reverberation System

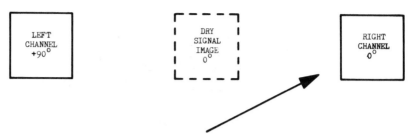

A. Phase of the right-channel reverberation is the same as the dry signal, so reverberation seems to come from the right.

B. Phase of both the right and left-channel reverberations are 90° off from the phase of the dry signal, so reverberations seem to come from the center.

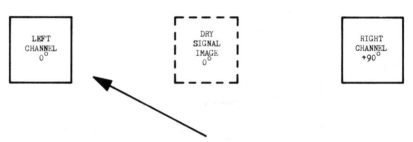

C. Phase of the left-channel reverberation is the same as the dry signal, so reverberation seems to come from the left.

D. Left and right-channel reverberations are 180° out of phase with each other, so reverberation seems to come from both directions.

Figure 6.26 The Effects of Phasing on Stereo Reverberation

(Figure 6.26), In Figure 6.25, an initial delay unit controls the time of the first reflection, affecting the apparent size of the room (the greater the initial delay, the larger the apparent room size). The independent reverberation unit has two separate pickups positioned to receive the signal at different delay times and, therefore, with different phases that are constantly changing because of reflections and feedback. Thus, the relationships of the "right," "left," and "direct" signals cause the reverberant field to surround the direct signal and the listener (Figure 6.26).

Doubling and Chorusing

One special effect that is often used in recording studios and has applications in the electronic music studio is called *doubling*. By delaying a signal for an extremely short time (only a few milliseconds) and allowing only one or two reiterations of the signal instead of the hundreds typical of normal reverberation effects, a slight phase shift is introduced that seems to make the single signal sound like two or more signals in concert, each producing the same sound but almost imperceptibly out of synchronization with each other. Using this effect, a single violin can be made to sound like a whole section of violins. This effect is also called *chorusing*, because a single singer can be made to sound like the whole section of a chorus. Chorusing or doubling effects can also be produced by overdubbing or multitracking the same instrument several times over. The slight differences between each performance will, of course, give the impression of several instruments, but this process is both time consuming and tedious. As with all overdubbing techniques, it can also add unwanted noise to the signal, while the original signal quality is progressively degraded with each overdub. An added benefit of chorusing is that it often covers up slight flaws in the initial or subsequent performances.

Reverse Reverberation

A somewhat unusual but useful effect, called *reverse reverberation*, can be produced by recording a reverberated sound and then playing the recording backwards, thereby reversing the normal sequence of the initial sound and its reverberations. In this way, the sound of a single held pitch and its reverberant decay can be made to grow steadily out of complete silence to a full sound.

EXPERIMENTS AND EXERCISES

1. Record several short passages of drum, piano, guitar, and violin sounds. Play these sounds back through various available reverberation and delay units, changing the delay time, the decay time, and the mixture of the direct and delayed sounds. Note the effects.

    - What is the longest delay setting possible before the repetition is perceived as an echo? Does it change for different instruments? Does it change for different frequencies?
    - What decay setting most realistically resembles the characteristics of: A concert hall? A gymnasium? A washroom? A football stadium?
    - What effect on the total sound does the mixture of direct and reverberated signals

have? Can one make the reverberation more prominent than the direct signal? If so, what is the result?

2. Using separate mixer inputs (each with pan pots) for a direct sound and its reverberated form, experiment with different spatial placements of the direct and the reverberated signals in the stereo (or quadraphonic) listening field.

   - What is the effect if the direct signal remains static in its spatial location while the reverberated signal is moved around the listening field?
   - What is the effect if it is the reverberated signal that is heard from one direction while the direct signal is moved about the listening field?

3. Play a recorded tape backwards, adding reverberation to it *as* it is playing.

   - What is the effect?
   - How is this effect different from adding reverberation while the tape is playing in the normal, forward direction?
   - What does this imply about the nature of reverberation itself? About the kinds of sounds that may be most effectively reverberated?

ELECTRONIC SWITCHES

An *electronic switch* is one of a number of devices normally used in scientific laboratories for which applications have been found in the electronic music studio. They are often used to permit the display of two different signals "simultaneously" on an oscilloscope by rapidly alternating between the two input signals and combining these alternations into a single output, which is then displayed on the oscilloscope. Because of the rapidity of the alternations, not perceivable by the human eye, the two signals seem to appear at the same time on the oscilloscope.

In its simplest form, an electronic switch has two inputs and one output. Switching between the two inputs is usually regulated by an internal square-wave oscillator, so the rate can be altered by merely changing the frequency of the oscillator.

Electronic switches designed for use in the electronic music studio often have additional refinements that greatly extend their usefulness. Many models are bidirectional; that is, they can switch between two inputs to produce one output, as in Figure 6.27a, or they can take one input and switch it between two outputs, as in Figure 6.27b. Another useful refinement is found in electronic switches that accept more than two inputs—often called *sequential switches*—that form the basis of the analog *sequencers* found in most voltage-controlled synthesizers. Switching rates of electronic switches found in the electronic music studio usually have a much wider range than their scientific counterparts. Alternations from as slow as once in 20 seconds and continuously variable up to as much as 20,000 times per second are common. When the switching rate exceeds about 20 times per second, the alternation of the separate "bits" of signal contained in the output (or outputs) is too fast to be heard as a succession of individual events, and the transformation of the resultant sound becomes similar to that produced by ring modulation (see Chapter 7). Some electronic switches allow the duty cycle of the internal square wave, which controls the switching rate, to be changed, creating a pulse wave. Thus, the two inputs would have different "on" and "off" times. Some studio versions of the electronic switch also incorporate the ability to voltage control the switching rate

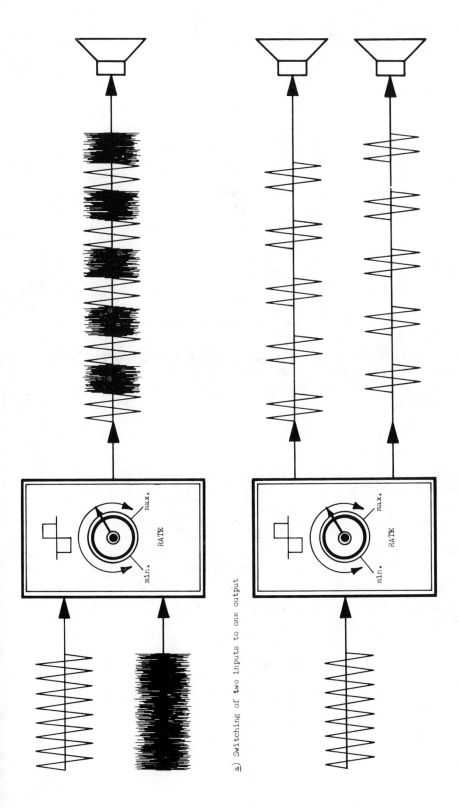

a) Switching of two inputs to one output

b) Switching of one input to two outputs

Figure 6.27 The Electronic Switch

185

(and sometimes even the pulse width) of the switching waveform. The voltage-controlled applications of electronic switches will be explored in Part II.

APPLICATIONS

The electronic switch offers one of the few means in the analog electronic music studio by which one may rapidly alternate between two or more signal inputs or outputs. The key to its usefulness is that this switching takes place *instantaneously*, without a loss of amplitude at the beginning and ending of each output "bit," as would be the case if one attempted to obtain the same result by the use of faders (2 inputs to 1 output) or pan-pots (1 input to 2 outputs) on a mixer. The only other way of producing the same effect would be to resort to tape splicing, a frightening and laborious prospect even at alternation rates as slow as 20 times per second!

EXPERIMENTS AND EXERCISES

1. Alternate between two different waveforms, set at different frequencies, at about 10 times per second.

    • What is the effect when the switching rate is increased to about 50 times per second? 100 times per second? 1000 times per second?
    • What is the effect when this experiment is repeated with two different waveforms having the same frequency?

2. Using one signal input alternating between two outputs, connected to two speakers, experiment with different switching rates as before.

    • At what switching rate does it become difficult to distinguish between the two sources of the sound?

3. Using a speaking voice as one of the inputs to an electronic switch and a waveform (or white noise) as the other, experiment with different switching rates.

    • What is the result if either of the inputs is disconnected?
    • Repeat this experiment using two different voices speaking two different texts as inputs.

4. If three or more electronic switches are available, connect the outputs of two of them to the inputs of the third. Use as many different input signals as there are inputs available on the first two electronic switches.

    • What is the effect when the switching rates of all three electronic switches are the same?
    • What is the effect when the switching rates of the several electronic switches are different?

LISTENING EXAMPLES

Arel, Bulent	*Stereo Electronic Music No. 2* CRI SD–268 Finnadar QD 9010 0798
Barron, Louis and Bebe	*Forbidden Planet* (soundtrack) Planet Records PR 001 (P.O. Box 3977, Beverly Hills, CA 90212)
Davidovsky, Mario	*Electronic Study No. 3* Turnabout TV–34487 Finnadar QD 9010 0798
Eimert, Herbert	*Selektion I* Philips 835 485/86AY Mercury SR–2–9123
Ligeti, Gyorgy	*Articulation* Philips 835 485/86AY Wergo 60059 Mercury SR–2–9123
Oliveros, Pauline	*I of IV* Odyssey 3216 0160
Pousseur, Henri	*Scambi* Philips 835 485/86AY Mercury SR–2–9123
Powell, Mel	*Second Electronic Setting* CRI S–227 *Events* CRI 227–USD
Semegen, Daria	*Electronic Composition* No. 1 Odyssey Y34139
Stockhausen, Karlheinz	*Study II* DGG LPEM 19322 DGG 16133

Chapter 7

Electronic Signal Modulators

MODULATION

The process by which any of the characteristics of one signal (frequency, amplitude, spectrum, and phase) are changed through interaction with another signal (or event) is called *modulation*. This relatively simple concept has been intrinsic to the development of electronic music since the early 1950s. Modulation was first used in electronic music to create complex and unusual sounds by mixing signals together in such a way as to take advantage of natural, acoustic phenomena with which we are already familiar—beats and combination tones. As the technology of electronic music developed, modulation became *the* basic operational principal of voltage-controlled synthesizers (see Chapter 8).

Vibrato

The human voice and most Western acoustic musical instruments are capable of producing a common and simple form of frequency modulation called *vibrato*. This "natural" vibrato that we have become accustomed to is actually a slight periodic variation in the frequency of a signal (in this case, a vocal or instrumental sound). The violinist moves his finger back and forth on the violin string as he presses it down against the instrument's fingerboard, varying the sounding length of the string slightly and, thus, changing the frequency of the sound produced by the string.

Carrier and Program Signals

The sound produced when the length of the string remains constant (the basic or "reference" frequency) is called the *carrier* signal, and the periodic frequency variation introduced by the movement of the violinist's finger on the string is called the *program* signal. When the violinist moves his finger back and forth, the carrier signal's frequency is modulated (changed) by the program signal he imparts to it by the movement of his finger. The result is a signal that combines characteristics of each of the two original signals—the basic frequency, timbre, and amplitude of the carrier signal and the speed (frequency) and amount (amplitude) of variation produced by the program signal.

Modulation Rates

If the frequency of the program signal (the speed of the violinist's vibrato) could be increased from the typical 4–8 cps normally employed to frequency rates well beyond the audio threshold (perhaps 40 to 100 cps) the resulting sound would begin to attain the complexity of more typical electronic signal modulations. The periodic characteristics of the program signal would then cease to be individually perceivable (as was possible with the slower, sub-audio rates of variation) and would begin to interact with the carrier signal to form *new* frequency, amplitude, and spectral relationships. In general, it can be stated that the effects of modulation of an *audio* carrier frequency (greater than about 20 cps) by a periodic *sub-audio* program frequency (less than about 20 cps) are perceived as periodic variations in some single characteristic of the carrier signal itself. Sub-audio *frequency modulation* is recognizable as vibrato (a periodic variation in frequency—as was the case with the violinist and his vibrato); sub-audio *amplitude modulation* is heard as *tremolo* (periodic variations in amplitude); and sub-audio *phase modulation* and *spectrum modulation* are perceived as periodic variations in the tone color or timbre of a sound (for example, using a "wah-wah" mute on a trumpet).

Modulation by a program frequency at audio rates (faster than about 20 times per second) results in a *transformation* of the carrier signal—regardless of the particular characteristic being modulated—into a completely different signal, often unrecognizable in relation to the original carrier signal. The effects of each variation in the program signal on the carrier signal are no longer perceivable as separate and distinct events.

Sideband Generation

Perhaps the single most recognizable effect of *all* forms of modultion at audio frequency rates is the creation of *sidebands*, specific frequencies that are generated above and below the frequency of the carrier signal. These sidebands occur at frequencies determined by the interaction of the two original signals (the carrier and the program) and the particular characteristics being modulated (frequency, amplitude, timbre, or phase). Paradoxically, the audible effect of amplitude modulation at audio frequency rates is the creation of frequency sidebands formed as the sums and differences of the carrier and program frequency components. Thus, amplitude modulation of a 600 Hz sine-wave carrier signal by a 100 Hz sine-wave program signal produces sideband frequencies at 700 Hz and 500 Hz. Other forms of modulation—frequency, spectrum, and phase—produce effects that are more difficult to predict precisely, particularly if spectrally complex waveforms or signals are used as carrier or program input signals. For the most part, audio modulation of these signal parameters will be discussed in Part II, since the devices that make such modulations possible are usually associated with voltage-controlled synthesizers. However, a few devices are used that do not involve the application of external control voltages. The *ring modulator, frequency shifter,* and *phase shifter* are each capable of sub-audio and audio modulations of input signals without the introduction of an external control voltage. (Though this is a narrow distinction, it is made here to facilitate the introduction of modulatory concepts before the introduction of the concept of voltage control. The voltage-controllable aspects of these devices will be examined in Part II.)

RING MODULATION

Audio Ring Modulation

A *ring modulator* (also known as a *balanced amplitude modulator*) is a passive circuit that, through a form of amplitude modulation, produces frequency sidebands at the sum and difference frequencies of the carrier and program signal components, while suppressing (or *squelching*) the carrier and program (input) signals at the output. Thus, if two sine waves at frequencies of 150 Hz and 600 Hz are the two signal inputs (the ring modulator does not normally distinguish the carrier signal from the program signal, particularly when they are both in the audio frequency range), the output signal will be a sideband frequency at the difference of the frequencies of the two inputs (450 Hz) *and* a sideband frequency at the sum of the frequencies of the two inputs (750 Hz), but the two input signals themselves will have been elminiated from the output. In this example, the input signals are harmonically related (600 Hz is two octaves higher than 150 Hz), but the output sidebands (450 Hz and 750 Hz) are inharmonically related. If either or both of the input waveforms were not simple sine waves but were more complex waveforms, perhaps sawtooth waves, many more sidebands would be created. *All* of the frequency components of one waveform would be added to and subtracted from *all* of the frequency components of the other waveform to produce an upper and lower sideband frequency for every combination of all components. In a much simpler case, where each input has only three components (far fewer than a sawtooth wave), eighteen different frequency combinations (sidebands) will be produced at the output. Notice in Figure 7.1, that the resulting frequency spectrum, while not itself harmonically related, *can* be thought of as harmonically related to an *implied* fundamental of 50 Hz. The sideband frequencies produced extend through the 27th harmonic of a 50 Hz fundamental, with harmonic numbers 1, 2, 3, 4, 8, 12, 16, 20, and 24 missing. Further, if the amplitudes of the six input components are all equal, the amplitudes of the 18 output components will also be equal. The ring modulation of two input waveforms with 12 components each would produce 288 sideband frequencies! In most cases, these sideband frequencies would not be harmonically related to the lowest sideband frequency produced but would form an extremely complex inharmonic spectrum. This is usually true even when the two input signals are themselves harmonically related. *In all cases*, when the exact frequency content of the two input signals is known, the number of sideband frequencies produced and their exact frequencies can be predicted with complete accuracy. This makes it possible to construct very complex harmonic or inharmonic spectra using relatively simple input signals.

Because of the ring modulator's ability to transform relatively simple signals into complex combinations of signals in unusual harmonic or inharmonic relationships, it has often been used by electronic music composers to change, more or less drastically, the context and meaning of commonplace signals and sounds—particularly the sounds used in musique concrète compositions. Figure 7.2 shows a typical set-up diagram for a simple experiment using a ring modulator. Try using different sound sources via the microphone with different waveforms at various frequencies from the oscillator, and note the wide variety of effects that are produced. Is there a difference in the output if the microphone and oscillator are switched between program and carrier inputs?

Sub-Audio Ring Modulation

When a sub-audio signal is used as an input to a ring modulator (usually as the program signal) along with an audio input (as the carrier signal), the result is a simple form of amplitude modulation that produces changes in the *amplitude envelope* (the change, in time, of the amplitude of the signal) of the carrier signal that follow the "shape" of the sub-audio program signal. For example, in Figure 7.3, a sub-audio sine wave used as the program input would cause a gentle variation (tremolo) in the amplitude of an audio triangle-wave carrier signal, periodically raising and lowering its amplitude in direct

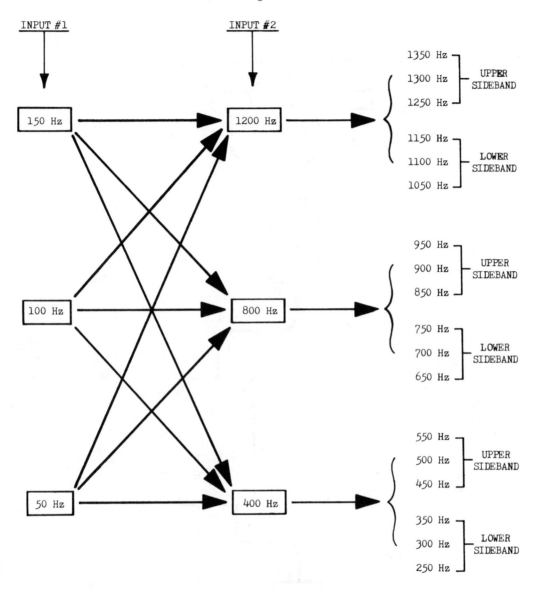

INPUT #1

INPUT #2

| 150 Hz | 1200 Hz |

| 100 Hz | 800 Hz |

| 50 Hz | 400 Hz |

1350 Hz ⎤
1300 Hz ⎬ UPPER SIDEBAND
1250 Hz ⎦

1150 Hz ⎤
1100 Hz ⎬ LOWER SIDEBAND
1050 Hz ⎦

950 Hz ⎤
900 Hz ⎬ UPPER SIDEBAND
850 Hz ⎦

750 Hz ⎤
700 Hz ⎬ LOWER SIDEBAND
650 Hz ⎦

550 Hz ⎤
500 Hz ⎬ UPPER SIDEBAND
450 Hz ⎦

350 Hz ⎤
300 Hz ⎬ LOWER SIDEBAND
250 Hz ⎦

Figure 7.1   Ring Modulation of Two Signals, Each with Three Components

relation to the rising and falling of the sub-audio sine wave. The width, or range, of this amplitude variation would depend on the signal strength of the sine wave. The greater the program input's amplitude, the greater the amount of variation in the amplitude of the carrier signal. Similarly, changes in the frequency of the sine-wave program input will change the frequency of the amplitude variations produced in the triangle-wave carrier input.

Amplitude Gating

A sub-audio square-wave program input would produce an on-off effect in the carrier signal (Figure 7.4), with the degree of attenuation and amplification determined by the

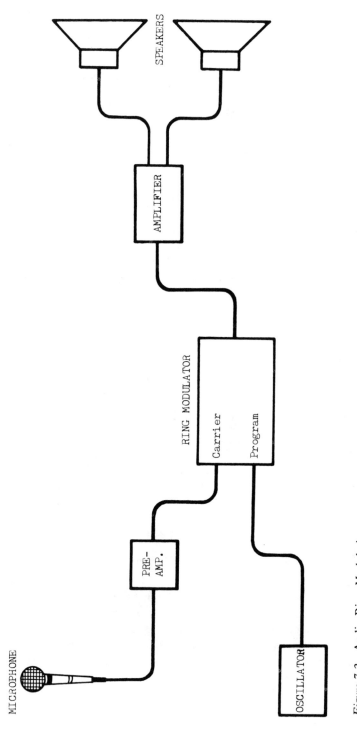

Figure 7.2 Audio Ring Modulation

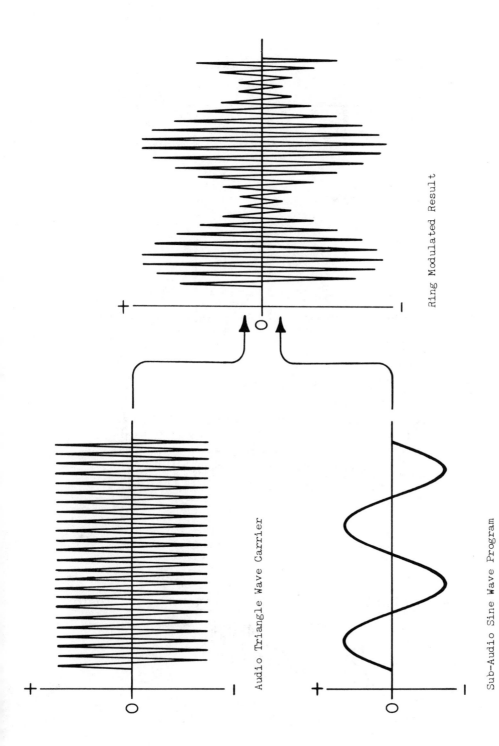

Audio Triangle Wave Carrier

Sub-Audio Sine Wave Program

Ring Modulated Result

Figure 7.3 Ring Modulation of an Audio Triangle Wave by a Sub-Audio Sine Wave

Sub-Audio Program signal <u>input</u>:

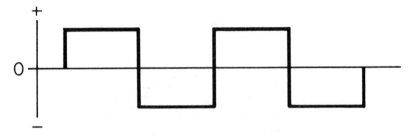

Sub-Audio Program signal <u>processed</u> in DC mode:

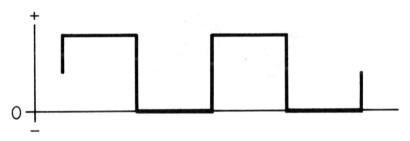

Audio Carrier signal <u>input</u>:

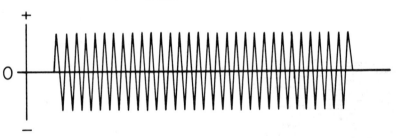

Carrier signal <u>output</u> from Ring Modulator:

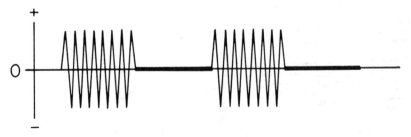

Figure 7.4 Ring Modulator in DC Mode with Sub-Audio Program Signal and Audio Carrier Signal

gain settings of both of the input signals. In this situation the ring modulator is actually functioning as an *amplitude gate*, since the audio signal (the triangle wave) is allowed through the circuit only when the square wave is positive (i.e., the "gate" is open). More complex amplitude gating and envelope-shaping techniques will be covered in Chapter 12, when we examine voltage-controlled amplitude modulation. Try the experiments shown in Figures 7.2, 7.3, and 7.4, using several different carrier signal sources (microphone, radio, another oscillator, white noise, etc.) and sub-audio program waveforms (sine, triangle, sawtooth, square/pulse). Notice the different effects on the various carrier signals as the frequency of the sub-audio input approaches the pitch discrimination threshold of about 20 Hz.

AC/DC Coupling

The controls of most ring modulators are generally very simple. There are usually volume controls for each of the input signals, and many models provide controls for the amount of suppression (squelching) of the two inputs in the output signal. Some ring modulators, such as the one found in the ARP 2600 synthesizer, have an AC/DC coupling switch that determines whether a square-wave input is only positive-going (DC) (Figure 7.4) or is both positive- and negative-going (AC) (Figure 7.5). In the AC (or Audio) setting, and with both inputs in the audio frequency range, this type of ring modulator functions just as described earlier, producing sum and difference sideband frequencies and suppressing the two input signals. However, if the program signal is a sub-audio square wave (or rectangular wave), this kind of ring modulator will pass the audio (carrier) signal only when there is a *change* in the direction (or "value") of the sub-audio signal input (Figure 7.5). Further, as shown, the amplitude of the output signal will vary in direct proportion to the amplitude of the sub-audio waveform.

In the DC mode (Figure 7.4), a square or rectangular wave is processed as only positive-going. If both of the input signals are at audio frequencies, the use of the DC mode allows a muted but audible amount of the input signals to pass through to the output along with the normal sum and difference sideband frequencies. If one of the input signals is a square or rectangular wave at a sub-audio frequency, the ring modulator functions as an amplitude gate, as described earlier.

Applications

Aside from its use for sub-audio amplitude modulations (including amplitude gating), the principal use of the ring modulator is to transform sounds with comparatively simple, harmonic spectra into sounds with complex, inharmonic spectra. In some cases, depending on the frequency content of the two input signals, the result is a "bell-like" clang; in others (particularly when the carrier signal is the human voice), it is a mechanical or otherworldly sound.

Although the effect of the ring modulator can be startlingly unpredictable, because of its dependence on the spectral complexity or the transient nature of the two input signals, the quality or characteristics of its effects on sounds is easily recognized by the listener after only a few experiences with it. Because of this, electronic music composers are generally cautious in using the ring modulator in compositions and, as with most "special effects," carefully avoid its overuse.

Sub-Audio Program signal <u>input</u>:

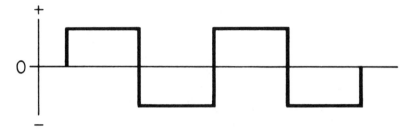

Sub-Audio Program signal <u>processed</u> in AC (Audio) mode:

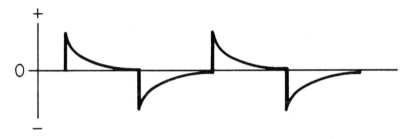

Audio Carrier signal <u>input</u>:

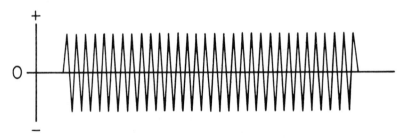

Carrier signal <u>output</u> from Ring Modulator

Figure 7.5   Ring Modulator in AC Mode with Sub-Audio Program Signal and Audio Carrier Signal

196

FREQUENCY SHIFTING

Operation

Frequency shifters have come to be known by a number of names (tone shifters, single-sideband generators, and *Klangumwandlers*, to list a few) and often work by very different means, but their effects are all the same: they shift the frequency of a *single* input signal (*and* all its components) up or down by a frequency increment set manually by the operator or by another, external signal. The resulting effect is much like that of a "one-sided" ring modulator, but it is more subtle and predictable than the effect produced by a ring modulator. Because of this, and their greater flexibility, frequency shifters often supplant ring modulators in current modular synthesizers.

Essentially, a frequency shifter separates the upper and lower sidebands produced by a ring modulator by using separate circuits to generate upper and lower sidebands. Many frequency shifters offer these upper and lower sidebands simultaneously, but at individual signal outputs (for example, the Moog model 1630 and the Bode model 735 Frequency Shifters offer individual outputs for the upper and lower sidebands as well as a mixed—ring modulated—output with a "balance" potentiometer to control the ratio of upper to lower sidebands in the output mixture). The amount of frequency shift, called the *shift index*, can be controlled manually or, in some models, by an external control signal.

Every frequency component of an input signal is shifted by an *equal* amount, so the effect is ultimately one of spectrum compression (upward shift) or spectrum expansion (downward shift). For example, in Figure 7.6a, if a signal with harmonically related component frequencies of 400 Hz, 800 Hz, 1200 Hz, and 1600 Hz (spanning a range of two octaves) is shifted upward by a harmonically related shift index of 800 Hz, the result is the compressed, but related, series 1200 Hz, 1600 Hz, 2000 Hz, and 2400 Hz (spanning only one octave). In this example, the resultant frequencies are harmonically related, but only as higher-numbered harmonics of an implied lower fundamental frequency, such as 400 Hz (harmonics 3, 4, 5, and 6) or 200 Hz (harmonics 6, 8, 10, and 12). In Figure 7.6b, the same frequency spectrum is shifted downward by a harmonically related shift index of 200 Hz. The result is the compressed, but related, series 200 Hz, 600 Hz, 1000 Hz, and 1400 Hz (spanning about three octaves). In this case, the resultant series is made up of harmonics 1, 3, 5, and 7 from a fundamental of 200 Hz. The series may also be considered as harmonics 2, 6, 10, and 14 from a fundamental of 100 Hz, or as harmonics 4, 12, 20, and 28 from a fundamental of 50 Hz, etc. Even when using a harmonically related spectrum as the input signal, interesting inharmonic spectra can be generated when the shift index is not harmonically related to the input components. For example, Figure 7.7 shows the same harmonically related input spectrum of Figure 7.6, this time shifted up and down by a nonrelated shift index of 220 Hz.

Applications

Several interesting and useful effects aside from those described above can be acheived with a frequency shifter. Very slight upward or downward shifts of an input signal (in the range of 0.1–10 Hz, depending on the frequency range of the input signal) will produce a *chorus* effect when the shifted output is mixed with the unshifted input. The effect of the frequency shifter on natural sounds can be quite subtle and evocative—

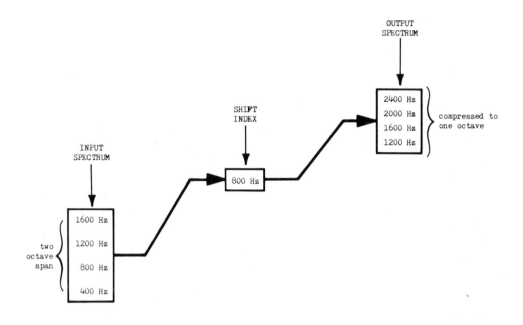

) Frequency Shifting of a harmonic spectrum upward by a harmonically related shift index (800 Hz)

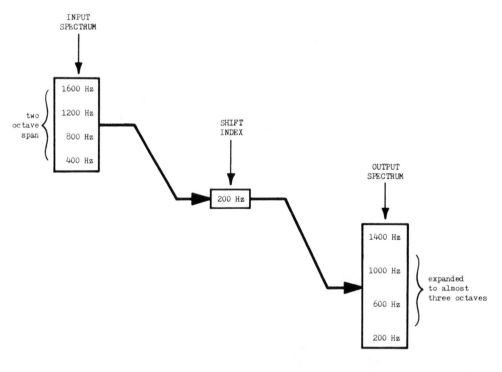

b) Frequency Shifting of a harmonic spectrum downward by a harmonically related shift index (200 Hz)

Figure 7.6   Frequency Shifting of Harmonic Spectra by Harmonically Related Shift Indexes

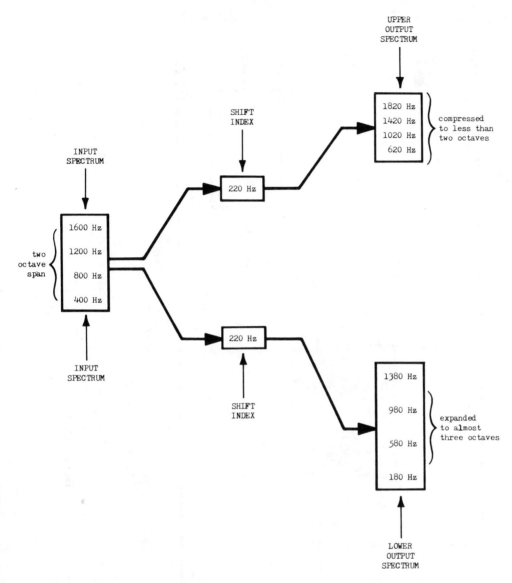

Figure 7.7   Frequency Shifting of a Harmonic Spectrum by a Nonrelated Shift Index

much less haphazard and over-rich than those often produced by ring modulation. By introducing a frequency shifter, using a small shift index, into a simple tape-delay system (Figure 7.8), it is possible to produce a gradual upward or downward "spiraling" of frequencies. If a frequency shifter is inserted into the mixer output line of a public address system so as to shift the frequency of the incoming signals up or down very slightly, acoustic feedback from the speakers can be reduced without seriously affecting the quality of the signal. Speech may also be processed by a frequency shifter with good results, normally preserving the intelligibility of the words even across fairly large shifts.

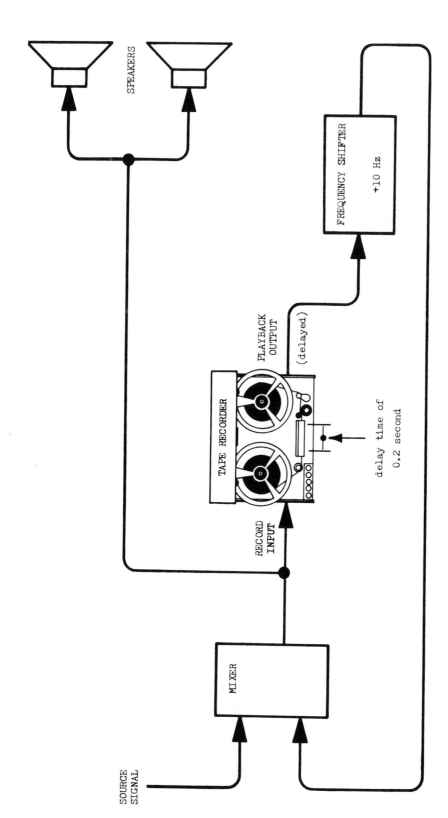

SPEAKERS

FREQUENCY SHIFTER

+10 Hz

PLAYBACK
OUTPUT

(delayed)

TAPE RECORDER

delay time of
0.2 second

RECORD
INPUT

MIXER

SOURCE
SIGNAL

Tape Machine Delay Time = 0.2 second

Frequency Shift = +10 Hz

The output frequency will increase by 50 Hz every second.

Figure 7.8   The Frequency Shifter Used with a Tape Machine Delay System

PHASE MODULATION

Operation

Unlike the effects of frequency or amplitude modulation, the effects of phase modulation are not, in themselves, humanly perceivable. For example, a waveform will sound the same whether its period is measured from 0° to 360°, from 90° to 450° (360° + 90°), or from any point in its period to the recurrence of that same point. Thus, the sine, cosine, negative sine, and negative cosine forms of the sine wave (see Figure 4.3) all *sound* alike. To be audible, phase modulation must be perceived according to its *context*, that is, the phase differences it creates between two or more copies of the same signal occurring slightly out of synchronization with one another. A *phase modulator, phase shifter,* or *flanger* (as various systems are known) functioning in the classic sense (there are devices of the same name that merely imitate these effects) splits a signal into two identical copies (as would a multiple), delays one of the copies by a very small fraction of time (usually variable from about 0.2 to 2.0 ms.), and then mixes the two signals back together again. The phase difference introduced between the two mixed signals (either of which would sound exactly the same as the other if heard separately) causes constructive and destructive interference patterns (amplitude variations) between them. The effect this has on the recombined signal depends on the amount of phase shift that occurs—a function of the frequency of the input signal and the length of the time delay applied to it—and of the harmonic or inharmonic complexity of the original signal.

If a sine wave is split into two identical copies, and one is then shifted 30° out of phase with the other, the only perceivable quality of the mixed signal that will be affected is their combined amplitude, which will be slightly reduced because of the periodic destructive interference occurring between the two copies. If the phase shift between the two signals is increased to 180°, the destructive interference will be complete, and the two signals will cancel each other out entirely (see Constructive/Destructive Interference in Chapter 4, Figure 4.18).

The effect of phase shifting on harmonically complex waveforms (or other complex signals) is more subtle. Each harmonic component of the waveform will be affected differently because the single delay time used will make up a different proportion of each harmonic's period—with the exception of a 180° phase shift, which will always cancel out both the original and delayed signals and all their harmonics completely. Thus, the effect of phase shifting on more complex signals is heard as a kind of spectral (or timbral) modulation in which the amplitudes of the harmonic components are either reinforced or reduced by periodic constructive and destructive interference.

If this were the only effect of phase shifting, it would be interesting and valuable enough. However, most phase shifters provide not only a manual means of changing the amount of phase shift applied to the input signal but also an automatic control that gradually changes the amount of phase shift at a rate determined by the frequency setting of a built-in low-frequency sine wave oscillator. This gradual but periodic change in the amount of phase shift causes the spectral characteristics of the mixed output signal to change periodically, resulting in what might be described as "ripples" in the output signal's harmonic spectrum.

Tape Recorder Technique

Although most currently available phase shifters use some form of digital delay circuitry to produce the phase shift, there are simpler ways of achieving the same effects, some of which have been used for many years. By recording a signal onto two tape machines at once, then playing the two machines back at slightly different speeds or delaying the start of one of the tape machines for a fraction of a second, the same basic phase-shifting effect will be produced when their output signals are mixed together. One method of delaying one of the tape machines—simply pressing a finger against the edge (flange) of the supply reel to slow it down slightly—gave phase shifting its nickname: *flanging*, from "reel flanging."

Comb Filtering

Another device used to produce an effect similar to that of actual phase shifting is the *comb filter*, which is essentially a set of widely-spaced band-pass filters with very steep cut-off slopes arranged in a preset frequency ratio. As the comb filter's center frequencies are changed (either automatically or manually—one control usually affects all of the center frequencies simultaneously), the spectrum of the input waveform or signal is changed in a manner similar to the spectral changes that occur as a result of true phase shifting. In fact, many phaser/flanger devices incorporate comb filters as part of their circuitry in order to enhance their basic phasing/flanging effects. By itself, the comb filter produces a somewhat disappointing and unsatisfactory illusion of phase shifting or flanging, since it is limited to a finite number of frequency bands. True phase modulation affects an infinite number of harmonics or frequency components; it *modulates* the signal. Filtering, even with a sophisticated comb filter, only *modifies* the signal.

Controls

An actual phase shifter should allow the amount of shift (time delay), the frequency of any automatic shift, and, in some cases, the relative amplitudes (mixture) of the delayed and undelayed signals to be controlled. Some models are also capable of accepting outside control sources, and some may have controls governing other special effects. Aside from the characteristic "rippling" effect produced by a phase shifter operating in its automatic mode, it can also be used to produce the *chorus* and *stereo* effects already discussed under Digital Delay Systems in Chapter 6.

THE PITCH TRANSPOSER

The final processing device to be discussed is a relatively recent addition to the tools of the electronic music studio. The effect of the pitch transposer on audio signals is quite different from those of the frequency shifter and the ring modulator in that the intervals between shifted frequencies or pitches of the original signal are maintained in the transposed signal. The most obvious use of such a device is to produce instant harmonies in real time or to accurately transpose the characteristics of an instrument or a voice into an unusual frequency range. Since the pitch transposer operates on digital principles, it is outside the scope of this book and not specifically related to this discussion of analog synthesis equipment and techniques. However, pitch transposers are becoming a commonplace and valuable tool in the modern electronic music studio, so some explanation of their operation is in order.

Operation

The basic operational principles of a pitch transposer can best be compared to the effects produced by tape speed transposition with which we are already familiar. When a recorded tape is played back at a speed faster than that at which it was recorded, the sounds recorded on it will be played back at a higher frequency (or pitch). When the tape is slowed down during playback, the sounds are played back at a lower pitch. However, the tape speed changes also affect the speed (or tempo) of the succession of sound events on the tape, making coordination or synchronization of the original and transposed versions impossible. To preserve the same timing of the original and the transposed versions of the tape it would be necessary to change the space between the sound events occurring in the transposed version to match the timing of the events of the original version, or vice versa.

If the transposed version is to be higher in pitch, the sound events will occur too fast; so space must be added between them, i.e., the sound events must be spaced out in time. The pitch transposer accomplishes this by filling these needed spaces with digital imitations or repetitions of the previous sound, creating the illusion of one continuous sound event with the correct duration. If the transposed version is to be lower in pitch, the sound events will occur at a much slower rate than in the original, so some of each sound event must be removed in order to fit it into the proper time span. To accomplish this, the pitch transposer merely removes minute "pieces" of each sound event, compressing them in time. This all occurs at an incredibly fast rate of speed, much too fast to be perceived by the human auditory mechanism, and is only made possible by digital techniques. This makes the slight additions to and deletions from the individual sound events relatively unnoticeable, depending on the quality of the unit. Better versions of the device, for example, employ additional circuitry to smooth out the beginning and end of each digital sample of the sound event.

Controls

The basic control offered by the pitch transposer allows the user to set the amount of upward or downward transposition that is to take place. Some pitch transposers, such as the MXR Pitch Transposer, provide multiple pots for this function. Each can be set to a different transposition level and, when lightly touched, will shift between them, enabling one to change the amount of transposition applied to the signal instantaneously. Some models of the device offer other controls that substantially extend the device's usefulness to the electronic music composer. For example, the MXR unit, which allows transposition up or down by as much as a full octave, has a mixture control that sets the proportion of processed to direct signal available at its output, allowing one to produce perfectly balanced two-part harmony in real time. This unit also has a "regeneration" control that allows any amount of the transposed signal to be fed back into the input of the unit, producing a continuous upward or downward transposition of the input signal. If the original signal is transposed up by a major third, for example, and then fed back to the input, it will be transposed upward by another major third, even while the direct signal is undergoing its first transposition. It should also be mentioned that small upward or downward pitch transpositions (as small as 1 or 2 Hz), when mixed with the direct signal, can even be used to produce chorusing effects.

PROJECT NO. 4: ELECTRONIC SIGNAL SOURCES AND ELECTRONIC SIGNAL PROCESSING

This project is designed to give students the opportunity to exercise their technical skills in using the equipment described thus far in a relevant compositional context. In contrast to the more rigid structuring of previous projects, this project allows for a number of individual creative options within a more loosely constructed framework. However, the focus of the project still remains on the development of technical skills, not on musical esthetics. Therefore, the project should be evaluated primarily on the following bases:

- Use of the available equipment
- Production plan completeness, accuracy, and efficiency
- Technical difficulty of the production plan
- Execution of the production plan
- Recording quality

Description

There are several, general guidelines that should be followed in the production of this project:

- The final tape should be recorded in two channels (stereo) at 15 ips (38 cm/s) using noise-reduction devices whenever appropriate.
- The duration of the piece should be from one to five minutes (depending on its complexity).
- A "score" should be made that illustrates the piece in sufficient detail that others would be able to duplicate the results without consulting the composers.
- A production plan should be developed showing each step of the production process, with particular emphasis on efficiency, speed, and quality of production.

A number of options will be open to the production groups (we still recommend that classes be divided into groups of two to four students for this project, depending on the available studio time). Each group should be allowed to choose the basic signal sources, signal processors, and formal structures it desires within the general constraints of the equipment that is available. However, there should be a few minimum requirements:

- Each piece should make use of at least two of the following signal sources: oscillators, noise generators, and electronically processed acoustic sounds.
- Each piece should involve at least three of the following modifying and modulating processes: filtering, reverberation/delay, electronic switching, ring modulation/frequency shifting, phase shifting/flanging/comb filtering, and pitch transposing.

- Each piece should be designed to require an extensive and careful use of the available mixer capabilities for the dynamic and spatial shaping of the piece.

Procedure

To many people new to composition, particularly electronic music composition, the most difficult part of the creative process is the formulation of an initial idea or concept around which a piece can be constructed. In most cases, this creative block is the result of having too many options available, not—as some might think—of having too few. In the words of Igor Stravinsky,

> I experience a sort of terror when, at the moment of setting to work and finding myself before the infinitude of possibilities that present themselves, I have the feeling that everything is permissible to me. If everything is permissible to me, the best and the worst, if nothing offers me any resistance, then any effort is inconceivable, and I cannot use anything as a basis, and consequently every undertaking becomes futile. (Stravinsky 1974)

This "terror" can only be eliminated by consciously reducing one's options, by deciding to use one sound and not another, by deciding to use a certain formal structure and not another, by deciding to use certain types of signal processing and not others; in other words, by choosing among the many options available. The temptation that must be strenuously avoided is the tendency to try to do too much in any one piece, to use too many sound sources, to use too many kinds of signal processing devices, in short, to try to put every idea one has into a single piece of music. A highly focused, well executed, and relatively simple piece using only a few basic sound sources will usually prove to be much more effective than a hodgepodge of unrelated sound events and processing effects that seem to be carelessly thrown together. Therefore, the first step in planning this project is to imagine a *few* possible basic sounds that can be produced with the equipment available and to attempt to produce them, carefully noting how they were produced and recording the results.

Once several complementary sounds have been gathered, an organizational structure should, and usually will, begin to insinuate itself from the material itself and the way in which the sounds seem to relate to one another. In a similar manner, possible, useful, or necessary manipulative effects (modifying, modulating, editing, mixing, etc.) should also gradually become apparent. The earlier recorded *sounds* are now ready to be transformed into *sound events*, in a manner that will focus the piece so that it effectively expresses the initial idea or concept. The use of the initial sounds, and any manipulations to be applied to them are now decided upon and defined *in terms of time*. How long is each sound event to be? What is its dynamic and spatial shaping? How and where is it to be placed in relation to other sound events? These and similar questions will lead to the kind of detailed imagining of the piece from which actual production step sequences can be derived.

At this point, each sound event chosen should be thoroughly described so that it could be reproduced by others, given similar circumstances and equipment. Once the *sound event descriptions* are complete, a *graphic score* should be produced outlining the relationships of the sound events and their transformations to time, to tape channeling (spatial location), and to each other. Finally, a complete, written outline of the production steps necessary to realize the piece should be made, describing each production step in the most efficient sequence possible, including sound event production, dubbing, editing, modification, modulation, mixing, and synchronization. Block diagrams should be used to illustrate all patches.

Admittedly, this production planning and record keeping may seem to be a time-consuming and tiresome process, especially in order to produce such a small piece. Some will prefer to "find" their piece in the studio rather than to "create" it out of their own imagination and their understanding of the capabilities of the equipment available. However, if electronic music composition is approached from this viewpoint, that one's piece can be "found" in the studio, one will be forever looking for it. This is not meant to denigrate the "free exploration" of the possibilities of the available equipment, particularly when one is new to it and to electronic music in general. Exploration of the possibilities (experimentation) is a never-ending process for the electronic music composer, but, as more experience is gained with the medium, one should begin to predict what might happen with a given sound and a given sequence of processing. It is only when this occurs that one can begin to "compose" what one *wants* to compose and not merely to string together haphazardly what one *finds* in the studio.

In a more practical vein, students should realize that at some point, unless they possess their own electronic music studio, their access to a studio is likely to be very limited and, in some cases, very expensive. With that in mind, it is obvious that time in the electronic music studio should be used for what the studio alone can provide—the facilities and equipment with which to *produce* a piece of electronic music. For the experienced electronic music composer, the actual *composition* of a piece takes place long before he or she ever enters the studio. (Refer to Chapter 15 for a more detailed discussion of the compositional process as it relates to electronic music.)

The resulting piece for this project should illustrate the students' ability to use the equipment of a standard, classical electronic music studio effectively. A short excerpt from a sample piece is shown below, including *sound event descriptions*, a *production outline*, and a *graphic score* of the result.

Sample Project: *Project No. 4* **(first 15 seconds)**

Event Descriptions

Sound Event #1: Take the output of a 100 Hz sawtooth wave into an equalizer or a fixed filter bank set to allow only frequency bands centered on or about 240 Hz, 480 Hz, 960 Hz, and 1920 Hz to pass. Record the output of the equalizer or fixed filter bank as the frequency of the oscillator is gradually raised. At the end of 5 seconds, the oscillator should reach 240 Hz, at which point the frequency should be held for 10 seconds. The patch without noise reduction devices is shown below:

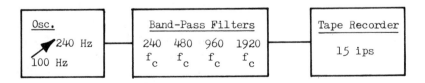

Sound Event #2: Record 10 seconds of white noise filtered through a band-pass filter with a center frequency of 4000 Hz and with very high regeneration (*Q*):

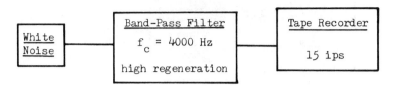

Sound Event #3: Mix the outputs of three sine oscillators set to the following frequencies: 800 Hz, 1200 Hz, and 1600 Hz. Route the mixed signal to a ring modulator as the carrier input, and use a 300 Hz sine wave as the program input. Record 10 seconds of the output of the ring modulator:

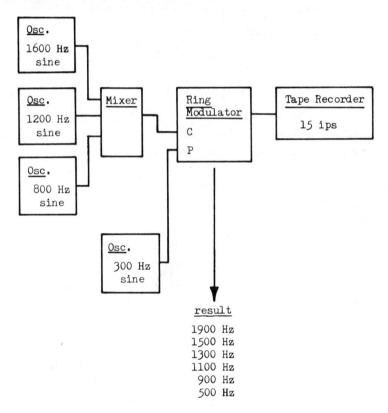

Production Outline

Using a four-channel tape recorder, record 15 seconds of Sound Event #1 onto Channel *A*. Splice leader tape at the beginning of this sound. On Channel *B*, synchronously record 5 seconds of silence followed by 10 seconds of Sound Event #2. Synchronously record 10 seconds of Sound Event #3 on Channel *C*, followed by 5 seconds of silence. A graphic representation of the resulting channel content is:

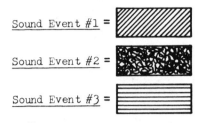

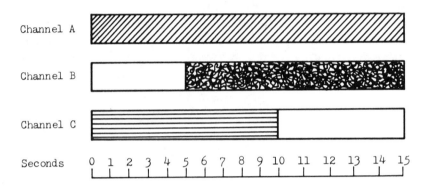

Now, connect the outputs of these three channels of the tape recorder to a 6-in/2-out mixer, and connect the stereo outputs of the mixer to a stereo tape recorder, as shown:

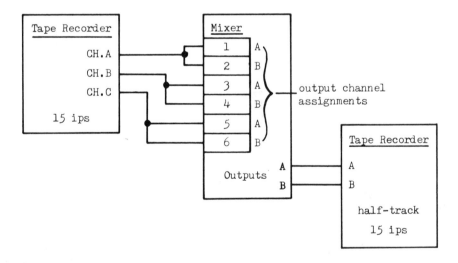

Record the outputs from the mixer onto the half-track stereo tape recorder, following these guidelines (All mixer levels are on a scale of 0–10, where 0 equals no output level and 10 equals the maximum output level.):

CH.A *Mixer Input 1* (*A*): start at +3—hold for first 5 seconds—decrease to 0 over the next 5 seconds—hold at 0.

Mixer Input 2 (*B*): start at 0—gradually increase to 10 over the first 5 seconds—gradually decrease to 0 over the next 10 seconds.

CH.B

Mixer Input 3 (A): start at 0—hold at 0 for 5 seconds—gradually increase to +5 over next 5 seconds—gradually decrease to 0 over last 5 seconds.

Mixer Input 4 (B): start at 0—hold at 0 for the first 5 seconds—gradually increase to +4 over the next 10 seconds.

CH.C

Mixer Input 5 (A): start at +10—gradually decrease to 0 over the first 3 seconds—hold at 0.

Mixer Input 6 (B): start at 0—gradually increase to +7 over the first 5 seconds—gradually decrease to 0 over the next 5 seconds—hold at 0.

Note: The mixer operation just described will very likely require more than one pair of hands. This cannot be avoided by attempting to provide the dynamic shaping during the initial recording on the four-track tape recorder, since each of the three sounds will appear twice, with two different dynamic shapings, in the final stereo result. However, if an eight-track tape recorder is available, each of the three original sounds could be recorded on *two* tracks simultaneously, with the correct dynamic shaping included, *before* the final mixdown.

Graphic Score

The graphic score below illustrates the relative amplitude of each sound event in each channel for the length of time designated in the production outline.

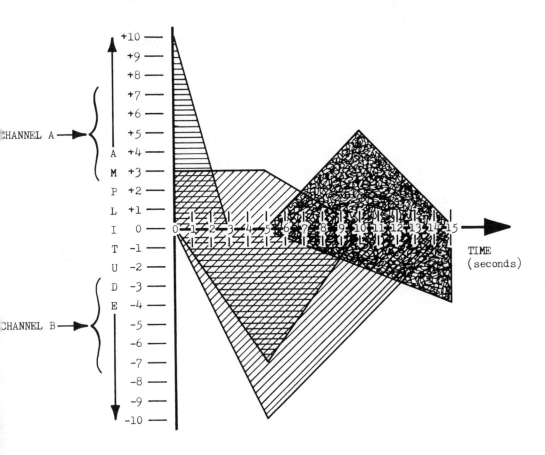

THE CLASSIC ANALOG ELECTRONIC MUSIC STUDIO

There is no absolute standard for the numbers or kinds of devices that are considered necessary or even desirable to make up a functional classic electronic music studio. To minimalists, a few oscillators, a filter bank, and a good tape machine might be sufficient. Others might want every possible piece of equipment currently available. It is certainly true that the variety and amount of studio equipment available in a particular situation will determine, to a large extent, the creative options open to the electronic music composer. The problem of designing an "ideal" electronic music studio, whether it is to function primarily as a teaching or as a production studio, or as both, is further complicated by the practical matter of the availability of the funding needed to build it.

With these variables in mind, *three* different lists of prospective studio equipment are compiled below. These lists are progressive; that is, the second list includes within it all of the equipment of the first, and the third list includes within it all of the equipment of the first and second. All three lists include the components that made up the Basic Tape Studio outlined at the end of Chapter 1.

In keeping with our designation of a "classic" electronic music studio, none of these lists includes voltage-controlled equipment (synthesizers) per se. However, some of the items that are included in the lists are often found as synthesizer modules capable of functioning without the application of control voltages and could, therefore, be substituted for some of the independent devices listed. Analog, voltage-controlled synthesizers (Part II of this text) can be added to any of the three studio lists.

The primary rationale for providing three different equipment lists is budgetary. Some studios are begun with small initial budgets, while others are begun with more substantial funding. It is much more common for a basic electronic music studio to be periodically augmented by infusions of new money and equipment as they become available. In this situation, the three progressive studio equipment lists should prove helpful, since equipment can be planned for and bought in distinct phases. Thus, the growth of a studio can be logical rather than haphazard. In any case, these lists represent a series of personal choices that may or may not be valid for a particular situation, so some degree of freedom should be used in choosing among them.

EQUIPMENT LIST #1: a basic, two-track (stereo), classic electronic music studio.

Tape Studio Equipment:

- two microphones
- one 4-in/2-out mixer
- one four-track ($\frac{1}{4}''$), quadraphonic tape machine with simultaneous synchronization
- one half-track ($\frac{1}{4}''$), stereo tape machine with simultaneous synchronization
- one stereo power amplifier
- two loudspeakers

Electronic Signal Sources:

- two oscillators (offering sine, triangle, sawtooth, square/pulse waveforms)
- one white noise generator

Electronic Signal Modifiers:

- one low-pass filter

- one high-pass filter
- one reverberation/delay unit

Electronic Signal Modulators:

- one ring modulator

Miscellaneous Support Equipment:

- patch bay
- one oscilloscope
- one VTVM (vacuum tube voltmeter)
- various cables, adaptors, and splicing equipment
- $\frac{1}{4}''$ splicing block and supplies

EQUIPMENT LIST #2: a medium-sized, four-track (quadraphonic), classic electronic music studio.

Tape Studio Equipment:

- four microphones
- one 8-in/4-out/2-out mixer with pan-pots
- one four-track ($\frac{1}{4}''$), quadraphonic tape machine with simultaneous synchronization
- two half-track ($\frac{1}{4}''$), stereo tape machines with simultaneous synchronization and variable speed capability
- one stereo pre-amplifier
- two stereo power amplifiers
- four loudspeakers

Electronic Signal Sources:

- four oscillators (offering sine, triangle, sawtooth, square/pulse waveforms)
- one white noise generator
- one stereo turntable

Electronic Signal Modifiers:

- one low-pass filter with regeneration (Q)
- one high-pass filter
- one fixed filter bank
- one parametric equalizer
- one reverberation/delay unit
- one electronic switch

Electronic Signal Modulators:

- one ring modulator
- one frequency shifter

Miscellaneous Support Equipment:

- patch bay
- one four-channel, noise-reduction unit
- one frequency counter
- one oscilloscope

- one timing clock
- one hand-held tape eraser
- one VTVM (vacuum tube voltmeter)
- audio test oscillator
- tape viewer
- various cables, patch cords, adaptors, splicing equipment, headphones, maintenance supplies and tools

EQUIPMENT LIST #3: a very complete, four-track (quadraphonic), classic electronic music studio.

Tape Studio Equipment:

- four to eight microphones
- one 12 to 16-in/4-out/2-out mixer with pan-pots, multiband equalizer system, and foldback system
- one four-track ($\frac{1}{4}''$), quadraphonic tape machine with simultaneous synchronization and variable speed capability
- two half-track ($\frac{1}{4}''$), stereo tape machines with simultaneous synchronization and variable speed capability
- one full-track ($\frac{1}{4}''$), monophonic tape machine
- one stereo pre-amplifier
- two stereo power amplifiers
- four loudspeakers

Electronic Signal Sources:

- six to eight oscillators (offering sine, triangle, sawtooth, square/pulse waveforms)
- one harmonic generator
- one white noise generator
- one stereo turntable
- one stereo AM/FM radio receiver

Electronic Signal Modifiers:

- two low-pass filters with regeneration (Q)
- two high-pass filters
- one band-pass/band-reject filter
- one fixed filter bank
- one parametric equalizer
- one one-third octave graphic equalizer (spectrum shaper)
- one stereo reverberation unit (spring or plate)
- one digital delay unit
- two bidirectional electronic switches
- one voltage inverter

Electronic Signal Modulators:

- one ring modulator
- one frequency shifter
- one phaser/flanger

- one pitch transposer
- one vocoder (see Chapter 12)

Miscellaneous Support Equipment:

- patch bay
- one four-channel, noise-reduction unit
- four noise gates
- two stereo compressor/limiters
- two frequency counters
- one dual-trace oscilloscope
- audio test oscillator
- two timing clocks
- one bulk tape eraser
- tape viewer
- one VTVM (vacuum tube voltmeter)
- various cables, patch cords, adaptors, splicing equipment, headphones, maintenance supplies and tools, tape machine test and calibration tapes

The studios outlined in lists #2 or #3 above *could* be built in an eight-track format simply by adding greater mixer (input/output) capability, an eight-track (1″ or $\frac{1}{2}$″) tape machine, and four more channels of noise-reduction. Each of these studios could remain substantially as given, and, if coupled with a good-sized, modular, analog, voltage-controlled synthesizer, would constitute a well-equipped analog electronic music studio.

LISTENING EXAMPLES

Eimert, Herbert	*Epitaph for Aikichi Kuboyama* Wergo 60014
Kagel, Mauricio	*Transition I* Philips 835 485/86AY Mercury SR2–9123
Mayazumi, Toshiro	*Mandara* Philips 6526 003 Nippon Victor SJX–1004
Shibata, Minao	*Improvisation* Philips 6526 003 Nippon Victor SJX–1004

Part II: Voltage-Controlled Synthesizers

Chapter 8

Concepts of Voltage Control

HISTORICAL BACKGROUND

It is hardly surprising that the development of electronic music can be linked to technological progress. Like the cinema, electronic music exists solely because of technological advancements and breakthroughs (by interesting coincidence initiated by the same person: Thomas Edison) that expanded the creative hardware available to existing art forms and artistic traditions. However, the expansion of creative means made possible by technological developments was far more profound than mere improvement to existing instruments. The static images of the visual artist and the fleeting sonic sensations of the composer could be made to take on each other's seemingly innate characteristics through the use of devices that allowed images to move in rapid, almost "melodic" succession and allowed sounds to be isolated and "sculpted" to fit the composer's ideal.

The "classic" electronic music studio of the 1950s was very often a hodgepodge of linked but unrelated electronic devices, ranging from simple sine-wave oscillators to ring modulators, multiband filters, and noise generators, many of which were actually designed for use as audio test equipment. Working in the classic studio required a thorough knowledge of recording techniques as well as the great patience and single-minded devotion that tape manipulation, editing, and mixing techniques demanded. Composers attracted to the medium primarily for the extensive possibilities it offered for the exact construction of sonic events were often inhibited in realizing these possibilities by the arduous task of assembling a complex tape of high quality.

It was at this point that technology again stepped in with another new development, one that set the stage for the dramatic increase in the influence and popularity of electronic music during the 1960s: the voltage-controlled analog electronic music synthesizer. The voltage-controlled synthesizer essentially freed the composer's hands by substituting another controller—electric voltage. Instead of the composer turning a knob by hand to increase the amplitude of a signal, a voltage (an electronic control signal) could be applied to a circuit (a voltage-controlled amplifier, in this case) that would accomplish the same thing automatically, and with more accuracy and predictability.

CONTROL SIGNALS

The individual modules of a voltage-controlled synthesizer either generate or process electric signals that carry information of some kind. Though this information may seem relatively meaningless in its "raw" state (e.g., an alternating current oscillating 100 times per second), it can be translated into a more relevant and meaningful form (e.g., the production of an audible 100 Hz tone by a loudspeaker). Of course, this kind of comparison is equally valid for the devices found in a classic electronic music studio. Yet, there is an important distinction between the sound production and processing devices found in the classic electronic music studio and the comparable modules of a synthesizer and that is voltage control. The modules of the voltage-controlled synthesizer have been designed to respond not only to information transmitted by manual controls (hand-operated gain pots, frequency verniers, and on-off switches, etc.) but also to information carried by certain control signals generated by the synthesizer itself. When a control signal is applied to the control voltage input of a synthesizer module, the control signal instructs the module how it is to behave. The information carried by the control signal, its instruction to the controlled module, is expressed in the control signal's voltage characteristics. (For our purposes, a change in a signal's voltage is equivalent to a change in the signal's amplitude.) If the control voltage is varying in some way, the module controlled by it will be instructed to vary some parameter (frequency, amplitude, or harmonic structure, depending on the type of module) of the signal it emits in an analogous way.

VOLTAGE TYPES

A synthesizer produces four basic types of voltages:

- *DC Voltage:* direct current voltage—a discrete voltage, unchanging in amplitude over time—it may have a positive or negative value (Figure 8.1a).
- *AC Voltage*: alternating current voltage—a voltage that changes direction and amplitude periodically, having the same characteristics (frequency, harmonic structure, amplitude) for each cycle or period—e.g. the voltage pattern of audio or sub-audio waveforms (Figure 8.1b).
- *Time-Variant Voltage*: a voltage that changes in its amplitude value predictably over time, but which is not periodic (i.e., repetitive)—sometimes termed "DC with an AC component" or "transient" (Figure 8.1c).
- *Random Voltage*: a voltage that changes direction and amplitude unpredictably over time, in a manner analogous to the voltage pattern of white noise (Figure 8.1d).

Variants of these four basic voltage types will be explored when we examine the synthesizer's various "control voltage generators" in Chapters 9, 10, and 11. With the exception of DC voltages, any of these types of voltage can communicate either *audio* or *control* information. The only distinction between a *control signal* and an *audio signal* is that an audio signal can be heard if it is amplified and sent to a loudspeaker. However, because a DC signal is a steady-state (unchanging) voltage, it cannot behave as an audio signal (to be heard via a loudspeaker, an electric signal *must* change its voltage in some manner, since a loudspeaker responds only to the voltage *changes* of its input signal).

Each type of voltage has particular characteristics that make it unique in terms of its applications in voltage-controlled synthesis. As we shall also see, each voltage type forms the basis for different kinds of control-voltage generators that are used for distinctly different purposes. The AC, time-variant, and random voltage signals may occur in either sub-audio or audio frequency ranges and can be used in either range to control a

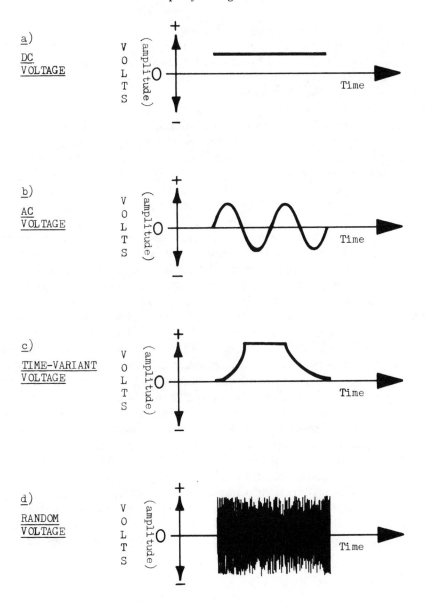

Figure 8.1 Voltage Types

voltage-controlled module. The different effects of the various control voltages, and of their combination, will be thoroughly explored in the next six chapters.

MODULAR SYSTEMS

The principal advantage of the modular organization of a voltage-controlled synthesizer is that it divides a seemingly complex machine into distinct and relatively simple functional units that may be combined in a wide variety of configurations. By learning how each unit works separately, then learning how it can work in combination with other units, one can gradually master the use of the entire system. However, due to different design approaches and goals on the part of different synthesizer manufacturers, there is no uniform standard as to how the different functions of a synthesizer should be divided among its various modules, or even which of many available functions to include. The designers of many of the most recently available synthesizers have put quite an effort into creating hybrid modules, which combine several different functions, in order to easily produce special effects currently in vogue. This aspect of synthesizer design is further compounded by the profusion of small synthesizers that are intended primarily for the live performance of popular music. These systems (ARP Axxe and Solus, Moog Source and Prodigy, Minimoog, Multimoog, Korg Sigma, Oberheim OB-1, and Roland SH-09, to name only a few of them) are often completely internally connected ("hard-wired") into preset signal paths that severely limit their possible configurations and serve to disguise their modular design. This, of course, makes them more suitable for the live performance situations for which they were designed, where quick access to a few preset module configurations is more important than the flexibility that a true modular system would offer. They are also less expensive and require less training and experience to use. Their big brothers, the polyphonic synthesizers (including Polymoog, Oberheim OB-SX, ARP Quadra, Roland Jupiter 8, Korg Trident, and Sequential Circuits Prophet 10, to name a few), tend by their very complexity to emphasize preset controls that further obscure the relationships of audio and control signal generators and signal processors. Even the popular ARP 2600, a standard instrument in many small studios in the United States, is limited by some of its hard-wired internal connections, but the basically modular division of its design remains both evident and accessible.

Since the design and construction of almost all analog synthesizers are based to some degree on the modular concept (even when this subdivision of functions may not be immediately apparent), and since a truly modular instrument permits the greatest system flexibility, the approach taken here assumes a completely modular system. Wherever a major synthesizer manufacturer has developed a unique or hybrid module or a special capability that is of particular interest and importance, it will also be discussed, but the primary emphasis will be on the basic functional modules common to all synthesizers, especially to such larger studio systems as the Moog System 55, ARP 2500, Aries System III, EMS, Buchla, Serge-Modular, and Polyfusion synthesizers.

Module Types

Every module in an analog voltage-controlled synthesizer either generates or processes an electric signal. Because of the voltage-controllable aspects of many of the synthesizer's modules, many of them can act in both ways, and a few of the modules (such as keyboard controllers and sequencers) actually produce several different kinds of control signals at once. However, for the sake of classification, most synthesizer modules can be categorized according to their primary function as either an *audio signal generator*, a *control signal generator*, or a *signal processor*. Audio signal generators consist mainly of oscillators and noise generators. Control signal generators include keyboard controllers, linear ("ribbon") controllers, sequencers, random-voltage generators (including sample/hold circuits), envelope generators, envelope and pitch followers, and sub-audio oscillators. Signal processors include a diverse range of filters, reverberation units, electronic switches, amplifiers, ring modulators and frequency shifters, mixers, phase modulators, X/Y controllers ("joysticks"), and a continual stream of newly developed devices. Most studio synthesizers also include a variety of accessory devices that do not belong specifically in the three categories mentioned above, such as multiple jacks, microphone pre-amps, and voltage or signal conversion devices.

Patching Systems

Although all of the components of a modular synthesizer will normally be housed in the same cabinet (or in interconnected cabinets) and will have the same power source, there will generally be few internal connections between the individual modules. Thus, there must be some external means of connecting (*patching*) the different modules together into various desired configurations. The simplest patching system relies on the use of standard *patch cords* to connect one unit to another (Figure 8.2a). The Moog, ARP 2600, Aries, and Polyfusion systems rely on phone-plug or mini-phone-plug patch cords. The Buchla and Serge systems use banana-plug patch cords. More complex but faster operating patching systems that involve hard-wired patching matrixes have been incorporated into the ARP 2500 and the EMS Synthi 100 systems. The former uses *sliding matrix switches* to indicate which X/Y (input/output) coordinate is being connected (Figure 8.2b), and the latter uses small shorting *matrix pins* that are inserted at the input/output crosspoint (Figure 8.2c). Although each patching system has its adherents and detractors, and all are completely flexible, none is truly ideal. A really complex patch using patch cords can easily take on the appearance of a plate of spaghetti in its wondrous confusion, but attempting to trace the seemingly circular signal paths of a matrix patching board is hardly less trying.

Miscellaneous Considerations

An important point to keep in mind when using any synthesizer is to make sure that all patches are made securely and accurately. Patch pins and plugs must be fully inserted, and matrix sliders must be placed precisely at the crosspoints desired. On some synthesizers, various modules will have attenuators at their inputs or gain controls at their outputs, both useful control additions. Be certain that these controls are not turned off; otherwise, the signal path will be interrupted. Extraneous noises, such as grounding hum, static, or even radio induction, can also occur in the patching network unless proper precautions are taken. Use shielded audio cable for patch cords whenever possible. These cables, while expensive, have a wire mesh shield that surrounds the signal conductors, shielding them from electromagnetic fields common in areas containing a good deal of electronic equipment. Matrix patching boards and jacks should be kept clean and dust-free in order to ensure a precise connection. Dirty matrixes often "leak" signals into places that they don't belong, causing a great deal of confusion and frustration.

BLOCK DIAGRAMMING/PATCH NOTATION

An accurate, yet simple system of block diagramming and patch notation is essential for the efficient use of a complex voltage-controlled synthesizer. In attempting to reproduce a patch devised and notated earlier, its sonic characteristics can be completely lost if only

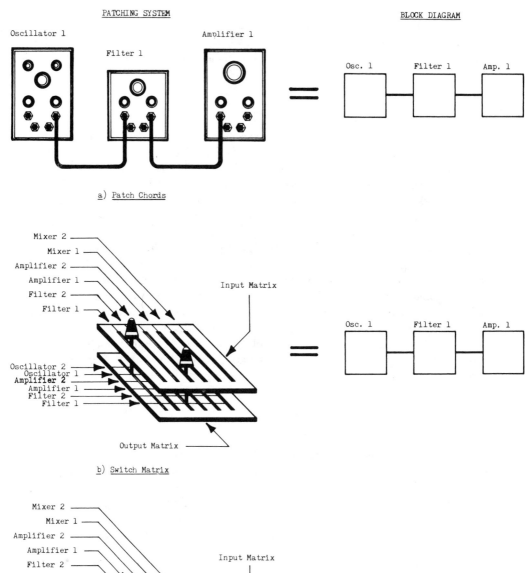

Figure 8.2 Synthesizer Patching Systems

222

a single portion of the signal path is misrouted or if the control settings of only a single module have not been made or notated with enough precision.

The basic system of block diagramming used in this book differs from some other commonly found patch notation systems in that no correlation is made between the shape of the different component modules in the diagram and their function. Instead, a simple system of labeling is used to distinguish between the different modules and their functions in the patch. This patch notation system is easily adapted to any model of synthesizer and, when specific control settings are added to the diagram, will result in a simple but accurate pictographic representation of a given patch. The list of abbreviations shown in Figure 8.3 should prove useful in labeling the diagram blocks appropriately and will be followed throughout the remainder of this text. The instructor or student may wish to develop his or her own set of block diagramming abbreviations or add to the above list to account for the particular modules or controls available on the equipment at hand.

Figure 8.4 illustrates the only absolute rules or principles to remember when using this patch notation system:

- *All audio signals* (those *not* being used as control or command signals) should enter a block from its left side.
- *All control and command signals* should enter a block being controlled from the bottom.
- *All output signals* (of *any* kind) should leave a block from its right side.

The arrow heads indicating signal path directions in Figure 8.4 are added only for additional clarity in this illustration. They are actually superfluous once the notational conventions outlined above are understood.

The proper functional abbreviation (what the module is or does) should appear *above* the block, and any pertinent control settings for the module should be placed inside the block itself. These settings may include waveform type, frequency, input attenuation, output gain, or any other relevant control feature of the module being used. If, as is often the case with many synthesizers, there are no precise markings on these controls, either estimate a percentage of whatever the maximum setting would be, estimate the setting on a convenient but arbitary scale, such as "0–10"; or—in the case of rotary dials—use the approximate position of the hour on the face of a clock. In all cases, be as consistent and precise as possible. Figure 8.5 is an example of this patch notation system used to notate a complete, detailed patch with all the required settings indicated.

Control Levels

In discussing the complexity of a particular patch, it is often useful to refer to the "level of control" being used in the patch. For example, if a VCO is being controlled by a KYBD (Figure 8.6a), there is one level of control being used. If the same VCO is being controlled by both a KYBD and another VCO, there is *still* only one level of control (Figure 8.6b). However, if the first VCO is controlled by a second VCO that is itself being controlled by a KYBD, there are now two *levels* of control. The first control level is the original VCO (the one producing the audio signal) being controlled by the second VCO; the second control level is the latter VCO being controlled by the KYBD (Figure 8.6c). Notice that the second VCO is a part of *both* control levels.

Voltage-Controllable Modules

VCO   -   voltage-controlled oscillator

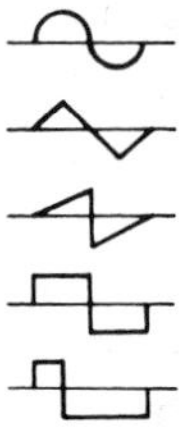

                  ⌇ - sine
                  △ - triangle
                  ◺ - sawtooth   } waveform outputs
                  ⊓ - square
                  ⊓ - pulse

              pw - pulse width
              f - frequency

VCA   -   voltage-controlled amplifier

VCF   -   voltage-controlled filter

              L-P   - low-pass
              H-P   - high-pass
              B-P   - band-pass
              B-R   - band-reject
              R/Q   - regeneration/"Q"
              cut-f   - cut-off frequency
              c-f   - center frequency
              b-w   - bandwidth

Control Voltage Sources and Associated Items

    KYBD   - keyboard
    LC   - linear controller
    ADSR   - envelope generator (attack, decay, sustain, release)
    AR   - envelope generator (attack, release)
    ENV.F. - envelope follower
    P.F.   - pitch follower
    SEQ   - sequencer
    SEQ.SW.- sequential switch (electronic switch)
    S/H   - sample/hold circuit
    V-TRIG - voltage trigger
    SW-TRIG- switch trigger
    GATE   - voltage gate
    V.P.   - voltage processor
    + or − - output polarity
    L.P.   - lag processor
    P.S.   - phase shifter

Miscellaneous

    NG   - noise generator
    FFB   - fixed filter bank
    EQ   - equalizer
    MIX   - mixer
    REV   - reverberation unit
    R.MOD. - ring modulator
    F.S.   - frequency shifter
    MULT   - multiple
    ATTEN - attenuator

Figure 8.3 Block Diagramming Abbreviations

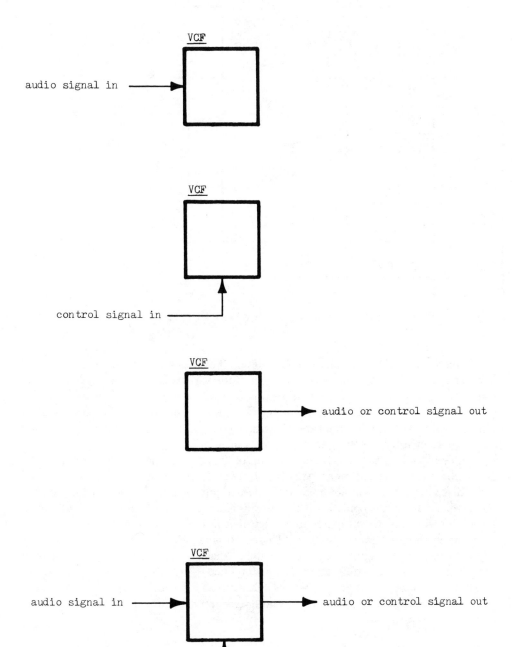

Figure 8.4 Block Diagramming Conventions

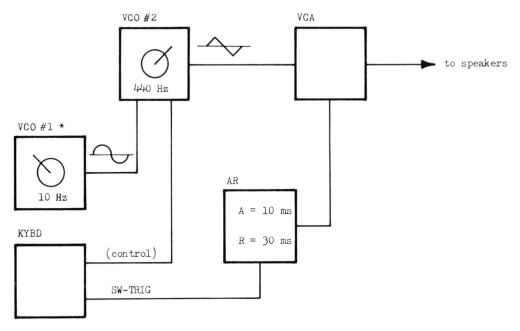

Figure 8.5 Block Diagram for a Sample Patch. *VCO #1 output at low amplitude provides "vibrato".

Complex patches often consist of many levels of control that must be carefully traced in order to appreciate the cummulative effect of the various controls on each successive level and the final result. Generally, it is easier to trace a complex patch backwards from the final signal output than it is to attempt to trace it from one of its many possible starting places. In this way, the various levels of control contributing to the final output signal become easier to follow to their points of origin.

While block diagrams have the advantage of providing a graphic representation of a patch, there are occasions when patches and module settings become so complex that block diagrams simply will not hold all the needed information. In such cases, a concise but detailed narrative explanation is the only option available. Often, experimentation in the studio will lead the composer to a patch that has several interesting options, each with slightly different control settings. These, too, may be explained in a brief narrative added to the block diagram. By saving patches that are carefully notated, sometimes along with a short recording of the sound produced, the electronic music composer builds a library or repertoire of basic sonic materials that can be used again or can function as an impetus to further exploration and refinement.

LISTENING EXAMPLES

Eno, Brian   *Ambient #1 Music for Airports*
                                    PVC 7908

Stockhausen, Karlheinz   *Gesang der Junglinge*
                                    DGG 138811

Subotnik, Morton   *Silver Apples of the Moon*
                                    Nonesuch 71174

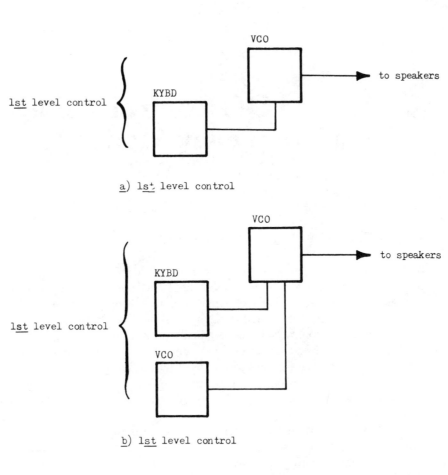

Figure 8.6 Control Levels

Chapter 9
AC and DC Control Voltages and Frequency Modulation (FM)

VOLTAGE-CONTROLLED OSCILLATORS

In some ways, it is possible to consider all the control voltages generated by the synthesizer as variants or combinations of simpler AC and DC signals. Even time-variant voltages are often described as DC signals with an AC component. Thus, it seems most natural to begin our examination of the applications of voltage control with the use of basic AC and DC control voltages, gradually progressing to the applications of other control voltages derived from them. In this and the next two chapters, all of the specific types of control voltages generated and used by the synthesizer will be discussed and illustrated by their effects on *voltage-controlled oscillators* (VCOs). The result of this kind of control, *frequency modulation* (FM), is the most easily perceivable control voltage effect.

The voltage-controlled oscillators found in synthesizers function in basically the same manner as the test oscillators found in classic electronic music studios (see Chapter 5). The only obvious difference may be the addition to the synthesizer oscillator of one or more input jacks marked "control." It is through these jacks that the control voltage is introduced into the oscillator circuit.

VCOs are designed to respond to changes in the voltage of a control signal with analogous changes in their output frequency. The *ratio* of the change in the control signal voltage level to the change in the oscillator frequency is most often set to 1 volt per octave (unattenuated). A positive or negative change of one volt in the control voltage input results in a change, up or down, of one octave in the output frequency of the VCO. The control voltage used may come from any control voltage source and may be any combination of AC, DC, time-variant, or random voltages, but the basic effect is always the same: a change in the control voltage results in a corresponding change in the oscillator's frequency.

Yet, there are often many differences in the design, features, and available controls of a VCO from those of a standard test oscillator. VCOs are designed specifically to meet the demands of electronic music composition and performance. Versatility, ease of use, and a consistent relationship to other synthesizer modules are the overriding concerns. Most of the variations in VCO design that equipment manufacturers have developed over the past 10 to 15 years have been motivated by a desire to create the most flexible, dependable, yet inexpensive device possible. One effect has been the creation of VCOs that only barely resemble their laboratory counterparts, due to all the special, synthesis related options and capabilities that have been added to them. Many of these additions have been motivated by the demands of the marketplace, but most also seem to have been carefully developed to satisfy the needs of adventurous composers. In such a fast-paced milieu, it is impossible to be absolutely comprehensive and up-to-date. However, the following descriptions of VCO functions and control voltage applications and effects should cover all but the most esoteric design whims of current and future analog synthesizer manufacturers.

VCO Controls

There are two essential characteristics of any oscillator signal output: frequency and waveform. Unlike laboratory test oscillators, whose controls are usually carefully calibrated to exact frequencies, VCOs generally use only relative frequency indications on the manual controls. A *coarse range* switch (*A* in Figure 9.1, which is a composite of the oscillator layout and controls found on a number of synthesizers) usually sets the oscillator to function in either sub-audio (low-frequency) or audio (high-frequency) ranges. The sub-audio frequency range, which is used to produce control voltage signals, usually extends from 0.1 Hz to about 100 Hz. The audio frequency range, which may be used to produce *either* control or audio signals, usually extends from 30 Hz to 20 KHz. (These are only average frequency ranges. The actual ranges of various popular modular synthesizer oscillators—as well as some of their other performance characteristics—are shown in Figure 9.2.) A second *range* control (*B* in Figure 9.1), when offered, sets the general frequency range of the oscillator in relation to the coarse range (audio or sub-audio) previously selected. This control may be continuously variable or changeable only in discrete steps. A further *fine tune* control, almost always a vernier pot or slider (*C* in Figure 9.1), then allows for the accurate tuning of the oscillator to the specific frequency desired. (Keep in mind that the actual placement and labeling of all of these controls will vary from synthesizer to synthesizer, though the function of the controls offered will probably be very much the same as those described here.) These three manual controls together set the *initial frequency* of the VCO *before* any control voltage is applied. To determine the precise initial frequency, it is necessary to route the output of the oscillator to a frequency counter.

Control voltage input jacks may be either unattenuated (*D* in Figure 9.1) or attenuated (*E* in Figure 9.1). The unattenuated inputs respond either *exponentially* (*D*), that is, at a ratio of 1 volt per octave, or *linearly* (*E*), at a ratio of as little as 1 volt per 10% change in the output frequency. The exponential response mode follows the perceptual characteristics of hearing (see Chapter 4) and the tuning of conventional scales. The variable linear response mode produces unusual frequency changes that do not relate directly to prior "acoustic" musical experiences and are particularly suited to the use of audio control signals. Some VCOs also offer a form of variable input attenuation (*F* in Figure 9.1) that changes the oscillator's response ratio roughly from linear at one end of the scale to exponential at the other.

Many VCOs have multiple control voltage input jacks (e.g., *D* in Figure 9.1). The control voltage finally applied to the oscillator is the *sum* of all of the control voltages present at the control voltage input jacks.

Unlike laboratory oscillators, which often offer only sine-wave or square-wave signal outputs, the VCOs employed in synthesizers generally offer a range of waveform outputs (see Figure 9.2 for the specific details on several standard systems), including sine, square (or variable pulse), triangle, and sawtooth (sometimes called "ramp") waveforms. A few synthesizers even offer variable-content waveforms (*G* in Figure 9.1),

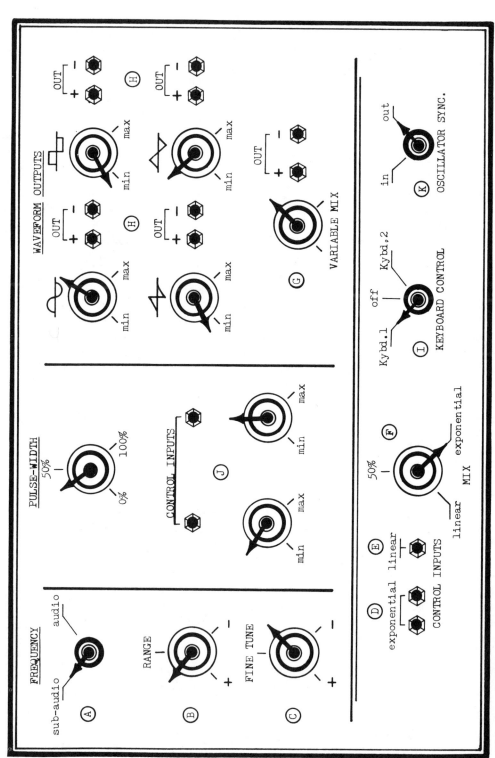

Figure 9.1 A Composite VCO

Note: Although rotary pots have been used in this illustration because they are used on most commercially available synthesizers, vertical or horizontal sliders could be used equally well (e.g., ARP 2600)

230

MODEL ➤ FEATURE ▼	Moog 900 Series (921)	ARP 2600	BUCHLA 200 Series (258)	Eμ 2200	SERGE NTO	ARIES AR-338
FM Control Input Attenuator		X	X	X	X	X
Waveshape Outputs:						
Sine	X	X	*	X	X	X
Triangle	X	X		X	X	X
Square (Pulse)	X	X	X	X		X
Sawtooth	X	X	X	X	X	X
Variable Mixture	X		X	X	X	X
Pulse Width Modulation	X	X		X		X
Oscillator Synchronization	X			X	X	X
Control Voltage Sync.						X
Output Attenuators				X		
Direct Keyboard Patching		X		X		
Keyboard Portamento Controls					X	
Phase Control (Clamping Trigger)	X			X		X
Polarity Inverter	X		X	X		
Overall Frequency Range	.01 Hz to 40 KHz in two ranges sub-audio/ x 100	.03 Hz to 10 KHz in two ranges LF & audio	.1 Hz to 30 KHz	.03 Hz to 30 KHz	.1 Hz to 100 KHz	.1 Hz to 20 KHz

Figure 9.2 The VCO Characteristics of Several Major Synthesizer Brands. *Can be derived from either saw tooth or pulse waveforms by adjusting waveshape control.

reducing the need to perform subsequent spectrum alterations of the normal output signals. Most VCOs allow for simultaneous access to all of the basic waveforms produced by the same oscillator, and some VCOs allow for variable attenuation of the output signal amplitude. A few VCOs even provide simultaneous positive and negative signal outputs (*H* in Figure 9.1).

The manual frequency settings, control voltage inputs, and signal outputs just described are essential parts of any VCO. Although not every VCO will offer every option they will usually offer some variant of many of these functions and controls. There are a number of other oscillator functions and control features, however, that have been added to the basic VCO by several equipment manufacturers, and the nature and effects of their operation may be quite different from synthesizer to synthesizer. The most commonly found of these "extras" are pulse-width modulation, phase synchronization, phase control triggers, and direct keyboard patching. The last of these, direct keyboard patching, is little more than a minor convenience, allowing a keyboard controller (discussed later in this chapter) to be internally connected to the control voltage input of the VCO by means of a simple switch, avoiding the need for patch cords (*I* in Figure 9.1). The obvious presumption is that this frequently used control patch warrants a special connection.

Pulse-width controls have become almost standard on high-quality VCOs. As discussed in Chapter 4, the pulse-width (or duty cycle) of a rectangular waveform is determined by the harmonic content of the signal, and vice versa. A variable pulse-width control allows the user to vary the spectral characteristics of the rectangular wave output (especially audible in the audio frequency range), which is synonymous with the *shape* of the output waveform (a much more important consideration when the output is used as a control voltage). This control capability usually consists of a pulse-width control pot, which sets the initial pulse-width, and one or more control voltage input jacks, which may or may not be attenuated (*J* in Figure 9.1), so that the pulse-width may be voltage controlled. The maximum response ratio is usually a 10% change of pulse-width per volt.

Waveform output phase synchronization is a much more recent addition to the complement of VCO features. It allows any oscillator in a synthesizer to be locked in phase with any other oscillator in the system. This is sometimes accomplished by an internal connection to a "sync bus," allowing the synchronization to be initiated at the flick of a switch (*K* in Figure 9.1). When the sync control is engaged, all of the harmonically related waveforms produced by the linked VCOs will be perfectly in-phase with each other. This is obviously useful for complex additive synthesis (particularly Fourier synthesis) in which the phase relationships of the component waveforms must be precisely controlled to avoid unwanted beats and beat frequencies. At least one syntheszer manufacturer (Aries Music) produces a VCO module (the AR 338) that permits the phase relationship of the synchronized oscillators to be varied, both by a manual pot and a control voltage input. The phase-shifting that results from the use of this control voltage input has become a much sought after effect in some synthesis applications (see Chapter 7). Another interesting and useful variation on phase synchronization is that offered by Moog synthesizers on their 921 VCO. The "waveform clamping" section of this oscillator allows the starting phase of the output waveform to be set at any point from 0% to 100% of its cycle and "triggered" (initiated) by either a switch trigger (a voltage gate) or a voltage trigger. Examples of the effects of this control on a sine-wave output are shown in Figure 9.3. Whenever a switch is closed or a voltage trigger occurs, the waveform automatically restarts its period at the phase position set by the "clamping point" pot. This feature has some very valuable applications, particularly when the oscillator is used as a control voltage generator in its sub-audio frequency range. If the onset of the triggers in Figure 9.3 were not "random" but periodic at some simple time multiple or factor of the output waveform's frequency, repetitive unusual "waveshapes" could be produced. A similar, though less sophisticated control is offered on the Eμ2200 VCO in the form of a "gate" control input that responds to control voltages greater than +2.5 volts by turning the oscillator off. When the gate voltage goes below +2.5 volts, the oscillator automatically starts again from the waveform's 0° phase position.

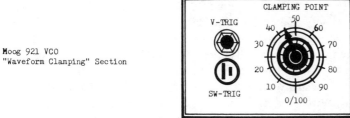

Moog 921 VCO
"Waveform Clamping" Section

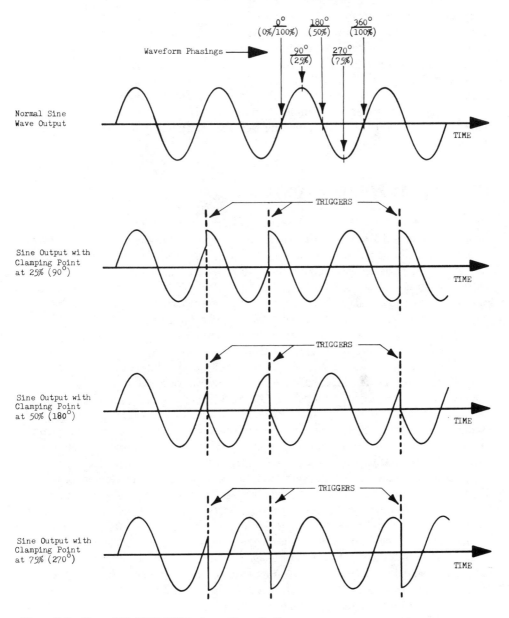

Figure 9.3   Moog 921 VCO "Waveform Clamping"

A few modular synthesizers offer VCOs with a shared oscillator driver or master oscillator controller, where one main oscillator exercises control over multiple secondary oscillators. The Moog 921-A and 921-B (901-A and 901-B on older models) VCO and VCO driver are probably the best known. The 921-A oscillator driver, which has both manual controls and voltage-control inputs for the basic frequency range and pulse-width of all the oscillators, is usually connected to two or more (up to 12) 921-B VCOs, which have independent controls for frequency range, fine tuning, phase synchronization, voltage control, and simultaneously available outputs for sine, triangle, sawtooth, and rectangular (variable pulse-width) waveforms. The principal advantage of this type of system is the ability to control an entire bank of VCOs concurrently, so that the response to applied control voltages remains absolutely consistent for the whole oscillator bank. Thus, if the "slave" oscillators in the bank were manually tuned in a certain harmonic or interval relationship, they would all respond equivalently to any control voltage applied to the "master" unit, always maintaining their relationships to each other. This can be an especially valuable capability in additive synthesis when it becomes necessary to shift an entire complex waveform mixture uniformly to other "fundamental" frequencies while maintaining the same relationship among the component waveforms.

SUB-AUDIO AC VOLTAGE CONTROL

Up to this point, oscillators have been considered primarily as sources of audio signals—carefully defined periodic waveforms of specific harmonic content. However, what has not been emphasized is that the *oscillations* that produce the periodic waveforms consist only of periodic variations in the voltage level of an electric current. Thus, the signals produced by an oscillator not only have definable harmonic characteristics and waveforms, but also exact voltage characteristics and values. These output voltages are the principal source of AC voltage control in the analog synthesizer.

Most VCOs produce signals in both the sub-audio (below 20 Hz) and audio (above 20 Hz) frequency ranges. Although signals in either frequency range may be used as a control voltage source, the voltage-control effects of the sub-audio signals are much more easily discernible. For example, if the sine-wave output of a VCO operating at 2 Hz is patched to the control voltage input of another VCO operating in the audio frequency range, the effect will be a gradual, periodic change in the frequency of the audio oscillator (see Patch No. 1). The *amount* of frequency change produced will depend on the *amplitude* of the control signal, and the *speed* of the change will depend on the *frequency* being produced by the control oscillator. If the output of the VCO producing the audio signal is monitored (through headphones, or an amplifier and loudspeaker) the aural effect is a very familiar one: periodic variations in the audio signal's frequency, or *vibrato*. If the audio signal is monitored on an oscilloscope, the visual effect will look similar to that of a spring expanding and compressing at a steady rate of two times per second (Figure 9.4c—Figure 9.4a shows the unmodulated audio triangle wave, and Figure 9.4b shows the sub-audio control signal). Notice in each case that the amplitude of the audio signal is unaffected by the modulation of its frequency. What is happening is that the frequency of the audio triangle wave is being controlled by the changing voltage level (the amplitude) of the sub-audio sine wave. When the sine wave's voltage level rises, the frequency of the triangle wave also rises, and when the sine wave's voltage level

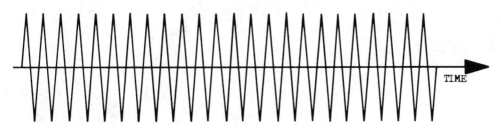

a) Unmodulated Triangle Wave

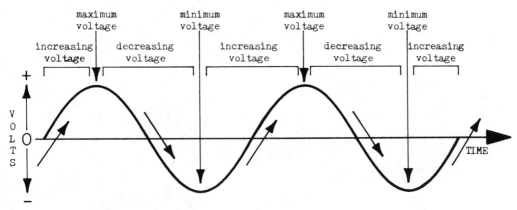

b) Sub-Audio Modulating Signal

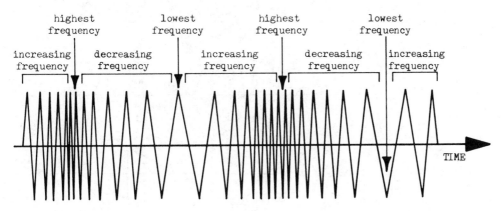

c) Frequency Modulated Resultant Signal

Figure 9.4   Sub-Audio Frequency Modulation (FM)

falls, the frequency of the triangle wave also falls. This is the essence of voltage-controlled frequency modulation (FM)—the frequency of one signal is directly controlled by the instantaneous voltage level of another signal.

By changing the shape of the control waveform, a variety of distinctive effects may be produced. Figure 9.5 shows the frequency modulation of the same audio triangle wave by the four basic sub-audio waveforms. Figures 9.5a and 9.5b are simplified versions of Figure 9.4, included for comparison. The control voltage effects of the

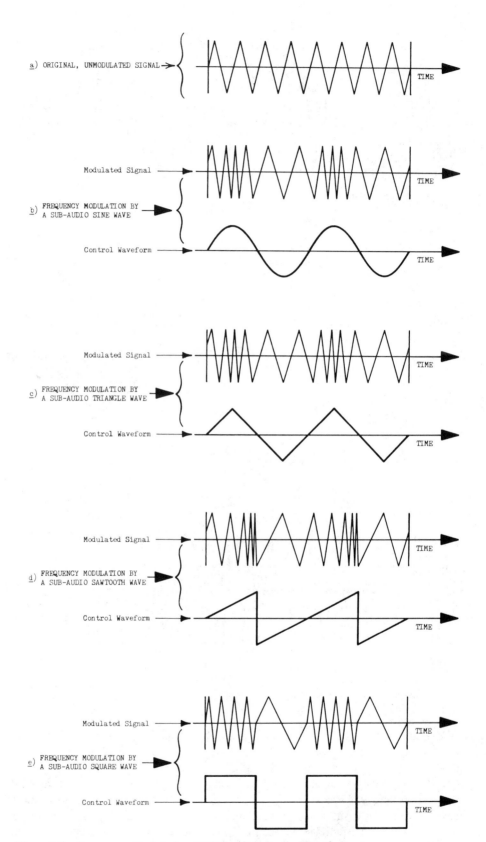

a) ORIGINAL, UNMODULATED SIGNAL

Modulated Signal

b) FREQUENCY MODULATION BY A SUB-AUDIO SINE WAVE

Control Waveform

Modulated Signal

c) FREQUENCY MODULATION BY A SUB-AUDIO TRIANGLE WAVE

Control Waveform

Modulated Signal

d) FREQUENCY MODULATION BY A SUB-AUDIO SAWTOOTH WAVE

Control Waveform

Modulated Signal

e) FREQUENCY MODULATION BY A SUB-AUDIO SQUARE WAVE

Control Waveform

Figure 9.5   Frequency Modulation (FM) by Sub-Audio Waveforms

sub-audio triangle wave (Figure 9.5c) are difficult to distinguish from those of the sine wave, since the two waveforms so closely resemble each other. The sudden drop followed by a gradual increase in the audio frequency resulting from sub-audio frequency modulation by a sawtooth wave has become an easily recognizable cliché (Figure 9.5d). Modulation by a sub-audio square wave results in the alternation of two distinct frequencies (Figure 9.5e). *The frequency interval (the distance between the high and low frequencies produced by the audio oscillator) can be changed simply by varying the amplitude of the control waveform.* Figure 9.6b shows the frequency changes in an audio triangle wave (Figure 9.6a) modulated by a sub-audio square wave with a voltage span of 2 volts. Figure 9.6c shows the effect when the voltage span of the square wave is increased to 4 volts. If the duty cycle of the sub-audio square wave in Figure 9.6 is changed (producing a pulse wave), the relative *duration* of the alternating high and low frequencies produced by the audio oscillator changes (Figure 9.7).

SUB-AUDIO WAVEFORM CONTROL VOLTAGE MIXTURES AND COMBINATIONS

Levels of Control

As discussed in Chapter 8, it is critically important to distinguish between the effects of various levels of control voltage applied to a signal generating or modulating device. Patch No. 1 and Figures 9.4, 9.5, 9.6, and 9.7 all illustrate the basic first-level control of an audio signal by a single sub-audio waveform. Although Patch No. 2 uses two oscillator control voltage sources (both are VCOs in their sub-audio frequency range), the resulting effect is still classified as a single level of control, because the two control signals are actually only added together: they do not affect one another in any way. The summation of control voltages is automatic when the VCO has multiple control voltage inputs. If this is not the case, the control voltages must be summed by an external mixer. Notice that the characteristic effects that the two control waveforms would have on the audio triangle signal if they were applied separately (Figures 9.8a and 9.8b) are still recognizable when the signals are summed (Figure 9.8c). The modulation of the audio triangle wave by the summed control waveforms is shown in Figure 9.8d.

Patch No. 3 shows a simple form of second-level voltage control using the same oscillators and oscillator settings that were used in Patch No. 2. In multiple-level voltage-control applications, each control signal interacts with (modulates) each successive control or audio signal. The sawtooth wave control signal shown in Figure 9.9a affects the frequency of the square wave control signal shown in Figure 9.9b, producing the composite control voltage shown in Figure 9.9c, which in turn affects the audio oscillator's frequency as shown in Figure 9.9d. The effect of the sawtooth control wave in the final audio signal (Figure 9.9d) can only be discerned in the periodically changing frequency (a rhythmic characteristic) of the square wave, *not* in a direct change in the frequency of the audio oscillator. Only the square wave output—the first-level control signal—*directly* affects the final audio signal. If the sequence of the two control oscillators in Patch No. 3 is reversed, the resultant effect should be noticeably different. As further levels of control are added to this patch, the rhythmic character of the frequency variations produced in the audio triangle wave will become increasingly complex, but the two frequencies produced by the audio VCO in response to the square wave will not

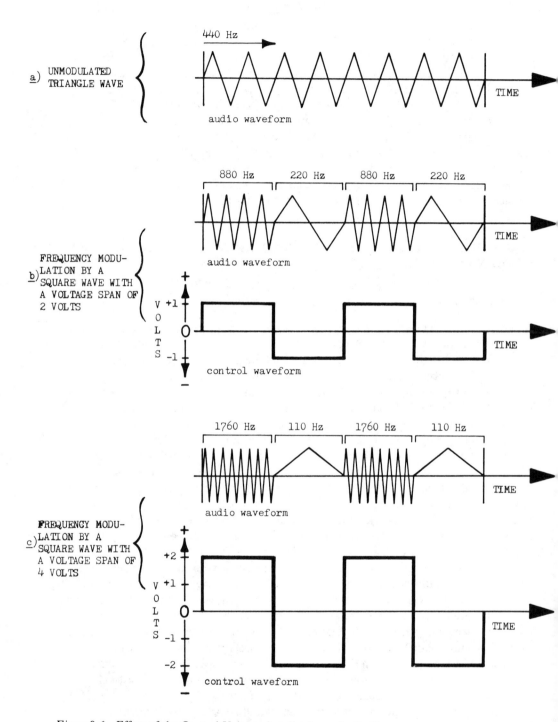

Figure 9.6 Effect of the Control Voltage Amplitude on Audio Frequency.

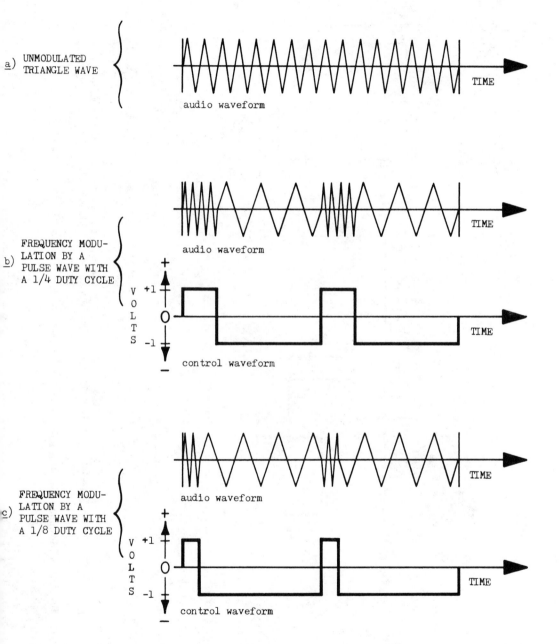

a) UNMODULATED TRIANGLE WAVE

TIME

audio waveform

b) FREQUENCY MODU-LATION BY A PULSE WAVE WITH A 1/4 DUTY CYCLE

TIME

audio waveform

VOLTS   +1   0   -1

TIME

control waveform

c) FREQUENCY MODU-LATION BY A PULSE WAVE WITH A 1/8 DUTY CYCLE

TIME

audio waveform

VOLTS   +1   0   -1

TIME

control waveform

Figure 9.7   Effect of the Control Voltage Pulse Width on Audio Frequency.

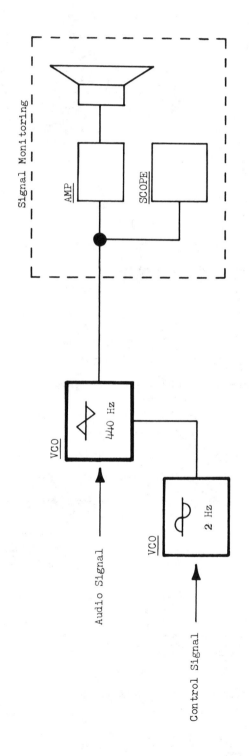

1. Set up the patch shown and note the effects produced.

2. Change the audio oscillator's waveform. Is the frequency modulation effect different?

3. Change the control oscillator's waveform. How is the audio signal affected?

4. Vary the amplitude (output level) of the control oscillator's output signal while using different control waveforms. How does the amplitude of the control signal affect the audio signal produced?

5. Vary the frequency of the control signal. How slowly can the modulation effect be made to occur? What happens as the frequency of the control signal reaches 20-30 Hz?

PATCH 1: **Frequency Modulation with a Sub-Audio Waveform**

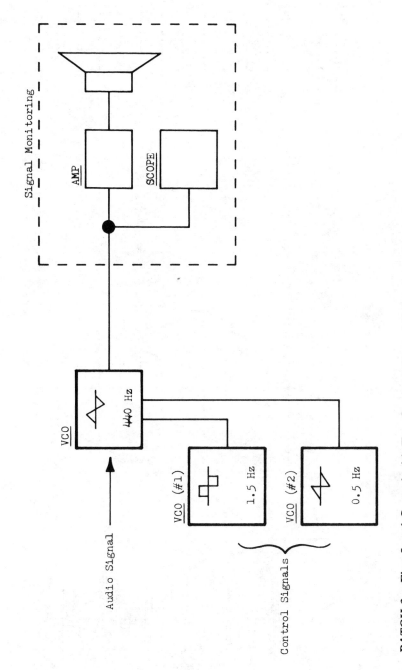

PATCH 2: **First Level Control with Two Summed Control Voltages**

241

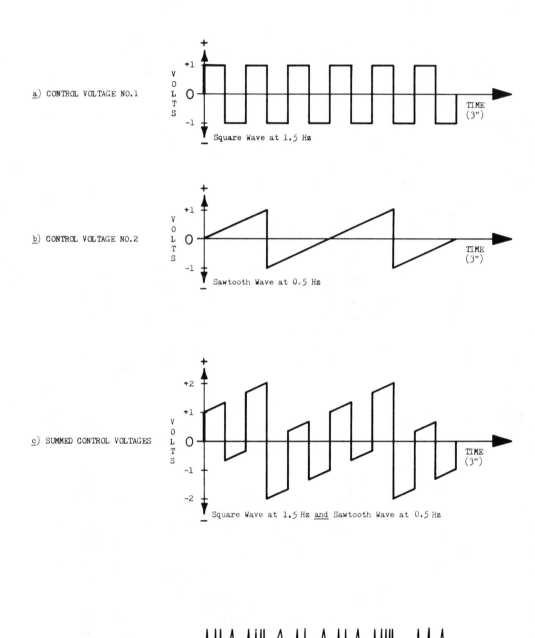

a) CONTROL VOLTAGE NO.1

Square Wave at 1.5 Hz

b) CONTROL VOLTAGE NO.2

Sawtooth Wave at 0.5 Hz

c) SUMMED CONTROL VOLTAGES

Square Wave at 1.5 Hz and Sawtooth Wave at 0.5 Hz

d) RESULTANT FREQUENCY MODULATION

Audio Triangle Wave

Figure 9.8   First Level Control with Two Summed Control Voltages (Patch 2)

242

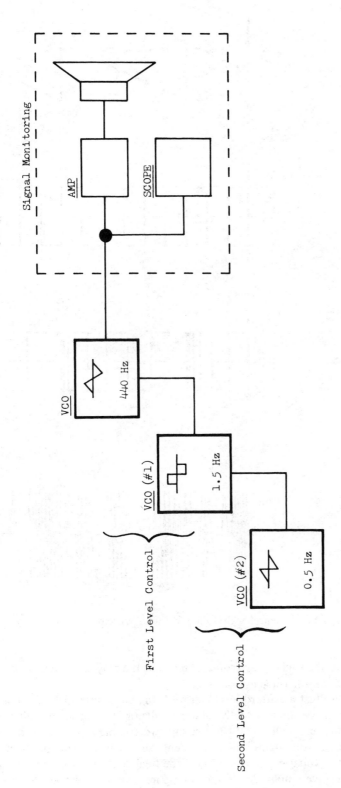

PATCH 3: **Second Level Control with Two Sub-Audio Waveforms**

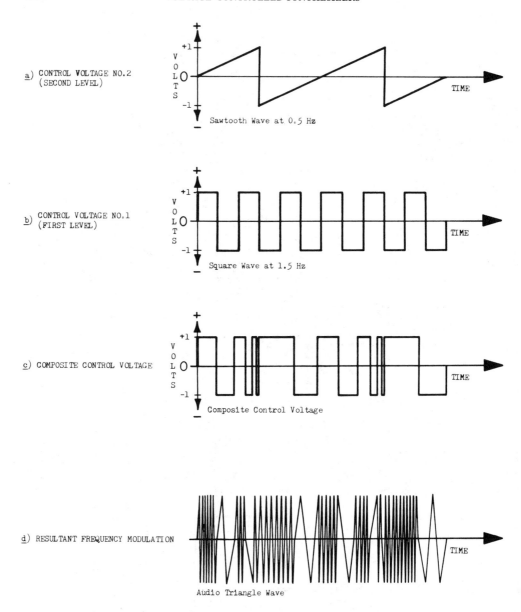

Figure 9.9   Second Level Control with Two Sub-Audio Waveforms (Patch 3)

change as long as the square wave control voltage is the only one patched directly to the audio oscillator control voltage input.

Patch No. 4 illustrates third-level control using an additional VCO. The resultant control voltage shape applied to the audio oscillator (having an overall period of 4 seconds) is shown in Figure 9.10 (illustrating two complete periods of the combined control voltage). In this figure, all component control waveforms occur at the same amplitude level (a voltage span of 2 volts). The final control shape could be altered by changing the relative amplitudes of the component control voltages. Notice that it is

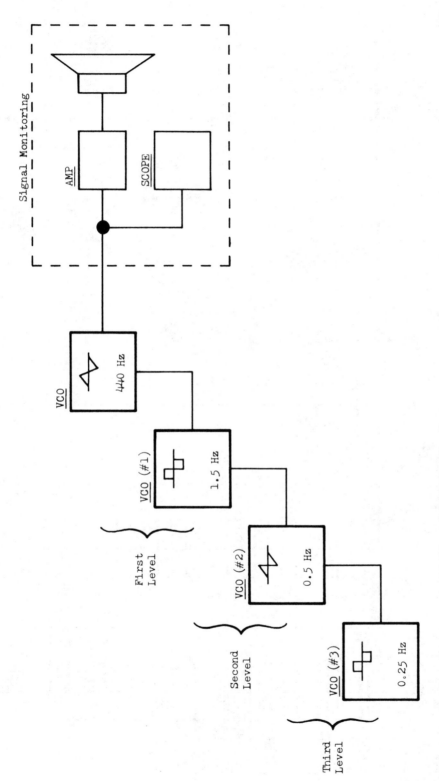

PATCH 4: **Third Level Control with Three Sub-Audio Waveforms**

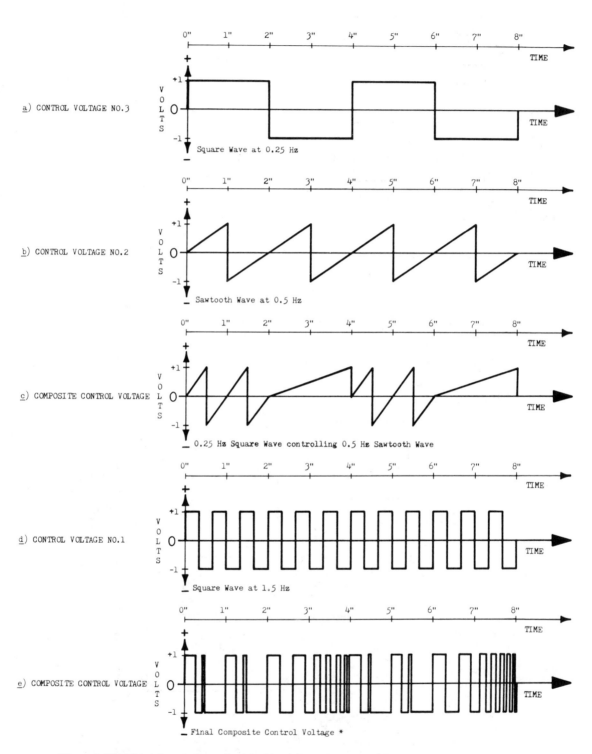

Figure 9.10 Third Level Control with Three Sub-Audio Waveforms.* This control voltage, applied to the audio oscillator, is the "first level" of voltage control.

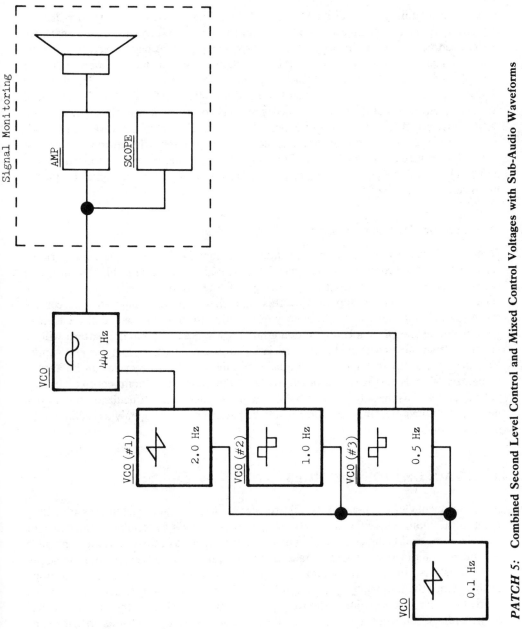

PATCH 5: **Combined Second Level Control and Mixed Control Voltages with Sub-Audio Waveforms**

generally most effective to have each successive level of control occur at a lower frequency, otherwise, its effect, which is *only* a periodic change in the rhythm of the final audio frequency changes, is even more difficult to perceive.

As should be obvious by now, the number of complex combinations of sub-audio AC control voltage levels and mixtures is limited only by the number of oscillator modules contained in the synthesizer. As this control voltage complexity increases, often accompanied by various processings of the component control waveforms, it becomes increasingly difficult to graph the final control voltage shape. The combined control voltage effect of Patch No. 5 would be very difficult to plot correctly on a graph. Yet, the aural effect of this patch will have several distinct characteristics: a carefully defined rhythm of frequency changes, periodic changes in the tempo (speed) of the rhythmic pattern, and a repeating "melodic" line or frequency pattern once every 10 seconds. Each level of control contributes to this cumulative result in its own way. The first control level of the patch (VCOs #1, #2, and #3) creates the basic melodic and rhythmic patterns (what could be described as a four-note "riff"). The basic time unit of the combined period of the three summed first-level control signals (VCOs #1, #2, and #3) is determined by the shortest time period in which all three of the waveform periods will coincide—2 seconds in this case. The second level of control (the sawtooth waveform at 0.1 Hz) controls only the overall tempo of the rhythmic pattern produced by the first-level control voltage combination; it has no effect on the audio signal frequency produced.

Periodicity and Pattern Repetition

One characteristic of all of the patches illustrated thus far has been the close periodic relationships of the control signals, which have created easily recognizable rhythmic and melodic patterns (*if* the frequency settings of the control oscillators were made accurately). It should be apparent by this time that if the frequency of one control voltage is a simple factor of the frequency of the other (or others), or if all of the control voltage frequencies have a common denominator, a repeated (periodic) pattern will be created. Often these combined periodic relationships are extremely complex and subtle. Yet, even a pattern that takes as long as a minute or more to recycle *can* be aurally recognized if it is distinctive enough. In fact, the creation of nonrepetitive control-voltage patterns using only sub-audio AC signals is much more difficult to do than one might at first imagine, since *any* control voltage pattern made up of only AC components must eventually repeat itself.

AUDIO AC CONTROL VOLTAGES

As the frequency of a sub-audio AC control signal increases, approaching the transition point to the audio frequency range, its "shape" becomes less discernible in the behavior of the audio signal being controlled. The frequency changes occurring in the controlled (modulated) audio signal begin to take place too quickly to be perceived as separate, periodic events. Instead, the audio signal begins to acquire an unfocused "buzzing" quality. Once the frequency of the control signal is above about 40 Hz and its amplitude is great enough, two separate audio frequencies, neither of which is the initial frquency of the audio VCO, will become easily audible. These frequency sidebands are caused by the extremely rapid alternations between the highest and lowest values of the control voltage. It is perhaps easiest to perceive this effect using a square wave as the modulating signal, since the square wave produces only two discrete voltage levels, a high voltage when the waveform is positive, and a low voltage when the waveform is negative. Figure 9.11a shows a simple first-level control patch, and Figure 9.11b shows the effect of a 40 Hz square wave control signal modulating a 440 Hz audio triangle wave. The amplitude of the control signal is very important, since it determines the amount of separation of the sidebands. Note that in this example (Figure 9.11b) the total amplitude of the voltage change of the 40 Hz square wave is set to 2 volts (1 volt above the 0 volt line and 1 volt

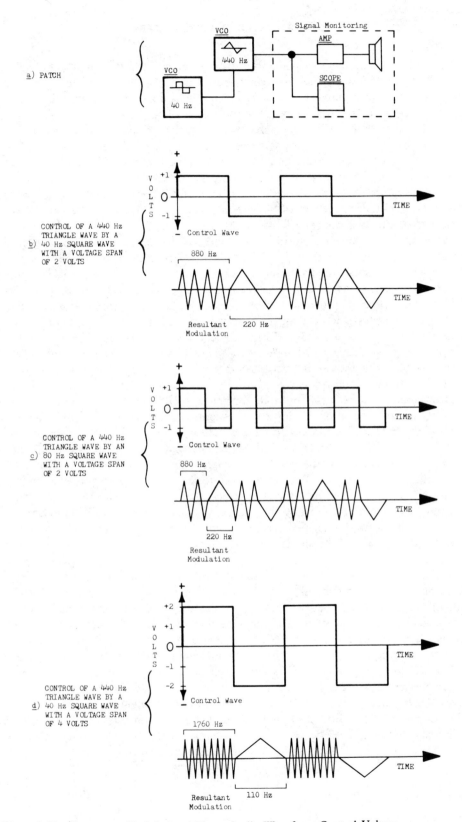

Figure 9.11 Frequency Modulation with an Audio Waveform Control Voltage

250 VOLTAGE-CONTROLLED SYNTHESIZERS

below the 0 volt line). If the modulation is exponential (1 volt/octave), the resultant sideband frequencies will be one octave above and one octave below the audio oscillator's initial frequency. In Figure 9.11b, this results in sideband frequencies at 880 Hz and 220 Hz. In Figure 9.11c, the frequency of the control signal has been raised to 80 Hz, while its voltage span has remained the same. Note that the *frequency changes* in the audio oscillator now occur *twice as fast* as earlier but that the actual sideband frequencies produced are still the same. In Figure 9.11d, the amplitude of the original (40 Hz) square wave control signal has been doubled to encompass a span of 4 volts (2 volts positive to 2 volts negative), resulting in sideband frequencies of 1760 Hz and 110 Hz. Thus, the greater the amplitude of the control signal, the greater the frequency differential will be between the generated sideband frequencies.

The square and pulse waveforms are the only AC signals that provide such a precise distinction between the frequency sidebands that are generated. Every other AC waveform contains a potentially infinite number of voltage values between its maximum positive and negative values because of the gradual slope of at least some portion of the wave shape. These intermediate voltage levels produce a correspondingly infinite number of frequency sidebands in the modulated signal within the limits of the total amplitude range of the control waveform (see Figure 9.12). A further point to be aware of is that *all* of the frequency components of the original audio signal (harmonics, etc.) will be modulated by the control waveform in a manner similar to that shown in Figure 9.12 for the fundamental frequency.

The combined effects of multiple control signals applied to a single VCO are extremely complex when one or more of the control signals is in the audio frequency range. If Patch No. 2 is modified so that the VCO producing the 1.5 Hz square wave control signal instead produces a 150 Hz square wave, the aural effect will be a two-second "glissando" of the two sideband frequencies as the audio oscillator also follows the shape of the 0.5 Hz sawtooth waveform. If the frequency of the sawtooth waveform is also increased into the audio frequency range, the two normally distinct sideband frequencies produced by the square wave control signal will be joined by a much less distinct band of frequencies produced by the sawtooth control signal. These sideband frequencies will be similar to those produced by the triangle wave in Figure 9.12.

If the same modifications are made to Patch No. 3, there will be a slightly different result. The change to an audio frequency in the square wave control signal will cause the formation of two distinct sideband frequencies that will change only their "definition" as they occur more and less often. The changing voltage level of the sub-audio sawtooth wave will make the square wave run "faster or slower." If the amplitude of the sub-audio sawtooth waveform modulating the sub-audio square wave control signal is great enough, the frequency of the square wave itself might range from sub-audio to audio frequency rates, creating a clear example of the gradual change from sub-audio to audio ranges. Obviously, complex mixtures and multilevel combinations of sub-audio and audio control signals at different frequencies and amplitudes will produce effects much too intricate and complex to be described here, but experimentation with these possibilities will greatly increase one's ability to get predictable results.

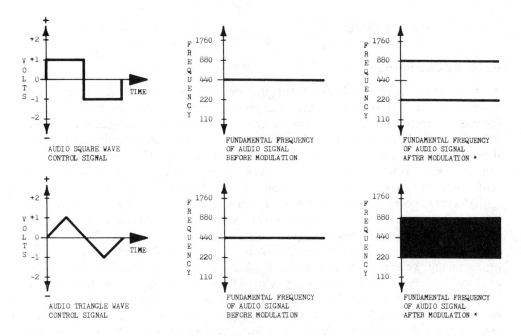

<u>a</u>) Audio Frequency Modulation with a 2 Volt Control Signal

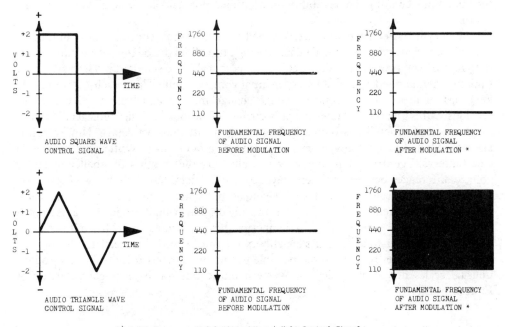

<u>b</u>) Audio Frequency Modulation with a 4 Volt Control Signal

Figure 9.12 Frequency Sidebands Produced by Frequency Modulation (FM) at Audio Frequency Rates. *All harmonic components of the audio signal will be similarly modulated.

251

DC VOLTAGE CONTROL

Keyboard Controllers

There are a number of a modules typically included in voltage-controlled synthesizers to produce DC control voltages. Unlike the modules that produce AC control signals (oscillators), these modules almost always serve *only* as control-voltage generators, since the DC signals they emit do not produce an audible result when amplified and played through a loudspeaker (except an occasionally audible "click" sound). One of the principal DC control-voltage generators is the *keyboard controller*, present in almost every synthesizer configuration except Serge and the early Buchla Series 200.

A keyboard controller (see Figure 9.13) usually consists of a series of switches that happen to resemble the keyboard of a piano or organ. This resemblance served to reduce the unfamiliarity of synthesizers when they were first introduced. The keyboard controller is the only control-voltage generator expressly designed to permit the production of Western, well-tempered scales and pitch relationships. Each switch (key) produces a discrete DC voltage that can be used to control any of the voltage-controlled modules of the synthesizer. If the keyboard controller is used to control a VCO (its primary function), a different and discrete frequency (pitch) will be produced for each key. Monophonic keyboards, which will be discussed first, produce only a single discrete DC voltage at a time, depending on which key is depressed. Polyphonic keyboards, which will be covered later in this section, can produce several discrete DC voltages at the same time, creating the possibility for multiple, independent "voices" and multinote chords.

Most synthesizer keyboards are designed to change their control voltage output by one volt per octave, the intermediate keys being "tuned" to divide the octave into voltage outputs that will produce a "tempered" chromatic scale (the standard modern system of tuning) when applied to a VCO's exponential control input. Thus, each octave on the keyboard divides a 1 volt control voltage change into 12 equal parts (Figure 9.13). Obviously, this greatly facilitates the performance of various melodies typical of Western music, most of which is based on a scale of 12 equal half-steps per octave. However, it is also possible to change the voltage/octave output ratio on many synthesizer keyboards (the "interval" control, A in Figure 9.13), allowing the creation of smaller or larger voltage differences between adjacent keys, so that it might actually take two octaves on the keyboard controller to produce a 1-volt output change (resulting in a one-octave change in the frequency of a VCO being controlled). This would produce what is known as a "quarter-tone" scale, having 24 distinct pitches per octave (at 1/24th volt per key), each one a quarter-tone from its neighbors on the keyboard instead of the normal half-tone difference. It is also often possible to tune the keyboard controller to produce unusual scales not at all typical of Western music but much more characteristic of Eastern music.

Additional Keyboard Features

Other controls that may be found on many synthesizer keyboard controllers include a "transposition" switch or pot (B in Figure 9.13), which allows for the shifting of the entire keyboard voltage range up or down by one or two octaves (in other words, a difference of 1 to 2 volts up or down in its output voltage range). This allows the

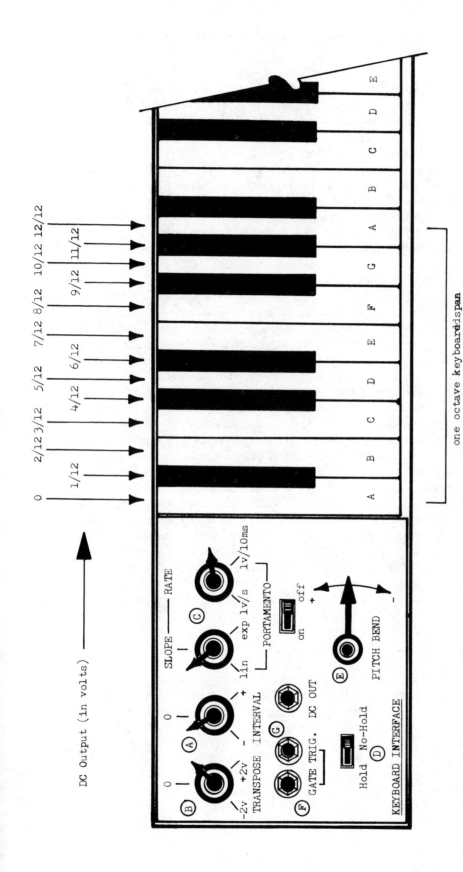

Figure 9.13 A Composite Keyboard Controller

253

keyboard to be "tuned" to match other instruments' pitches or the pitch of a prerecorded tape, for instance. A variable "portamento" control (C in Figure 9.13) allows the voltage output of the keyboard to "slide" (glissando) between successively depressed keys, rather than change instantaneously, as is normally the case. It often has an "on/off" switch and a variable "rate" pot (controlling the speed of the voltage change). Sometimes, a "slope" control (either a switch or a variable pot) that determines the linear/exponential characteristic of the portamento slope is included. A control-voltage "hold/no-hold" switch (D in Figure 9.13) determines whether the keyboard maintains the control-voltage value of the last key depressed after the key is released or returns to a "0" volt output after the key is released. Performance-oriented keyboard controllers also often offer a "pitch bend" control (E in Figure 9.13). This is usually a lever, a pot, or a pressure-sensitive pad used for creating slight variations in the voltage output of the keyboard while a key is depressed and, therefore, slight variations in the output frequency of an oscillator controlled by the keyboard.

The keyboard mechanism itself can be constructed in any of several ways, largely determined by the degree of sophistication and precision desired. The simplest and most common type of keyboard is little more than a long resistance strip (see the description of a "ribbon" controller below) with which wire arms connected to the individual keys make contact when the keys are depressed. The voltage output of a given key is determined by the exact place on the resistance strip at which the key connects, so precise spacing of the wire contacts is essential to the accurate tuning of the keyboard. Problems with the contact wires making a firm connection with the resistance strip and problems with poor alignment are frequent, annoying, and often unavoidable with this type of construction. Some Moog synthesizers have a more sophisticated keyboard controller that allows individual control of the voltage difference (from 0 to 2 volts) between any pair of adjacent keys—a helpful feature that not only solves tuning problems but also permits the creation of unique pitch scales. To improve the accuracy of the Eμ System keyboard, digital circuitry has been substituted for the usually analog resistance circuit. A further useful characteristic of both Buchla and EMS keyboard controllers is their sensitivity to either the velocity or the pressure applied to the keys during performance. The control-voltage output produced as a result of the velocity/touch-sensitivity is separate from the keyboard's normal discrete DC voltage output and can, depending on where it is applied, be used to create minor variations in pitch (frequency modulation), loudness (amplitude modulation), or timbre (spectrum modulation).

Gate and Trigger Voltages

Aside from the normal, discrete DC control voltages produced by the individual keys, the keyboard controller usually produces a *gate voltage* (F in Figure 9.13) and a *trigger voltage* (G in Figure 9.13). (The Moog and Korg keyboards produce a special "switch-trigger" output, which functions as a combination of both a passive gate and a trigger voltage.) The gate voltage is produced whenever a key is pressed and remains at a preset voltage level until the key is released. It is used to control the timing of various other synthesizer modules whose operation may be related to the event being produced or controlled by the discrete DC voltage output of the keyboard, such as envelope generators (see Chapter 10). The trigger voltage is a voltage "spike" that is used to initiate envelopes, sequences, or other "triggered" events elsewhere on the synthesizer (see Chapters 10 and 11).

Capacitance Sensitive Keyboards

An early distinction of Buchla synthesizers was their lack of a conventional black-and-white keyboard. Instead, Buchla created a "touch-controlled DC voltage source" that consisted of a series of individually tunable, capacitance-activated, pressure-sensitive "keys" (actually, only the division of a metal foil on a smooth or fretted surface). The original intent of this design was to free the user from making conventional and simplistic use of the synthesizer as an electronic organ. There certainly was no reason why synthesizers *had* to be treated in the same manner as traditional acoustic musical instruments, and, in fact, many of the early pieces created on Buchla synthesizers took advantage of the gestures, phrasings, and articulations that would have been impossible on conventional keyboards. However, the pressures of the consumer marketplace have since caused most manufacturers to move away from capacitance keyboards in favor of the more familiar "organ" keyboard. The philosophical and esthetic impact of this limitation has yet to be fully recognized, but it is true that when most people new to the possibilities of synthesizers first see one, with its conventional keyboard so prominently displayed, they automatically think of using the synthesizer for creating or playing "diatonic" Western music.

POLYPHONIC KEYBOARDS

The polyphonic (many voice) capabilities of the keyboards of most modular, voltage-controlled synthesizers are usually either very limited or totally nonexistent. True polyphony may be defined as the ability to obtain an independent "voice" (voltage) from *all* keys simultaneously. This is quite different from using the keyboard to produce two or more tones from separate oscillators by pressing only a single key, which all monophonic keyboards are capable of doing simply by splitting the control voltage output and routing it to several differently tuned oscillators. There are, however, several means of achieving more truly polyphonic or at least limited polyphonic effects. Moog's Polymoog (and a host of imitators, including the ARP Quartet and Omni II, the Korg Lambda, and the Crumar Stratus) produces a separate voice for each of its 71 keys using a process called "top-octave division." The frequency of a supersonic oscillator, built into the keyboard itself, is electronically "divided" to create the individual output frequency produced by each key. Each key has its own independent frequency, amplitude, and spectral characteristics (limited to the degree of "brightness"), as well as its own attack envelope (see Chapter 10). The Polymoog actually uses two supersonic oscillators, which are then slightly mistuned, in order to produce a richer tone color (due to phase interference and the interaction of different waveforms). The keyboard may also be "split" so that each of the two oscillators is controlled by either the lowest or the highest key pressed.

Some kind of keyboard splitting (or partitioning) is the most commonly employed means of deriving two or more simultaneous voices from the standard synthesizer keyboard. Either specific octaves on the keyboard will be set aside to produce independent control voltage outputs, or logic circuits incorporated into the keyboard will sense the order in which the keys are depressed (the Oberheim and Eμ Systems use this method), assigning a different control voltage output bus to each successive key depressed (up to a limit determined by the sensing and output circuitry employed, usually 2–10 separate "voices"). When the maximum number of "voices" is reached, the circuit restarts at the beginning of its counting series. Each of these sensing/output voice units may have completely different spectral, amplitude, and frequency characteristics, because the separate control voltage outputs are usually assigned to different signal generating and processing modules elsewhere in the synthesizer.

LINEAR CONTROLLERS

Linear (or "ribbon") controllers are simple resistance strips that produce a DC control voltage proportional to their length. The length is changed when a separate metallic conducting strip (about an eighth of an inch of vertical separation is normally used) is pressed against the resistance strip (Figure 9.14). If a finger is moved along the conducting strip while pressing it against the resistance strip, the control voltage will vary continuously in proportion to the placement of the finger along the strip, producing a unique kind of "time-variant" DC control voltage output not obtainable elsewhere on the synthesizer. If the finger's movement is stopped anywhere along the length of the ribbon, the output signal will remain steady at the selected DC voltage level.

Variable controls are usually included on the device that allow the operator to set the total voltage span of the ribbon (often from as little as 0 volts to as much as 10 volts) (Figure 9.14a) and the position of the 0-volt reference point on the ribbon (Figure 9.14b). The sliding pitch effects (glissandos, pitch bends, etc.) that result when the linear controller modulates a VCO have become a commonplace performance effect, especially with popular and rock musicians. An example of the subtle control-voltage shapes that the linear controller can produce is shown in Figure 9.14c.

JOYSTICK CONTROLLERS

Many people have encountered joystick (or "X/Y") controllers on quadraphonic amplifiers or video games. Essentially, they operate in two directions simultaneously (Figure 9.15a), producing a DC control voltage for the "X" axis (horizontal) position and a separate DC control voltage output for the "Y" axis (vertical) position. Figure 9.15b shows the "X" and "Y" outputs for two possible positions of the joystick. The control voltages may be applied independently, or they may be mixed to produce a single averaged or summed control output. Although joystick controllers can be used to control two different oscillators, with some interesting results, their outputs are more typically applied to voltage-controlled amplifiers and filters in order to produce spatial modulation and phasing effects. Voltage-controlled joystick controllers have also been devised in which the levels of the "X" and "Y" voltage outputs may themselves be controlled by another control–voltage producing module.

AC AND DC CONTROL VOLTAGES:
EXPERIMENTS AND COMBINATIONS

The control-voltage generators examined in this chapter are among the most important modules of analog synthesizers. A liberal amount of studio time should be devoted to exploring their uses, individually and in combination. The following outline lists a few experiments that will help transform a theoretical knowledge of their use into a practical, "hands-on" understanding.

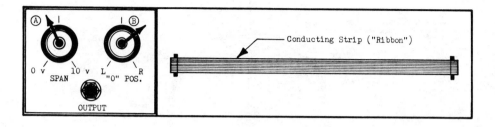

<u>a</u>) Overhead View

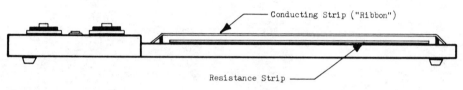

<u>b</u>) Front View

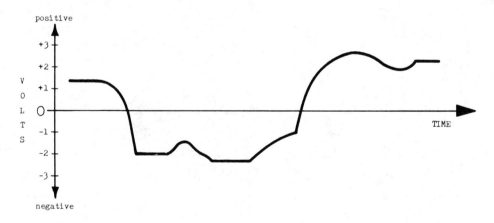

<u>c</u>) A Possible Control Voltage Output

Figure 9.14 The Linear ("Ribbon") Controller

257

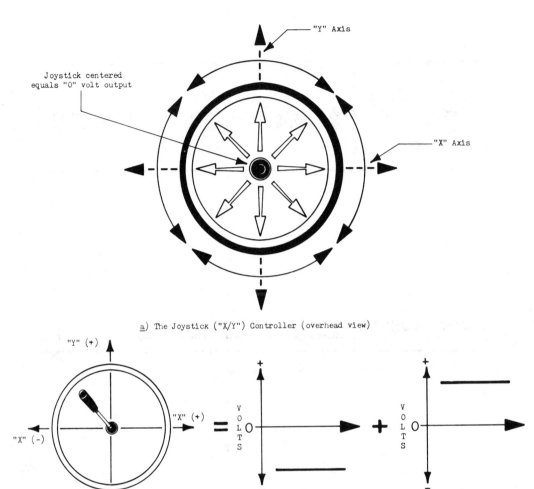

<u>a</u>) The Joystick ("X/Y") Controller (overhead view)

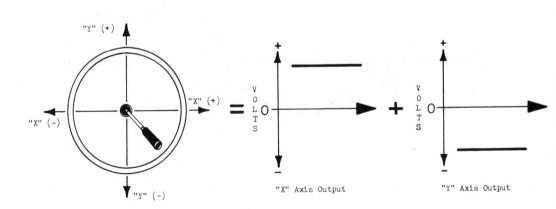

<u>b</u>) Two Possible Output Settings

Figure 9.15   The Joystick ("X/Y") Controller

AC Control Voltages

1. Voltage control a single VCO with each of the basic waveforms in their sub-audio frequency range.

   • What is the effect of different control signal amplitude settings?
   • What is the effect of different control signal frequency settings?
   • What is the effect of different pulse-width settings when using a rectangular control waveform?

2. Mix two or more sub-audio AC control signals together to control a single audio oscillator.

   • What is the effect of each possible combination of the sub-audio waveforms when: their frequencies and amplitudes are the same? their frequencies and amplitudes are different?

3. Repeat #1 and #2 above, using two audio VCOs:

   • one controlled by an inverted form of the control voltage applied to the other.
   • one controlled by a different control voltage from the other, at a different rate, so that it changes frequency at a simple factor of the other.

4. Experiment with some of the above sub-audio control voltages applied at the same time to three or more oscillators that have been tuned to form a widely spaced chord.

5. Repeat some of the above experiments, setting one or more of the AC control signal frequencies

   • around the transition point to audio frequency rates (20–40 Hz).
   • above the transition point to audio frequency rates (greater than 40 Hz).

6. Repeat some of the above experiments using:

   • second-level voltage control.
   • third-level voltage control.

DC Control Voltages

7. Experiment with the different scale tunings possible on a keyboard controller.
8. Experiment with the effects of a linear controller, trying different voltage ranges for its output level.
9. Experiment with a joystick controller by using its "X" and "Y" axis outputs to control two audio oscillators that have both been tuned to produce the same frequency when the joystick's voltage outputs are "0".
10. Use both a keyboard controller and a linear controller to control the same audio VCO.
11. Repeat #10, using a joystick controller in place of the linear controller.

Combined AC and DC Control Voltages

12. Repeat some of the experiments under *AC Control Voltages* (#s 1 through 6) using a keyboard controller, linear controller, or joystick controller as alternate control voltage inputs

    - to the audio oscillator(s).
    - in place of some of the second and third-level control voltage signals attempted earlier.

13. Combine a keyboard controller (for discrete pitches) and a sub-audio oscillator sine wave with a 4–10 Hz output (for vibrato) as a mixed control voltage input to an audio VCO.

14. Repeat #13, using a linear controller to control the frequency of the sub-audio sine-wave oscillator.

The above experiments suggest only a few of the possibilities of using AC and DC control voltages to control audio VCOs. Students may wish to begin a "library" of these and other patches by making accurate block diagrams.

PATCHING PROJECT NO. 1

The purpose of this project is to produce a fairly complex patch based on the modules and control-voltage concepts covered to this point. Frequency modulation will be the only control-voltage application used, so the challenge presented will be to create as many subtle frequency relationships as possible. However, the patch and the sound it produces should have a perceivable organization over time—some particular sonic characteristic that makes it distinguishable from other possible patches.

At this point in our study of the voltage-controlled synthesizer, planning is less important than it would be in the organization of a complete piece of electronic music. But, if some beginning approach is decided upon (i.e., choices are made, as they must always be) and certain objectives are set, work with the synthesis equipment will be more rational and productive. Prior planning may also make it easier to trace and diagram the patch.

Project

Produce a patch employing at least three levels of voltage control and making use of both AC and DC control-voltage generators. A block diagram containing sufficient detail to enable its reconstruction by a person uninvolved in its creation should be made, as well as a recording of the final result.

The quality of the resulting patch may be assessed in several ways: use of available equipment, complexity and organization, flexibility in terms of possible variation, clarity of the block diagram, reproducibility from the block diagram, and esthetic appeal.

Chapter 10

Time-Variant
Control Voltages and FM

Time-variant control voltages have been variously described as "DC voltages with an AC component," "transient signals," and "biased AC." As far as we need be concerned, a time-variant voltage is any signal that changes its amplitude (its voltage level) over time but is not inherently periodic. Because time-variant voltages are not periodic (as are AC signals) and do not usually occur at audio frequency rates, they are generally inaudible when applied to an amplifier and loudspeakers (except perhaps as occasional "clicks" caused by instantaneous voltage changes they may contain). However, they are extremely versatile when used as complex control voltages. Their varying amplitude shapes (known as the "envelope" of the signal) can be used to control a wide variety of synthesizer functions, including VCOs, VCFs, and, most typically, VCAs in ways that more simple DC control voltages or periodic AC control signals could not duplicate.

There are three principal devices that produce time-variant signals: the *transient envelope generator*, *envelope follower*, and *pitch follower*. The last two devices produce a DC output voltage contour that is analogous to the amplitude envelope (for the envelope follower) or the pitch contour (for the pitch follower) of an input signal.

ENVELOPE GENERATORS

The transient envelope generator is the usual source for time-variant control voltages in the analog synthesizer. It creates specific, variable voltage contours that are determined by the settings of various timing and amplitude controls. It requires no input signal to be sampled or "read," as do the envelope follower and the pitch follower. Although the signals that the envelope generator produces are normally used to control the *amplitude envelope* of another signal, through their application to a voltage-controlled amplifier (VCA) (see Chapter 12), their time-variant characteristics are most easily perceived when they are used to control a VCO, as in the following technical description of the envelope generator's operation.

The AR Envelope Generator

The voltage output of an envelope generator is actually a sequence of mutually dependent events. Each of the principal segments of the total envelope (regardless of how many segments there may be) can be completely defined in terms of its time span and its voltage amplitude. The simplest envelope shape usually available on a synthesizer is that produced by a "two-stage" (AR) envelope generator (Figure 10.1a) consisting of

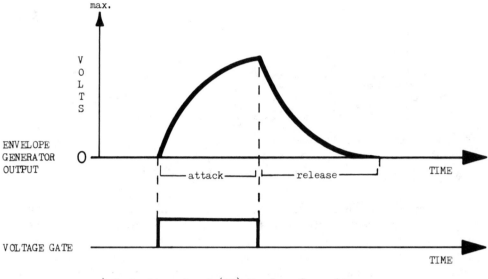

a) Basic "two-stage" (AR) Envelope Generator

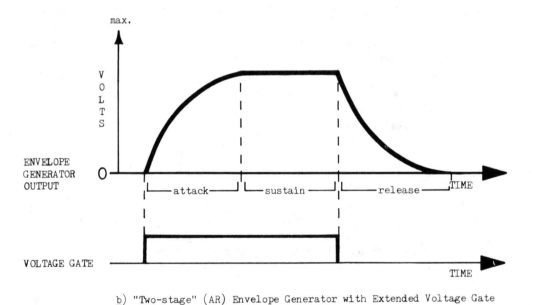

b) "Two-stage" (AR) Envelope Generator with Extended Voltage Gate

Figure 10.1   The "Two-Stage" (AR) Envelope Generator

an *attack* segment (the *time* it takes the envelope generator output to reach a predetermined maximum voltage once the envelope is initiated), and a *release* segment (the *time* it
takes for the envelope generator's output voltage to return to its initial or "0" voltage
level). These two timed segments of the envelope generator output may be initiated by a
switch being closed or by a key being pressed on a keyboard controller. When the
resulting voltage gate or switch trigger is initiated, the "attack" segment of the envelope
generator's output begins. When it is removed (i.e., the switch is opened or the key is no

longer depressed) the "release" segment begins. If the switch is closed or the key is depressed for a longer time than the attack time set on the envelope generator, the maximum voltage level output of the generator will be sustained until the switch is opened or the key is released. Thus, there may actually be three segments to the control signal produced by an attack/release (AR) envelope generator: an attack stage, a sustain stage, and a release stage, all of which are functions of time (Figure 10.1b). In most cases, the slopes of the attack and release voltage changes that are produced by the envelope generator are exponential, not linear, since an exponential change most accurately reflects the response characteristics of the human ear. Both the attack and the release times are usually continuously variable from as little as 0.002 seconds to as much as 10 to 20 seconds (the Aries 344 and 345 AR envelope generators can spread their output changes over as long as 200 seconds). The maximum output voltage actually produced varies according to the manufacturer but may be as high as +10 volts DC, from an initial starting value of 0 volts. AR envelope generators are found as a part of many systems, including the ARP 2600, Buchla 280, Serge, and many other performance-oriented synthesizers. Patch No. 6 shows a typical set-up for an audio VCO controlled by an AR envelope generator, which is activated by a gate from a keyboard controller. Note that the keyboard's discrete DC control voltage output is not used, only its ability to produce voltage gates or switch triggers. The audio result will be the same no matter which key is actually depressed.

The ADSR Envelope Generator

It is obvious that this two- or three-segment envelope shape is relatively simplistic. A much more complex and typical envelope shape is that produced by the four-stage (ADSR) envelope generator, in which two additional functions (*decay time* and *sustain level*) are introduced. (For comparison with Moog synthesizer systems, Attack Time = T_1, Decay Time = T_2, Sustain Level = E_{sus}, and Release Time = T_3.) The sustain level control determines the *voltage level* at the end of the decay time that will be maintained as long as the gate voltage is present, *not* the duration of the sustain stage, which is still a function of the length of time the switch is closed (or the key is depressed) and the voltage gate is present. The sustain voltage level can usually be set anywhere between the envelope generator's maximum predetermined value and 0 volts. Two of the many possible envelope shapes that can be produced with an ADSR envelope generator are shown in Figure 10.2. There are occasions when the maximum voltage output of the envelope generator (preset by the manufacturer) may be too high or too low for the intended use. In these cases the use of a separate attenuator (to lower it) or amplifier (to raise it) may be required.

Gate Delays

Several envelope generators (including the Em 2350 and the Polyfusion models) offer an *initial delay* control that delays the start of the attack portion of the envelope after a gate voltage is present. On Moog synthesizers a "Dual Trigger Delay" (Moog module 911-A) can coordinate or sequence two separate delay times. The need for this capability arises when two or more envelope generators are being used to form complex envelope shapes. Patch No. 7 and Figure 10.3 illustrate a possible control–voltage output when the outputs of two ADSR envelope generators, one of them with an applied delay of three

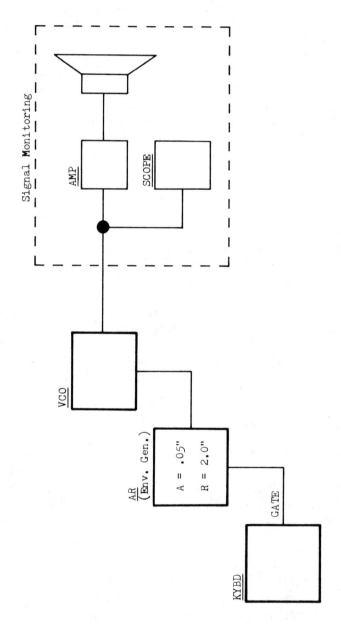

PATCH 6: **Use of an Envelope Generator (AR) to Control a VCO**

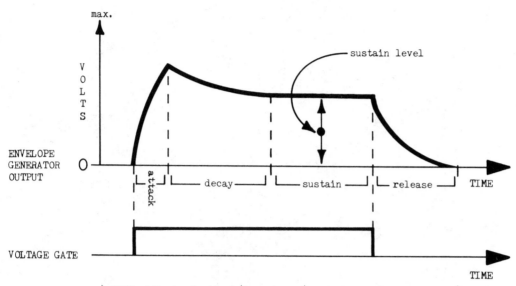

a) ADSR with short attack/long decay/long, high voltage sustain/ moderate release

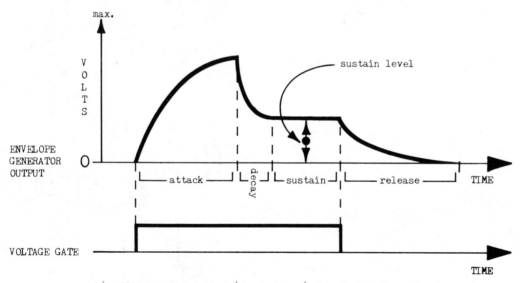

b) ADSR with long attack/short decay/moderate length, moderate voltage sustain/long release

Figure 10.2 The "Four-Stage" (ADSR) Envelope Generator

seconds, are summed to form a more complex control voltage envelope. Note, in this patch, that while the onset of the gate voltage for ADSR #2 is delayed by three seconds, the gate voltage ends at the same time for both envelope generators. To end the gate voltage at different times for each envelope generator would require a separate gate voltage for each ADSR unit. The Moog "Dual Trigger Delay" mentioned above actually permits the sequencing of three envelope generators, since it is capable of separately

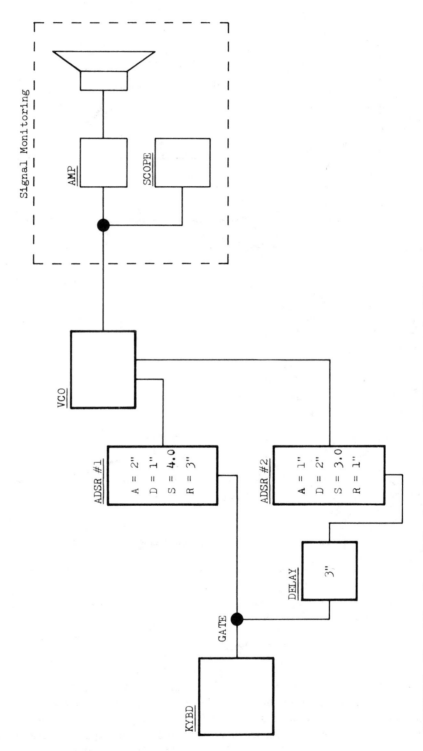

PATCH 7: Use of Two Summed Envelope Generators (ADSR) to control a VCO

266

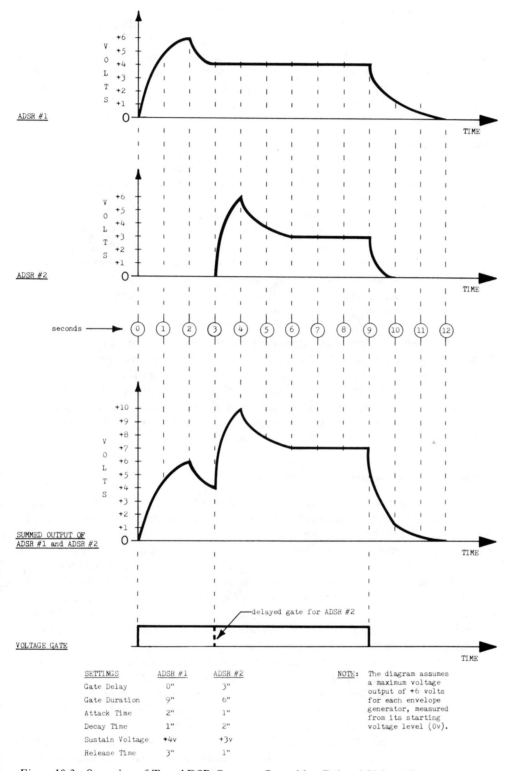

ADSR #1

ADSR #2

seconds

SUMMED OUTPUT OF
ADSR #1 and ADSR #2

VOLTAGE GATE

delayed gate for ADSR #2

SETTINGS	ADSR #1	ADSR #2
Gate Delay	0"	3"
Gate Duration	9"	6"
Attack Time	2"	1"
Decay Time	1"	2"
Sustain Voltage	+4v	+3v
Release Time	3"	1"

NOTE: The diagram assumes a maximum voltage output of +6 volts for each envelope generator, measured from its starting voltage level (0v).

Figure 10.3 Summing of Two ADSR Outputs, One with a Delayed Voltage Gate

delaying two trigger outputs. By carefully combining control voltage envelopes from several envelope generators, and attenuating or amplifying the separate or combined output signals as desired, very complex control of sonic events can be achieved. This capability can be especially important in the synthesis of the transient harmonic characteristics and amplitude envelopes of complex sounds (to be discussed at greater length in Chapters 12 and 13).

Timing Controls

As has already been noted, the envelope generator can be activated by the simple closing of a switch, which is equivalent to starting a voltage gate. If the voltage gate is present for longer than the combined attack and decay times set on the envelope generator, a sustained voltage level will be held until the gate is removed, at which point the release segment of the envelope will begin (Figure 10.4a). However, if the voltage gate is present for a shorter period of time than the attack time, the attack segment of the envelope will be interrupted, and the release segment will commence immediately (Figures 10.4b and 10.4c). In this situation there will be no decay or sustain segments. The voltage output at the time the release segment begins will determine the voltage change encompassed during the release stage.

There are several sources on most synthesizers for voltage gates capable of activating envelope generators. (Remember that the Moog 911 envelope generator uses a switch trigger, not a voltage gate. This is usually derived from the "voltage trigger/switch trigger" conversion section of a special "interface" module on the Moog synthesizer designed to "translate" one kind of signal to another.) Various electronic timing circuits available in most analog synthesizers, including electronic switches, sequencers, and even some low-frequency square wave oscillators are capable of producing voltage gates that can initiate and maintain the functioning of an envelope generator.

Schmitt Trigger Generators

Another device found on many synthesizers, called a *Schmitt Trigger Generator*, is also used to provide voltage gates needed for the operation of envelope generators. This device "reads" an input voltage amplitude from some other signal (a sub-audio waveform or a microphone input, for example), producing a voltage gate when the input signal's amplitude goes above a level set by a "threshold" pot (Figure 10.5). This voltage gate will remain on as long as the amplitude of the input signal remains above the threshold setting. If the input to the Schmitt Trigger Generator is periodic (a sub-audio waveform), the voltage gates will be produced periodically. If the input signal is aperiodic or random, then the voltage gates will be produced aperiodically or randomly.

Although all of these voltage gate sources provide a very useful and potentially "automatic" function that can be used to simultaneously control many parameters of the signal or signals being shaped, it should be remembered that the gate voltage must be present for longer than the combined times of the first two segments of the envelope if the complete envelope is to be produced. If the gate voltage is too brief, only part of the envelope will actually occur. If several overlapping gate voltages are used to control only a single envelope generator, the initial segments of the envelope will reoccur with each reinitiation of the voltage gate, but the final envelope segment (the "release" portion) will not occur until the last gate voltage has been removed (Patch No. 8 and Figure 10.6).

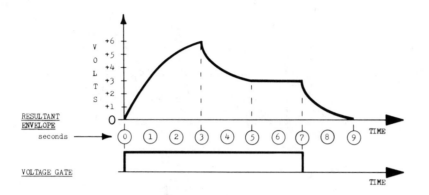

a) ADSR Output with a Seven Second Gate

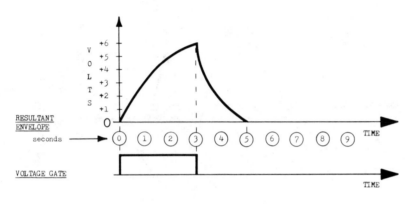

b) ADSR Output with a Three Second Gate

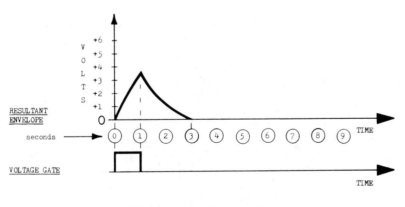

c) ADSR Output with a One Second Gate

SETTINGS		
	Attack Time	3"
	Decay Time	2"
	Sustain Voltage	+3v
	Release Time	2"

Figure 10.4 Effect of Voltage Gate Duration on Envelope Output

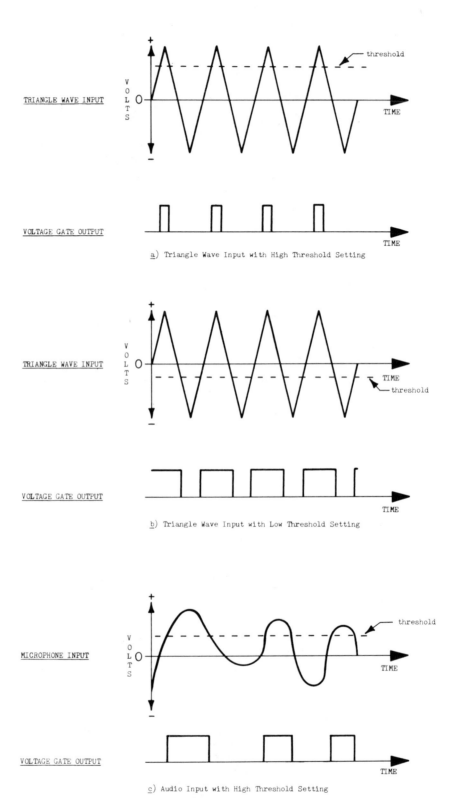

TRIANGLE WAVE INPUT

VOLTAGE GATE OUTPUT

a) Triangle Wave Input with High Threshold Setting

TRIANGLE WAVE INPUT

VOLTAGE GATE OUTPUT

b) Triangle Wave Input with Low Threshold Setting

MICROPHONE INPUT

VOLTAGE GATE OUTPUT

c) Audio Input with High Threshold Setting

Figure 10.5 The Schmitt Trigger Generator

270

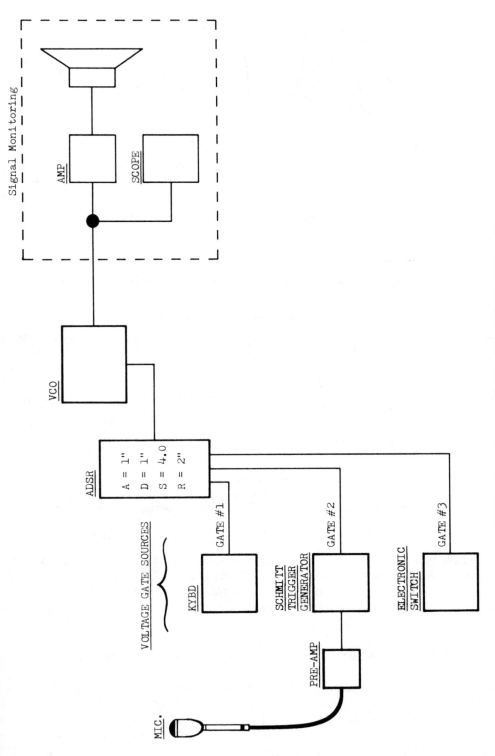

PATCH 8: **A Single Four-Stage (ADSR) Envelope Generator Initiated by Multiple Voltage Gates**

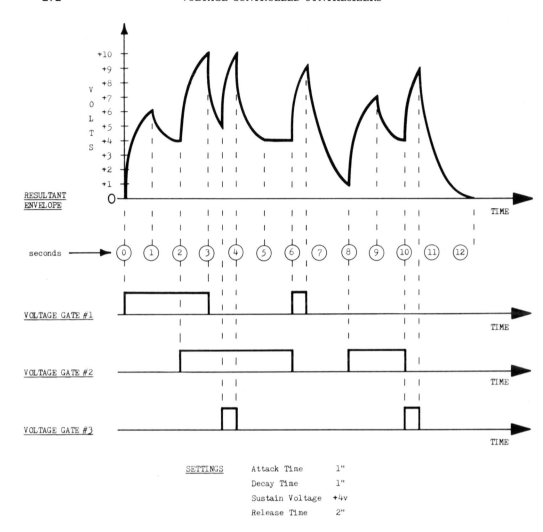

Figure 10.6   A Single Four-Stage (ADSR) Envelope Generator Initiated by Multiple Voltage Gates

The effect produced when each of several gate voltage sources is used to initiate a separate envelope generator (three ADSRs altogether), which in turn control three separate audio VCOs, is quite different (Patch No. 9 and Figure 10.7), since each envelope generator is allowed to act separately.

ENVELOPE FOLLOWERS

An envelope follower produces a time-variant voltage proportional to the logarithm of the average amplitude envelope of any input signal (AC, DC, time-variant, or random). Thus, the continuously changing amplitude envelope of an acoustic or other external signal can be translated into a time-variant voltage that can then be used to control a VCO, VCF, or VCA. If the envelope follower's output is used to control a VCO (as is the

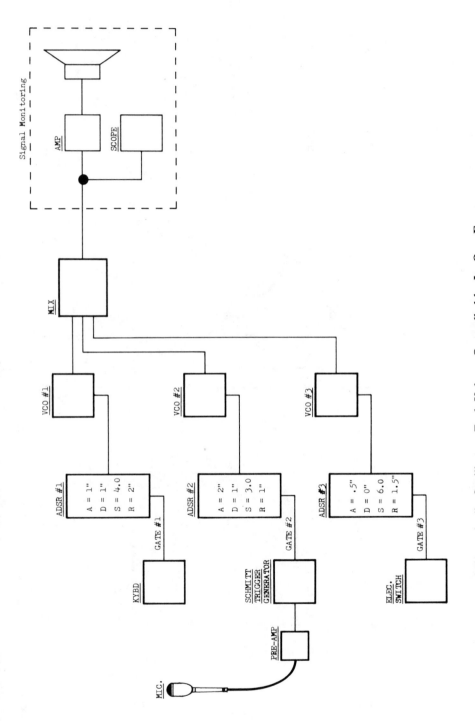

PATCH 9: **Mixing of Three Audio Oscillators, Each Voltage-Controlled by Its Own Four-Stage (ADSR) Envelope Generator**

273

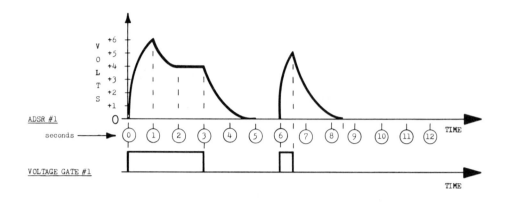

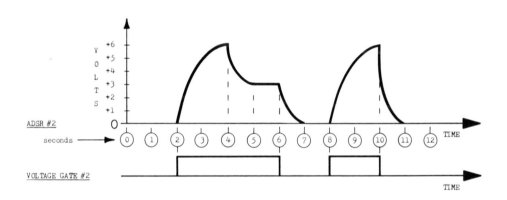

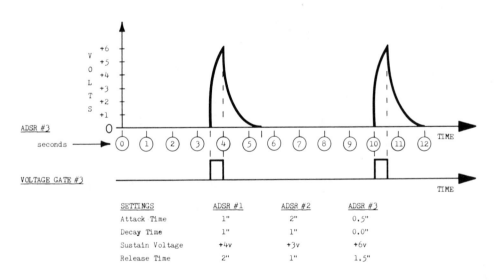

SETTINGS	ADSR #1	ADSR #2	ADSR #3
Attack Time	1"	2"	0.5"
Decay Time	1"	1"	0.0"
Sustain Voltage	+4v	+3v	+6v
Release Time	2"	1"	1.5"

Figure 10.7 Three Four-Stage (ADSR) Envelope Generators Initiated by Separate Voltage Gates

274

case in Patch No. 10), it produces changes in the oscillator's *frequency* proportional to the changes in the *amplitude* of the input signal—the louder the input signal, the higher the VCO's frequency, the softer the input signal, the lower the VCO's frequency. The ratio of the input signal level to the output voltage is often controlled by a built-in "sensitivity" pot, which functions as an attenuator of the input signal.

When an AC signal is used as the input to the envelope follower, the resulting effects can be very difficult to predict. The voltage characteristics of the signal produced by the envelope follower will be largely determined by the frequency of the input signal, its waveform, its amplitude, and the envelope follower's *response-time* setting. The response-time control found on many envelope followers allows the user to determine how quickly the envelope follower will respond to amplitude changes in the input signal. Its effect is similar to that of a lag processor. At one extreme, it may instantaneously follow even the most minute amplitude changes of the input signal. At the opposite extreme, it will often "smooth out" all but the most drastic amplitude changes in the input signal. If the input signal is a sub-audio waveform and the envelope follower has a short response time, it will attempt to follow the voltage (amplitude) variations in each cycle of the waveform (Figure 10.8a).

Since the average amplitude of such a signal will always equal 0 volts, resulting in no DC output from the device at all, the envelope follower incorporates a special circuit that transforms any negative (below the 0-volt line) AC voltage input component into a positive component, much as would a very selective voltage inverter. Thus, the envelope follower will actually produce *two* derived envelope shapes, one for the positive component and a second for the negative component, as is shown in Figure 10.8a, which illustrates two different response-time settings with a maximum sensitivity setting. Figure 10.8b shows the resulting DC control voltage output when an external audio signal (perhaps from a microphone) is used as the input signal, this time with a short response time and two different threshold settings.

Since the envelope follower is often used in conjunction with a Schmitt Trigger Generator (as in the Moog 912, Aries AR-331, Em 2440, and Buchla 230 modules), voltage triggers and voltage gates can also be produced and used to activate other events (usually with an envelope generator) in synchronization with the output of the envelope follower.

PITCH FOLLOWERS

Just as the envelope follower produces a time-variant voltage proportional to the amplitude envelope of an input signal, the pitch follower (often called a "pitch-to-voltage converter"—PVC) produces a time-variant voltage that is proportional to the frequency envelope of an input signal. Because of the nature of the device, only one input signal may be used at a time. Like the envelope follower, the pitch follower is often combined in one unit with several other complementary circuits (often including an envelope follower as well) (Aries AR-333, Serge), making it possible to control the synthesizer from the frequency or amplitude of any audio signal input. By patching a microphone into the synthesizer's pre-amp section, which is often hard-wired to both the envelope follower and the pitch follower, and carefully adjusting the sensitivity controls of the two devices, reasonably similar amplitude and frequency envelopes can be derived from the same audio signal in a form that the other signal generating and modifying modules of

276

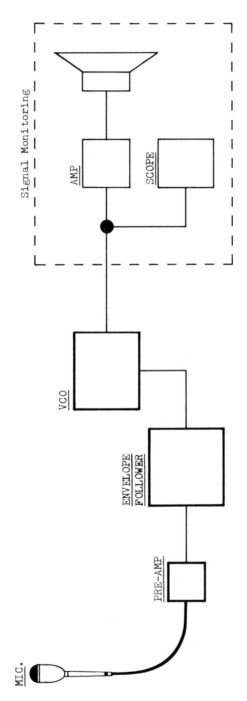

PATCH 10: **Use of an Envelope Follower to Control a VCO**

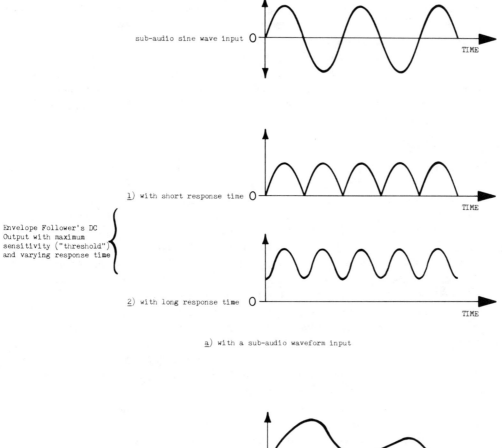

sub-audio sine wave input

TIME

1) with short response time

TIME

Envelope Follower's DC
Output with maximum
sensitivity ("threshold")
and varying response time

2) with long response time

TIME

a) with a sub-audio waveform input

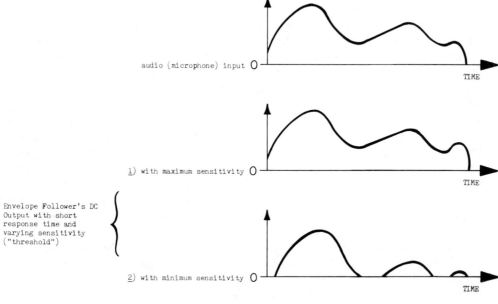

audio (microphone) input

TIME

1) with maximum sensitivity

TIME

Envelope Follower's DC
Output with short
response time and
varying sensitivity
("threshold")

2) with minimum sensitivity

TIME

b) with an audio (microphone) input

Figure 10.8 Envelope Follower

277

the synthesizer can "understand": time-variant control voltages. These voltages can then be used to control the same characteristics (amplitude or frequency) from which they were derived (by applying them to a VCA and a VCO, respectively), or they can be applied to different modules, adapting conventional relationships of amplitude, spectrum, and frequency to quite different sound contexts. For example, the output of the envelope follower could be used to control the frequency of a VCO, and the output of the pitch follower could be used to control a VCA or VCF (see Chapters 12 and 13).

Controls and Functions

The many possible variations in the design and construction of a pitch follower module—especially one that also includes a variety of support circuits—makes generalizations about controls and module functions difficult. However, assuming the composite configuration of a pitch follower shown in Figure 10.9, there are several important controls and functions that are often found. Figure 10.10 shows the various signal routes possible in the idealized pitch follower illustrated in Figure 10.9. As can be easily seen, such a module provides a very wide array of outputs from its four discrete sections: pre-amp, pitch follower, envelope follower, and Schmitt Trigger Generator. The first segment of the module consists of a *pre-amp* that accepts either a *mic* or a *line* input. The *level* control is an attenuator to limit the amplitude of the input signal (line or mic), and the *overload* indicator shows when the capacity of the circuit is being exceeded. The pre-amp is usually hard-wired to all of the other component segments, and its output is often separately available in both direct and compressed versions. The signal available at the *compress* output has usually been compressed to a reduced amplitude range according to a predetermined compression ratio chosen by the manufacturer (see Chapter 1 for a discussion of compression). Compression is usually necessary for the signal to be used by the pitch follower.

The pitch follower circuitry first analyzes the frequency content of the incoming signal and extracts its fundamental frequency (this is why only monophonic signals may be used as an input to the pitch follower). The extracted *fundamental frequency* is then made available as a direct, square wave output and is also passed on to the *frequency-to-voltage converter* section of the device, which performs the most essential function of the pitch follower, the conversion of the fundamental frequency into a DC voltage output. By setting the *track/hold* switch found on most pitch followers to the track position, the fundamental frequency of the input signal is followed almost precisely as it changes. The DC control voltage output will end when the input signal is no longer present. The hold function allows the circuit to keep producing its final DC voltage output and to keep the voltage gate on until a new signal is received at the *hold input*. The *tuning* control adjusts the proportion of the DC output voltage to the fundamental frequency of the input signal, and the *volts/octave* control adjusts the output voltage range in a manner similar to the "scale" pot on a keyboard controller.

The *envelope follower* section of the device usually produces both logarithmic and linear DC voltage outputs. Its sensitivity to the amplitude changes of the input signal is primarily determined by the *line level* setting. Voltage triggers and voltage gates are simultaneously produced by the *Schmitt Trigger Generator* circuit, which is usually internally linked to the track/hold control so that any voltage gate produced remains on for the duration of any hold, as described above.

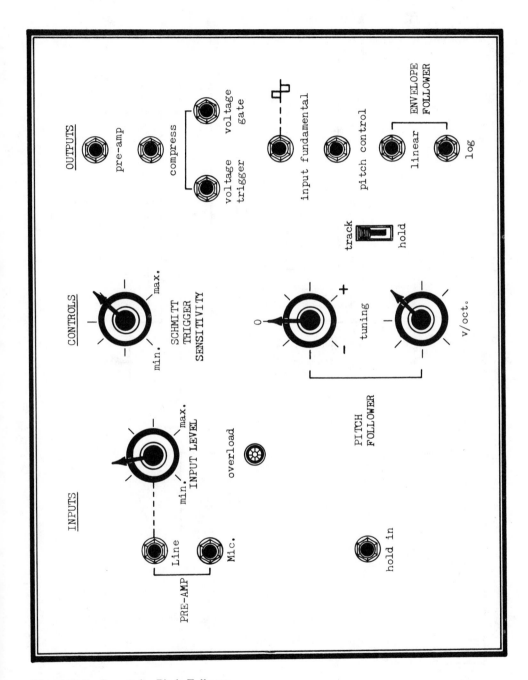

Figure 10.9 Composite Pitch Follower

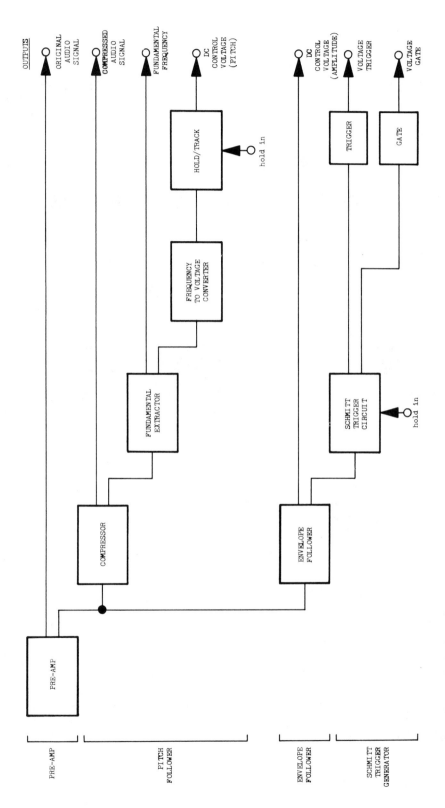

Figure 10.10 Signal Paths in a Composite Pitch Follower

280

TIME-VARIANT CONTROL VOLTAGES: EXPERIMENTS AND COMBINATIONS

The patches illustrated so far in this chapter can only serve as a brief introduction to the time-variant voltage-control applications that are often available on all but the simplest of analog synthesizers. The experiments with time-variant control voltages and voltage-controlled oscillators that are listed below will help in the exploration of these possibilities and can serve as a starting point for further explorations.

Envelope Generator Control Voltages

1. Control a single audio oscillator with the output of a single AR or ADSR envelope generator.

   - How do the different envelope generator controls affect each other?
   - How does altering the amplitude of the envelope generator output affect the frequency of the VCO?
   - Can the action of the envelope generator be initiated by a sub-audio square wave or pulse wave as well as by the standard voltage-gate source?
   - What is the effect on an envelope when the duration, timing, and frequency of the initiating voltage gate are changed?
   - What is the effect when the envelope generator's output is: inverted? Lag processed? Used as the only input to an electronic switch before it is routed to the VCO?
   - How fast may the envelope generator be made to recycle—what happens when it is recycled more than 30 to 40 times per second?

2. Using the outputs of two or more envelope generators to simultaneously control the same VCO:

   - What is the result, and how do the envelope generators interrelate when they are initiated by the same voltage gate?
   - What is the result when they are initiated by different voltage gates?
   - How are these effects altered by changes in the settings on one or more of the envelope generators?
   - How is the result altered when the amplitude of the envelope generator outputs are separately attenuated or boosted before application to the VCO?
   - What is the effect when the envelope generators' outputs are used as the inputs to an electronic switch before routing to the VCO?

3. If some means of delaying the application of voltage gates to the envelope generators is available:

   - Experiment with the effects that are possible when two or three envelope generators are timed to operate one after the other, all controlling the same VCO (see Patch No. 7). How complex an envelope can actually be constructed?
   - Tune two or three VCOs to the same starting frequency and, controlling each by a separate envelope generator, experiment with different settings and delay times.

4. Use a Schmitt Trigger Generator to initiate an envelope generator controlling a VCO.

- What is the resulting effect when the input to the Schmitt Trigger Generator is a sub-audio waveform, and how will this effect be altered: if the input waveform is changed? If the frequency of the input waveform is changed? If the threshold setting of the Schmitt Trigger Generator is changed? If the timing controls on the envelope generator are changed?
- What happens when the input to the Schmitt Trigger Generator is a microphone picking up an acoustic sound, and how will this effect be altered if different sound sources (voice, guitar, piano, etc.) are used?

5. Use the Schmitt Trigger Generator to synchronize synthesizer operations with a prerecorded tape. This is usually done by using one track of a multitrack tape to record high-amplitude sounds (an audio waveform will do) at the proper tape locations and for the proper durations. Route this tape signal to the Schmitt Trigger Generator, where the voltage gates produced can then initiate an envelope generator in perfect synchronization with the other prerecorded tape tracks.

Envelope Follower Control Voltages

6. Using the output from an envelope follower to control a VCO, experiment with its available sensitivity and response-time controls while using:

- various sub-audio waveform inputs to the envelope follower.
- various acoustic inputs (via a microphone) to the envelope follower.

7. Using the output from an envelope follower to control one VCO, experiment with the use of the voltage gate output of the Schmitt Trigger Generator (if available) to initiate an envelope generator used to control a second VCO. What kinds of combined or interrelated effects can be produced?

8. How can some of the above effects be altered if the envelope follower's control output is processed by a voltage inverter? A lag processor?

Pitch Follower Control Voltages

9. Using the DC control output of a pitch follower to control a VCO, experiment with various acoustic input signals (via a microphone) to determine how accurately and quickly the pitch follower is able to extract the fundamental frequency of the various input signals (the results may vary with different types of input signals).

- Can the initial frequency of the VCO be set so that the sound source pitches are exactly duplicated by the VCO?
- Can the initial frequency of the VCO be set so that the pitch follower's output results in synthesizer pitches at a fixed interval above or below the sound source pitches? (In this situation the pitch follower can function as a "pitch transposer.")

10. How can some of the above effects be altered if the pitch follower's control output is processed by a voltage inverter? A lag processor?

Combined Time-Variant Control Voltages

Patch No. 11 illustrates one of many ways in which modules producing time-variant control voltages can be made to interact. Although this patch is not entirely typical—since it deals only with frequency modulation—it can nevertheless serve as an illustration of the many subtle variations of time-variant voltage-control combinations that are available.

COMBINED AC, DC AND TIME-VARIANT CONTROL VOLTAGES

If the control voltages discussed in Chapter 9 (AC and discrete DC) and Chapter 10 (time-variant) are freely combined and used to control VCOs, the potential for complex control voltage applications becomes almost limitless. Students should take ample studio time to explore these possibilities. Specific experiments will not be given here, since doing so in only a perfunctory manner might limit the possible directions and scope such experimentation should take. If students keep in mind that each control voltage generator discussed in these two chapters is designed to produce a very specific type of control-voltage, some useful combinations should come to mind and serve as an impetus to further exploration. Some basic combinations are obvious (such as keyboard and envelope-generator control of the same VCO, or sub-audio AC and pitch-follower control of the same VCO), and should lead the student to other, more complex possibilities.

PATCHING PROJECT NO. 2

Based on the modules and the concepts covered in Chapters 8, 9, and 10, create a patch that makes distinctive use of AC, DC, and time-variant voltages to control one or more VCOs. Attempt to develop the temporal relationships of the patch—for example, the use of complex periodic sound events or intricate aperiodic sound events—in a way that will give the patch a definable sonic character. The texture or density of the sounds produced should also be considered. Several layers of simultaneous sound events and different timbres can be assembled by careful attention to the timing and combination of complex control-voltage relationships.

Project

Produce a patch, employing one or more levels of voltage control, using AC, DC, and time-variant control-voltage generators. Make a block diagram of the patch containing sufficient detail to enable its reconstruction by a person uninvolved in its creation, and record the final result.

The quality of the patch may be assessed by its use of available equipment, complexity and organization, flexibility in terms of possible variation, block diagramming, reproducibility from the block diagram, and esthetic appeal.

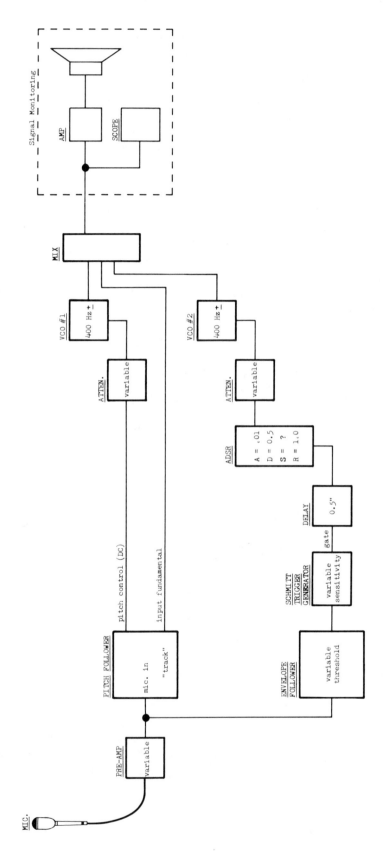

PATCH 11: **Combined Time-Variant Control Voltages**

284

Chapter 11

Random and Sequential Control Voltages and FM

Time-variant voltages that cross the zero-volt line (Figure 11.1a) are often distinguished from those that do not (Figure 11.1b), but there is absolutely no discernible difference in the resulting *effect* when either signal is used as a control voltage source, since the 0-volt line is merely a relative point of reference. Although many people would classify the first signal as "random" and the second as "time-variant," we have chosen to make no such distinction. Thus, this chapter does not introduce a new type of control voltage but only several very interesting and useful synthesizer modules that employ and produce a variety of complex time-variant, DC, and—in one very particular case—AC signals. The first modules that will be covered employ some form of noise to produce random control-voltage signals (thus, the necessity of defining this term so carefully). The use of random control voltages is so peculiar to electronic music in general and to voltage-controlled synthesizers in particular that the sounds produced by them (especially by modulating VCOs) are often identified as the quintessential "electronic music" or "computer" sounds.

FILTERED NOISE

The most basic random control voltage is produced by filtering the output of a noise generator. Although unfiltered white noise could be used as a control signal, the effect would rarely be usable, because the overall amplitude of the noise would not vary enough to produce a clearly discernible effect. However, if the noise is first filtered, the normally rapid variations in amplitude that are characteristic of noise become much more apparent. This is most noticeable when the noise is processed by a low-pass filter (Patch No. 12) so that its extremely dense high-frequency content is reduced to only a few discrete components (or perhaps only one) that vary randomly in both frequency and amplitude (Figure 11.2).

Although somewhat more effective than unfiltered white noise, the control signal produced when the noise is processed by a high-pass filter suffers from the same lack of discernible change. It still has too many components to be used effectively as a control voltage. A much more effective use of middle- and upper-range noise frequencies can be achieved by using a narrowly focused band-pass filter. A narrow band of random frequencies can be isolated and then applied to a VCO to produce characteristically unpredictable frequency changes.

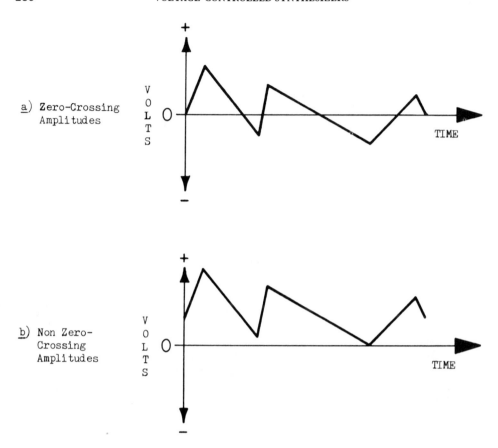

Figure 11.1   Voltage Patterns Referenced to Zero Volts

Other Uses of Filtered Noise

As with any time-variant control voltage, the random voltages produced by filtered noise can be used in a number of ways to trigger other events. By sending the random signal through a Schmitt Trigger Generator, an envelope generator can be initiated in response to the random amplitude variations of the signal. An envelope follower could be used to smooth out, to a greater or lesser degree, the normally rapid changes in the amplitude of the noise signal, or a pitch follower could be used to produce a second random voltage that changes its amplitude in relation to the frequency variations of the noise signal. Another particularly effective way of using filtered white noise is to apply it to one of the inputs of a ring modulator. Used as the carrier signal, filtered noise will cause random sideband frequencies to be generated in the program signal. This is an especially interesting effect when the program signal is a voice (see Patch No. 13). In this case, experimentation with the width of the noise band used will cause a wide variation in the characteristics of the output of the ring modulator.

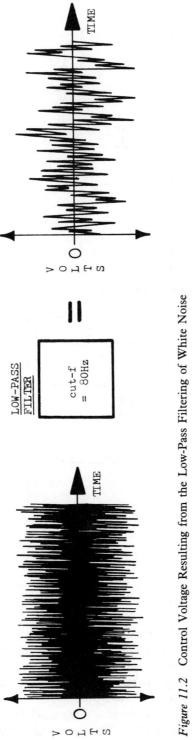

Figure 11.2 Control Voltage Resulting from the Low-Pass Filtering of White Noise

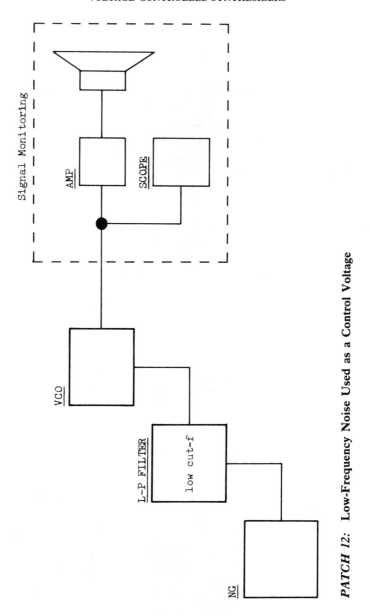

PATCH 12: Low-Frequency Noise Used as a Control Voltage

SAMPLE/HOLD CONTROLLERS

Appropriate to its name, a sample/hold circuit periodically *samples* an input signal and *holds* whatever voltage is present until the next sample is taken. The output of the sample/hold controller is a series of discrete DC voltages or, in some instances, a smoothed-out version of these discrete changes that slides gradually to each new voltage level. (The same effect can be produced by routing the normally discrete voltage changes through a lag processor.) The randomness or predictability of the DC voltages produced is determined solely by the character of the signal being sampled. The rate at which the sampling occurs is usually set by an internal "clock," which is actually a voltage-

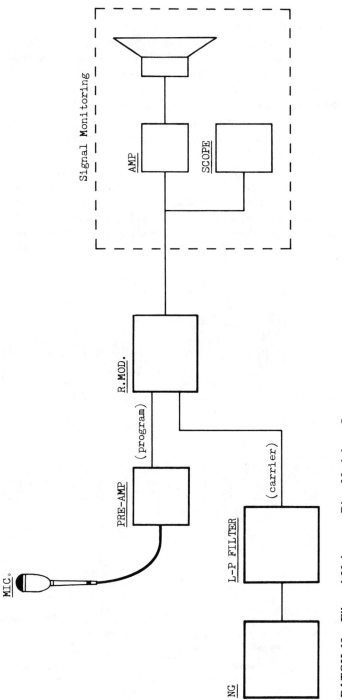

PATCH 13: **Filtered Noise as a Ring Modulator Input**

controlled square-wave generator. The amplitude range of the output voltages is often controlled by a built-in attenuator or "level control," but, barring this, a separate attenuator can be used for the same purpose.

The use of noise as the sampled signal is so common that many sample/hold modules include a built-in noise generator (Aries AR-318, Buchla 265, ARP 1036, and the Serge "Random Source" are some models with this feature). Since the sample time required can be made extremely brief—often 10–20 microseconds—the sample/hold circuit can extract discrete DC voltage levels even from the dense, rapid fluctuations of unfiltered white noise. Naturally, the succession of DC voltages produced by sampling unfiltered white noise is completely random. It may be somewhat easier to illustrate the functioning of a sample/hold module, however, by showing the result of sampling extremely filtered, low-frequency noise (Figure 11.3).

On the other hand, if the signal being sampled is periodic, it is likely that a much more distinguishable pattern (or sequence) of DC voltages will be produced. Figure 11.4 shows a 2-Hz sawtooth waveform being sampled at a consistent rate of 8 Hz. Notice that a single pattern of output voltages (four per sawtooth-waveform cycle) is repeated, because the sample rate and the sample signal frequency are related, the former being a

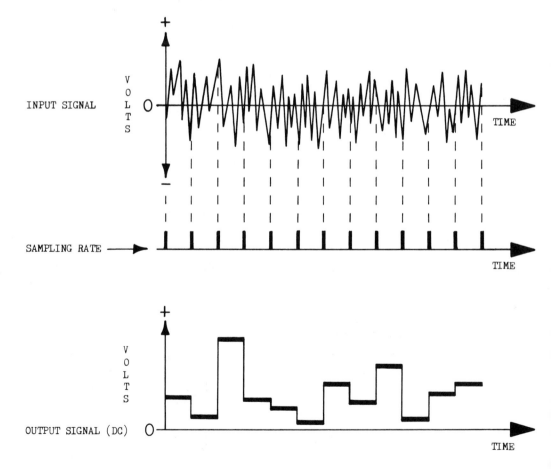

Figure 11.3 Sample/Hold Circuit with an Input of Low-Frequency Noise

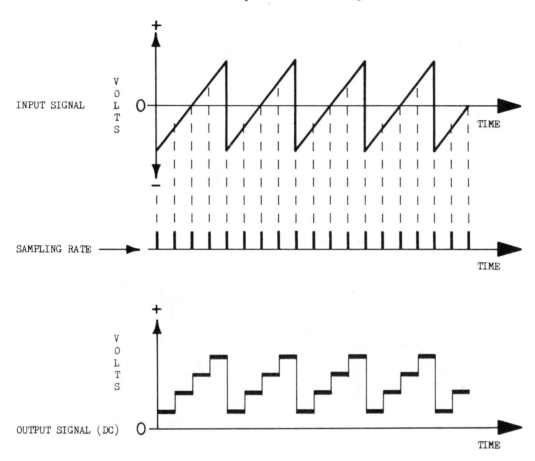

INPUT SIGNAL

SAMPLING RATE

OUTPUT SIGNAL (DC)

Figure 11.4 Sample/Hold Circuit with a Sub-Audio Sawtooth Waveform Input

simple multiple of the latter (a 4:1 ratio in this case). This repetitive pattern of output voltages would not occur if the sample rate was not itself periodic, but, because of the extremely identifiable shape of a sub-audio sawtooth waveform, it is still likely that the same "stairstep" pattern of output voltages would eventually make its influence apparent. Thus, the frequency/amplitude characteristics of the sampled signal input and the sampling rate are the principal factors determining the output characteristics. The more complex or variable the input signal (for example, a VCO undergoing second-level frequency modulation) and the less periodic the sampling rate (perhaps the square-wave generator, or "clock," being modulated by highly filtered low-frequency noise) the more obscure the pattern of the output voltages produced (Patch No. 14).

External Trigger Sources

Since the sample/hold circuit samples in response to the command of a voltage trigger (its internal "clock") which causes a voltage gate to be held open (providing the "hold" function), several external triggering sources can be used instead of, or in combination with, the internal square-wave generator. Keyboard controllers, Schmitt Trigger Generators, electronic switches, and external pulse or square waveform generators can

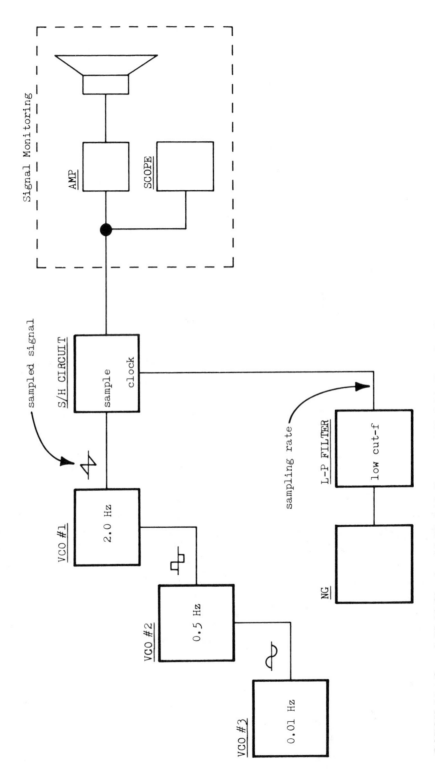

PATCH 14: **Sample/Hold Circuit with Variable Input and Variable Sampling Rate**

also trigger the sampling, making it possible to synchronize the sampling with any number of other events. By carefully mixing or switching between various trigger sources, very complex, but discernible rhythmic patterns can be set up in the sampling rate, which can be closely related to or in constant variation with the frequency of the sampled signal.

The controls of a sample/hold module are generally quite simple, even when a number of separate features are combined in the same unit, such as a white noise source and an internal clock. Figure 11.5 shows a composite, general design for a sample/hold module. The essential features are the sample signal input (which may be hard-wired to a noise generator) and the sample rate control. External signal inputs (often with "level" controls) and external trigger ("clock") inputs are also fairly standard. Output signal level controls and an internal oscillator output, as well as the expected DC voltage output, allow other events to be synchronized with the sampling rate of the circuit.

SEQUENTIAL CONTROLLERS

The very essence of all music is the realization of a sequence (a succession) of sound events occurring in time. A "melody" is nothing more than a sequence of pitches, and "harmony" (or polyphony) is merely what we call the result of the coincidence of two or more melodic "voices" (independently identifiable sequences). The character of the sequence is in all cases determined by two factors: 1) the relationship of each sound in the sequence to the other sounds in the sequence, and 2) the division of time among the component sound events. The first characteristic can be either *conjunct* (closely related) or *disjunct* (distantly related). For example, the components of an eight-event sequence producing the pitches *A, B, C, D, E, F, G,* and *A* in upward succession would be considered conjunct. On the other hand, a five-event sequence consisting of a gunshot, the sound of a buzz saw, a dog's bark, the sound of a baby rattle, and the squeak of a door hinge would probably be considered disjunct (though, through proper manipulation over several repetitions of the sequence, a close relationship among all of these disparate sounds could conceivably be produced). The second characteristic—the division of time among the component sound events—is directly analogous to the conventional effects of rhythm (the relative length of the sound events) and tempo (the rate of change) except that the term *division* of time is a little misleading, since many analog synthesizers actually produce rhythmic effects and changes in their tempo by *adding* discrete units of time together, not by subdividing a single block of time into separate units. Although this may seem to be an insignificant distinction, since the practical effects and the sonic results may be the same in either case, it represents two quite different approaches to the relationship of music and time, one of them occidental (the division of larger units into smaller units) and the other, oriental (the addition of smaller units to form larger ones).

The analog sequential controller (sequencer) functions much the same as a standard keyboard controller—producing a series of discrete DC voltages, voltage triggers, and voltage gates—except that it is preprogrammed to "perform" automatically the same series of events that would have to be manually produced in "real time" on the keyboard controller. In its simplest form, the analog sequencer is only a series of automatic switches, which control the choice of control voltage outputs, and a timing mechanism that controls the rhythm and tempo of these choices. Since the selection of the events

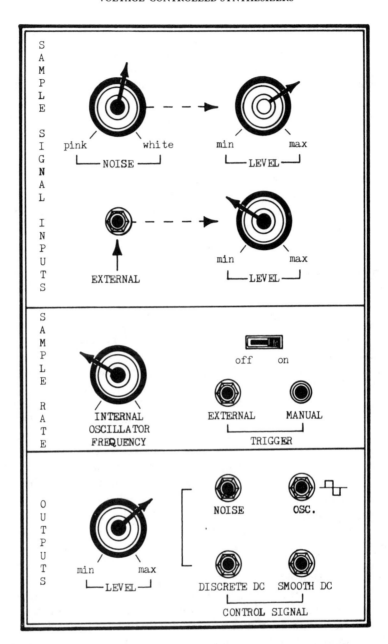

Figure 11.5   Composite Sample/Hold Module

(control voltages) and their temporal relationships are *preprogrammed*, the sequencer is a kind of analog memory, capable of *remembering* the characteristics of a given sequence of control signals for some future use.

Controls and Functions

The specific characteristics of an analog sequencer may vary considerably from model to model, especially in the case of some of the newer analog/digital hybrids. However, there are several basic characteristics attributable to most analog sequencers, and the actual effects produced in most cases are remarkably similar. Figure 11.6 shows a highly simplified, single-row, eight-stage sequencer unit and its complement of controls, trigger inputs, trigger outputs, and DC control voltage outputs. Each of the eight stages of the sequencer has two primary functions, producing 1) a discrete DC voltage output whose exact value (amplitude) is determined by the setting of a level control pot or fader (often ranging from 0 to +10 volts) and 2) a voltage trigger—normally available from a jack at the base of each component stage. A small indicator light at the top of each of the eight stages is illuminated whenever that stage is active. Normally, *only one stage of the sequencer can be active at one time.* The voltage trigger input ("V-TRIG. IN") advances the sequence from one stage to the next whenever a voltage trigger is present. Usable voltage triggers can be derived from any conventional source, including a high-amplitude pulse generator, a keyboard controller, or a Schmitt Trigger Generator. In Figure 11.6, the sequence would progress from stage 1 to the right, through each successive stage up to and including stage 8, after which it would automatically return to stage 1 and repeat the sequence, continuing to do so as long as voltage triggers were provided.

The sequencer shown in Figure 11.7 functions in essentially the same way as the more basic design of Figure 11.6, except that there are now two separate rows of eight stages each and several additional control functions. The two separate rows of this sequencer operate and are active simultaneously as the sequence progresses from stage to stage, producing two concurrent sequences of discrete DC voltages and (on many models) one sequence of voltage-trigger outputs. (A simple application of this expanded capability would be to use the two series of DC voltages to control two separate VCOs, producing a simple two-part harmony.) The additional controls indicated are a composite of most of the kinds of controls offered on the majority of sequencers (particularly the Moog 960 Sequential Controller, which is the prototype for many other models). Some of them may not be included on some manufacturers' models, or if they are they may be arranged differently so that certain functions are offered on separate auxiliary modules (as is the case with the Eμ Modular Sequencer).

One of the principal additions to this sequencer illustration is the self-contained pulse generator (the section furthest to the left), which is hard-wired to the voltage-trigger input ("SEQUENCE RATE"). The sequence can be advanced by both an external voltage trigger (as before) and the internal pulse generator, which functions just like any other voltage-controllable oscillator. The controls that are offered set the frequency (rate) of the sequencing, provide for turning the pulse generator on and off by either a manual switch or an external voltage-trigger at the "on" or "off" input jacks, allow the frequency of the pulse generator to be voltage-controlled (at the "FREQ. CONTROL INPUT" jack), and provide a jack for the internal pulse generator's output that allows other events (including other sequencers) to be triggered simultaneously with each step of the sequence.

The additional controls and jacks offered at each stage of the sequencer set the DC voltage output level for each component of rows A and B ("LEVEL"); determine whether the component stage will be included in the sequence, omitted (skipped), or held indefinitely (halting the sequence at that point); provide a voltage-trigger output ("V-TRIG. OUT") whenever the stage is active; allow an external voltage-trigger input ("V-TRIG. IN") to start the sequence from that stage; and allow the stage to be activated manually by a push button ("MANUAL TRIGGER"), from which point the sequence would progress as usual. The DC voltage output level controls for rows A and

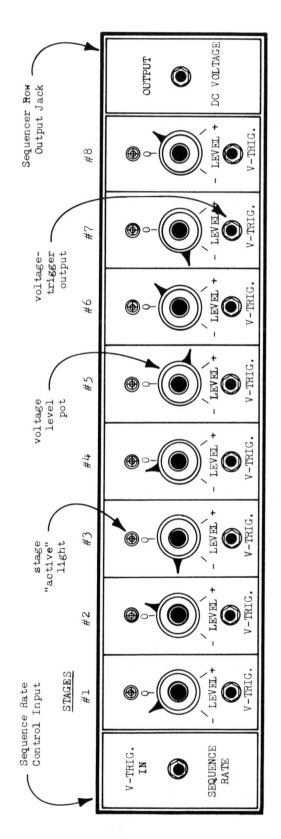

Figure 11.6 Basic Eight-Stage Sequencer Module

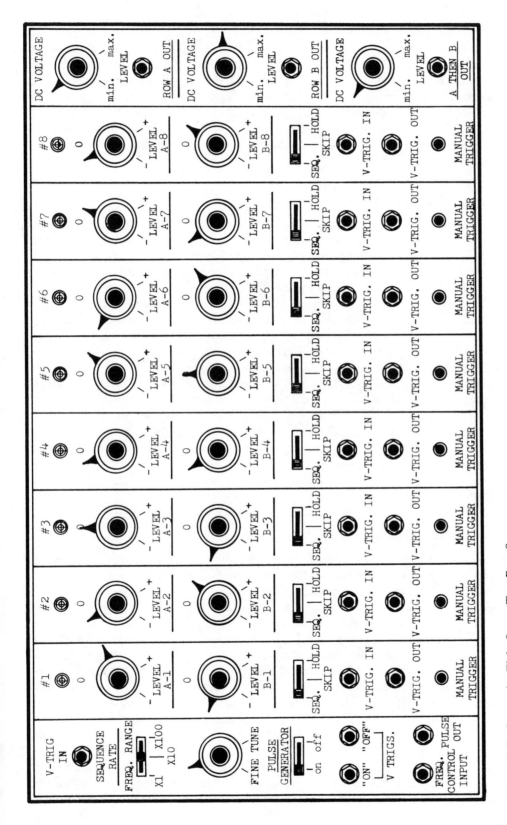

Figure 11.7 Composite Eight-Stage, Two-Row Sequencer

B provide a convenient way to control the voltage range (overall amplitude) of the entire sequence of voltages. These output "level" pots may operate in discrete stages (as with the Moog 960 Sequencer voltage "multipliers"), or they may be continuously variable. Some units may have a separate output that offers the DC voltages of the A row, *then* the DC voltages of the B row, producing a 16-stage sequence. This may also be determined by a switch that selects "*A and B*" (simultaneously) or "*A then B*" operations. (Another way of sequencing the different rows consecutively using an electronic switch will be shown later.)

Additional Functions and Modes

Among the many variations of this composite sequencer that frequently occur are the addition of more rows (Moog has three, Buchla four, and Serge can have from two to four) and different numbers of discrete stages (up to 16 in one row on the Buchla 246). The Buchla 245 and 246 sequencers also include a unique voltage-control input (called "Analog") that varies the stage assignment according to the amplitude level of the voltage present; the higher the voltage, the higher the number of the sequencer stage selected. This amounts to voltage-controllable stage selection. In this way, the sequencing order of the stages can be made to follow the amplitude shape of low-frequency waveforms or other varying control voltage inputs, as shown in Figure 11.8. Notice in Figure 11.8 that the type of low-frequency waveform used for this purpose will determine the relative "on-time" of each of the sequencer stages, as well as which stage is active at the moment. Serge provides a circuit called a *quantizer* on some of its sequencers. It "rounds-off" the DC voltage outputs produced by the individual stages of the sequencer rows to the nearest voltage corresponding to the equal-tempered scale (i.e., in 1/12th volt increments). Serge sequencers also provide voltage-trigger inputs that determine the *direction* of the sequence (up or down), hold the sequence at one stage for the duration of a voltage-gate, and reset the sequence to stage 1 whenever a voltage-trigger is present.

Sequence Rate Controls

There are several ways of controlling the sequence rate, the most obvious being the use of the internal pulse generator. Variations in the normally steady frequency of the internal pulse generator may be created by turning it on and off automatically or manually, by combining it with an external voltage trigger input, or by using any available control-voltage source (including an envelope generator) to control its frequency, just as can be done with any other VCO. One potentially interesting application of a voltage-controlled sequencing rate is to route the discrete DC control voltage output of one of the sequencer rows into the pulse generator's frequency control input (Figure 11.9). In this way, the voltage setting of each sequencer stage of the row used will determine the length of time that stage will remain active. A high setting of a given stage, temporarily increasing the frequency of the pulse generator, will cause the sequence to move on rapidly, while a low setting will have the opposite effect. By carefully coordinating the voltage settings of the individual stages, very subtle rhythmic patterns can be constructed. (Moog Sequential Controllers provide this feature through an internal patch called "third-row control of timing.") Since the voltage-trigger outputs of each stage can be used to trigger external modules (envelope generators, in particular),

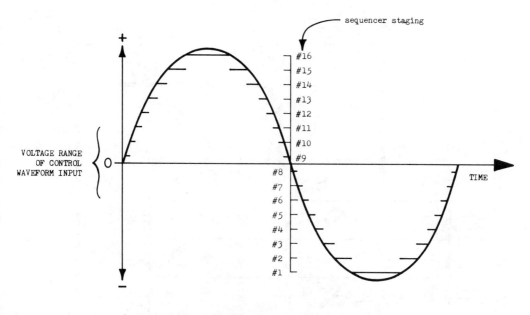

a) with Sub-Audio Sine Wave Input

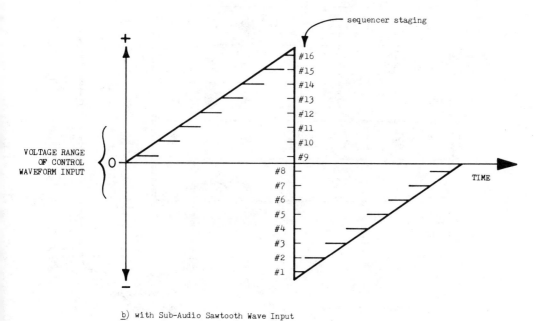

b) with Sub-Audio Sawtooth Wave Input

Figure 11.8 Voltage-Controlled Sequencer Staging

299

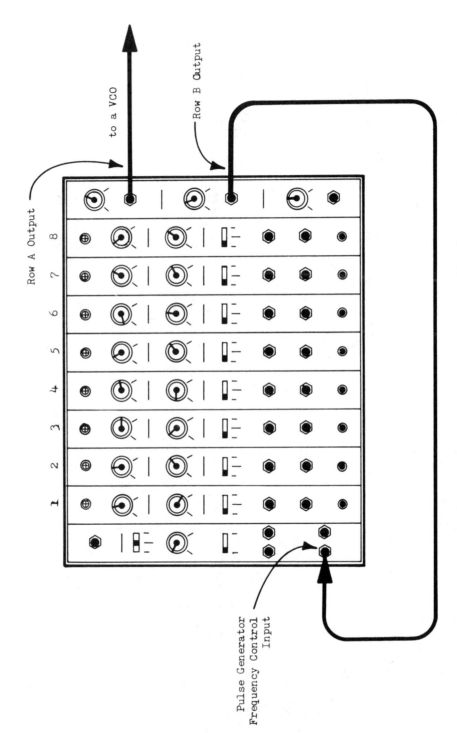

Figure 11.9 The Use of One Sequencer Row Output to Control the Sequencing Rate of Another

300

the rhythmic pattern of the sequence could be extended to any number of other synthesized events. Patch No. 15 illustrates one possible set-up that combines the control of a VCO by Row A of a two-row sequencer, control of the sequencer's pulse generator (sequencing rate) by Row B, and the triggering of two envelope generators by voltage triggers produced at the first and the fifth stages of the sequence. Note that if the pulse generator's initial frequency is increased, the rhythmic pattern will accelerate intact. The speed of the sequencing rate will also affect the operation of the two envelope generators. At higher sequencing rates, the full attack time (0.3 seconds) of the second envelope generator may not occur, since the voltage gate will only be produced while stage 5 is active. Further, if the sequencing rate becomes fast enough, the release times of the two envelope generators will eventually overlap. (It should be noted that the Moog 960 Sequential Controller voltage-trigger outputs would have to be converted to switch triggers by the Moog 961 Interface to control the envelope generators.)

Audio Frequency Sequencing Rates

Many sequencers can be triggered and advanced at audio frequency rates (the internal pulse generator of the Moog 960 Sequential Controller has a frequency range of 0.25 Hz to 500 Hz, well into the audio frequency range), creating an extremely versatile "waveform controller/generator." In such cases, the DC control-voltage (row) output may be used in the same way as any low-frequency periodic control voltage. The rapid variations in voltage steps become the equivalent of the more familiar oscillations of a periodic waveform, except that every individual section of the waveform is controlled by a separate stage of the sequence (Figure 11.10). The abrupt changes in voltage that make the waveform uneven and "jerky" can be smoothed out by sending the sequencer output through a lag processor. Naturally, the greater the number of sequenced stages used, the better the definition of the waveform will be. To determine the frequency of the waveform created, simply divide the frequency of the internal or external pulse generator driving the sequencer by the number of sequencer stages being used (for example, if the frequency of the pulse generator is 400 Hz and eight sequencer stages are being used, the frequency of the output waveform would be 50 Hz). This is actually a good example of how digital waveform synthesis is accomplished, though such a discussion is outside the scope of this text.

Extended Sequences

Some modular sequencers, particularly three- or four-row models, do not have the internal logic that makes possible a choice between sequencing the rows concurrently or consecutively; the rows function only concurrently. However, by connecting the DC control-voltage outputs of the sequencer rows to an electronic (or sequential) switch, as shown in Patch No. 16, each row can be passed through consecutively. When the first position of the electronic switch is active, the input from Row A is passed through the switch; in its second position, Row B is passed; in its third position, Row C is passed, and so on, depending on the number of rows the particular sequencer model has and the number of signal inputs the electronic switch can handle.

Any device as complex as the composite sequencer described above requires a good deal of experimentation for its capabilities to be fully understood and for the many interactive possibilities it presents to become apparent. A good deal of studio time should be set aside for these possibilities to be thoroughly explored.

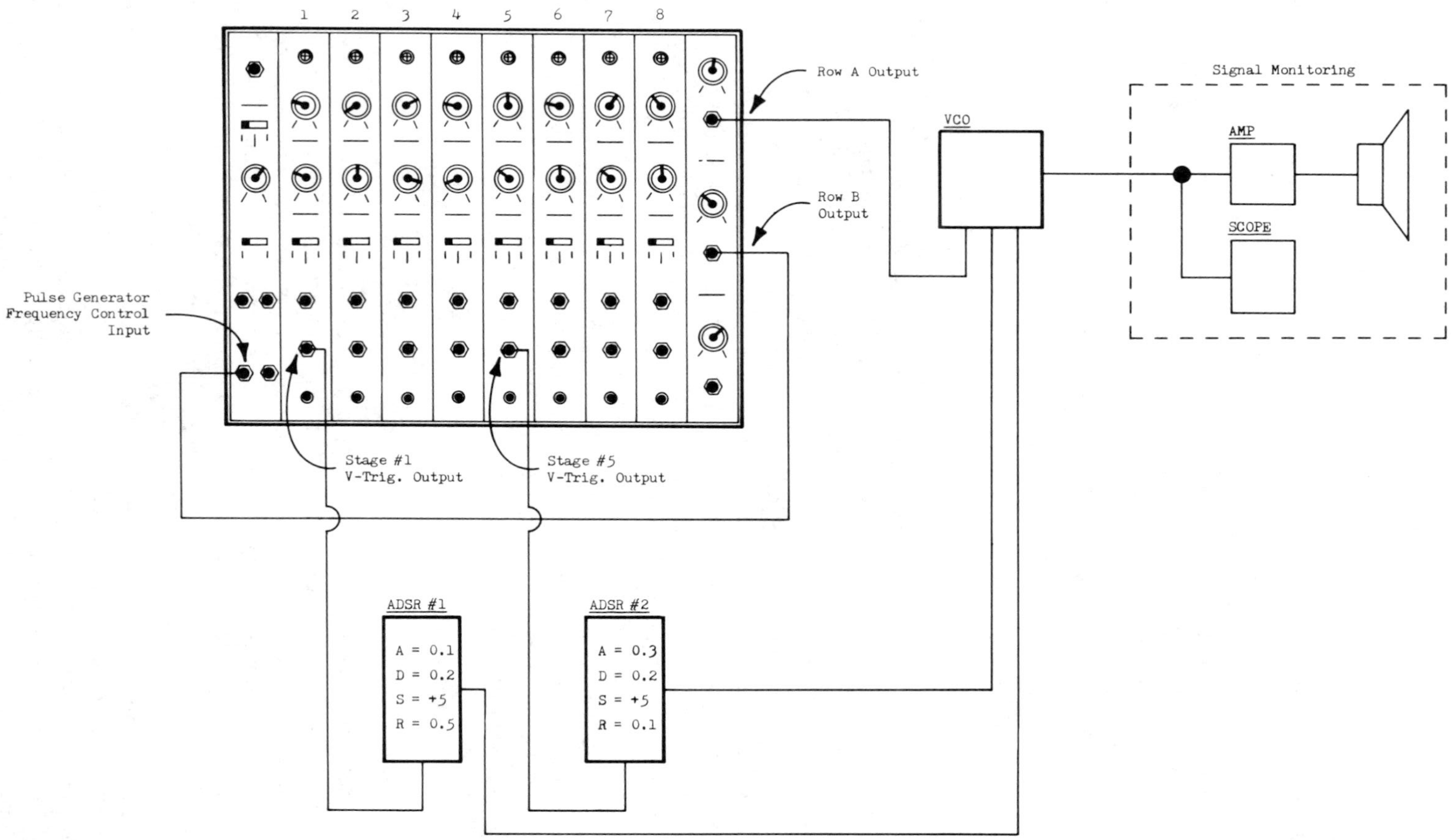

Signal Monitoring

AMP

SCOPE

VCO

Row A Output

Row B Output

Stage #5 V-Trig. Output

ADSR #2
A = 0.3
D = 0.2
S = +5
R = 0.1

Stage #1 V-Trig. Output

ADSR #1
A = 0.1
D = 0.2
S = +5
R = 0.5

8 7 6 5 4 3 2 1

Pulse Generator Frequency Control Input

PATCH 15: **Combined Sequential Controls**

302

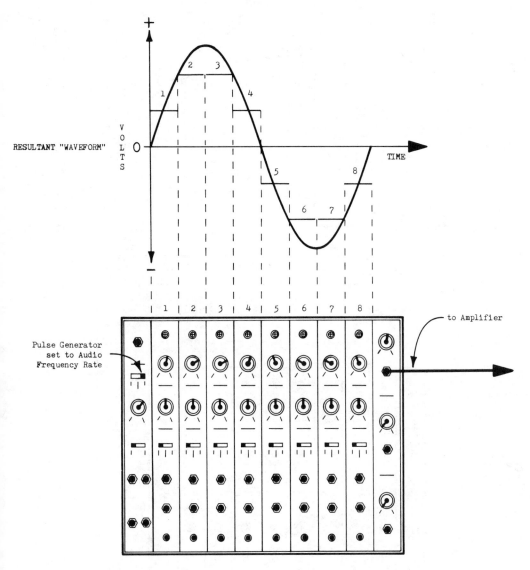

Figure 11.10   Audio Waveshape Synthesis Using Sequences of DC Voltages

Auxiliary Sequencer Modules

Every analog synthesizer has its special characteristics that have been developed to suit the particular synthesis goals of its designers. Often these design choices create the need for unusual or special modules that may have no direct counterpart in the synthesizer systems of other manufacturers. It would be impossible to cover (or to even anticipate) all of these designs here. However, it is probably fair to single out the Moog 961 Interface module for special comment. This module, which has no counterpart on most other analog synthesizers, can become one of the most important crossing points in the Moog synthesis system, because it acts as a translator of the synthesizer's control and command signals, allowing the special voltages or signals of one module to communicate

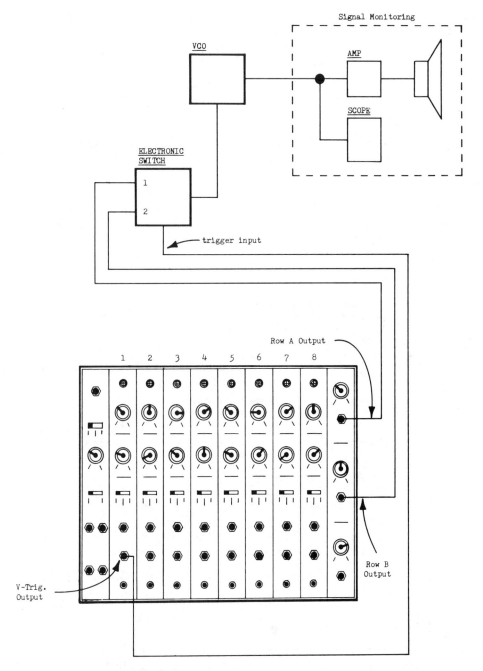

PATCH 16: **Extending the Sequence Using an Electronic Switch**

their effect to and be used by other synthesizer modules. The Moog 961 Interface is made up of three separate units. The "Audio-to-Voltage-Trigger" section of the module is nothing more than a Schmitt Trigger Generator in a different guise, deriving a voltage gate from an input signal (internal or external to the synthesizer). Its only control is a variable threshold setting. Another section of the device converts a switch trigger (produced only by the keyboard controller—a Moog peculiarity) into a voltage trigger (which can be used by the Moog 960 Sequential Controller and the Moog 962 Sequential Switch—a three-input/one-output electronic switch). The "voltage-trigger-to-switch-trigger" converter portion of the unit (necessary to permit the sequencer to initiate and control an envelope generator) has two totally separate sets (columns) of eight voltage-trigger inputs (one for each of the sequencer stage's voltage-trigger outputs). Column A of the unit translates the voltage-trigger (or gate) inputs presented to it into a switch-trigger output whose duration is the same as that of each of the voltage-trigger inputs. Column B of the unit allows the duration of the switch-trigger output to be set anywhere from 40 milliseconds to 4 seconds by a variable timing pot, regardless of the duration of any voltage trigger presented at its input. Without this interface, the Moog Sequential Controller's ability to interact with, to control, or to be controlled by other modules of the synthesizer would be severely limited.

RANDOM AND SEQUENTIAL CONTROL VOLTAGES: EXPERIMENTS AND COMBINATIONS

While AC and DC control voltages are generally used with equal frequency to control VCOs, VCAs, and VCFs, and time-variant control voltages are used to control VCAs and VCFs, more often than not, random and sequential control voltages find their most frequent applications in the control of VCOs. Owing to this, the experiments outlined below, which cover many frequency modulation applications, are extremely pertinent. As was mentioned at the beginning of similar sections in Chapters 9 and 10, these experiments are only intended to serve as preliminary explorations of the potential of the control voltage generators used in them. Students should be encouraged to extend these explorations further, particularly those that involve random and sequential control voltages in combination with control voltages covered in earlier chapters.

Random Control Voltages

1. Control the frequency of an audio oscillator with white noise.

   - How is the effect modified by various filterings of the noise (high-pass, low-pass, various band-pass center frequencies and bandwidths)?
   - When filtering noise with a band-pass filter, how narrowly may the passed band be focused and still remain usable as a control voltage?
   - Are the effects produced above audibly different from the effects produced when various filtered versions of white noise are simply mixed with the audio output of an oscillator?

2. Compare the effects produced when filtered or unfiltered white noise is used as an input:

   - to a Schmitt Trigger Generator whose output is used to initiate an envelope generator, which in turn is used to control a VCO.
   - to an envelope follower whose output is used to control a VCO.
   - to a pitch follower whose output is used to control a VCO.

3. What is the effect when filtered or unfiltered white noise is used as one of the inputs to a ring modulator, with various other signals (including the human voice via a microphone) used as the other input? Does it make any difference whether the noise is used as the "program" or as the "carrier" input to the ring modulator?

4. Using the output of a sample/hold controller to control the frequency of an audio oscillator:
   - experiment with a wide variety of input signals to the sample/hold circuit, including sub-audio waveforms, white noise, audio signals, and acoustic sounds via a microphone.
   - determine the resulting effects when the signals above are sampled at speeds approaching and even exceeding audio frequency rates.
   - explore the effects produced when two or more of the above input signals are mixed before being sampled.
   - experiment with the possibilities of voltage controlling the signal(s) to be sampled.
   - voltage control the sample/hold circuit's sampling rate (if possible), experimenting with various control-voltage inputs.
   - determine what kinds of sample/hold input signals and sampling rates can be effectively used to initiate an envelope generator (via a Schmitt Trigger Generator or similar signal conversion device), which is then used to control the same or a different VCO.

Sequential Control Voltages

5. Using the DC output of one row of a sequencer to control a VCO, determine:
   - the effect of changes in the sequencing rate. What happens when the sequencing rate is close to or beyond the minimal audio frequency threshold?
   - the variety of melodic and rhythmic effects that may result from different adjustments of the individual sequencer stage voltage level pots and the number of stages used.
   - the effect on the VCO of changes in the output amplitude level.
   - the result when the sequencer's internal control oscillator is itself controlled by various sub-audio waveforms or waveform mixtures.

6. Using the DC outputs of a multirow sequencer to control the same oscillator, determine how extended and complex a sequence can actually be made when the sequencer rows are themselves "sequenced" (either by an "A then B" output or by an external electronic or sequential switch).

7. Using two or three oscillators, each controlled by the DC output of a different row of the same sequencer, set them to produce two- or three-voice harmony.

8. Experiment with using the sequencer as a "waveform" generator by operating it at audio frequency rates. Different sequencer stage voltage level settings should produce different "waveforms."

9. If the voltage-trigger outputs of multiple sequencer stages are mixed and sent directly to an amplifier, what kinds of rhythmic ostinati can be obtained, depending on the "sequence/skip/hold" switch positions of the individual sequencer stages? Can these rhythm outputs be combined with DC control of an

oscillator, producing pitched *and* percussive sequences at the same time?

10. If two separate sequencers are available, what kinds of control voltage configurations may be obtained by using the DC control outputs and voltage-trigger outputs of one sequencer to control the sequencing rate, staging, "on/off" operation, and recycling point of the other sequencer?

Combined Random and Sequential Control Voltages

11. Using white noise as the input to a sample/hold circuit having a very slow sampling rate, can the sample/hold circuit's output be used to control the sequencing rate of a sequencer controlling an audio oscillator in a manner that produces random rhythmic effects?

12. Use the output of a sequencer row having a very slow sequencing rate to control the sampling rate of a sample/hold circuit.

COMBINED AC, DC, TIME-VARIANT, AND RANDOM/SEQUENTIAL CONTROL VOLTAGES

At this point we have discussed and explored the use of virtually every control-voltage generator and support module (voltage processors, trigger delays, signal translation devices, etc.) that any analog synthesizer is likely to offer the user, whether it be a simple live-performance preset unit or a large studio model requiring dozens of patch cords. Even restricting ourselves, for the time being, to the single aspect of frequency modulation, the combined control-voltage possibilities available are staggering. Even with seemingly simple patches, carefully thought out variations in the available control settings and possible voltage processings can lead to a wealth of different sounds obtainable from the same basic patch. With the use of multilevel control-voltage configurations, the potential variations of frequency modulation really do become endless.

There are many complete works of electronic music that have been conceived and produced using only a single patch. A little experimentation with a patch as multifunctional as Patch No. 17, presented as an example of these possibilities, should prove to be very entertaining as well as informative. Variations in any of the control settings of this patch can substantially alter the effects produced. Notice that each control voltage generator, signal processor, and signal translation device has a very specific role to play in the production of the final sound. The thought process used in constructing such a complex patch is the same as that used in the construction of the simplest patch imaginable: i.e., "What audible results do I want to produce *and* what items of the synthesizer, configured in what way, will produce those results?"

PATCHING PROJECT NO. 3

Using the sequential and random controllers described in this chapter, as well as the control modules and concepts covered earlier in Chapters 9 and 10, devise a patch that uses the characteristics of these various devices in an audibly distinctive manner. As

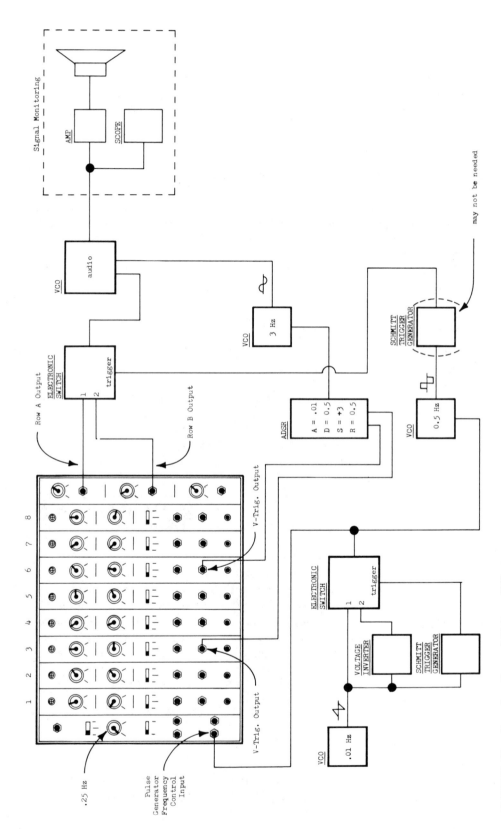

PATCH 17: **Complex Control Voltage Effects**

might be expected, the patch should attempt to combine and contrast both patterned (periodic) and random sound events, perhaps including a wide range of rhythmic variation. Study the patches already presented in this chapter; then, develop your own ideas. But have some idea of what you want to accomplish *before* you begin to work out the configuration of your own patch. The possibilities are so numerous that some sort of preplanning is now a necessity.

As with the earlier patching projects, accurate block diagramming, the reproducibility of the patch, and the creative use of the modules and concepts thus far discussed should be the criteria for evaluation. Remember that the mere complexity of the patch is not the final objective. The subtle combination or interaction of only a few control voltage effects will often prove much more interesting and effective than a dense clutter of uncomplementary, unrelated sound effects.

Chapter 12

Amplitude Modulation (AM)

VOLTAGE-CONTROLLED AMPLIFIERS (VCAs)

The concepts and applications of voltage control have thus far been presented only in terms of frequency modulation, primarily because the human hearing mechanism is more sensitive to changes in frequency than it is to changes in any other parameter of sound. Now that the sometimes intricate workings of control-voltage generators have been mastered—or at least a reasonable acquaintance established—it is a fairly simple task to transfer the application of these control modules to voltage-controlled amplifiers (the subject of this chapter) and to voltage-controlled filters (the subject of Chapter 13). Since the essential principle of voltage control is that a change in the control voltage produces an analogous change in whatever characteristic of sound is being controlled by it—whether it be frequency, pulse width, amplitude, or filter cut-off frequencey—there should be little difficulty in transferring a basic understanding of this cause-and-effect relationship from the voltage-controlled oscillator to any voltage-controllable module.

Function

The function of a voltage-controlled amplifier (VCA) is to vary the gain (amplitude) of a signal (AC or DC) in relation to changes in the amplitude level of a control voltage. The automatic gain control provided by the VCA not only frees the composer from having to operate gain or level controls manually, but is usually more subtle and immediate. This becomes very important when synthesizing the amplitude characteristics of electronic sounds that approach the same level of complexity as acoustic sounds. Although the human hearing mechanism is most acutely aware of changes in frequency, it is nevertheless a superb analyzer of amplitude characteristics, particularly when they are combined with similar transient harmonic structures (to be explored in Chapter 13). The ear depends to a very great extent on the shape of the amplitude envelope to identify the nature and, hence, the aural significance of a sound. Of particular importance is the attack, since the ear depends heavily on the initial 20 to 30 milliseconds of a sound to identify or categorize it. Accurate manual control of such a complex and quickly changing sound characteristic would be virtually impossible.

The importance of carefully defined and controlled amplitude characteristics does not stop at the attack, nor is it confined to the attack, decay, sustain, and release functions produced by controlling a VCA with an envelope generator. Gradual changes in loudness (*crescendo* and *decrescendo*, in musical terms), periodic variations in loudness (tremolo), and any number of other complex combinations of controls and effects may also be created. These effects, though essential in synthesizing "lifelike" imitations of acoustic instruments (if this is one's goal), can also play a significant role in creating pure electronic sounds that have a complexity and subtlety comparable to or exceeding those of "natural" sounds. Careful attention to the amplitude characteristics of a sound will ultimately contribute to the creation of a personal electronic music composition style.

It should also be remembered that control signals as well as audio signals may be modulated. Since it is the variation in the amplitude (voltage) of a control signal that will affect the device being controlled by it, the VCA makes it possible to produce these variations in a much more refined or complex manner. Particular applications of a variety of these techniques will be covered below.

Controls

Although there are a number of variations in the design of VCAs, their essential controls are generally fairly simple, such as on the Moog 902, the Aries AR-316, the Eμ 2000, the Serge Dual VCA, and the VCA section of the ARP 2600. Figure 12.1 shows a composite representation of a VCA possessing the range of controls and control options normally found in a studio version of the device (though even simpler VCAs are offered on some synthesizer models). If multiple signal inputs are available (as in this illustration), they are automatically summed within the VCA—in this case equally, though some VCAs permit the independent and variable attenuation of signal inputs. Signals are passed through the circuit at an amplitude level determined, in part, by the "INITIAL CONTROL VOLTAGE" setting. The initial control-voltage pot is set manually and is

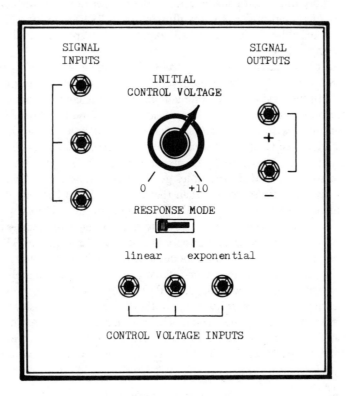

Figure 12.1 A Composite VCA

usually variable from 0 volts (for complete attenuation) up to +10 volts (for complete pass-through). This control is not quite the same as a typical amplifier gain control; it is actually a source of a DC control voltage that is added to the effect of the external control-voltage inputs to the unit. At its "0" setting no voltage is produced, and at its fully open position the maximum voltage acceptable by the VCA is produced. The effect of any external control-voltage inputs is thereby minimized, since the amplifier is protected from being "overdriven."

In the VCA of Figure 12.1, both positive and negative signal outputs are offered, the latter producing an exact inversion of the input signal, as shown in Figure 12.2. (The positive and negative outputs of the Moog 902 VCA are not labeled, but the signal output exactly across from the signal input used will be inverted.) Figure 12.2a shows the result when a DC envelope generator input is inverted (keep in mind that the "0" volt line is only a relative reference point) and Figure 12.2b shows the result when the VCA is used to invert a sub-audio waveform.

Linear and Exponential Response Modes

The control voltages present at the control-voltage inputs of the VCA are summed (mixed) with the manually set initial control voltage in order to control the amplitude of the VCA's signal output. Although none is shown here, the Aries AR-316, the Eμ 2000, and the ARP 2600 VCAs each provide at least one attenuated control input—a welcome convenience, but a capability that can be provided equally well by external mixers or attenuators. A more important consideration is the *manner* in which the control-voltage affects the gain of the amplifier. In this illustration, a "RESPONSE MODE" switch offers a choice of either a linear *or* an exponential response to changes in the control-voltage input level.

A linear response, as shown in Figure 12.3, provides an equal increase in the amplifier's gain for every increase in the level of the control voltage (in this example, a 10% change in amplifier gain for each one-volt change in the control-voltage level). This occurs because both gain and voltage are linear or *arithmetic* functions. On the other hand, the *intensity* of a sound (as measured in decibels) is *not* an arithmetic but an *exponential* function (see Chapter 4); that is, each increase of 10 decibels increases the intensity level of a sound by a factor of 10, also shown in Figure 12.3. Thus, the intensity level of a given sound at 0 dB is 100 times greater than the intensity level of the same sound at −20 dB, 1000 times greater than that at −30 dB, and 10,000,000,000 times greater than the intensity level at −100 dB. The change, in this example, from complete attenuation to "unity gain" (gain = 1)* is equal to the difference between −100 dB and 0 dB (which is the same exponential response ratio that is used in the Aries AR-343 and the Eμ 2000 VCAs). In the linear response mode, a control voltage of 5 volts, produces 50 percent of unity gain, so the resulting intensity level is approximately −6 dB—or one-half the intensity of the same signal at 0 dB. The first 5 volts of control voltage raise the output level to 50 percent of unity gain, but they increase the intensity level by 90 dB or 1,000,000,000 times. This would seem to indicate an extreme increase in the loudness of the signal as the control voltage is increased from 0 to 5 volts. However, since the human auditory system responds to changes in intensity level exponentially, the

---

* GAIN = $\dfrac{\text{output level}}{\text{input level}}$, so "unity gain" is when the output level of the VCA equals the input level.

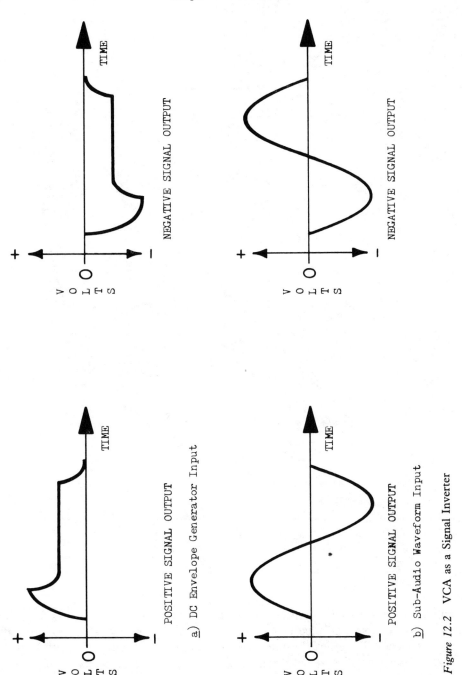

Figure 12.2 VCA as a Signal Inverter

perceivable difference in the loudness of a signal at −100 dB and the same signal at −60 dB is very small. The most significant increase in the perceived loudness of the signal would actually occur from about −30 dB to 0 dB. In the linear mode, this increase in loudness occurs from about 70 to 100 percent of unity gain.

By contrast, the exponential mode imitates the response of the human auditory

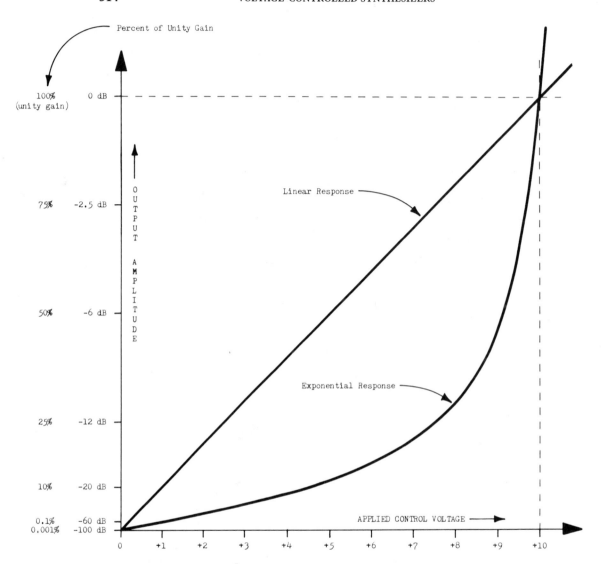

Figure 12.3   The VCA's "Linear" and "Exponential" Response Modes

system much more accurately, increasing in perceived loudness much more evenly, This change is so effective that some VCAs (all Serge VCAs, for instance) operate *only* in the exponential mode. By setting the initial control voltage pot at about 5 or 6 volts, virtually no audible signal will be passed through the VCA when it is in the exponential mode because of the extremely low gain (about 0.1 to 1.0%) and the low intensity level (−60 to −40 dB). Then, with a relatively small increase in the control voltage (3–4 volts, totaling 8–10 volts) a tremendous increase in both gain and perceived loudness will occur. On the other hand, if the VCA is set in the linear response mode, and the initial control-voltage pot is set low enough so that virtually no audible signal is passed (less than 1 volt, for example), a very substantial increase in control voltage (up to 9 volts) is required to cause anything even approaching a substantial increase in gain and perceived loudness. Thus, except in those particular instances where the most minute and subtle response to control-voltage changes is desired, the exponential mode will prove most useful. This is especially true when using an envelope generator as the primary control voltage input to a voltage-controlled amplifier.

Design Variations

Although the composite VCA shown in Figure 12.1 is fairly typical of the standard synthesizer modules, there are several variants of this basic design that should be mentioned even though the basic operational principles remain quite similar (especially in one of the most frequently encountered design variations: the voltage-controlled mixer). The Buchla Quadraphonic Monitor/Interface (Model 226) and Quad Spatial Director (Model 204) each allow the amplitude of the signal outputs to be determined by a combination of initial and external control voltages. There is, in essence, one VCA provided per output channel of the mixer, each operating in the same manner as the simpler VCA module already described. The Buchla modules (as well as the Serge Universal Audio Processor) have additional voltage-control capabilities that allow the input signal to be panned from one output channel to another output channel in response to applied control voltages. In the structuring of some complex patches, this can be extremely helpful. A more common way of achieving the same effect ("auto-panning") will be discussed below.

The most important variant of a VCA is the ring (balanced amplitude) modulator, whose operation and applications were discussed in Chapter 7. When the program signal input to a ring modulator is either a sub-audio waveform or a DC signal, the effect on an audio signal input is the same as it would be if the program signal were acting as the primary control voltage applied to a VCA with the audio signal as the carrier input. This is because the basic operational principles of the ring modulator rely on a form of amplitude modulation. However, the general lack of control over the exact response of the ring modulator makes this an unlikely alternative to a VCA in all but the simplest gating operations.

OPERATION AND APPLICATION

The principal use of amplitude modulation is to control the amplitude envelopes of audio signals. As such, the VCA is often found as one of the last modules in the audio signal path, altering the signal just before (and sometimes just after) it is combined with other signals in the mixer. Any number of low-frequency AC waveforms, DC voltages and gates, time-variant voltages (particularly the voltage envelopes derived from envelope generators or envelope followers), and even random and sequential voltages may be used as control sources. Yet, in discussing these operations and their applications it should always be remembered that other, less immediately perceived uses for amplitude modulation (such as the processing of control voltages) do exist. Indeed, these can prove to be among the most creative and individually expressive capabilities of the voltage-controlled amplifier and the analog synthesizer as a whole. These applications may involve the modulation or modification of low-frequency control waveforms or of DC voltage sequences, perhaps controlled by other sub-audio frequency AC voltages or envelope generator outputs.

AC CONTROL VOLTAGES

Sub-Audio AC Control Voltages

Most uses of AC signals as control voltages occur when they are in the sub-audio frequency range. The typical arrangement shown in Patch No. 18 produces a smooth, periodic variation in the amplitude of the audio signal known as *tremolo*. If a square wave or a pulse wave is used as the control signal in this patch, the VCA acts as a simple gating mechanism, allowing the audio signal to pass only when the duty cycle of the control waveform is positive. This effect would normally require the VCA to be set in its exponential mode, with some degree of initial gain. In a similar vein, it is possible to take the square wave output from the internal pulse generator ("clock") of a sequential controller, as shown in Patch No. 19, and to use that signal as a gate voltage to control the amplitude of an audio VCO (which is being controlled by the same sequencer).

In a different kind of application, the shape of the sub-audio sawtooth waveform makes it ideal for creating a gradual increase (using the normal upward waveform slope) or decrease (using an inverted or downward waveform slope) in the output amplitude of a VCA. In musical terms, these effects are called *crescendo* and *diminuendo*, respectively. Extremely low sub-audio control frequencies can produce very slow changes in amplitude, often lasting as long as 90 seconds with some synthesizers (depending on the minimum frequency limits of the control oscillator).

An effective stereo panning effect (called "auto-panning") can be produced by using a very low-frequency sawtooth waveform in both its normal and its inverted forms to control two separate VCAs, as illustrated in Patch No. 20. The audio signal from VCO #1 is gradually panned from the left to the right channel of a stereo amplifier by using the sawtooth waveform produced by VCO #2 to increase the gain of one VCA (modulating the signal produced by VCO #1) as its inverted form simultaneously decreases the gain of a second VCA (also modulating the signal of VCO #1). Although the exponential mode is designated in this patch, the linear mode might also be useful in situations requiring a more subtle effect. With the frequency setting of VCO #2 that is

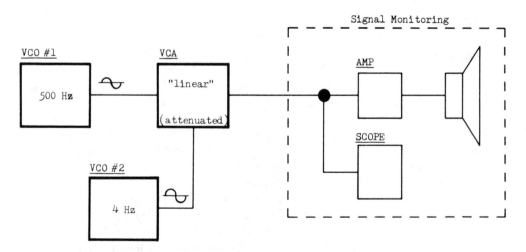

PATCH 18: **VCA Used to Produce a Tremolo Effect**

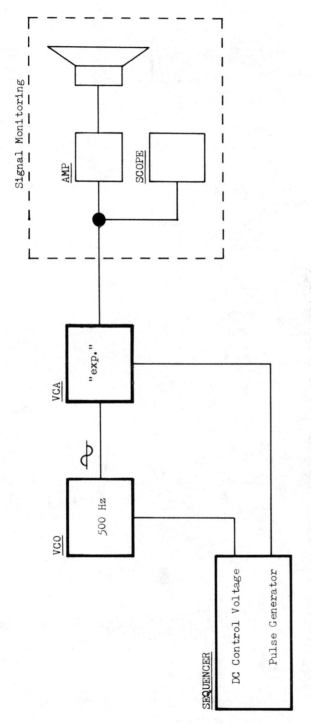

PATCH 19: **The Use of the Sequencer's Pulse Generator Output for VCA Gating**

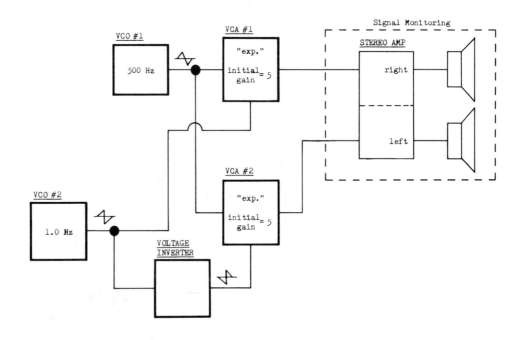

a) The "Auto-Pan" Patch

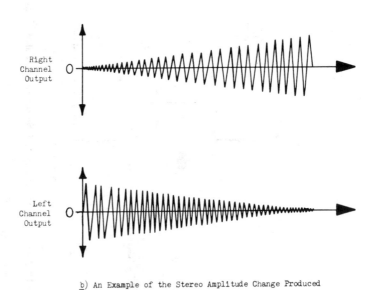

b) An Example of the Stereo Amplitude Change Produced

PATCH 20: **The Use of Two VCAs for Automatic Stereo Panning**

318

shown in Patch No. 20 (1.0 Hz), this gradual stereo panning effect would take place once every second. The use of either a sine wave or a triangle wave output from VCO #2 would produce variants of this same effect. However, if the waveform of VCO #2 were changed to a square wave, the result would be an instantaneous "bouncing" of the audio signal from one stereo output channel to the other, and the two VCAs would function as amplitude gates, producing the same effect as a one-input/two-output electronic switch placed directly between VCO #1 and the stereo amplifier. The use of VCAs as amplitude gates, controlled by sub-audio pulse or square waves, or by envelope generators with sharply defined component times, is one of the VCA's most frequent applications.

Audio AC Control Voltages

The use of audio AC signals to control VCAs produces an effect very similar to audio frequency modulation: frequency sidebands. The complex output signals that can be created contain not only the frequencies of both the modulating and modulated input signals but very strong sum-and-difference sideband frequencies as well. Such amplitude modulation effects are primarily useful in developing complex, rich timbres or textures with no particular harmonic balance, because the resulting conglomeration of spectral characteristics usually overshadows any specific harmonic or melodic characteristics in the final output signal. As was the case with frequency modulation at audio rates, the shape of the control waveform input especially affects the degree of complexity of the output. A square wave used as the control signal input will normally produce the most precisely defined results, due to the instantaneous transition that occurs between its two voltage levels. Sawtooth waveforms used as the control signal input produce the broadest, most unpredictable sideband generation effects, because the sawtooth waveform has a constantly changing output amplitude that continually blurs or changes the sideband frequencies produced.

DC CONTROL VOLTAGES

DC control voltages, even when rapidly varied, tend by their very nature to produce relatively static events, because the collection of voltages they produce represent discrete quantities. As we saw in Chapter 9, when used to produce and control changes in frequency, the static character of DC voltages can be very important (if not absolutely essential), because the ear is extremely sensitive to very minor changes in frequency. Western music, at least, has traditionally been concerned, if not obsessed, with producing discrete, almost static pitches with carefully preserved relationships between them. The amplitude characteristics of sound are quite a different matter. In this realm, composers, performers, and listeners seem generally to have favored the expressive qualities of continual, subtle variations in amplitude. Consequently, the effective use of discrete DC signals to control amplitude via voltage-controlled amplifiers is very limited.

As we know, the ear is relatively insensitive to small changes in loudness; yet, constant variation in the loudness of sounds is necessary to maintain our interest as listeners. The importance of transient amplitude characteristics to our perception of a sound, especially at the beginning of the sound, has already been discussed. It should also be noted that acoustic musical instruments, natural sounds, and even environmental noises seldom maintain a steady, unchanging amplitude for any appreciable length of time. This is partially because the energy that causes the sound naturally dissipates over time and distance. Although electronically synthesized sounds may be sustained at the same amplitude level for a virtually unlimited time, the human auditory network quickly becomes bored with such a sound and soon ignores its existence entirely (unless the sound is either painful or annoying—hardly desirable esthetic goals in most situations), preferring, instead, to concentrate on sounds that incorporate changing amplitude characteristics.

The principal use of DC voltages in controlling the amplitude of a signal is to set a reference level from which either sub-audio AC or time-variant control voltages can be used to actually modulate the signal. This is usually the function of the initial gain control of the VCA, which provides a DC control (or "offset") voltage internally. The use of other DC control voltages from external sources is rare because of the limitations outlined above, but there may still be instances in which the discrete changes in amplitude they can produce may be effective. The keyboard controller, the linear controller, the joystick controller, and even the sequencer are all usable sources for DC control voltages that have some interest. For example, it is possible to produce a very definite, audible correlation between an audio signal's frequency range and its amplitude (not an unusual characteristic of many naturally occurring sounds) by controlling both a VCO and a VCA from the same DC control-voltage generator, as is shown in Patch No. 21. A similar, though random effect would result from using the DC voltage output of a sample/hold module, with white noise as the sampled input, to control both the VCO and the VCA. A further variant of this patch might be to use an inverted form of the sample/hold DC control voltage output to control either the VCO or the VCA. Both the envelope follower and the pitch follower are designed to allow the control of the synthesizer from external, usually acoustic, sources. The output of either device may be used to control a VCA or a VCO, or both. Individual frequencies may be produced by controlling the frequency of a VCO with the output of a pitch follower and controlling the amplitude of the frequencies generated by the output of an envelope follower, as is shown in Patch No. 22. An alteration of this patch, well worth experimentation, would be to reverse the use of the control voltage outputs of the envelope follower and the pitch follower. The use of only one or the other of these devices to control *both* the VCO and the VCA should also be explored. In any of its possible configurations, this patch truly represents the possibility of using a sound source external to the synthesizer to control it, almost by "remote control." Much more typical is the case where a keyboard controller would be used to initiate a transient control voltage produced by an envelope generator, which would subsequently be used to control the VCA discussed in the next paragraph. The subtlety of quickly changing, discrete DC levels from either the keyboard or sequencer may also be quite effective.

Other DC control voltage sources that are frequently used to control a signal's amplitude usually have some transient characteristics. Both linear controllers and joystick controllers rely, to a significant extent, on their ability to move smoothly through different voltage levels, instead of remaining static on one voltage level or changing instantly between discrete voltages. The linear controller can be especially effective in producing crescendos and diminuendos, as well as in producing the slight variations in loudness typical of live performers on acoustic instruments, because the operator's hand movements on the device can provide an extremely versatile and, presumably, sensitive control mechanism (assuming that human beings can function more subtly than machines). Joystick controllers are used mostly for panning between

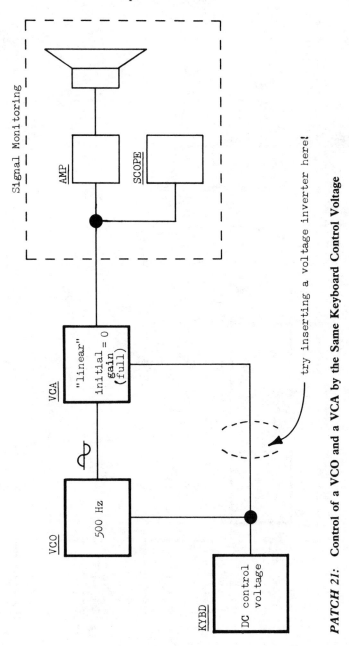

PATCH 21: **Control of a VCO and a VCA by the Same Keyboard Control Voltage**

two or more different audio output channels, effectively controlling the spatial location of the sound in the listening environment. Patch No. 23 illustrates how a four-output joystick controller could be used to control the localization of a signal produced by a single VCO. Notice that a separate VCA is needed for each of the four output channels and that the amplitude level of each channel corresponds to the position of the joystick. As the joystick is moved further into any particular quadrant (labeled A, B, C, and D in the diagram), that quadrant's DC voltage, in turn, determines the amplitude level of the

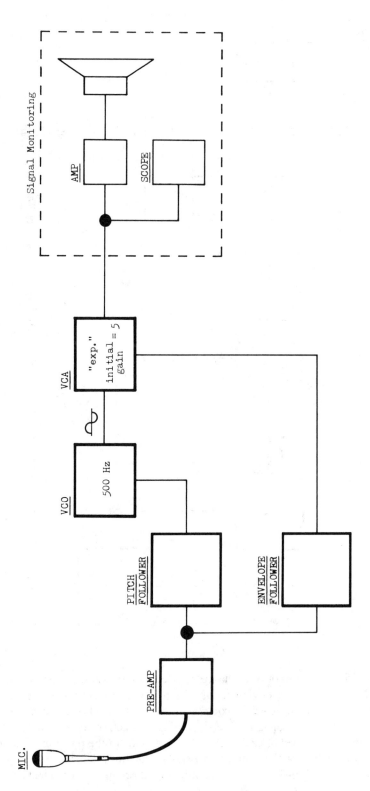

PATCH 22: **External Control of Synthesizer Frequency and Amplitude**

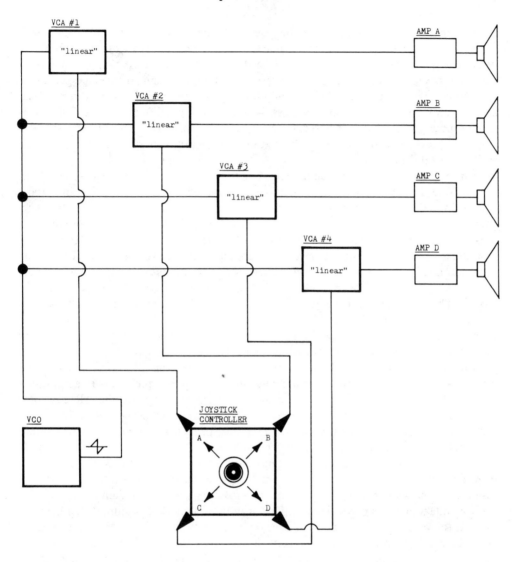

PATCH 23: **The Use of a Joystick Controller for Quadraphonic Panning**

signal in the appropriate output channel. The Putney VCS-3 and the Buchla Quad Spatial Director (Model 204) units are good examples of very versatile joystick controllers designed primarily for sound localization. The Buchla unit makes many of the patch cords indicated in Patch No. 23 unnecessary, since many of the patching connections shown are made internally.

TIME-VARIANT CONTROL VOLTAGES

The primary use of time-variant voltages is the control of amplitude envelopes. The complexity of the amplitude characteristics of most acoustic sounds, and the human auditory network's resulting reliance on the complex amplitude envelopes of these sounds for their identification, make the plastic qualities of time-variant control voltages often essential in the synthesis of amplitude envelopes. Thus, because of the flexibility of its control parameters, the real workhorse of the time-variant control voltage generators is, not surprisingly, the multistage envelope generator. Although an envelope generator can control any voltage-controllable module, it is primarily intended—as even its name and its control functions seem to suggest—to mold the amplitude characteristics of a given sound. By specifying the attack, decay, sustain, and release portions of a sound's amplitude envelope, the basic criteria necessary for sound recognition and interest can easily be established.

Since the operational principles and functions of envelope generators, envelope followers, and pitch followers have already been covered in Chapter 10, this discussion will be limited to a few ways in which the application of time-variant control voltages to amplitude modulation differ significantly from the analogous frequency modulation uses. Perhaps one of the best ways to become familiar with the potential uses of these modules is to repeat some of the patches and experiments that were given in Chapter 10, substituting a VCA for the VCO being controlled, and using the VCO as an audio signal source for the patches. For example, Patch No. 6 might be changed as shown in Patch No. 24. The keyboard controller would now be used both to control the discrete changes in pitch of the VCO and to initiate and maintain the functioning of the envelope generator controlling the VCA, thereby providing a definable amplitude envelope for each pitch. Experimenting with the envelope generator's control settings, and changing the length of time a key is held down, will result in several amplitude effects, ranging from short, percussive sounds to sustained sounds with no sharp changes in amplitude. These control possibilities could be further enhanced by replacing the AR envelope generator by an ADSR envelope generator. Replacing the VCO by a noise generator would produce percussive sounds very close to those of acoustic percussion instruments.

The effect that was illustrated in Patch No. 7 and is here applied to a VCA as Patch No. 25, is perhaps of greater significance to this discussion, since any means of increasing the subtlety of a given audio signal's amplitude envelope greatly increases the resulting sound's interest and credibility. Careful attenuation of the amplitudes of the control voltages used is particularly important in this patch. The beginner's tendency to use control voltages only at their full level should be overcome as soon as the student becomes familiar with the effect the control voltages produce. Although the intention may not be to reproduce natural or instrumental sounds, one of the primary challenges of electronic music has always been to create sounds that equal their subtlety.

Spectral Control

An often forgotten characteristic of naturally produced sounds is that their higher frequencies tend to diminish in loudness more quickly than do their lower frequencies. This effect can be reproduced to a certain extent on the synthesizer by using several VCAs, each one controlling the amplitude envelope of a different portion of a sound's frequency spectrum. Patch No. 26 illustrates one way in which the different spectral dimensions of a sound can be carefully shaped and varied by controlling the amplitudes of several different frequency ranges separately. As usual with such a patch, plenty of time should be taken to experiment with all of the control parameters provided: the frequency and waveform of the VCO, the cut-off frequencies of the filters, the timing and sustain level controls of the three envelope generators, the gain settings on the VCAs, and the input settings on the mixer.

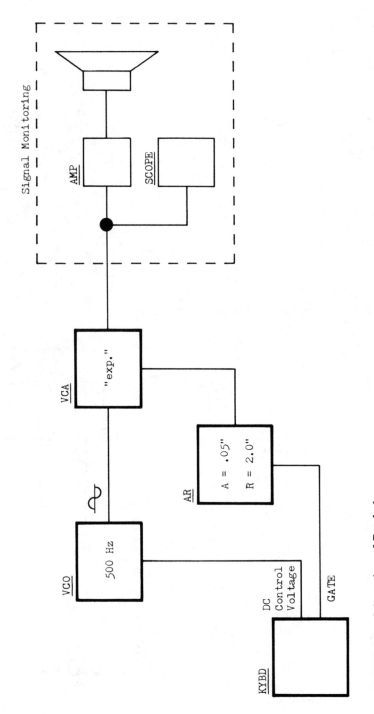

PATCH 24: **Adaptation of Patch 6**

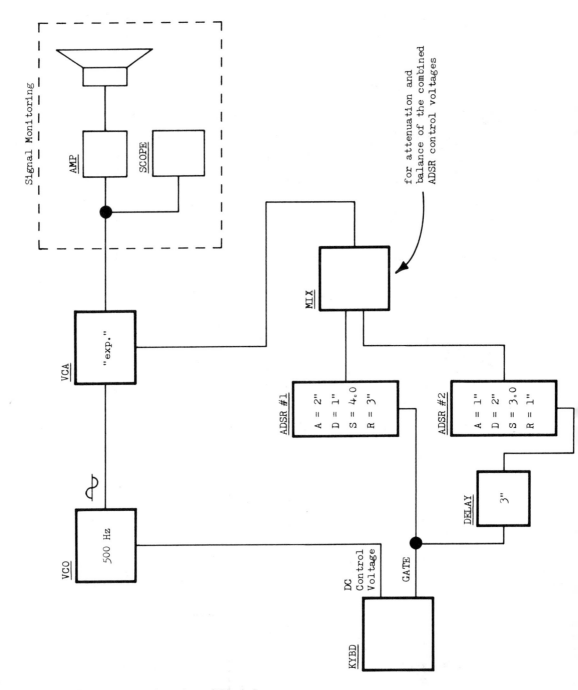

PATCH 25: **Adaptation of Patch 7**

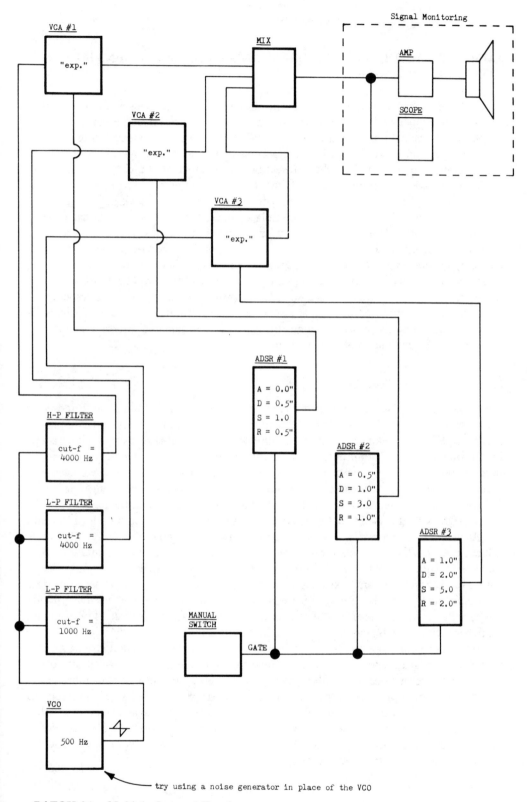

PATCH 26: **Multiple Spectral Envelopes**

try using a noise generator in place of the VCO

COMBINED AC, DC, TIME-VARIANT, AND RANDOM/SEQUENTIAL CONTROL VOLTAGES

It should be clear by now that control of the amplitude characteristics of a signal involves much more than simple gating or even the use of a single envelope generator. The amplitude of a signal must usually be in constant flux to keep the listener's interest. This interest occurs on two different but interrelated structural levels, that of the individual sound event and that of the overall direction and context of the composition. Every sound must have a carefully articulated dynamic shape and must contribute in some way to an overall dynamic contour involving continuous building, relaxing, or contrasting amplitude levels. This is such a commonplace concern in traditional musical training that it may seem odd to even bother stating it here, but one of the primary criticisms leveled against many electronic music compositions is their lack of subtle articulation, shaping, variety, and interplay. To a great extent, these shortcomings, when they do exist, are due to a lack of careful attention to the refining of the amplitude characteristics of sounds in relation to the other sounds that surround them. In this respect, the electronic music composer must act as a superior "orchestrator," completely designating the exact characteristics of every sound, the relative importance of different sounds and the variation of articulations among them.

Combined Control Processes

Since amplitude plays an important role in defining the rhythmic and temporal characteristics of complex sounds by determining event duration and dynamic emphasis, it is possible to create an almost infinite number of rhythmic patterns and relationships by thoroughly mastering amplitude modulation techniques. The obvious on/off amplitude gating effects produced by square or pulse waveform control voltages can themselves be voltage controlled to create more subtle or complex changes in speed (frequency modulation) and duration (pulse-width modulation), and the use of multiple control signals can be used to define rhythmic relationships among the sounds produced.

As was the case with frequency modulation, an appreciation of the effects that can be achieved with VCAs can only be obtained through extensive experimentation. Any number of control-voltage levels and combinations is possible, but, it should be re-emphasized, patching complexity for its own sake is not the best motivation, nor does it produce the best results. Some adjustments or additions to earlier patches may provide the best illustration of the effects of control voltage signals and their levels. For example, a further refinement to Patch No. 26 might be the addition of a slight tremolo (via a low-frequency sine wave) to one or more of the VCAs. This patch might also be given a subtle bias toward a specific frequency range by using the DC control-voltage output from a keyboard or linear controller (probably attenuated) to control one or more of the VCAs. The overlapping and interrelated events occurring in Patch No. 27, provided as an example of the kinds of control-voltage combinations now available, require that careful attention be given to several levels of voltage control and to complex mixtures of control voltages. In developing similar patches on your own, try to pay particular attention to these control characteristics.

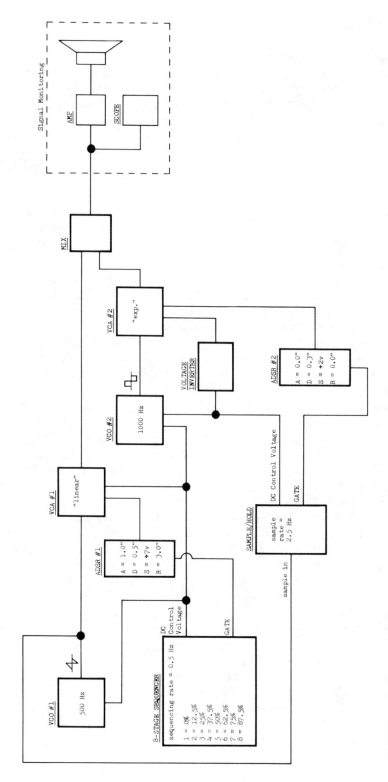

PATCH 27:** **Interrelated Events

THE VOCODER

The vocoder is a rather specialized device, not normally a part of the analog synthesizer, but using its technology, which has become increasingly common in electronic music studios. It is discussed here because its operation relies so heavily on the use of voltage-controlled amplifiers. The vocoder combines in the same unit two sets of matched fixed-filter banks with identical center frequencies and bandwidths, a set of envelope followers, and a set of voltage-controlled amplifiers. The device is used to sample the spectral characteristics of one sound and to impose the resultant formant envelope on another sound. Figure 12.4 illustrates the basic structure and operating principles of most vocoders. A sample signal (sometimes referred to as the "voice" input, since vocoders were originally designed to duplicate the formant characteristics of the human voice) is fed into a bank of band-pass filters and into a single high-pass filter (the purpose of the high-pass filter will be explained later). Each band-pass filter passes only the part of the sample signal that lies within its preset frequency range. The outputs of each band-pass filter are then fed into a separate envelope follower which produces an envelope voltage proportional to the amplitude of the signal passed through the filter; the greater the intensity of the signal in a particular frequency band, the greater the voltage output of that band's envelope follower. This completes the sampling process.

A separate carrier signal is simultaneously fed into a second bank of band-pass filters (and a high-pass filter) with the same center-frequency and bandwidth characteristics as the bank of sampling filters. The output of each of these filters is then processed by a voltage-controlled amplifier that is being controlled by the corresponding envelope follower. For example, if a large portion of the total amplitude of the *sampled* signal occurs in the 400-Hz frequency band, the control-voltage envelope derived from the sample signal causes a similarly large amount of the *carrier* signal to be passed through the VCA in the 400-Hz band. If little of the sampled signal is present in a particular frequency band, a small amount of the carrier signal is allowed through that band's VCA. Thus, the vocoder responds to changes in the frequency content (formant envelope) of the sampled signal by producing analogous changes in the formant envelope of the carrier signal. If the sampled signal is a person speaking and the carrier signal is an audio sawtooth waveform, the formants or timbral characteristics produced by the spoken words will be imposed on the harmonic content of the sawtooth signal, perhaps even preserving the intelligibility of the words, but without the speaker's voice.

The high-pass filters incorporated in the unit are used to reproduce the high-frequency characteristics of consonant sounds, such as s, c, ch, t, p, or k, as well as other percussive sounds with high-frequency components. The high-pass filter in the carrier signal path generally uses a pink-noise generator as a signal source, instead of the carrier signal itself, thereby preserving the effects of consonants or other high-frequency noises.

Although any number of variations are possible, most vocoders employ from 16 to 24 discrete frequency bands to cover most of the audio frequency range (in one-third-octave increments), with the high-pass filter adding in the highest frequencies. It should be obvious that the more discrete frequency bands there are, and the more narrowly they can be focused, the more accurate and realistic the formant transfer will be. However, most of the important frequency information necessary to produce an accurate formant translation lies in the 50–5000-Hz range; so this is the frequency range which most manufacturers concentrate on.

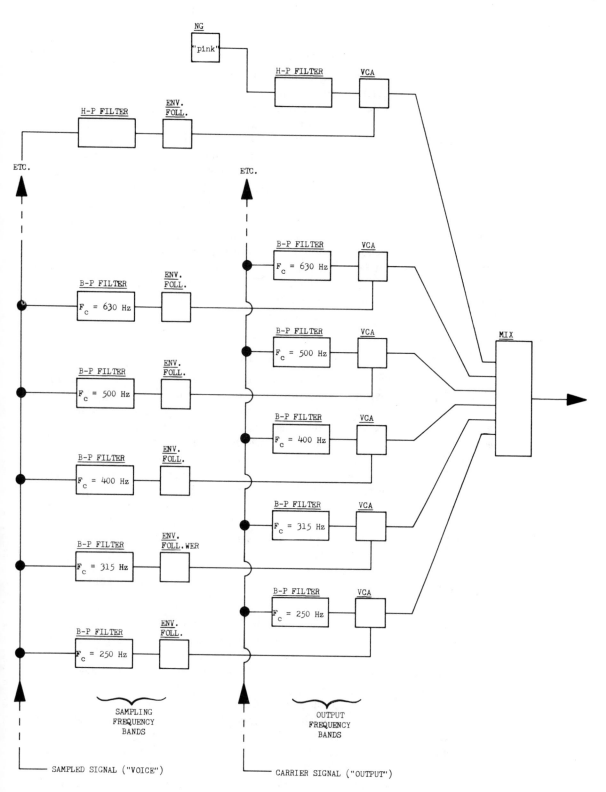

Figure 12.4 The Vocoder

Controls

Standard operation of the vocoder requires only a sample signal input (usually with a level control) and a carrier signal input (also with a level control). Since an exact frequency relationship must be maintained between the analysis and synthesis sections of the instrument, most vocoders provide no frequency or bandwidth controls for the two sets of filters. However, the high-pass filter may often be switched in or out of the circuit, and there is usually a control for balancing the amplitude level of the pink noise with the carrier signal. Some models of the vocoder also allow the user to choose between a "constant tracking" mode, in which the carrier signal is passed only when a sample signal is actually present, and a "hold" mode, in which the relationships of the most recent formant sampled are maintained, allowing the affected carrier signal to be sustained even after the sample signal ends. A bypass switch may also be included, permitting the user to choose between the unaffected sample signal and the processed carrier signal at the mixer output, making it easier to compare the two. Individual control voltage inputs to each frequency band's VCA and individual control-voltage outputs from each frequency band's envelope follower are found in more sophisticated vocoders.

Operational Uses

The vocoder is most typically used to transfer the spectral characteristics of the human voice onto other sounds, particularly the harmonic structure of audio waveforms. For example, a common set-up allows the user to sample his own speaking or singing voice as he plays a melody on a keyboard controller, using the keyboard's control-voltage output to control the frequency of a VCO that produces the carrier signal, giving the impression in the resultant processed carrier signal that the words he speaks or sings are being electronically "spoken" or "sung." It is, of course, possible to use any signal for a sample input and any signal for a carrier input. If the control-voltage inputs and outputs of the individual frequency bands are also accessible, even greater timbral flexibility is possible, since the unit can then be used as an extremely sophisticated signal analyzer and frequency-dependent voltage-controlled amplifier.

PATCHING PROJECT NO. 4

Combine the use of frequency and amplitude modulation techniques in a patch that employs at least one of each of the four principal control-voltage types: AC, DC, time-variant, and random/sequential. This patch should be controlled to some degree both manually and automatically and should particularly attempt to develop both distinctive amplitude envelopes (the dynamic shape of the individual sound events) and a large-scale amplitude structure (the overall dynamic shape of the patch as a whole). Diagram the patch in sufficient detail for other members of the class to reconstruct the patch accurately without further instructions. The quality of the patch can be assessed by its use of the available control-voltage options, the accuracy of the block diagram and any written instructions, its reproducibility by others, the development of distinctive and interesting sound events, and its attention to the balance and interplay of the component sound events. Try to make the patch as expressively satisfying as possible (on whatever terms are decided upon) by emphasizing subtle detail and variation of the individual sound events within an *episodic* structure that has some definable shape as a whole and some sense of movement toward an objective. Although many of these guidelines are subjective, any degree of forethought and any conscious attempt at defining the characteristics to be achieved will usually be apparent in the resulting patch.

Chapter 13

Spectrum Modulation

Of the several primary characteristics that define a sound, its spectral structure is the least easy to quantify or control. The spectral content of a sound is defined by the intricate relationships of many component frequencies and their relative amplitudes (which may be static or transient in nature). Most naturally occurring sounds have such finely articulated spectral structures that it would take an impractical number of VCOs (all perfectly tuned) and VCAs (all perfectly matched in their amplitude response) to create them by additive synthesis. Thus, the principal means of shaping the spectral characteristics of signals produced by an analog synthesizer is subtractive synthesis, or filtering (a discussion of the basic effects and uses of filtering is contained in Chapter 6).

VOLTAGE-CONTROLLED FILTERS (VCFs)

A voltage-controlled filter (VCF) allows voltages to be used to control such parameters as cut-off frequency, cut-off slope (resonance or Q), bandwidth, and center frequency. Although the voltage-controlled filter offered on live-performance synthesizers is often only a simple low-pass circuit allowing voltage control of the filter's cut-off frequency, several other filters—including high-pass, band-pass, and band-reject—are generally provided on more sophisticated studio synthesizer systems, often assimilated into a single unit called a *multimode VCF* (such as found on the Aries AR-3390, the Em 2120, and the ARP 2500). Since the functions of all basic filter configurations are integrated into such a unit, the following discussion will use the multimode VCF as a composite example of VCF operations and applications (Figure 13.1). It will also be assumed that the student is already familiar with the general operational and functional characteristics of filters as described earlier in Chapter 6.

Controls

The signal input of a VCF may be a single, unattenuated jack, or it may (as in Figure 13.1) consist of several independently attenuated jacks that act as a simple passive signal mixer. Since some analog synthesizers use VCFs as the dominant form of envelope formation (as opposed to the use of VCAs for this purpose), the ability to mix several input signals may be an essential final step before the signal is output from the synthesizer.

An initial cut-off frequency or center frequency can be manually set using a combination of the coarse and fine tuning controls. The cut-off frequency control-voltage input may be either attenuated or unattenuated (responding at a ratio of 1 volt/octave). This response ratio ensures that the filter's cut-off frequency will react in the same way to

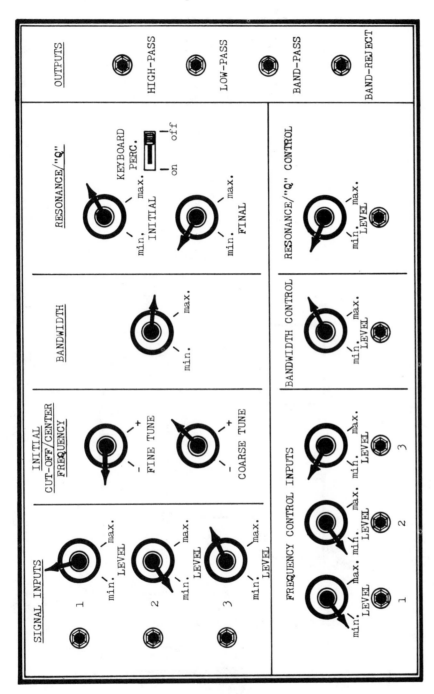

Figure 13.1 Composite Multimode VCF

changes in the control voltage as a VCO being controlled by the same voltage. Thus, as the frequency of a VCO input signal to the filter increases, the filter cut-off frequency controlled by the same voltage will increase at the same rate, producing a similar transient spectral envelope at each frequency (Patch No. 28).

The bandwidth controls normally provided consist of an initial bandwidth setting

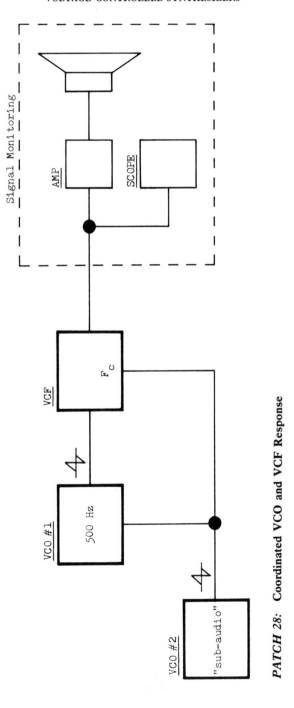

***PATCH** 28*: **Coordinated VCO and VCF Response**

pot and a control-voltage input jack (either attenuated or unattenuated). As the control voltage level increases, the bandwidth increases, allowing a wider range of frequencies to pass when the filter is used in the band-pass mode and a wider range of frequencies to be excluded when it is used in the band-reject mode. Naturally, the bandwidth control will have no effect when the filter is used in either the high-pass or the low-pass modes.

Resonance (Q or regeneration) can often be added at the cut-off frequencies of the filter (in some models this capability is limited to the low-pass filter component only, or to the low-pass section of the band-pass component), creating a particularly sharp cut-off slope and the potential for sufficient internal feedback at the cut-off frequency to make the filter "ring" or even oscillate on its own. The initial Q control is, of course, always active, but the final Q control will work only when the "keyboard percussion" control is activated. The keyboard percussion circuit merely links the resonance (Q) control of the filter directly to the keyboard's trigger and gate voltage outputs so that, when any key is depressed, a sudden increase in filter resonance will occur. The sharp, virtually instantaneous response of this circuit can enable the production of percussive effects from the filter that closely resemble "wooden" or "metallic" percussion instrument timbral envelopes, depending on the kind of audio signal fed into the filter. If the keyboard's DC voltage output is used to control the filter's cut-off frequency and its trigger/gate output is used to control the final resonance control, a variety of such effects can be obtained from different keys (Patch No. 29). When the keyboard percussion control is engaged, the final Q control pot is used to set the amount of filter resonance or regeneration that will be allowed after the keyboard's trigger/gate voltage has ended and the filter's initial resonance setting has subsided. Thus, a kind of "resonance envelope" is produced. The coordination of resonance control capabilities with other voltage-controllable signal characteristics (frequency or amplitude) is not as common or typical as it is with the filter's f_c and bandwidth, since resonance is not inherently or specifically related to changes in frequency.

In describing the application of the various control voltages to the VCF, control of the filter's cut-off frequency will be discussed first, since it is the predominant functional characteristic of the VCF and produces the most distinctly audible effects. Bandwidth and resonance (Q) modulation will be explored after the basic techniques of cut-off frequency modulation have been covered. Many of the following examples and patches will also assume the use of a low-pass filter, the workhorse in most filtering applications.

AC CONTROL VOLTAGES

Sub-Audio AC Control Voltages

Periodic variations in spectral content—such as those produced by modulating a VCF with an AC signal—do not normally occur in natural acoustic sounds, principally because all physical systems change their spectral characteristics as they gain or lose signal energy, making the spectral envelope more akin to transient envelopes than to AC variations. However, the special characteristics produced by periodic spectral modulation techniques have become commonplace in synthesized electronic music, particularly in its more popular forms. The colorful "sweeping" or "swooshing" sounds that may be produced by modulating the spectrum of an especially "rich" or complex signal source with a sub-audio sine wave controlling a band-pass or a low-pass filter can be very effective in many contexts, resembling the unique timbral cascading produced by a phase shifter.

Naturally, this type of periodic spectral modulation normally occurs at sub-audio frequencies, though the range over which the f_c varies might be as much as several octaves (by using a relatively unattenuated control signal). Figure 13.2 shows a typical

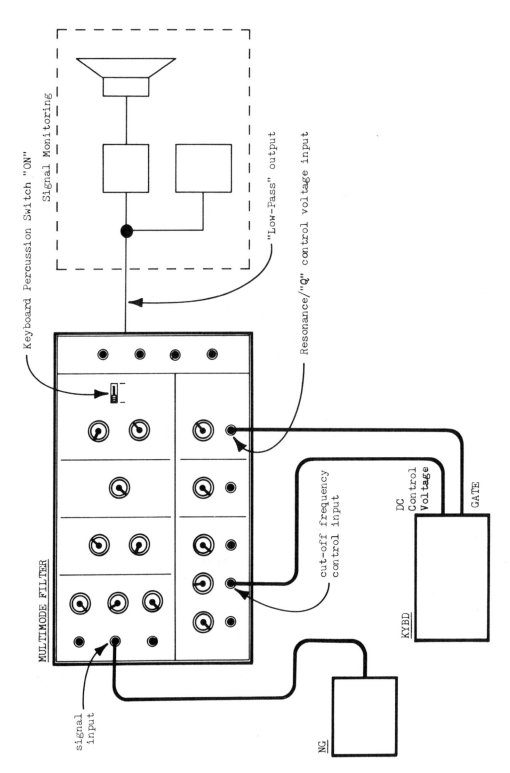

PATCH 29: **Keyboard Percussion**

338

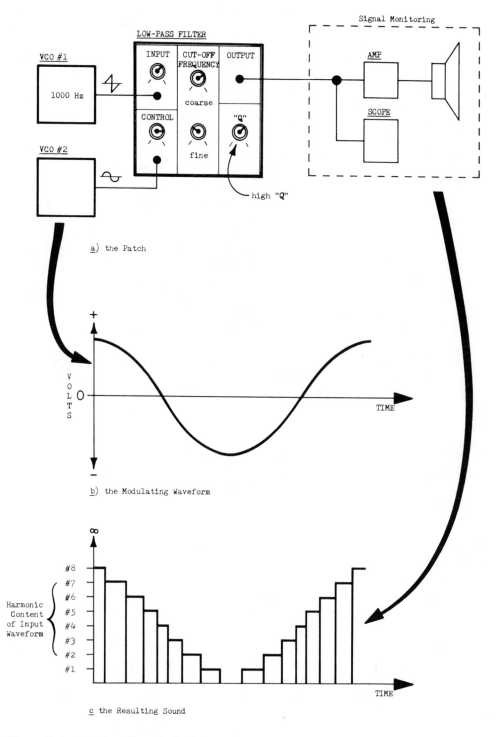

Figure 13.2 Filtering Through the Harmonics of an Audio Signal

set-up for simple spectrum modulation using an AC signal (sine wave) as the control signal, as well as a simplified graph of the effects of such modulation. Notice that the change in spectral content does not occur smoothly over time. Instead, the gradual change in the amplitude of the sine wave is translated into definite stages at which each harmonic of the audio input signal is filtered out or allowed to pass. If the resonance (Q) setting of the filter is high enough, an arpeggio on the harmonic components of the input waveform will be heard. (This effect is even more apparent if a band-pass filter with a high Q setting and a relatively narrow bandwidth is used instead of the low-pass filter.) It is also possible, as shown in this example, to drive the filter's f_c so low as to eliminate the input signal entirely, though the total effect then loses some of its subtlety.

The effects produced by using other sub-audio AC waveforms to control the cut-off frequency of a filter are easily predictable from what has already been learned about both frequency and amplitude modulation. Sawtooth waveforms may be used to create "stair-step" arpeggios of the harmonics of waveform inputs (if a high initial Q setting is used) or to produce gradually diminishing or increasing spectral complexity. Since a characteristic of most naturally occurring sounds is a gradual attenuation of their upper harmonics or partials—as the vibrating body producing the sound loses energy—the use of the inverted sawtooth waveform as a control signal can create an analogous (though less subtle) effect, particularly if the filter's action is coordinated with the simultaneous action of a VCA, as shown in Patch No. 30.

Owing to their instantaneous rise and decay times, pulse or square waveform control signals are very effective in producing percussive effects using either complex periodic waveforms or noise as the audio signal input. Variations in the filter's cut-off frequency, its resonance, and in the pulse-width of the control signal may be made to adjust the overall effect produced, which can be made quite subtle. Patch No. 31 illustrates a particularly interesting use of the variable pulse-width control input of an oscillator to produce delicate changes in the timbral characteristics of the audio input signal. (Try using a noise generator instead of the VCO as an audio input signal in this patch.) The percussive effects produced can be refined by carefully setting the initial f_c and by attenuating the f_c control signal input to various degrees. The use of a band-pass filter instead of a low-pass filter in this patch will also increase the definition of the timbral characteristics that are possible, especially if white noise is being used as the audio signal input.

Audio AC Control Voltages

As the frequency of the control waveform is increased, the usual "fuzziness" in the output signal will occur when the control frequency reaches about 20 to 40 Hz. Also as expected, when the frequency of the control waveform exceeds this frequency range, sideband frequencies will be produced. In effect, the filter's f_c is being changed fast enough to oscillate at an audio rate, resulting in the formation of a complex mixture of the audio input signal's frequency spectrum and the control waveform. This effect is much less pronounced or distinct than were the comparable effects of either frequency or amplitude modulation at audio frequency rates. However, this very obtuse quality can, in certain applications, be an asset. As in all forms of high-frequency modulation, the square and the pulse waveforms will produce the most precise results, due to their "binary" shape (either "on" or "off"). The other standard waveforms (sine, triangle, and sawtooth) produce a continually changing series of sideband frequencies, obscuring

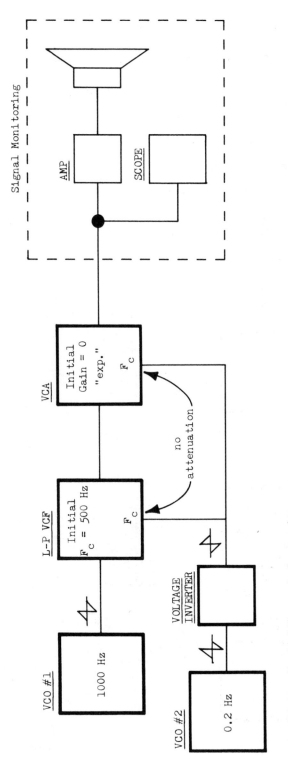

PATCH 30: **Gradual Harmonic Attenuation**

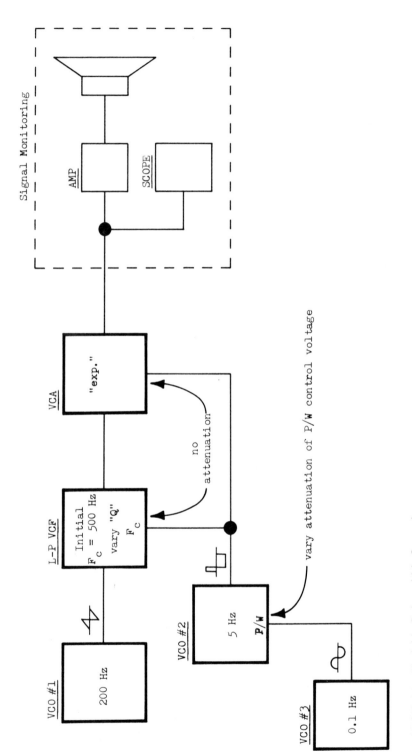

PATCH 31: **Variable Pulse-width Control**

the spectral results in the range between their maximum positive and negative amplitude values.

Processed AC Control Voltages

There is a noticeable tendency among those new to voltage-controlled synthesis processes to largely ignore the possibility of modifying the "basic" shapes of control waveforms in any way. It is often forgotten that the shape of a periodic control waveform is merely the result of its harmonic structure, and not the reverse; therefore, the waveform shape can be modified simply by altering that harmonic structure in some way, a process which is usually accomplished by selectively filtering out unwanted components. Figure 13.3 shows, in a simplified manner, what happens to the waveform shape when the upper harmonics of a square wave are gradually eliminated by a low-pass filter. Note in particular that the first change, when the filter has a relatively high cut-off frequency (Figure 13.3b), is a slight delay, or "lag," in the normally instantaneous rise of the waveform. Because the instantaneous voltage rise of a square wave (in particular) will often cause a VCA to "clip" (producing a "clicking" sound), a "lag processor" is offered on many analog synthesizers to alter this characteristic at will. But the same effect can be produced by processing the waveform using any available low-pass filter. As the cut-off frequency of the filter is lowered, the resulting shape of the waveform becomes less and less distinct (Figure 13.3c), until it finally becomes no more than a sine wave (the reasons for this were explained in the discussion of Fourier synthesis in Chapter 4). Patch No. 32 shows one possible arrangement for processing a control signal in this way using a lag processor or a low-pass filter. If the lag processor or the filter is itself voltage-controllable (dotted line), a number of different and unusual effects can be produced by the changing control signal waveform.

Other commonly available techniques for obtaining unusual control waveforms might involve the inversion of the waveform (especially the sawtooth waveform), the mixing of several different waveforms or waveform frequencies, or extending the number of levels of voltage control that are used (i.e., controlling the controller). A different example of the last of these techniques is shown in Patch No. 33, which produces a percussive sound in a rhythmic pattern determined by the frequency of the second-level control voltage (the sub-audio sawtooth waveform). A still different effect would be produced if the sawtooth waveform were inverted by a voltage inverter. In contrast, Patch No. 34 produces a varying timbral character by interjecting a second VCA to control the amplitude of the primary control signal. The subtle variations of control that are possible are virtually unlimited due to the numbers of, and manipulations of control voltage parameters, as implied in Patch No. 35.

DC CONTROL VOLTAGES

Since DC control signals are by their very nature discrete and gradual change is the natural characteristic of spectral modulation, the use of discrete DC signals to control spectral content is often too static to be of interest. However, there are exceptions to this general principle. As illustrated in Patch No. 36, discrete DC voltages (from a keyboard controller, in this example) can be used to coordinate the frequency produced by an audio VCO with the cut-off frequency of a VCF, resulting in a similar timbre being

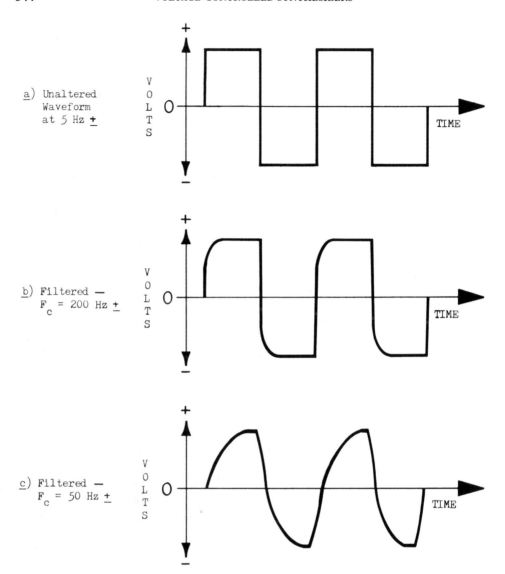

a) Unaltered
   Waveform
   at 5 Hz +

b) Filtered —
   F_c = 200 Hz +

c) Filtered —
   F_c = 50 Hz +

Figure 13.3   Low-Pass Filtering of a Sub-Audio Square Wave

produced for each pitch. (This is quite a different effect from that which would be produced if the filter's cut-off frequency remained always at one setting as the frequency of the audio input signal changed.)

The primary reason for using linear controllers or joystick controllers is their ability to introduce a transient effect into what is, as already stated, a static condition. If the resonance control of a narrowly focused band-pass VCF is set high enough so that the separate harmonics of an input signal are individually emphasized, the linear controller can then be used to move quickly from one harmonic or partial of the input signal to another, making it possible to actually "play" the overtones of a given tone.

As in most uses of the joystick controller, spatial movement of the sound in the

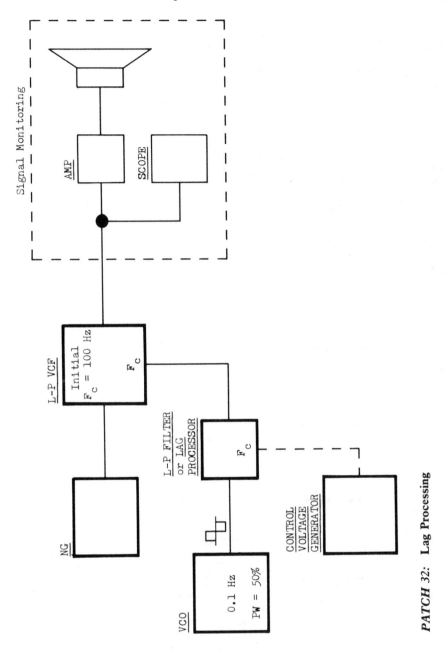

PATCH 32: **Lag Processing**

listening field is the most common objective. In using the joystick controller for spectrum modulation, one can control the spatial location of timbre, which may provide a very subtle or a very pronounced effect, depending on the control-voltage range. One possible set-up for this type of effect is shown in Patch No. 37. Notice that only one audio signal is being processed by the four different VCFs. Assuming that the final outputs of the four amplifiers are routed to loudspeakers spread around a room, the spectral characteristics of the perceived sound will shift in space as the joystick is moved around its axis. Whenever the cut-off frequency of one of the four VCFs is driven lower

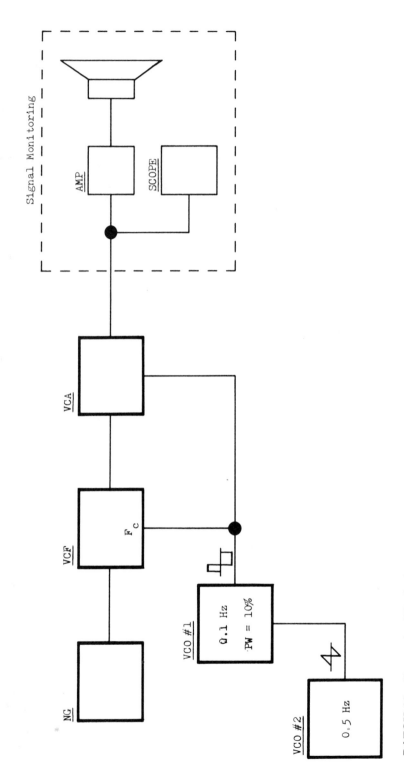

PATCH 33: **Percussive Rhythmic Patterns**

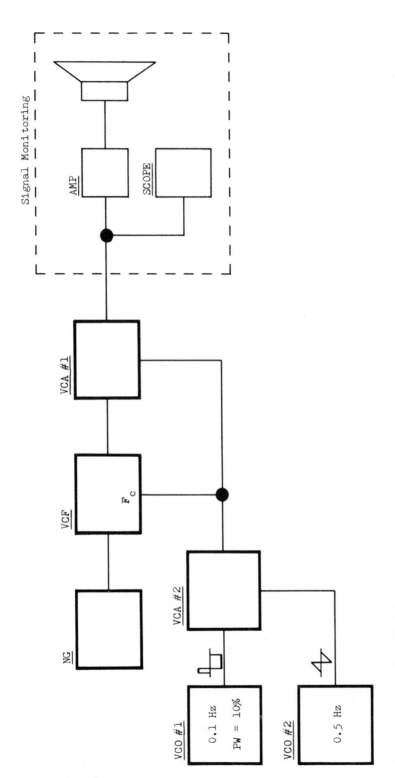

PATCH 34: **Timbral Variations**

347

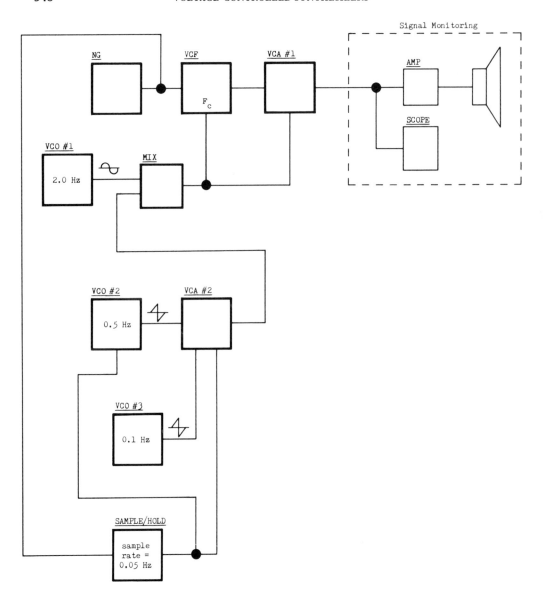

PATCH 35: **Control Variations**

than the audio input signal's fundamental frequency, the signal will be completely attenuated in that filter's speaker, producing a "null" in the movement of the sound.

TIME-VARIANT CONTROL VOLTAGES

As was the case with amplitude modulation, time-variant control voltages generally offer the greatest range of control contour and the greatest delineation of spectral character. The complexity of naturally occurring spectral envelopes is one of the basic means by which we define and differentiate the sounds of various instruments and natural sounds.

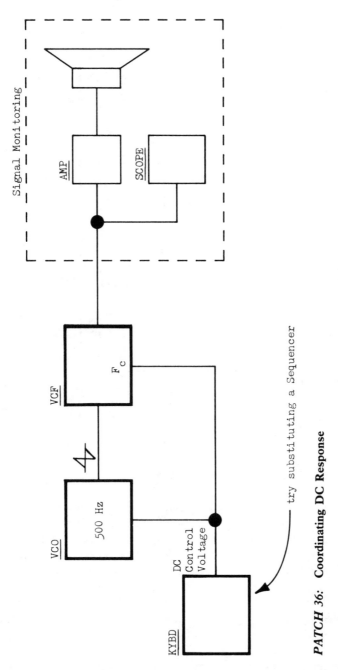

PATCH 36: **Coordinating DC Response**

The human auditory mechanism is so finely attuned to these transient spectral cues that, once trained by experience, it can easily distinguish among the individual characteristics of dozens of different instruments playing simultaneously, a feat no computer can yet match!

Thus, the importance of transient spectral envelopes makes the special characteristics of time-variant control voltages particularly useful. Although there are no significant differences in the operational characteristics of time-variant control-voltage generators,

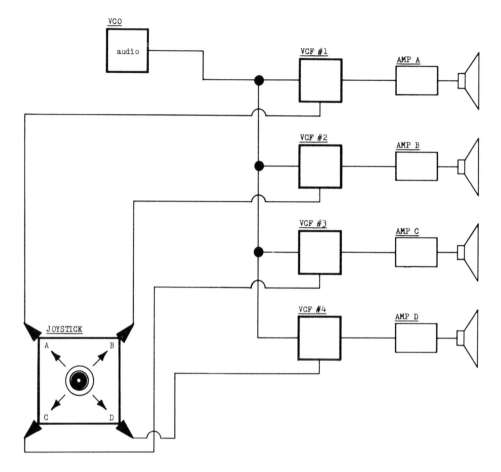

PATCH 37: **Spatial Control**

whether they are used for frequency, amplitude, or spectrum modulation, it might be useful to point out the exact effect a transient envelope can have on the spectral content of an audio input signal. Figure 13.4 illustrates in a very simplified manner how complex the careful control of transient spectral characteristics can become and how essential it is for the exact definition of a sound. Not only does the actual harmonic content of the sound change over time, but the relative energy levels of its different frequency components also vary over time (represented in the figure by different shadings). Further, all these spectral changes may occur very rapidly. Some sounds exhibit an even greater complexity than that shown in Figure 13.4 in as short a time span as several milliseconds.

There are several ways of achieving the kind of subtle, rapidly changing timbral effects implied in the example just given. As one might imagine, the use of multiple envelope generators to control the response of several VCFs and VCAs would be a basic requirement. One possibility is illustrated in Patch No. 38. (Ideally, all the filters shown in this patch, particularly VCFs #2 and #3, would be band-pass filters set to different pass-bands, but this may prove impractical in most studios. The filters shown here are all low-pass filters.) Notice that two envelope generators are used to control the three spectral ranges produced (high, medium, and low) as well as their relative amplitudes.

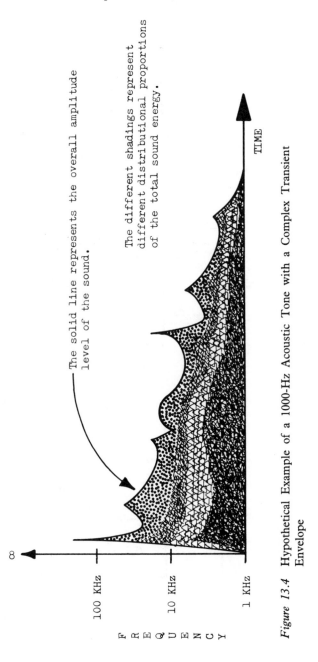

The different shadings represent different distributional proportions of the total sound energy.

The solid line represents the overall amplitude level of the sound.

TIME

100 KHz

10 KHz

1 KHz

FREQUENCY

Figure 13.4 Hypothetical Example of a 1000-Hz Acoustic Tone with a Complex Transient Envelope

The high-frequency range (VCF #1 and VCA #1) is controlled by the first envelope generator, producing an immediate surge of energy in this frequency range. This ADSR also controls the amplitude of the fundamental component in the low-frequency range (VCA #3). The second envelope generator produces more gradual response in the middle frequency range (VCF #2 and VCA #2) and in the low-frequency range (VCF #3). By carefully adjusting the initial cut-off frequencies of the three VCFs, the initial gain controls on the three VCAs, and the timing and level controls on the two ADSRs,

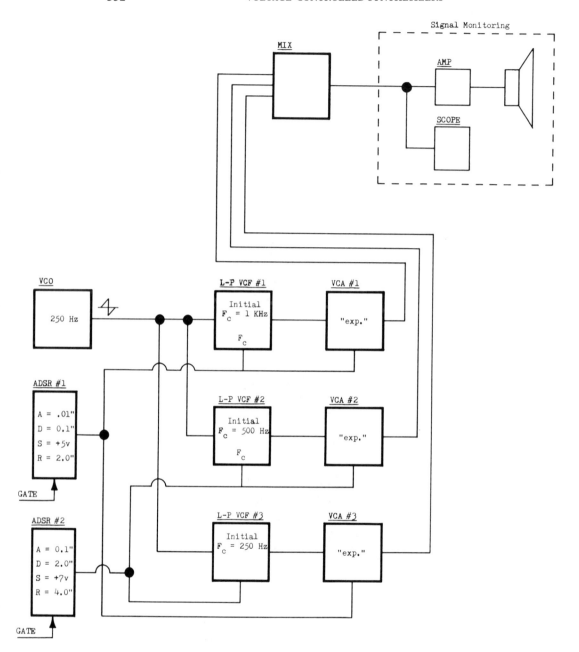

PATCH 38: **Complex Envelopes**

then balancing the three VCA outputs with the mixer, a fairly subtle spectral envelope for the final sound can be produced. Of course, the envelope generators can be triggered from any standard sources—keyboard controllers, electronic switches, low-frequency square wave oscillators, sequencers, etc. (actual trigger/gate sources are not shown in the illustration). In addition, the use of trigger/gate delays could further enhance the subtlety and complexity of the resulting effect.

The potential applications of other time-variant voltage-producing control modules, such as the envelope follower or the pitch follower, are essentially the same as those outlined in Chapters 10 and 12. Since the envelope follower produces a time-variant control voltage that is fairly analogous to the amplitude envelope of *any* signal input to the device, it is possible to use the control-voltage produced to control the spectral characteristics of one signal in coordination with the changing amplitude characteristics of a separate signal being analyzed by the envelope follower. Likewise, the pitch follower makes it possible to produce a spectral envelope for one signal that changes in relation to changes in the fundamental frequency of a different input signal.

One of the more commonly heard criticisms of electronic music is, ironically, that the equipment suffers from its too consistent response. The numerous quirks of acoustic musical instruments (and their human performers), which create all sorts of extraneous and sporadic buzzes, clicks, overtones, and noises, are to a large extent responsible for the unique "personality" of the sounds they produce. A good example of only one of these acoustic phenomena that was at first totally ignored, then successfully incorporated in the instrument's basic sound, is the "chiff" of a pipe organ. The chiff is a sudden, short-lived burst of upper harmonics that occurs whenever an organ key is depressed and a note is sounded. It is produced by the initial blast of air and the sudden increase in air pressure that follows within the organ pipe itself and is a natural part of the sound of the instrument. Disparaged by most nineteenth-century organ builders, who tried, with varying degrees of success, to remove this characteristic sound from their instruments, it was virtually essential to the delineation of separate contrapuntal melodic lines in music of earlier centuries. The creators of the first electronic organs totally ignored the significance of the chiff in attempting to create an "authentic" synthesis of organ sounds—perhaps due to a residual nineteenth-century distaste for the sound. However, contemporary electronic organ manufacturers have been extremely careful in their recreation of acoustic organs by producing a fairly realistic chiff in their instruments and sometimes even by allowing the amount of chiff to be regulated by the performer.

Another significant characteristic of acoustic instruments that has been too seldom taken into account in creating electronic "voices" is the timbral (spectral content) change that occurs in the sound of most instruments in their different frequency ranges. For example, the clarinet is said to have at least four *timbral registers* (discrete frequency ranges) (Figure 13.5), each of which emphasizes different spectral characteristics of the instrument's sound. (This can be easily demonstrated by having a clarinetist play several tones in each register and monitoring the results with a loudspeaker and an oscilloscope.) The lower part of the instrument's range (*a* in the figure) is called the "chalumeau" register and is dark and rich in spectral quality. The next higher group of notes (*b*) are called the "throat tones" and are pale and even "fuzzy" by comparison. The next higher octave (*c*) is made up of pitches which seem "bright" and "lively" while the highest register of the instrument (*d*) has pitches which may sound like those of a flute when played softly but which become chrill and piercing when played loudly. Generally, the lower frequencies of the instrument emphasize a more complex mixture of harmonics, while the amplitude energy of the tones become increasingly focused on the first few harmonics as the pitch (frequency) gets higher. These subtle registral differences can be very difficult to reproduce on electronic instruments.

The acoustic instrument examples of the organ and the clarinet are offered not as a suggestion that students strive to duplicate existing acoustic instrumental timbres (in the authors' opinion, an ultimately unrewarding application of electronic music) but to make

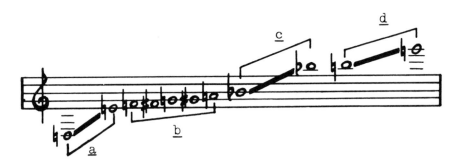

Figure 13.5 Timbral Registers of a Clarinet (sounding pitches)

students aware of the complexity of natural acoustic sounds and the consequent burden on the electronic music composer to create sounds of corresponding complexity and interest to the listener. The most dramatic and influential capability of electronic music is its capacity for creating new timbral resources and new ways of thinking about timbre as a compositional device. Thus, it cannot be overstated that careful attention to the spectral characteristics of synthesized sounds (particularly their transient relationships) is essential in the electronic music studio.

RANDOM AND SEQUENTIAL CONTROL VOLTAGES

Random Control Voltages

Random changes in spectral content are not idiomatic to acoustic musical instruments; however, they are quite easy to produce using electronic devices such as filtered noise generators or sample/hold controllers. A control voltage derived from filtered noise may be extremely complex or relatively simple, depending on the kind and degree of filtering used. Patch No. 39 illustrates the use of highly filtered white noise to control the random selection of the harmonics resulting from a complex waveform mixture (a square wave at 1000 Hz and a sawtooth wave at 1500 Hz, the amplitude balance between them being controlled by the mixer). As the degree of resonance (Q) of the filter is reduced, the final modulation effect will become more sinuous and difficult to characterize. The student should experiment with different cut-off frequency and Q settings of both low-pass filters used in this patch.

The use of a sample/hold controller to modulate a VCF results in the cut-off frequency of the VCF being set to various random but discrete frequency levels at a pace or "tempo" determined by the sampling rate. This effect is related to the discrete control that could be provided by keyboard controllers or sequencers, except that it is random to the extent that the signal being sampled is random. If a periodic waveform is the sampled signal, a periodic pattern of spectral changes would result, as is the case in Patch No. 40, where a "stair-step" control signal is produced by the sample/hold controller sampling a sawtooth wave. The characteristic effect of these discrete changes can, of course, be mitigated or even blurred altogether by using a lag processor between the sample/hold controller and the VCF, but the general character of the sample/hold circuit is the production of discrete DC voltage changes. The complex, unpredictable results of

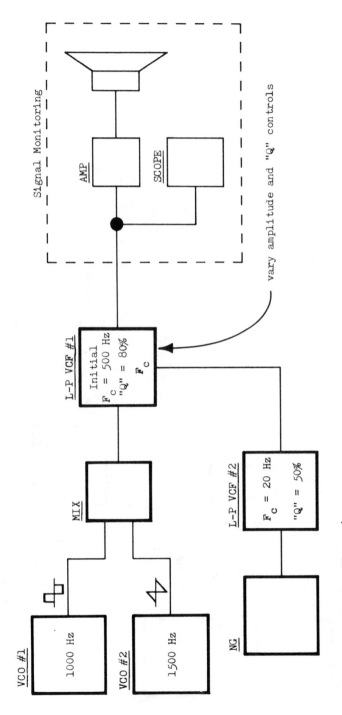

PATCH 39: **Random Harmonics**

355

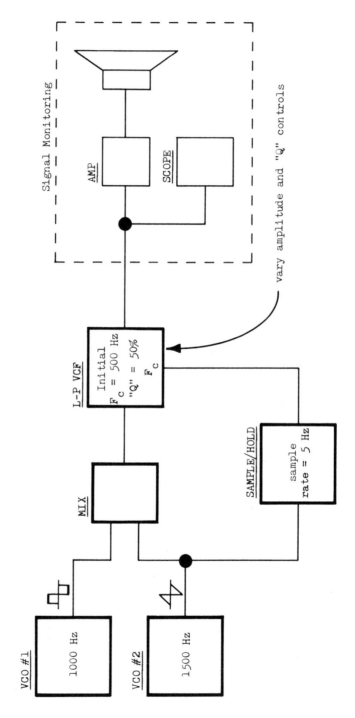

PATCH 40: "Stair-step" Control Signals

raising the sample rate into the audio frequency range will be similar to the effects produced by using AC control signals in their audio frequency range.

Sequential Control Voltages

As previously discussed in this chapter under *DC Control Voltages*, the usefulness of producing discrete changes in the spectral content of an audio signal is limited. Tying the cut-off frequency of a filter to the frequency produced by a sub-audio VCO is advantageous in some applications (as was shown in Figure 13.2). Other sequential effects, such as arpeggiation on the harmonics of an audio signal (shown in several previous patches), or the production of rhythmic ostinati (via the sequencer) made up of percussive noises, are also possible. As was the case with the sample/hold controller, if the sequencing rate rises into the audio frequency range, some very complex timbral effects may be produced. The many adjustable stages of the sequencer make it possible to fine tune these effects very accurately. If patches such as Patch No. 15, No. 16, and No. 17 (Chapter 11) and No. 26 (Chapter 12) are adapted so that the sequential controller is controlling a VCF instead of (or in addition to) the VCOs and VCAs that are indicated, the possibilities of a wide variety of spectral effects will become apparent.

OTHER FORMS OF VCF CONTROL

Voltage-Controlled *Q*

Since the resonance (*Q*) setting of a filter determines the cut-off slope of a simple high- or low-pass filter to such a great extent, it can be advantageous to use a control voltage to make changes in a filter's resonance. The dramatic effect that changes in the resonant response of a VCF can have are hinted at in Patch No. 41. Here the resonance of the VCF varies periodically (at a rate of 0.3 Hz) during the production of a tone (from VCO #1) that is rapidly repeated (10 times per second) at the same time that the cut-off frequency of the VCF is being slowly modulated. The coordinated use of the VCA heightens the repetitive effect that is produced. Resonance control can also be extremely useful in shaping the spectral content of white noise, especially in conjunction with a narrow-bandwidth, band-pass VCF. Try Patch No. 40 using a noise generator as the audio signal source instead of VCO #1, and use a band-pass filter in place of the low-pass VCF indicated.

Voltage-Controlled Bandwidth

The effects of bandwidth modulation can best be shown with a patch similar to the resonance example (Patch No. 40). Simply substitute control of the *Q* (of the low-pass filter) with control of the bandwidth of a band-pass filter. (Note that variations in the resonance or *Q* of the filter will largely determine how easily perceivable the results of the bandwidth modulation are.) Naturally, the most noticeable variation occurs when the initial bandwidth is very narrow, since the applied control voltage will cause the bandwidth to expand. Try the same set-up using the band-reject mode of the filter (if your synthesizer offers it), and note the differences.

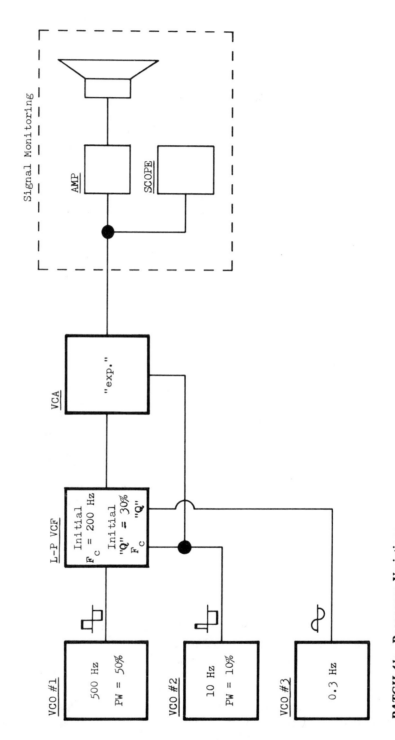

PATCH 41: **Resonance Variations**

COMBINED AC, DC, TIME-VARIANT, AND RANDOM/SEQUENTIAL CONTROL VOLTAGES

Given that a certain degree of timbral complexity and variety is desirable in most sounds, different control-voltage combinations and multilevel control functions are often used simultaneously. It is difficult to make specific recommendations as to which combinations will prove the most effective or even the most typical, since "anything goes," and "anything" has at least the chance of achieving a usable effect. The only advice that can be given with any degree of confidence is to try everything, every possible single- and multi-level control-voltage configuration, and note the effects produced. With that in mind, Patch No. 42 is offered as an incentive to further experimentation. Try changing the various control parameters shown and listen for the audible changes produced. Of course, the goal is to learn to *predict* what changes will occur before they actually happen. Patch No. 42 *looks* very complicated, but how many control voltage levels are actually used? Which control parameters have a more important or noticeable effect on the patch than others? What would happen if some of the control voltage sources indicated were switched with other control-voltage sources, or replaced by others not indicated?

PATCHING PROJECT NO. 5

Plan, produce, and diagram a patch that involves spectrum modulation as the most significant element of its organization and development over time. Particular attention should be given to the development of subtle and complex timbral relationships. Specific requirements may be determined, and evaluation guidelines developed, according to the outlines for earlier patching projects.

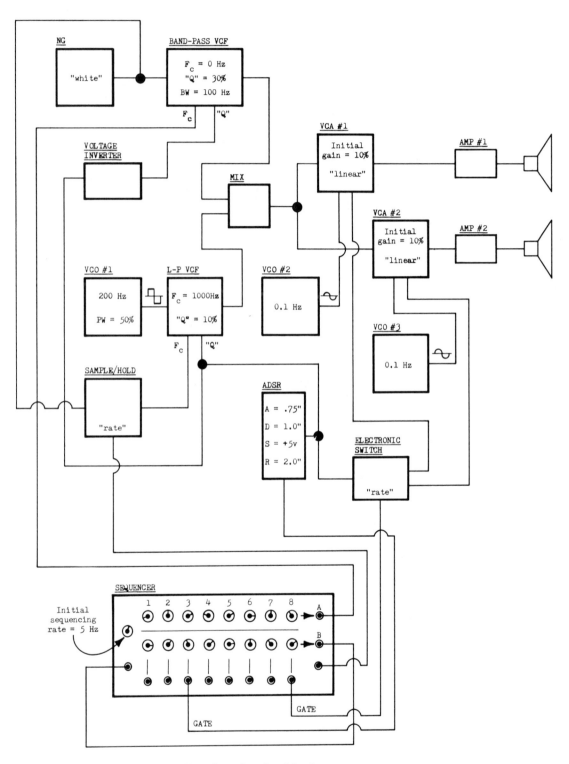

PATCH 42: Very Complex Combinations

Chapter 14
Combined Modulations

Any discussion of combined frequency, amplitude, and spectrum modulation must be prefaced with a disclaimer: no such discussion could hope to be comprehensive. The purpose of this chapter is to merge the individual modulation concepts and applications covered so far in Part II into a rational approach to the synthesis of complex sound events having a variety of simultaneously controlled parameters. The many patching configurations that might occur from the application of this all-encompassing approach to voltage-controlled synthesis are limitless. In fact, it is quite rare that a synthesizer patch will involve only one form of voltage-controlled modulation at a time. Accurate synthesis of the subtleties of a perceived or imagined sound will, more often than not, require the composer to consider the simultaneous application of all types of modulation.

Naturally, it is assumed that the need for a more or less rational and systematic approach toward voltage-controlled synthesis is necessary. Although the point can be made that improvisation with the available synthesis equipment can often lead to esthetically satisfying results, and is certainly necessary when one is new to the voltage-controlled synthesizer, it is also usually true that some type of planning takes place even in the most casual circumstances, because the electronic music composer—unlike any other musician—must actually define and "build" his instrument before he can begin to "play" it.

TOTAL VOLTAGE-CONTROLLED SYNTHESIS

Starting Points

The discussion of control-voltage applications and their effects has thus far been fairly limited to modulations of only one parameter (frequency, amplitude, and spectrum) at a time. In actual synthesis situations, such a narrow focus would be very rare indeed. Most synthesized sounds result from the application of several concurrent means of modulation and modification. Added to this must be the many possibilities of processing synthesizer signals by devices external to the synthesizer, devices such as those discussed in Chapters 6 and 7. Such processing is not limited to the final synthesizer output signal but can occur at any point or at many points in the synthesizer patch. The fact that this text has so far been divided into two parts, "Tape and Electronic Music" and "Voltage-Controlled Synthesizers," is not meant to imply that these two approaches are mutually exclusive. Well-equipped studios such as those found in large universities are usually designed to permit the integration of both kinds of equipment and both approaches.

ADDITIVE PROCESSES

There are several ways in which total voltage-controlled synthesis may be approached. Patch No. 43, given in six increasingly complex stages, shows how the characteristics of a single sound (a 1000-Hz square wave tone, in this case) can be increasingly controlled and manipulated by adding processing modules and control-voltage sources. The first stage shows one of the very simplest sound-producing configurations: a sound source that is merely amplified and reproduced. Simple frequency modulation of this tone by a sub-audio sine wave (in Stage 2) produces vibrato. Control of the amplitude envelope of the resulting audio tone is introduced in Stage 3 by adding a VCA to the signal path. The VCA is shown in a somewhat typical set-up, with a four-stage envelope generator as its control-voltage input. A simple voltage-gate (switch) source for the ADSR is shown at this stage. The configuration shown in Stage 4 shifts the control source emphasis to a keyboard controller, which produces discrete DC voltages to control the frequency of the audio signal source and the necessary trigger/gate voltages for controlling the operation and timing of the envelope generator. This is one of the simplest keyboard-oriented patches possible, permitting the simultaneous control of both the pitch and the amplitude of the sound.

The addition of spectrum modulation to the patch in Stage 5 produces a very basic but fully realized sound. Although the VCF could just as well have been controlled by the same envelope generator that is used to control the VCA, the contrasting envelopes produced by the two envelope generators are used to form a more complex transient envelope. Notice that the keyboard controller's DC voltage output, used to control the frequency of the audio signal source VCO, is also used to control the cut-off frequency of the VCF. Thus, every pitch produced by the audio VCO will have the same spectral content and amplitude shape. The final stage shown in this illustration (but not the limit of our possibilities!) changes the focus of the primary control-voltage source from the manual keyboard to an "automated" sample/hold module. The unique aspect of this stage of the patch is the use of the sub-audio (2 Hz) sawtooth waveform to produce both the trigger/gate voltages (through a Schmitt Trigger Generator) needed to control the two envelope generators. The relationship between the frequency of the sawtooth waveform and the sampling rate of the sample/hold controller will have a substantial effect on the final sound.

Throughout the multiple stages of Patch No. 42, the underlying motivation is to produce a "tone," which might be defined as any single pitch with a relatively independent character. As the sequence of stages in this patch progresses, the character of this tone becomes increasingly refined, until the specific amplitude and spectral dimensions applied to it create the sense of individually distinct sound events occurring. The additional control (manual, then automated) of the frequency of the tone produced does not obscure the basic identity of the "voice" created, a term which can loosely be defined as any sound or set of sounds that maintains a definite and recognizable identity, with relatively little regard to the frequency range in which it occurs or to changes in its overall loudness.

Obviously, the concept of "tones" and "voices" is implicit in most instrumental music, where an instrument maintains a more-or-less definite and identifiable character, regardless of the actual frequency of the tone produced (though relatively minor changes in spectral character that normally occur over the different frequency ranges of most acoustic musical instruments are essential to their subtle expressiveness). Thus, the

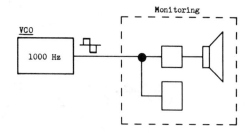

Stage 1

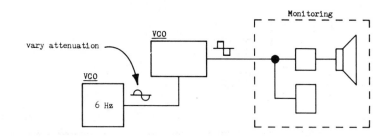

Stage 2

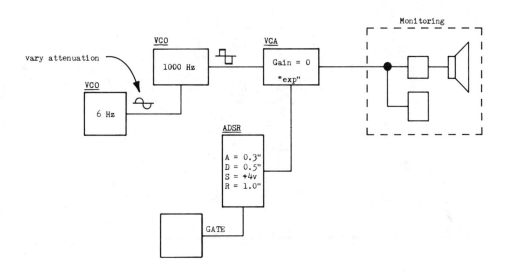

Stage 3

PATCH 43: **Possible Stages of Synthesis**

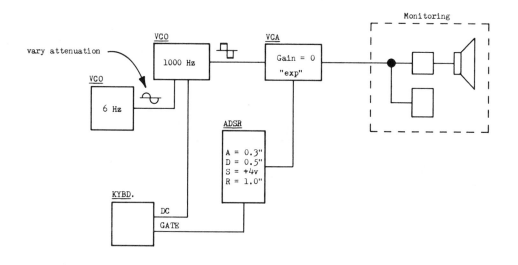

Stage 4

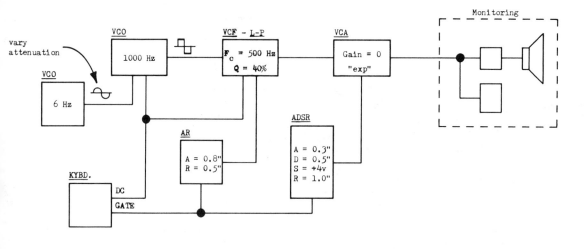

Stage 5

PATCH 43   Continued

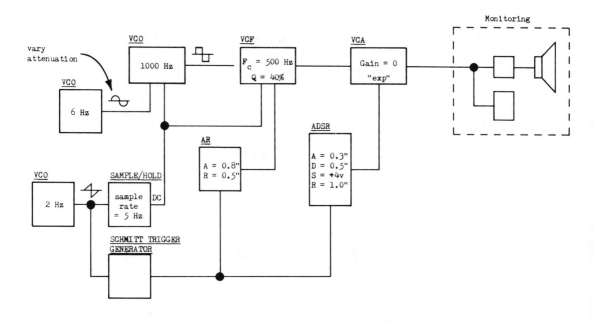

Stage 6

PATCH 43   *Continued*

approach to synthesis that is shown in Patch No. 43 is entirely conventional in that the "instrument" that is gradually created from the available synthesizer modules resembles (in its effect) the acoustic musical instruments with which we are already familiar. There is nothing inherently wrong with this mimicry of familiar acoustic properties. However, there are other ways of approaching sound synthesis.

ABSTRACT PROCESSES

Whenever you stand in front of the synthesizer and attempt to use it to create a sound, you are, in essence, creating the instrument you will be working with by determining how the modules of the synthesizer will interrelate. The creative process in electronic music synthesis is, therefore, potentially much more complex than is the case when a composer is working with a collection of known accustic musical instruments. However, there are a few general approaches to this aspect of sound synthesis that can illuminate some of the more abstract processes involved. Figure 14.1 outlines, in a very simplified form, some of the qualities, parameters, and options that must be considered in creating a particular synthesized sound and, hence, the resources required for its production. The available modulating and modifying options (including those covered in Chapters 6 and 7) remain fairly consistent for each functional stage in the creation of abstract sounds.

The first and most important step in producing an abstract sound, especially one with which we are not familiar through prior experience, is to have a somewhat detailed mental image of what the sound should be. This may be more difficult to do than it might at first seem. There is something particularly vague about purely imagined sounds

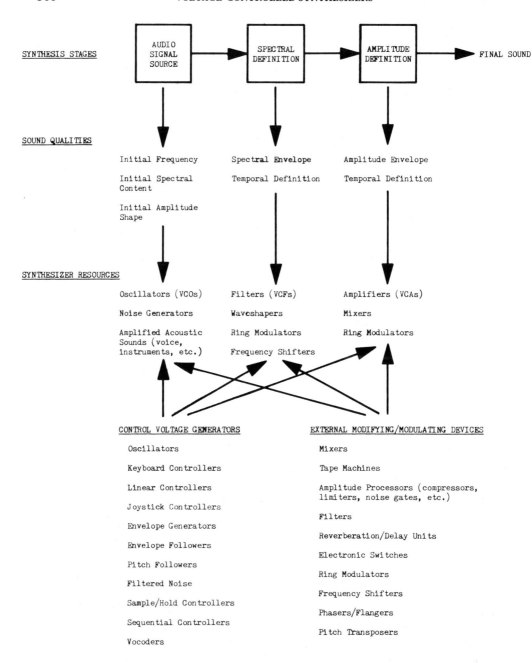

Figure 14.1   Synthesized Sound Resources

that makes them difficult to analyze, especially in terms of available synthesis options when one is still new to analog synthesis. But, the ability to discern the component characteristics of an imagined sound, and the understanding of how to actually produce it in the studio, improves with experience—especially if one begins to listen more carefully to everyday sounds and attempts to hear their constituent elements. For example, what are the primary qualities that distinguish the sound of a police car siren? Of thunder? Of various bird calls? Of the sound of waves breaking on a beach?

Once an initial mental image of the desired sound is formed, creation of the sound depends on the definition of the sound's basic characteristics. Each of the sounds mentioned above has its own unique frequency, spectrum, and amplitude characteristics, all of which usually change over the passage of time. As an example, imagine and analyze the sound of a thunderclap. Its basic sonic material is obviously very low-frequency noise. Its spectral character is more-or-less random, composed of several unevenly dispersed transient spectral envelopes, and its amplitude envelope can also be complex and random. The temporal definition of the sound (how it changes over time) is irregular, sometimes even occurring in several overlapping stages or distinct layers. Having determined these qualities of the sound, it should be possible to choose the appropriate arrangement of synthesizer modules (signal sources, control sources, processing devices, etc.) required to produce the sound we have imagined. Patch No. 44 illustrates how this synthesis process might work by proceeding in several stages from the production of the most basic elements of the desired sound to the production and control of its more subtle spectral, amplitude, and temporal qualities, until the desired sound is finally achieved. Stage 1 of the patch shows the identification and use of the basic sound source required: white noise—though at this point the audible output of the noise generator hardly resembles the desired final result. There is too much high-frequency content in the signal. Stage 2 more clearly defines the desired final sound by manually filtering out all of the middle- and high-frequency signal content so that all that remains of the white noise sound source is a low-frequency rumble. Some filter resonance (Q) will tend to emphasize and amplify these remaining low frequencies. Stage 3 allows the low-pass filter's cut-off frequency to be varied by an envelope generator, which causes the filter to pass a changing but limited range of low-frequency noise. The control settings of the envelope generator may vary depending on the temporal/spectral characteristics of the thunderclap desired, and its output may have to be attenuated.

A more sophisticated and convincingly complex amplitude envelope is created in Stage 4 by combining the effects of two envelope generators using two independent gate sources. Finally, Stages 5 and 6 show two different ways of producing the voltage-gates needed for the two envelope generators automatically, and in a more-or-less random fashion. In any of the six stages of this patch the possibility of using signal processing devices external to the synthesizer should be apparent. Perhaps the most obvious of these possibilities would be to use a reverberation unit to "fatten" the sound, probably by placing it after the VCA indicated in the signal path.

Obviously, the production of a thunderclap is still a fairly simple example of what can prove to be a much more complex process, but the mechanics of the process remain much the same for the synthesis of any desired sound, real or imagined. At each stage in the development of a desired patch it is necessary to carefully adjust amplitude levels and control parameters, as well as to consider what the next stage of control should entail, generally following the approach set out in Patch No. 44, with its multiple stages of increasing complexity and subtlety. Even after the desired sound has finally been created, there is always the possibility that further "fiddling" with the available controls might produce an imaginative, unexpected, and potentially useful variant of the original sound.

VARIATION PROCESSES

The capacity of the analog voltage-controlled synthesizer to produce an enormous variety of sonic relationships with relatively minor variations in signal and control module

Stage 1

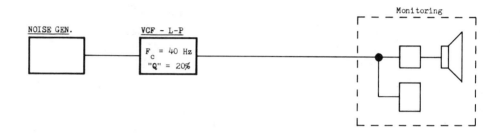

Stage 2

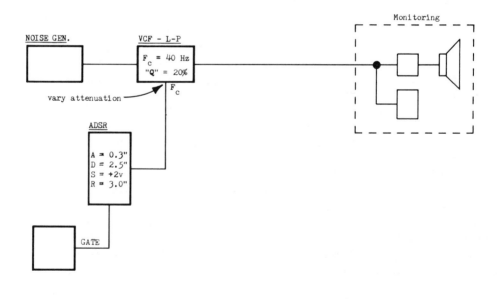

Stage 3

PATCH 44: **Synthesizing a Preconceived Sound**

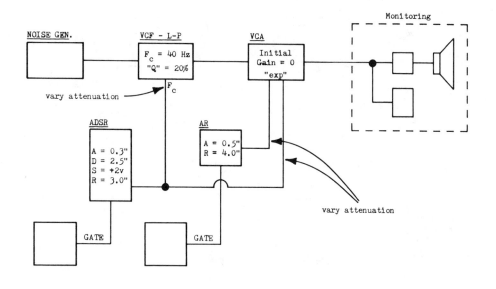

Stage 4

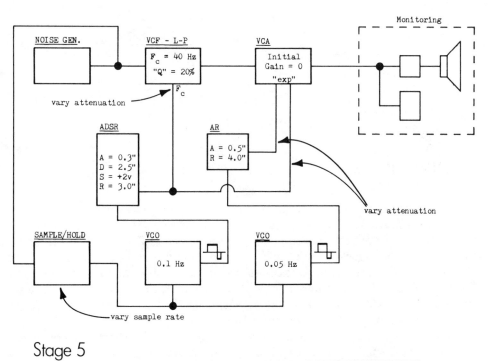

Stage 5

PATCH 44   Continued

369

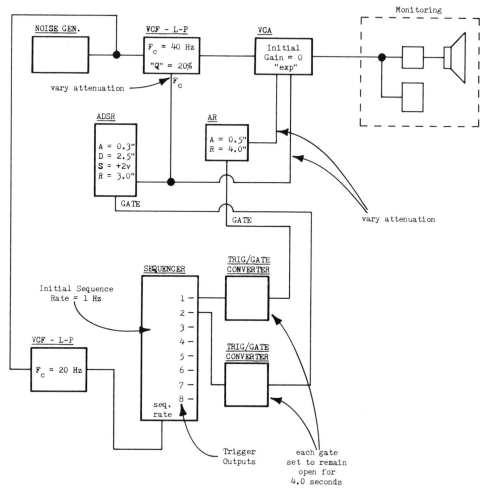

Stage 6

PATCH 44   **Continued**

settings is probably one of its most frustrating but uniquely valuable aspects. There are occasions when the production of variations of the original synthesized sound can become an integral part of the composer's creative process. The object of this kind of exploration is not to meander aimlessly from one sound to another, but to gradually change certain module settings and control parameters while noting the different sonic effects produced. Even more important is to discover and understand *why* these changes are produced, providing the kind of knowledge that will lead to ever more consciously creative and imaginative work with the synthesizer.

Patch No. 45 shows the progress of a patch through several distinct variations. First, the synthesizer configuration is broken down into its basic elements in Patch No. 45a: sound production, spectral control, amplitude control, frequency control (of which there are two distinct components shown), and timing control. Each of these elements can be varied, but, to ensure that it is possible to hear and to understand the effect of any

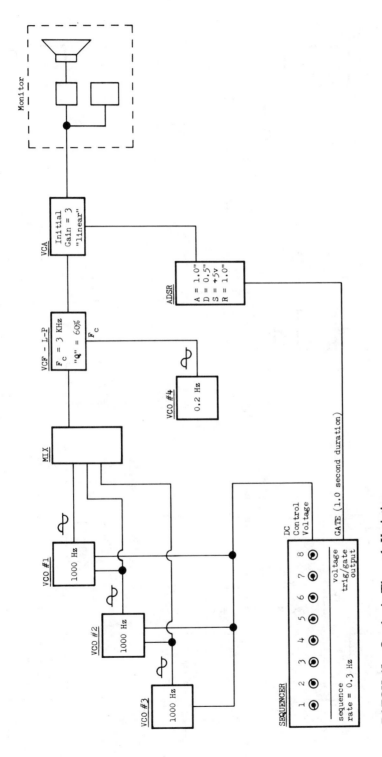

PATCH 45: **Synthesis Through Variation**

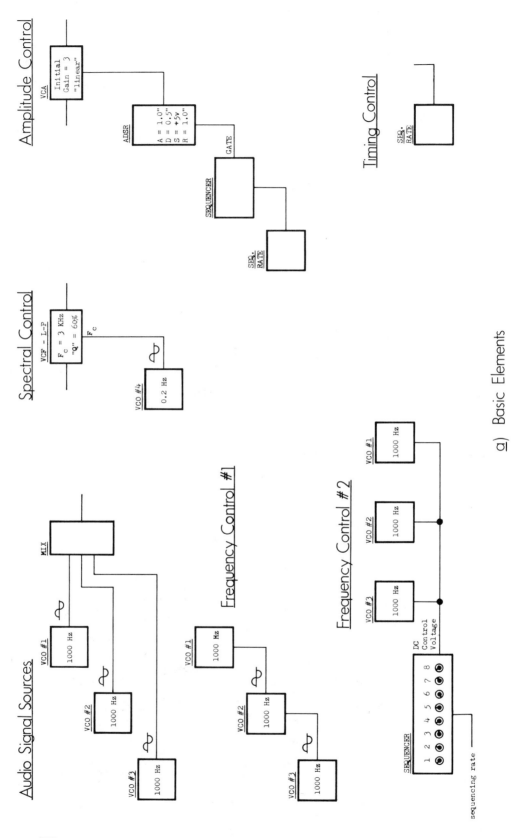

Amplitude Control

VCA
Initial Gain = 3 "linear"

ADSR
A = 1.0"
D = 0.5"
S = +5v
R = 1.0"

GATE

SEQUENCER

SEQ. RATE

Timing Control

SEQ. RATE

Spectral Control

VCF - L-P
F_c = 3 KHz
"Q" = 60%

F_c

VCO #4
0.2 Hz

Audio Signal Sources

MIX

VCO #1
1000 Hz

VCO #2
1000 Hz

VCO #3
1000 Hz

Frequency Control #1

VCO #1
1000 Hz

VCO #2
1000 Hz

VCO #3
1000 Hz

Frequency Control #2

VCO #1
1000 Hz

VCO #2
1000 Hz

VCO #3
1000 Hz

DC Control Voltage

SEQUENCER
1 2 3 4 5 6 7 8

sequencing rate

a) Basic Elements

PATCH 45   Continued

372

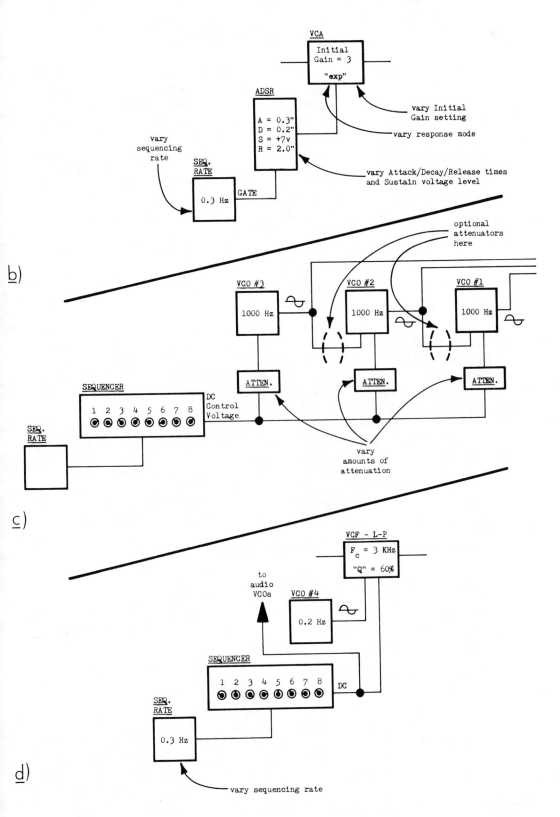

b)

VCA

Initial
Gain = 3

"exp"

vary Initial
Gain setting

vary response mode

ADSR

A = 0.3"
D = 0.2"
S = +7v
R = 2.0"

vary Attack/Decay/Release times
and Sustain voltage level

vary
sequencing
rate

**SEQ.
RATE**

0.3 Hz

GATE

c)

optional
attenuators
here

VCO #3

1000 Hz

VCO #2

1000 Hz

VCO #1

1000 Hz

SEQUENCER

1 2 3 4 5 6 7 8

DC
Control
Voltage

**SEQ.
RATE**

ATTEN.

ATTEN.

ATTEN.

vary
amounts of
attenuation

d)

VCF - L-P

F_c = 3 KHz

"Q" = 60%

to
audio
VCOs

VCO #4

0.2 Hz

SEQUENCER

1 2 3 4 5 6 7 8

DC

**SEQ.
RATE**

0.3 Hz

vary sequencing rate

PATCH 45   Continued

373

changes made, only one element should be worked with at a time. For example, Patch No. 45b shows a few of the changes that can be made in the basic amplitude envelope. The change is from a gradually undulating amplitude in the envelope of the original sound to a more forcefully dramatic attack and decay in the amplitude shape of the sound. An even more extensive variation occurs in Patch No. 45c where, by attenuating the control-voltage inputs to the three audio VCOs by differing amounts, not only is the audio signal mixture directly affected, but so is each VCO's control of the next VCO's frequency. The possible results are so complex that they are virtually unpredictable. The last variation illustrated (in Patch No. 45d) requires a change in the sequencing rate and the subsequent use of the DC control voltages to control the VCF as well as the three audio VCOs. At this point, if all of the variations outlined above were to be combined, the resulting patch would be quite different from the original patch, and many more variations could still be made.

PATCHING PROJECT NO. 6

Develop a complex patch that makes use of at least three different types of control-voltage generators to control and modulate the frequency, spectrum, and amplitude characteristics of a synthesized sound. Begin with a written description of the qualities of the basic sound you would like to produce. Then, draw a block diagram of the basic patch that you believe will result in the desired sound. Try the patch and make any alterations and adjustments to it that are necessary to approximate the desired sound, noting any changes that are needed. Make an accurate block diagram of the final patch, including those places where control settings may be effectively varied, and record the resulting sound(s) on tape. As a check on the accuracy and completeness of your block diagram, have another student reproduce the patch without your guidance and compare the results with your own. Last, produce a series of "variations" on your patch that you can "perform" and explain before the class within a five- or ten-minute period.

PROJECT NO. 5: *Voltage-Controlled Synthesizer Tape Project*

Many, if not most, electronic music compositions require that a practical knowledge of voltage-controlled synthesis techniques be combined with a fairly comprehensive use of both tape music techniques and classical electronic music techniques, which, in part, explains the organization of this text. Having covered the operation of the various synthesizer modules and examined some of their potential relationships in an exploratory rather than a creative context, it is now important to exercise the techniques of voltage-controlled synthesis in conjunction with the tape and electronic music practices covered earlier in Part I.

For the purposes of this project, it may be useful for the instructor or the students to set a few, perhaps arbitrary, guidelines requiring the use of a specific range of the available equipment, several voltage-controlled synthesis, tape, and electronic techniques, and a prescribed time limit. Regardless of the number and the degree of the restrictions placed on this project, or of the range of the synthesizer equipment available, the planning, documentation, and evaluation procedures used in earlier projects should also be followed here. The suggested sequence of production steps listed below may be helpful in defining your own procedures:

1. Define the basic "structure" of the production process, that is, the number of "voices" or channels used, the basic formal design of the project (the development of one basic sound idea or concept throughout, the alternation of different sound ideas, the juxtaposition or layering of several sound ideas, etc.),* and its overall length.
2. Determine the nature of the sound events to be used, then make block diagrams for all of the patches needed to produce the desired sounds.
3. Diagram the relationships of the chosen sound events and the "voices" in some form of score that is precise enough to illustrate to someone unfamiliar with the work how it is structured.
4. Produce a thorough set of written production steps that reduce the actual production process to the most efficient routine possible.
5. Create the source sound events, refining the concepts and patches earlier sketched in the block diagrams. Revise all block diagrams to indicate any changes and annotate them thoroughly and accurately enough so that the sounds they represent may be reproduced by someone not involved in their original production.
6. Execute the score, being certain to make complete notes of any necessary deviations from the production plan.
7. Evaluate the final project results according to the quality of the tape production, the complexity and subtlety of the relationships of the sounds used, the accuracy and reproducibility of the score and block diagrams, and the efficiency of the production process.

THE VOLTAGE-CONTROLLED SYNTHESIZER STUDIO

The three equipment lists for voltage-controlled synthesizer component modules given below are meant to complement the three classic analog equipment lists that were given at the end of Part I. For minimally funded studios, the only equipment from the lists at the end of Part I that is absolutely essential are those items found under the headings of *Tape Studio Equipment* and *Miscellaneous Support Equipment*. Many of the items listed under *Electronic Signal Sources, Electronic Signal Modifiers,* and *Electronic Signal Modulators* are found as components of most voltage-controlled synthesizers.

The voltage-controlled synthesizer requirements of list number one, and to a lesser extent list number two, can often be met by a self-contained synthesizer, such as the popular ARP 2600 or the newer live-performance oriented instruments made by Moog, Roland, ARP, and other manufacturers. The needs of list number three, and to a lesser extent list number two, will be best met by a large, completely modular synthesizer (no hard-wired patches at all), such as the Serge or Moog studio models. In these cases, the exact module configuration of the synthesizer is determined by the user (and the user's budget!) at the time of purchase. The goal of this type of truly modular design is that of maximum flexibility, for which the live-performance capability of hard-wired or pre-patched and self-contained synthesizer units is generally sacrificed. A further point to be kept in mind is that such truly modular design formats can be added onto at any

---

* Formal design will be covered more thoroughly in Part III, when we discuss compositional concepts in relation to electronic music. At this point, formal structure is still less important than technical expertise.

time, permitting the user to start out with a relatively simple configuration (such as that of list number one) and gradually add more modules.

EQUIPMENT LIST #1: a basic voltage-controlled synthesizer consisting of at least the following items:

- three voltage-controlled oscillators (possibly two audio, one sub-audio)
- one noise generator
- one voltage-controlled low-pass filter
- one envelope generator (AR or ADSR)
- one voltage-controlled amplifier
- one ring modulator
- one monophonic keyboard controller
- one mixer
- miscellaneous attenuators, multiples, etc.

EQUIPMENT LIST #2: a moderate sized synthesizer consisting of some combination of the following modules:

- four or five voltage-controlled oscillators
- one noise generator
- one voltage-controlled low-pass filter
- one voltage-controlled high-pass filter
- one voltage-controlled multimode filter (low-pass/high-pass/band-pass/band-reject)
- two or three envelope generators (AR and ADSR)
- two voltage-controlled amplifiers
- one ring modulator
- one electronic switch
- one monophonic or duophonic keyboard controller
- one sample/hold circuit
- one envelope follower
- one voltage processor unit (inverter, lag processor, etc.)
- one external input pre-amplifier
- two mixers
- miscellaneous attenuators, multiples, etc.

EQUIPMENT LIST #3: a large modular synthesizer consisting of some combination of as many of the following modules as is possible:

- six to eight voltage-controlled oscillators
- two noise generators (white/pink)
- three voltage-controlled low-pass filters
- two voltage-controlled high-pass filters
- one voltage-controlled multimode filter (low-pass/high-pass/band-pass/band-reject)
- one multiband fixed filter bank
- four to six envelope generators (AR and ADSR)
- two envelope trigger delay units
- four to six voltage-controlled amplifiers

- two ring modulators
- one frequency shifter
- two electronic or sequential switches
- two keyboard controllers (one monophonic, one duo- or polyphonic) (one with touch/velocity sensitive capability)
- one linear (ribbon) controller
- two sequential controllers
- two sample/hold circuits
- two envelope followers
- one Schmitt Trigger Generator
- one pitch follower
- one joystick controller
- two or three voltage processor units (inverter, lag processor, etc.)
- two external input pre-amplifiers
- three mixers (one a matrix mixer)
- miscellaneous attenuators, multiples, etc.

LISTENING EXAMPLES

Babbitt, Milton — *Ensembles for Synthesizer*
Columbia MS 7051

Maxfield, Richard — *Night Music*
Odyssey 3216 0160

Pousseur, Henri — *Trois Visages de Liege*
Columbia MS 7051

Smiley, Pril — *Kolyosa*
CRI S–268

Stockhausen, Karlheinz — *Hymnen*
DGG 2707 039

Subotnik, Morton — *The Wild Bull*
Nonesuch 71208
Until Spring
Odyssey Y 34158

Part III:
Electronic
Music
Composition

Chapter 15

Compositional Concepts in Electronic Music

INTRODUCTION

The development of electronic music has been historically tied to the reevaluation of what may be considered musically meaningful or relevant. Born out of the Modernist and Dadaist movements of the early part of this century and nurtured during the Post World War II era, electronic music has presented composers, performers, and listeners alike with some of the most profound questions about music composition, interpretation, and appreciation that have ever been posed to Western culture. Thus, it is hardly surprising that composers must approach electronic music with a willingness to openly question what it means to create "music," and they must be prepared to continually expand their awareness of the infinite musical potential of sound.

There are no absolute esthetic values that can be attributed to the medium of electronic music. Like most musical instruments, the "instruments" of electronic music are esthetically neutral. Rather, each composer must define the expressive and esthetic potential of the "instrument" in his or her own way. The esthetic approach adopted by the electronic music composer may simply be predetermined by the prejudices the individual brings to such an encounter, or it may develop from a more open-minded (though certainly not uncritical) desire to understand the possibilities of musical expression made uniquely available through electronic technology. Certainly, most contemporary composers in the electronic music medium (or in any medium, for that matter) tend to believe that it is the obligation of every composer, performer, and listener to make esthetic judgments based on the broadest possible understanding of the medium.

As a practical matter, most people, even many practicing musicians, never consciously consider that they have esthetic criteria or perspectives—though they will, more than likely, have strongly held opinions about what particular pieces, styles, or types of music they like or dislike. It is only in the last 20 years or so that electronic music has begun to have an effect on this broad popular audience, although that effect may be largely undefinable. Unconscious esthetic judgments are not easily seen or measured—except perhaps as broad popular trends; the most important and noticeable measures of which may be record sales and radio broadcast programming, both of which respond quite immediately to the demands and tastes of their listener/consumers. Only recently has the extreme popularity of technology-based musics (involving electronic instruments and production techniques) begun to have a strong, definable effect on the popular listening audience. Though the "popular" forms of electronic music tend to rely most heavily on fairly traditional harmonic, melodic, and rhythmic constructions, there are significant exceptions whose subtlety, complexity, and "newness" are equal to those of the most abstract of the "art" music forms. The very timbral dexterity of the electronic medium is in itself a progressive influence, subtly yet pervasively expanding the audience's perception and definition of what is meaningful sound. The composer of electronic "art" music (unlike his more cloistered brethren who compose using only traditional acoustic musical instruments) must be open to the forms of expression taking place in "popular" electronic music—if only to be aware of the progress continually being made in advancing the esthetic perceptions of the vast majority of the listening audience.

DEFINING MUSIC

Although everyone makes esthetic judgments, artists (and their critics) have an obligation to fully explore and develop the esthetic criteria that define their artistic expression and viewpoints. Sadly, the vast majority of traditionally trained musicians confuse technical analysis according to certain theoretical or historically imposed "rules" of musical practice with esthetic perception and understanding. The poet Wallace Stevens referred to this imposition of technical values in the place of esthetic understanding as *ideas about the thing* that are not *the thing itself*. We perceive its form and its structure but not its essence. But what is the *thing*; what is *music*; and what makes it *beautiful*?

There can hardly be a question of greater personal importance to a composer, yet there is no absolute answer that can be offered here or anywhere else. Beauty—like Truth—is not easily dissected and analyzed, even if it may be perceived. The more one becomes aware of the perception of beauty, the more there is to perceive and the more there is to question. There is even a strong case to be made for the importance of *non*rational creative processes (whether they are called instinct, impulse, or even inspiration). The Bachs, Mozarts, and Beethovens of the past were instinctual geniuses, often improvising with little or no forethought what many people have since spent lifetimes trying to rationalize. The incredibly perceptive teacher Nadia Boulanger refused to accept the young George Gershwin into her rigorous music composition classes for fear of damaging his already highly developed musical instincts. Yet, merely because musical instinct cannot be dissected and quantified does not mean that it cannot or should not be accommodated in the formation of one's esthetic conceptions or—more important to this discussion—creative processes.

To a great extent, each creative act is an attempt to understand beauty and to define it as perfectly as possible according to one's own creative and technical abilities and one's own ways of perceiving things. Thus, the development of esthetic sensitivity is the development of self-knowledge and an enhanced awareness of the world in general. There are no "ethics" involved in this; there can be no "right" or "wrong." There can be only one person's attempt to apprehend beauty in every way at his or her disposal. Some people will find that their way of defining beauty is shared by many others—giving the illusion of communication to what is essentially an utterly abstract, personal expression. Others may find that no one seems to understand or appreciate their creative efforts. Neither condition is preferable in and of itself, except in a purely egoistic or monetary sense. It is not merely that beauty may be relative, but that it is so multifaceted that one person may perceive it entirely differently from another merely by approaching it from a different point of view.

Thus, there are no recipes for the composition of a flawless, beautiful piece of music. There are no litmus tests to certify the profundity of the composer's artistic perceptions. So where does a composer begin? How do you go about perceiving—then creating—what has never existed before? Well, you start with your own unique imagination and a good deal of sensitivity to cultural stimuli. These are up to you. Then there is the matter of basic technique or compositional craft, the sort of nuts-and-bolts, how-do-I-get-this-thing-to-work knowledge that this book is all about. Training in the techniques and craft of electronic music should give you the ability to translate imagined sounds into real sounds (however imperfectly they may be realized at this stage of your experience). By manipulating and organizing the sounds you create, you *are* composing. So the compositional *process* encompasses the *imagination, creation, manipulation, and organization of sound*. It's that simple, whether your beginning sounds are chord progressions or white noise. And, though this is only the definition of a *process* (not "the thing itself"), it can be significant in developing your own unique awareness of esthetic considerations, which may eventually lead to a greater understanding of "the thing itself": Beauty.

AUDIO/ELECTRONIC TRANSLATION

Late nineteenth-century and early twentieth-century composers did not spring from the womb with the whole gamut of known orchestral "colors" already ringing in their ears. The colorful and subtle orchestration techniques that they frequently employed were the result of a gradual accumulation or cataloging of instrumental sounds that they had listened to and analyzed, carefully noting the use and combination of the many orchestral instruments available to them. The experienced composer, having heard and analyzed the sound of the orchestra for many years, was then able to "think for" the orchestra, imagining the sounds of various instruments and instrumental combinations without actually having to hear them.

The composer of electronic music must also learn to imagine potential electronic sounds and their possible combinations without actually hearing them. He or she must also be able to analyze these imagined sounds, breaking them down into their component characteristics and proposing means of synthesizing these characteristics in the studio. Students of electronic music quickly learn to characterize the sounds they hear in electronic music compositions in terms of the equipment, set-ups, and techniques used. In fact, this active audience becomes so quickly discerning that it is the constant challenge of the composer to avoid predictable and easily classified (perhaps even clichéd) compositional techniques or electronic "effects." The tendency of poorly conceived electronic pieces to become mere collages of clever or outlandish effects is an early discovery to intelligent students in the medium, who often get at least some enjoyment from knowing how each effect was produced.

COMPOSITIONAL DELIBERATION AND IMPROVISATION

Music composition is a deliberate act of creation—it does not occur by accident or without human intervention. Even good jazz improvisation, seemingly so free, is actually the result of experience, insight, and training. Yet, as stated earlier, there is room in this strategy for essentially nonrational processes, such as impulse, instinct, or inspiration.

Even these acts, though seemingly not elicited through or confined by rational processes, are the result of a conscious effort by the composer to be open and receptive to them and—most importantly—to develop and organize them. The legends of Handel's "Messiah" aside, whole works do not suddenly create themselves in all their details from impulse alone. Creative insight must always be accompanied and followed by a prodigious amount of deliberation, which is just one way of saying that, inspired or not, there's a lot of hard work involved.

Basically, there are two opposite ways of approaching a new composition, and they aren't necessarily mutually exclusive, though they may seem so to the beginner. One can thoroughly imagine, conceive, and organize a complete piece before even creating a single sound or setting up a single patch. And one can, without forethought, merely begin to create sounds in the studio, gradually varying them or developing them until one finds something pleasing to work with further. Though the latter of these approaches may seem to be rather haphazard, it can actually be an extremely rational process when carried on by an experienced electronic music composer, a process in which many possible options are quickly weighed and discriminated among, gradually exploring and defining an idea that might perhaps be too complex to mentally apprehend immediately and without such experimentation. However, such an approach, used exclusively, requires a large amount of studio time, which may be a very rare and a very expensive commodity.

Even if access to extensive studio time is not a problem, there are good reasons to have an organized approach to electronic music composition. The most obvious and basic of these is that most types of music composition require some form of organization—that is, the elements (sound events) of the piece must be carefully shaped and interrelated in some kind of formal structure or pattern (discussed later on in this chapter). Although there is ample historical proof that complex formal structures can indeed be improvised (Bach was famous for his fugal improvisations), it should be noted that, in most cases, the analog electronic music studio has not been designed for complex "real-time" sound production. Even live-performance synthesizers have their limitations in this regard. In very practical terms, one must also plan a composition in order to have the needed equipment and resources available, particularly in the composition of Musique Concrète.

Having begun to make general assumptions about how one composes, there are a few points that should be made on the precarious nature of such speculations. Today, we invent our compositional language even as we create the work in which it is used. In the most forceful and expressive works of music made today, the musical language and the essence of the music become one, and inspiration and craft are truly inseparable. The corollary to this is that no compositional perspective or approach is closed to us, that concepts discarded at one time in our development may be picked up and explored at a later time, yielding results that would not have been possible earlier.

DEFINING INDIVIDUAL SOUND EVENTS

Duration

By this time it may seem obvious and unnecessary, but it may still be useful to reexamine some of the qualities of a sound that define it as a specific, perhaps meaningful event.

There are two characteristics that all sounds have in common: a beginning and an end. The length of time between these two boundaries is significant because it defines the sound in time, making rhythm, tempo, simultaneity (harmony, in traditional musical terms), and contrast possible. As a result, the type of beginning or ending that is given to a synthesized sound event can be very important. A sound that starts very softly and gradually swells in volume to become loud, then suddenly ends, is altogether different in its effect from a sound with a sudden and loud "attack" which then gradually diminishes in volume until it is no longer audible.

Rhythm and Tempo

For rhythm or tempo to exist, a sound must occur more than once or more than one sound must occur sequentially. Figure 15.1 illustrates a few examples of rhythm. Note that for a single sound to create a rhythmic pattern there must be some silence between its reiterations, or it must have a strong attack. Otherwise, no beginning or end to the sound will be perceived. However, if two or more sound events occur in sequence, as in Figure 15.1b, their time spans may overlap without intervening silence and still produce a combined rhythmic effect. The combined rhythmic relationship formed in Figure 15.1c presents a problem to traditional rhythmic notation but may be precisely calculated and produced using tape splicing or voltage-control techniques. More complex transient amplitude envelopes would further complicate the perceived rhythmic character of the music. As an example of this aspect of sound, play a tape recording of a familiar piece of music backwards and notice how its rhythmic structure seems much more awkward or unclear. This is a result of the reversed amplitude envelopes of the component sound events more than it is the result of the mere reversal of the time relationships they exhibit. More subtle variations in the attack and decay characteristics of sounds occur constantly in music.

Tempo, for our purposes, can be identified as the overall or average rate of change in the component sound events. For example, the rate of change (reiteration) of the quarter notes shown in Figure 15.1a was once every second or 60 times per minute, which is traditionally indicated as ♩ = 60. As long as traditional rhythmic values are used in creating electronic music, it is feasible—though occasionally difficult—to ascribe various tempos to them. However, more abstract electronic music compositions may require a more statistical approach (arriving at an average number of sound-event changes per minute) if precision is desired. A more general sense of fast, slow, or moderate changes in event succession is easily created and perceived, serving a function closely related to the more strict delineation of traditional musical tempi.

Spectral Content and Structure

The most prominent characteristic of any single sound event is its spectral or timbral content, particularly as it changes over time. Frequency, amplitude, and duration may all be important to the function of the sound, but these characteristics become meaningful, for the most part, only in the context of the whole composition. Only the spectral structure of a sound is at least potentially immediately meaningful. Naturally, the degree to which the spectral content and structure of a sound are meaningful is influenced by its frequency, amplitude, and duration, since many sounds take on very different qualities when these characteristics are varied—even if the spectral content of

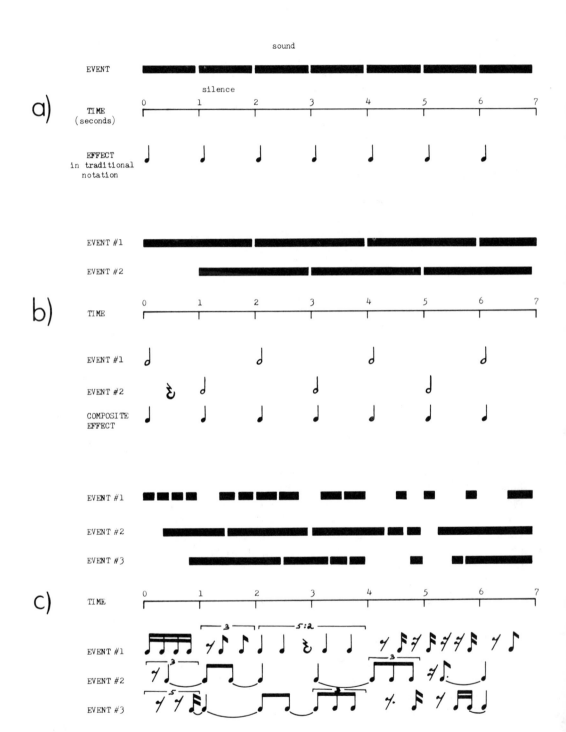

Figure 15.1 Rhythm Characteristics

386

the sound remains the same. For example, the sound of someone saying one word, or even one syllable or phoneme, that is then tape recorded and played back at a slower speed is very different from the same sound occurring at its "natural" speed, frequency, and duration. However, the difference in potential meaning of a pure sine tone transposed upward or downward by several octaves is irrelevant unless the sine tone occurs in the context of other sounds. Thus, its frequency is not particularly meaningful except in comparison to the frequency of those sounds around it. In most cases, frequency, amplitude, and duration are only relative characteristics that derive most of their meaning from the context in which they are used, but spectral structure has a much higher potential for conveying meaning within the bounds of only a single event.

The importance of spectral content and structure has been particularly emphasized by the special capabilities of electronic music devices to produce virtually any conceivable spectral structure through either additive or subtractive synthesis techniques. In fact, a strong case can be made that electronic music's greatest contribution to contemporary music (in any of its forms) has been the consequent expansion of possible timbral (spectral) structures and the ability of spectral content to convey meaning—thus, to become an important, perhaps primary part of the organization of a composition. In some cases, this ability has taken the focus of the composer away from the traditional Western concern with pitch as the basic organizational parameter of music. In other cases, including such highly pitch-organized works as Milton Babbitt's *Ensembles for Synthesizer*, spectral structure and spectral relationships have been manipulated as an additional level of compositional organization, complementing the use of pitch structures.

One should also remember that the transient characteristics of any spectral structure are extremely important in defining the nature of its sound. The amplitude envelope of the hypothetical cymbal crash shown in Figure 15.2a is actually a composite of the amplitude envelopes of the individual component harmonics and partials shown in Figure 15.2b, which may vary greatly in both their shape and duration. Defining sound events to this level of complexity is one of the real challenges of electronic music, because the subtlety of synthesized spectral structures, including their complex transient relationships, is automatically compared by the listener with the wide-ranging spectral variety of "natural" and acoustic sounds.

DEFINING SPECTRAL CHARACTER

There are three basic forms of spectral structure: harmonic, inharmonic, and random. Yet, many sounds can be very difficult to classify. For example, the noiselike sounds made by some percussion instruments (e.g., triangles, tuned gongs, various tuned drums) might seem to be randomly or even harmonically structured, when, in fact, they exemplify complex inharmonic spectra.

Each of these three discrete classes of spectral quality can be easily produced with most analog synthesizers. For example, the unmodulated output of any VCO is obviously harmonically structured. The signal spectrum produced by a ring modulator (even with two inputs from harmonically structured signal sources) will more than likely be inharmonic. And the spectral output of the white noise generator is, of course, quite random in nature.

These are only the basic materials of synthesis. They are the raw, static forms that

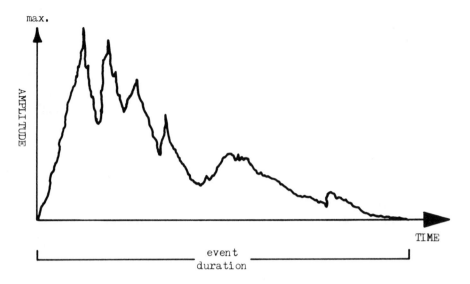

a) Composite Amplitude Envelope

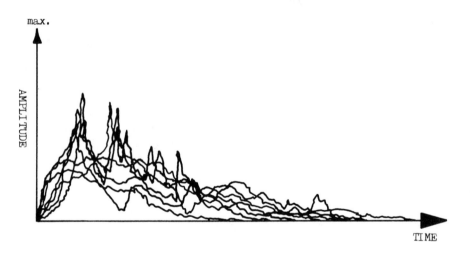

b) Amplitude Envelopes of Spectral Components

Figure 15.2 Spectral Characteristics of a Hypothetical Cymbal Crash

must be given shape by the composer. Since it is change in the spectral character of a sound that gives it a definition, the control of the spectral elements of the sound must be achieved—usually by either additive or subtractive synthesis. Of the two techniques, additive synthesis is potentially the more complex and difficult approach to use, since all of the component elements of the desired sound must be produced separately, then combined to make the whole sound. However, if enough precision equipment is available, it would be possible to specify the amplitude envelope of each component (harmonic or inharmonic) in any relationship with the others, thereby making it feasible to construct sounds with extremely subtle transient spectral characteristics. Figure 15.3 illustrates a simplified version of this technique, using only four sound components. The equipment configuration that would be required to produce this composite spectral effect is shown in Patch No. 46.

In many ways, the subtractive synthesis process is easier to apply in the studio, since even the simplest oscillator is usually capable of producing extremely complex, harmonically rich waveforms. The careful frequency and amplitude calibration and phase alignment of entire banks of oscillators that is required with additive synthesis is entirely unnecessary. The set-up shown in Patch No. 47 is infinitely more simple and reliable than that shown in Patch No. 46, yet, its effect and its audible result are certainly much more likely to be perceived as a single, unified and well-integrated sound event. However, it is also possible to add even greater subtlety to this sound event. Notice that this relatively simple patch allows for the production of a single spectral envelope for the entire sound produced. Although this envelope effectively simulates a much more complex event than might at first be imagined—note the individual component harmonic envelopes resulting from the waveform structure, shown in Figure 15.4—there is very little variation in the sound's harmonic content between the initial attack stage and the final decay stage. But, by combining several control voltages to produce more complex variations in the spectral content of the sound, and by using a VCA to control the overall amplitude envelope of the sound (allowing the initial F_c of the single low-pass filter to be set higher, thereby increasing the spectral complexity of the tone produced), the behavior of the individual harmonically related component envelopes can be varied consistently while control of the overall amplitude envelope is maintained. Patch No. 48 uses this technique resulting in the fairly subtle and complex spectrum variations shown in Figure 15.5.

SOUND EVENT DEFINITION

Of course, the basic aim of composition is the organization and manipulation of individual sound events in relationship to others occurring either simultaneously or sequentially (corresponding to harmony and melody, respectively, in more traditional music). Although a few electronic music works have been composed that emphasize the use of only a single sound event, such as Steve Reich's *Come Out*, it is much more usual that a composition will contain several different sound events that are either *complementary* or *contrasting*. These relationships usually define the formal structure of the composition on both large- and small-scale terms. The large-scale compositional structure of a work is generally defined by the relationships of entire sections of the work to each other. Each section of the work, in turn, generally has its own small-scale structure. Although it is quite typical for the composer to have some sense of the large-scale structure of a piece before producing it, the actual composition of a piece is mostly concerned with the building of small substructures from individual sound events, then linking these together to form larger sections and, eventually, an entire piece.

The distinction made between complementary and contrasting sound characteristics is relative to the composer's musical perceptions and experience. Although it can be stated with a fair degree of certainty that a cymbal crash and a bird song have contrasting sound characteristics, it would not be difficult to imagine that a composer could create

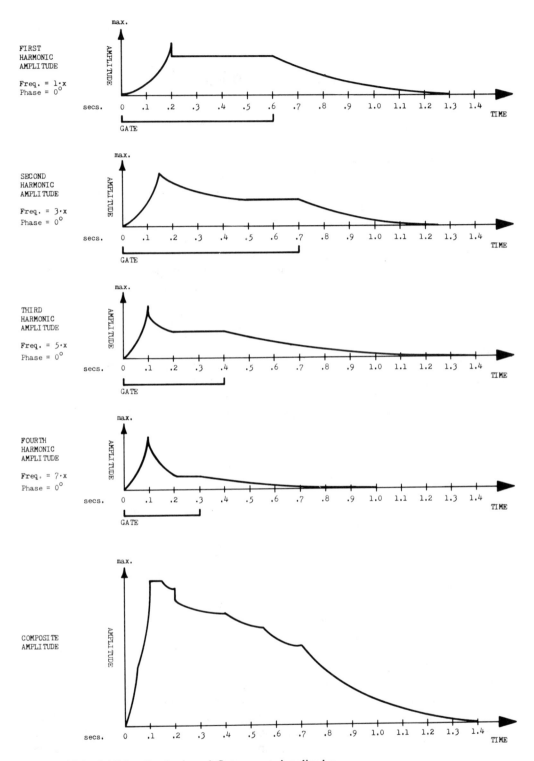

Figure 15.3 Additive Synthesis and Component Amplitudes

390

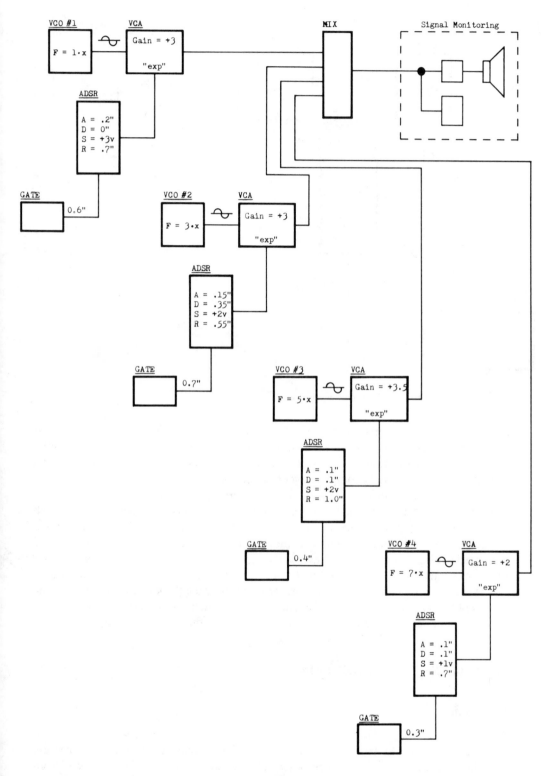

PATCH 46: Additive Synthesis Note: The output levels of the envelope generators need to be carefully controlled. If the VCAs do not have attenuated control inputs separate attenuators must be used.

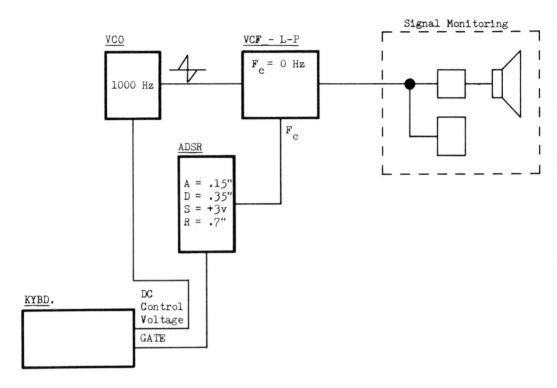

PATCH 47: **Simplified Spectral Variation**

complementary characteristics for both of these sounds by various electronic means. It is not the sound materials themselves that absolutely dictate the character of the sound event, but how the composer chooses to use them. The ways in which a composer uses sound materials to create a complete event can be described, again in relative terms, as *conjunct* or *disjunct*, *simple* or *complex*, *static* or *varying*. A fast succession of bursts of white noise could be described as *conjunct*, since the sounds used are similar to each other; *simple*, because only one distinct sound occurs at a time; and *varying*, since there are definite, though rapid, changes in the amplitude of the sound. The last of these characterizations is the one that presents the most problems for the composer, because the only characteristic of the sound that changes in a noticeable manner is its amplitude. The overall spectral character of the sound remains the same throughout the event. If the attacks of the sound (reiterations) occurred rapidly enough, even the amplitude changes would become less distinguishable, eventually making the event seem more static.

SOUND EVENT ORGANIZATION

Repetition

A thorough discussion of musical structure, organization, and form is somewhat beyond the scope of this book. However, there are some basic concepts of sound organization that should provide the novice composer of electronic music with a good base from which to explore and refine his or her understanding of formal structures. The most

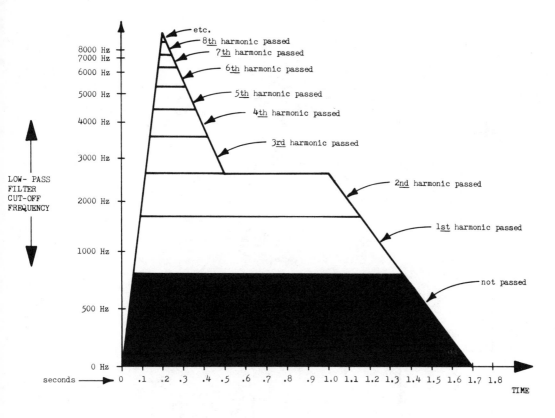

a) the ADSR Control Voltage Envelope

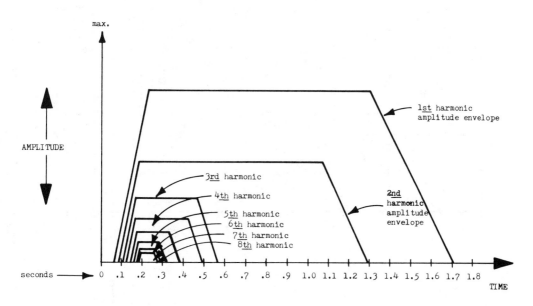

b) the Amplitude of the Component Harmonics

Figure 15.4   The Spectral Results of PATCH 47

393

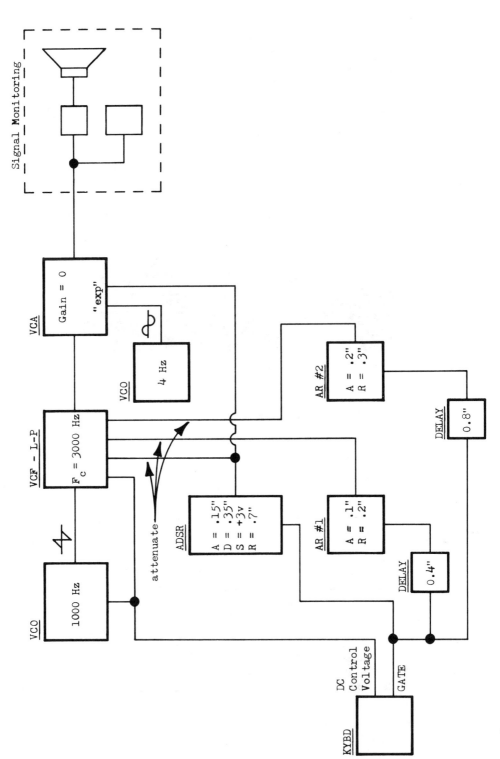

PATCH 48: **Variations in Spectral Content Produced by Combined Control Voltages**

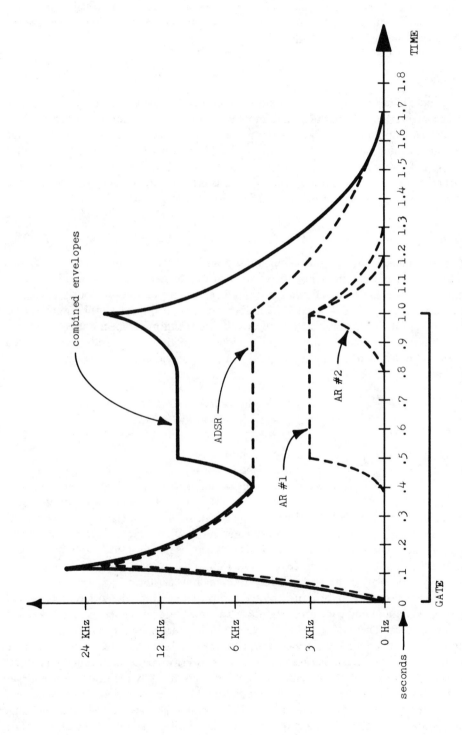

Figure 15.5 The Combined Envelope Control Voltages from PATCH 47

395

elemental of these concepts is that of *repetition*, which, obviously, involves the reiteration of a single sound event. Actually, this is rather rare as an *extended* musical form. However, it is not at all unusual to repeat a sound event once or twice before exposing a second, probably contrasting sound event.

Variation

It is also possible to repeat a single sound event effectively many times over if it is *varied* in some way, perhaps through changes in its frequency, timing, filtering, or amplitude. Similarly, variation may also take the form of gradual changes in the phase relationships of repeated sounds, as is the case in Steve Reich's *Violin Phase*. The "layering" of a single sound event over itself presents many possibilities in this case, since the constructive and destructive interference patterns created actually alter the character of the sound while maintaining its original identity to a large extent.

Contrast

The use of *contrast* is probably the single most prominent aspect of most music. One idea (or "theme") is presented, then contrasted with one or more subsequent ideas. Such contrast can take the form of relative differences in any of the previously discussed characteristics of a sound event, including conjunct/disjunct, simple/complex, or static/varying qualities. Many structural possibilities resulting from the use of contrast have been identified and standardized as follows (each letter stands for a unified "section" of music, which may correspond to a single sound event or to a large group of related sound events):

a a b b	binary form
a a b a b a	rounded binary form
a b a	ternary form
a b a c a	rondo form
a b c a b	sonata form
a b a c a b a	sonata-rondo form

Every composer brings to these simple formal structures the perspective, imagination, and individuality that will give them a greater subtlety and expressiveness than these strings of letters would seem to imply. Musical "form" is not an actual end to be pursued in its own right, but merely a choice of a mold into which musical ideas are to be poured. It is a means of structuring and relating different musical ideas.

There are also many hybrid or invented forms that combine the different aspects of repetition, variation, and contrast in unique ways, most often designed to fit the needs of a particular piece. These often highly complex musical forms are typical of a great many nineteenth- and twentieth-century compositions, particularly those that espouse or take their structure from extra-musical influences, such as a story plot, a painting, or a natural event (e.g., a storm at sea). In some cases, there is no carefully delineated form as was described above, but only a seemingly random or "stream-of-consciousness" succession of events that are subtly complementary and contrasting (perhaps only sharing the same "mood"), the desired result being an accumulation of different but related effects. The music of the late romantic and impressionist periods was often cast in this unrestrained form.

PERFORMANCE SITUATIONS

Unlike most other forms of music, it is possible to "perform" an electronic piece without the use of a live performer. Start the tape, and the music happens, sounding exactly the same as in each previous performance (assuming that no technical problems intervene). This appears to be an ideal situation if what you want is a perfect performance every time, without any superfluous distractions. The only problem is that even the best of audiences soon becomes uncomfortable in this setting. People have eyes, and they seem to be constantly obliged to do something with them. Without a performer or something else to focus their visual attention on, the members of the audience soon begin to become distracted by the lack of visual stimuli and by their own self-consciousness. There is, after all, something less than satisfying about studiously watching a pair of loudspeakers sitting on the stage.

The answer to this problem is not simply to turn out the concert hall lights unless you purposefully want to play on the listener's subconscious connection of darkness with either apprehension or sleep. It is also possible that a large group of people sitting quietly together in a darkened hall might begin to feel quite silly about it all, interjecting yet another uncontrollable aspect into the performance. It is usually far more profitable to take the problems of tape music performance into account and provide some sort of visual stimulus for the audience that complements the music. Various forms of light shows and film or slide projection techniques have been developed that offer the electronic music composer many creative options, either on his own or in collaboration with a visual artist. Videotape productions and laser displays have also become increasingly available in the past few years, greatly expanding the possibilities for a variety of mixed-media presentations. Another time-honored collaboration is that of electronic music and dance. Electronic music is particularly suited to the needs—both economic and expressive—of small modern dance troupes. Especially since the music is generally available for rehearsals *just* as it will be performed, does not require the services of live musicians, and is generally apt for the dancers to work with.

Another solution, often more closely tied to the esthetic goals and parameters of the piece, is to include some form of live musical performance. This can range from actual live synthesis to various combinations of tape and live instrumental or vocal performers. Each of these options places very specific demands on the composer.

Live Synthesis

There is a tendency for live synthesis to be equated with improvisation or "chance" music. Formal improvisation may be conducted in several ways, depending largely on the equipment being used and the abilities of the performers involved. Studio analog electronic music systems are often somewhat limited by the complexity of the patching required to produce even a single sound or combination of sounds, so live improvisation with this kind of equipment often consists of gradual changes made to a single complex patch. Of course, it is also possible that an entire set of patching changes could be carefully worked out in advance of a performance, more strictly defining the structure of the piece and avoiding the possibility that the improvisation might become aimless and ineffective. It should also be noted that audiences usually find the manipulation of the synthesis equipment on stage very fascinating in itself, which is certainly a minor concern in creating the music but not in performing it.

Naturally, it is also possible to coordinate live, real-time synthesis with other forms of live performance, including instruments, voices, visual media, or dance. The only problem that may arise in all of this is the incredible complexity that can result from trying to control the actions and interactions of many people simultaneously. But it is no less a feat to bring off a good production of Puccini's *Turandot* than it is to produce *Einstein on the Beach* by Philip Glass. The technical demands are different in each case, but the need for coordination and direction of the production, and their possibilities for truly spectacular success or failure are the same.

Recorded Tape and Live Performers

Music involving prerecorded tape and live performer(s) presents much more unique problems to the electronic music composer. Usually, when two or more musicians play together, there is a certain amount of give-and-take between them. Tempos and dynamic (loudness) levels can be adjusted between the members of the ensemble. In most performer/tape collaborations, there is no room for such flexibility, since the tape procedes at an absolutely stable tempo and adheres to preset loudness contours (unless someone is continually monitoring and changing the levels during the performance). Pieces that require the performer to play in precise synchronization with the tape and to adjust his dynamic levels to it may, therefore, require a lot of rehearsal before the correct relationships between the two are achieved. Of course, once the performer gets the proper timings and dynamics down it will likely result in a near perfect performance every time, since the tape will "respond" precisely the same way in each performance.

There are essentially two ways of coordinating live performers with a prerecorded tape. One involves the use of a continuous tape part with precise timings of all its musical cues indicated in the score, either through the use of traditional notation or through the indication of elapsed time in seconds from the beginning of the piece. This latter method puts a tremendous burden on the live performer, especially if the tape sounds employed by the composer are very abstract and relatively undifferentiated. It is often difficult (though never impossible) for the live performer to develop an aural sense for the placement of his cues, and long periods of time when the tape may be silent are very tenuous. Also, most musicians are unaccustomed to watching clocks or stopwatches during a performance for the needed precise timings. An additional problem arises when singers are required to locate their pitches in the midst of an abstract electronic music texture. Very few vocalists have the necessary sense of absolute pitch needed for this task, so carefully placed pitch cues in the tape part are essential for the majority of singers to have even a chance of producing accurate pitches.

A second method of coordinating live performers with a prerecorded tape can be used when the tape part is made up of several different segments that alternate with the live performance. Cues are provided in the score for the tape machine operator (who starts and stops the tape machine at the appropriate places) as well as for the performers. This method of synchronization provides at least some flexibility in the live performer's timing, tempo, and dynamics when the tape is not playing, but the tape machine operator must have some time before the entrances of his "part" in order to carefully set up each cue, and he must be a musician capable of following the score.

It is also possible to construct pieces for tape and live performers in such a way that precise cues or timings are not necessary for either the performers or the tape operator. Naturally, these pieces would not be concerned with creating absolute, predetermined relationships of pitch, rhythm, or simultaneity, but would, instead, involve an exploration of the possible relationships that might be formed, sometimes at the performer's discretion, within the limits of the composer's intentions. A hypothetical example of this sort of piece would be a song in which the singer is asked to wait for an approximate amount of time from the start of the tape, then sing a melody at a given pitch level (specified or not) within general rhythmic parameters lasting for only an approximate length of time. The composer would obviously be trying for only a general effect in which the live performer would have a certain degree of freedom and creative input with the work. Each performer's interpretation of the piece—which would actually determine most of the small-scale relationships—would be somewhat different. Yet, so long as the general guidelines determined and stated by the composer were actually followed, each interpretation of the work would be equally valid.

Tape Delay and Live Performers

Most electronic music compositions using tape are created entirely before the perform-ance. The complexities of mixing and editing—let alone the creation of the actual electronic sound materials—normally require many hours of studio work. However, a significant exception to this rule is the use of tape delay systems to alter and enhance the live performance sounds *as they are created* by the performer. Initially, this would seem to be a rather simplistic technique, adding little more than a superfluous echo to the live sound. Yet, through extremely careful planning, tape delay techniques can create a successful interactive counterpoint between the live sounds and the recorded sounds that result from them. There can be an entire series of carefully selected single or multiple echoes, since the microphone that picks up the live performer may also pick up the tape-recorded sounds as they are played back over the loudspeakers. This cumulative effect must be controlled by the composer to avoid an eventual oversaturation of the texture.

Figure 15.6 is an example of a tape delay set-up that produces fairly complex and continually changing interactions between the live performer and the tape delay system. This is from a work titled "Alone, in the night's loud silence . . ." for amplified solo oboe, prerecorded oboe, and tape delay system by Joel Naumann. A sample score page is also given, as Figure 15.7. The carefully orchestrated use of a mixer is crucial to this work, since it allows both the number and the dynamic levels of the successive reiterations of a sound to be strictly controlled. A further complication in this example is added by a prerecorded oboe part. As is the case with all tape delay systems, the distance between the recording head of the recording tape machine and the playback head of the playback tape machine, in conjunction with the tape speed (here set to three seconds, or 22.5 inches of tape at $7\frac{1}{2}$ ips), determines the actual length of the resulting delay. Notice how the three separate parts (live amplified oboe, prerecorded oboe, delayed sounds) can each by cycled into the delay system to produce whatever complexities and simultaneities the composer wishes. In performance this work is almost as difficult for the mixer operator as it is for the oboist, since the precisely synchronized changes in input/output channel assignments is critical. The extensive performance notes are included here as an example of the careful specifications the composer must provide to the performers in such a work. Almost any electronic music piece involving live performers will include such precise instructions.

It is not at all unusual to combine many or even all of the above-mentioned performance arrangements in the production and performance of a single piece. Many contemporary "performance artists" combine prerecorded tape, live synthesis, live

Performance Notes

This work is notated using three staves. The upper stave ("Solo Oboe") is performed live; the middle stave ("Prerecorded Oboe") is recorded by the soloist prior to the performance and is played back during the performance; the lower stave ("Tape Delay System") is used for the sounds resulting from the tape delay system. Dynamics and rests are not indicated on this stave since these will be determined by the performance of the other two staves. The total sound heard during the performance is the simultaneous combination of all three staves.

Partial vertical 'bar lines' are provided at one second intervals, for synchronization purposes among the three staves. The tempo is a steady quarter-note = 60 throughout. Each second, or 'measure' therefore equals one quarter-note.

Square noteheads are used in the notation of the "Prerecorded Oboe" part. This notation is also used in the lower (tape delay) stave when delayed soundings of this part occur, to distinguish these sounds from those originating in the "Solo Oboe" part.

The work is realized by first recording the "Prerecorded Oboe" part on one channel (Channel II) of a multi-track tape recorder. This tape is then played back during the performance of the "Solo Oboe" part, while the electronics technician produces the sounds on the lower stave ("Tape Delay System") using Channel I of the same tape.

Accuracy in the production of the "Prerecorded Oboe" part is of primary importance. The dynamic level of this part will determine the overall balance of the total sound since dynamic levels for the other two parts must be adjusted in relation to it. The accurate placement of the "breathing spaces" in this part, and in all the parts, notated by a comma (') in the score, is necessary for the proper placement of all grace-notes and also to enable the electronics technician to accomplish the delay system routing via the mixer correctly, as indicated in the score. Further, accuracy in tempo and timing for this part is an absolute necessity, since the other parts are performed in relation to it. In effect, this part functions as a 'click track', or metronome for the realization of the entire work. Any inaccuracy in it can not be corrected during the performance, therefore great care should be exercised in its production.

OBOE NOTATION

, = 'breathing space', a definite separation between notes, needed by the technician.

m.v. = molto vibrato
s.v. = senza vibrato
n.v. = normal vibrato
ord. = ordinary manner of playing

m.v. 〰〰〰 s.v. = gradual transition from molto vibrato to senza vibrato

s.v 〰〰〰 m.v. = gradual transition from senza vibrato to molto vibrato

note: the notation indicates both the speed and the width of the vibrato!

= a glissando, occupying the full duration of the note from which it is indicated, up or down as shown

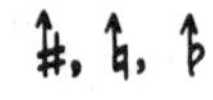

= pitches that are a quarter-tone (or more) sharp

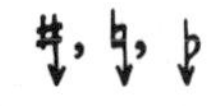

= pitches that are a quarter-tone (or more) flat

note: accidentals apply only to those notes which they immediately precede, except in the case of tied notes.

Grace-Notes: Single grace-notes should be played as short as possible, highly accented, as a 'percussive' sound. What is sought is a quality of sound for these isolated notes that will make them stand out from their surroundings, but done in relation to them. Therefore, in

Figure 15.6 Performance Notes for a Work for Solo Performer and Tape Delay System

softer dynamic surroundings (pp, p, etc.) they may be softer
themselves, as long as they have this quality; in louder (f, ff, etc.)
surroundings they will have to be correspondingly louder and more violent.

Groups of grace-notes should be played as fast as possible, and are
usually notated with a violent dynamic change, as in p ————— sf,
or sf ══════► p, or as otherwise indicated.

Care must be taken in the correct placement of all grace-notes; some
are intended to occur before 'bar lines', some after them, usually in
a place which coincides with a 'breathing space' in another part. At
times there are grace-note 'chords' which will be mis-played if this
caution is not carefully observed. Further, the mixer technician must
perform most of his channeling assignments during these 'breathing
spaces'.

DYNAMICS   The dynamic range used is from a minimum of 'pp' to a maximum of 'ff'.
                        Cutoffs of notes should be abrupt, even articulated if the performer
                        wishes, but, in any case, without any 'fade' just prior to the cutoff
                        of the tone. The extremes of the dynamic range ('pp' and 'ff') should be
                        those levels that the performer is still able to control and articulate.

EQUIPMENT NEEDED   A 7" reel of tape, with the "Prerecorded Oboe" part recorded on Channel II
                        A highly directional (cardoid) microphone, preferably a condensor microphone
                        Two tape machines, 2 channel, running at $7\frac{1}{2}$ ips
                        A mixer with at least 3 inputs and 3 outputs
                        A stereo amplifier or two mono amplifiers
                        Two speakers
                        Assorted connecting cables, as indicated in the diagram

EQUIPMENT SETTINGS   1.   The "Prerecorded Oboe" part is to be recorded before the performance
AND CONNECTIONS   on Channel II of the tape. All echoes from the tape delay system
(refer to diagram)   will be produced on Channel I of the same tape, while Channel II will
                             be used only for the playback of the "Prerecorded Oboe" part.

                        2.   The "Prerecorded Oboe" tape is threaded from the feed reel of
                             Tape Machine #1 to the take-up reel of Tape Machine #2.

                        3.   Tape Machine #1 is set in the "record" mode for Channel I only. Its
                             function is to record material for the Tape Delay System. Channel II
                             is not used at all on this machine!

                        4.   Tape Machine #2 is set in the "playback" mode for both channels.
                             Its function is to play back both the "Prerecorded Oboe" part on
                             Channel II and the "Tape Delay System" results on Channel I.

                        5.   The microphone is patched to Mixer Input #1

                        6.   The playback output from Tape Machine #2, Channel I is patched to
                             Mixer Input #2

                        7.   The playback output from Tape Machine #2, Channel II is patched to
                             Mixer Input #3

401

8.   Mixer Inputs #1, #2, and #3 are all assigned to Mixer Outputs #2 and #3 throughout the performance, feeding the stereo speaker system.

9.   Mixer Output #1 (the source for all echoes in the tape delay system) is patched to Tape Machine #1, Channel I input.

10. Mixer Outputs #2 and #3 are patched to the amplifier(s) and the loudspeakers.

DELAY TIME

The tape delay time must be exactly 3 seconds in order for the work to to be realized correctly. With both tape machines running at 7½ ips, their distance apart should measure exactly 22½ inches when measured between the record head of Tape Machine #1 and the playback head of Tape Machine #2. The 3 second delay time remains constant throughout the performance.

TECHNICAL OPERATION and SCORE NOTATION

There are three different kinds of electronic manipulation which take place in the course of the performance:

1.   Live amplification of the "Solo Oboe" part occurs through Mixer Input #1, assigned to Mixer Outputs #2 and #3 throughout the performance. The volume level of the amplification is controlled by the fader setting of this mixer input.

2.   "Prerecorded Oboe" playback occurs through Mixer Input #3, assigned to Mixer Outputs #2 and #3 throughout the performance. The volume level of this playback is controlled by the fader setting of this mixer input.

3.   "Tape Delay System" (and score notation). The tape delay system is designed to produce various combinations of single and multiple echo effects, from various sources. The volume level of these effects is controlled by the fader setting of Mixer Input #2.

    Single Echoes: For single echoes of the "solo Oboe" part Mixer Input #1 is also assigned to Mixer Output #1. This effect is indicated in the score by the sign ①↘. It is terminated by the sign ①↗.

                 For single echoes of the "prerecorded Oboe" part Mixer Input #3 is also assigned to Mixer Output #1. This effect is indicated in the score by the sign ③↘. It is terminated by the sign ③↗.

    Multiple Echoes: Multiple echoes use the single echoes as sources in a 'feedback' loop between Mixer Output #1 and Tape Machine#1, by also assigning Mixer Input #2 (the Tape Delay playback) to Mixer Output #1. This is indicated in the score by the sign ②↘. It is terminated by the sign ②↗.

                 NOTE: All three of the above signs refer only to to the assignment of their respective Mixer Inputs to Mixer Output #1, the only source for all the echo effects. Ideally, aside from adjustments to the output levels of the Mixer during the performance, in order to maintain a proper balance of the various

402

electronic effects in relation to the soloist, the technician need only be concerned with the accurate operation of these channeling assignments as indicated in the score. These channeling assignments usually occur during the 'breathing spaces' (ᵎ) shown in one or both of the upper two parts. ALL desired echoes are indicated on the lower of the three staves--any others that appear are the result of an error on the part of one of the two performers.

VOLUME LEVELS   All volume levels for: Tape Machine #1 (recording on Channel I), Tape Machine #2 (playing back on Channels I and II), Mixer Inputs #1, #2, and #3, Mixer Outputs #1, #2, and #3, and the Amplifier(s) should be pre-set, as much as possible, through adequate rehearsal in the acoustic space used for the concert. The two tape machines, once started, do not stop, and should require no adjustment during the performance.

The volume level of the amplification of the "Solo Oboe" part (Mixer Input #1) should be loud enough so that its presence is heard and so that it can provide an adequately strong signal to the tape delay system. It should not overpower the 'live' sound of the oboist.

The volume level of the "Prerecorded Oboe" part (Mixer Input #3) should be loud enough to balance with the "Solo Oboe" part. Although it is generally intended to be heard as 'background', it must be loud enough so that its attacks and cutoffs can be heard by both the oboist and the tecnician.

The playback level of the "Tape Delay System" (Mixer Input #2) should be slightly less than the volume of the live performer (with amplification). It is not necessary that multiple echoes 'fade' in any great degree since their appearance is controlled only by the signs ②⌐ and ②⌐ in the score. However, the volume setting of Mixer Output #1 should be high enough to produce at least four clearly audible echoes when multiple delays of any of the three Mixer Inputs are called for.

TIMINGS   Accurate timing on the part of both participants is a necessity. The 'partial barlines' are an aid for local synchronizations. As a further aid, cummulative timings are given at all major structural points in the piece. These are located just above the "Prerecorded Oboe" part.

STAGING   The two loudspeakers should be positioned as far apart as the stage width will allow. The oboist and the microphone should be positioned midway between the two loudspeakers and behind a line connecting them, to avoid acoustic feedback between the loudspeakers and the microphone. The mixer operator should, ideally, be positioned well in front of and between the two loudspeakers where he can monitor the performance and adjust balances as needed.

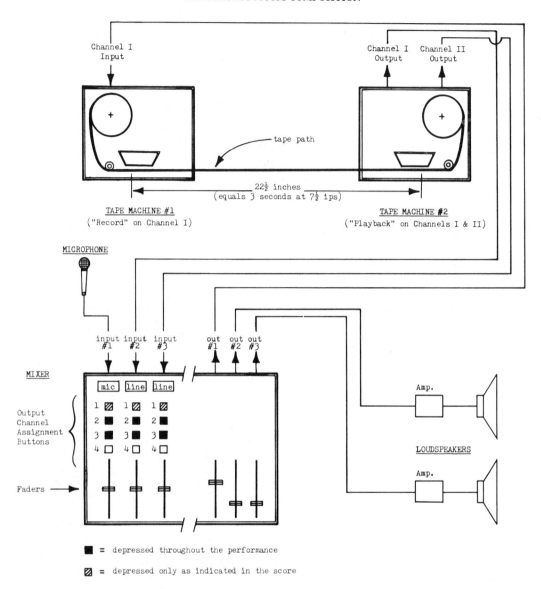

performance, lighting effects, and multi-media (film, dance, theatre, etc.) presentations in a single work. The technical demands of such pieces can be both monumental and astounding, but they are never insurmountable, assuming that all the equipment needed is available and that enough trained performers and technicians can be assembled in the same place at the same time. If you are esthetically inclined toward such large-scale, intricate production schemes, take into account the practical obstacles.

Planning

The now familiar litany of this book still bears repeating: *Know what you want to do, know how it may be done, plan how you intend to do it, then, do it!* The planning necessary

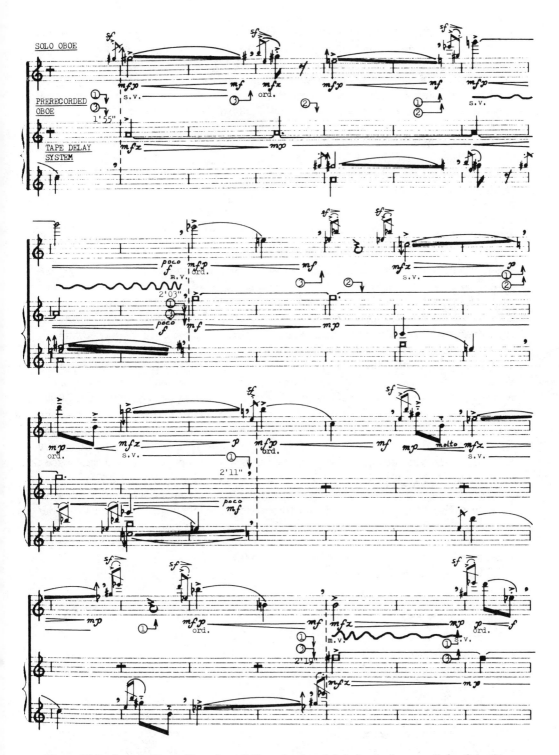

Figure 15.7 Sample Score Page from "Alone in the night's loud silence..." for Solo Oboe, Prerecorded Oboe, and Tape Delay System

for a well-thought-out electronic music composition often includes producing accurate, detailed descriptions of the sound events to be used in the piece, working out and diagramming the patches and studio production routines for making the sounds, and plotting out the separate sequence of production steps that will be necessary to properly assemble the sound events into a completed work. Each of these activities has been described in relation to specific projects throughout this book. It would be impossible to anticipate the planning and organizing requirements needed for every possible electronic music composition or style of composition, but it can be stated that even the most improvisatory piece will normally require some type of planning. It can certainly be said that a complex multi-media work will require extensive planning at all levels and stages of its creation and production.

SCORING AND NOTATION

There is hardly any other issue that has resulted in more argument or whose solution has proved to be so elusive as the pursuit of an ideal means of notating or scoring modern music. Electronic music has often been caught in the very center of this multifaceted debate, since every extreme of notation has been tried for this medium, including the most disturbing answer of all to traditional musicians—no score at all. (There certainly is no inherent need to produce a score for a work that exists completely on tape. In fact, the U.S. Music Copyright Office will accept tapes of electronic music works for copyright purposes, with or without a written score.) There is no one solution to this problem except for the general rule that if it works, use it. If a graphic score consisting of nothing but a bunch of ink blots and a timeline gives you the results you want, then that notation is eminently satisfactory. If, however, your piece requires the participation of others and the score you have created for it causes them to be confused about your intentions, you need to rethink your scoring. If you want a performer's cooperation (much less a good performance!), take into account what is meaningful to the performer and what that person must know from the score to play the work effectively, and attempt to notate your ideas in such a way that they will most accurately and efficiently communicate your intentions. The most innovative system of notation devised is absolutely useless if it does not convey your ideas accurately or if no performer is willing to take the time to understand it.

Electronic music scores generally fall into one or more of the following classifications:

- No score (only a tape realization)
- Traditional music notation
- Graphic notation
- Verbal notation (written instructions and diagrams)

If there is no score to the piece, as is often the case with many solo tape pieces, it obviously cannot be reconstructed. The only version of the piece is the one actually produced by the composer. Even with a score, the chances of reconstructing an electronic music piece precisely are slim. Generally, traditionally trained musicians as well as many listeners find this disturbing. It is as if a piece of music is not valid if it is not set forth in a score the way traditional music is.

Traditional notation and scoring techniques are only appropriate to electronic music when a traditional concern for pitch, dynamic, rhythm, and tempo relationships is evident or required. Otherwise, it is of little use to try to impose a notational system designed for entirely different requirements on this kind of music. Often, when writing for tape and an instrument or a voice, a composer will combine graphic representations of the tape sounds along with the traditional notation required for the instrumental or vocal part. This is usually a very workable compromise, since it provides a system of needed visual cues to the performer and can also show specific pitches.

The variety of forms that graphic notation may take are virtually limitless, ranging from extremely specific pictographic representations of frequency, amplitude, and temporal relationships to completely abstract visual shapes and images meant only to evoke musical ideas. Particularly as far as the latter case is concerned, there are no rules for the construction of a graphic score and, therefore, no general notation techniques that must be used. However, there are several factors that can influence the creation of an effective graphic score that attempts to show some form of quantifiable, reproducible sound relationships, or to at least provide the user with some insight into the actual sound events intended and how they fit together. The most simple graphic score notation shows the amplitude envelopes and the time sequences of all of the sound events. If more than one channel (loudspeaker) is used, parallel graphs are usually provided to show the sound activity of each channel (refer back to Figure 3.15), giving some sense of the spatial interchange of the piece's sound events and their relationships to time. It is also possible that the individual sound events can be labeled, numbered, or lettered in the score in reference to either a verbal description or a patch diagram given as preliminary notes to the score. If specific frequency relationships are important in the work, but fall outside the notation of traditional pitches or even pitch temperaments, a separate frequency graph can be placed alongside the amplitude graph(s) to show these changes in frequency. The graphing of spectral characteristics and changes in a score is a much more complex undertaking, since the spectral components of a sound may be transient and largely unquantifiable. Thus, verbal descriptions and patch diagrams may be the only meaningful notation alternatives for representing spectral content and change. Figures 15.8 and 15.9 are examples of some of the diverse techniques currently being employed by composers.

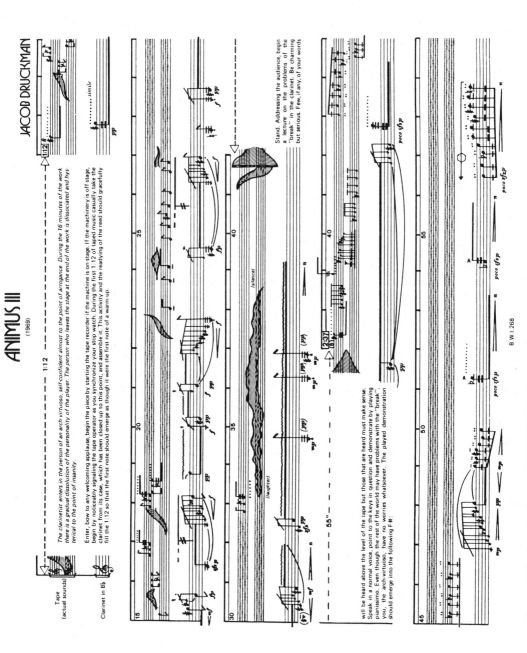

Figure 15.8 Sample Score ANIMUS III, for clarinet and electronic tape, p. 8, by Jacob Druckman. c 1978 by Boosey & Hawkes, Inc. Used by permission.

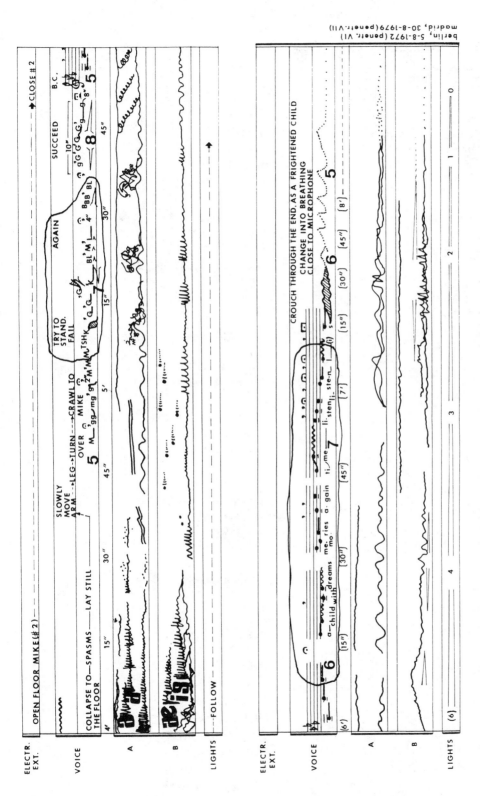

Figure 15.9 Sample Score "penetrations VII (1972-iii)," for voice, lights, electronic music, and electronic extensions, p. 4, by Alcides Lanza. Boosey and Hawkes, Inc. Used by permission.

409

LISTENING EXAMPLES

Anderson, Laurie	*Big Science* Warner BSK 3674
Austin, Larry	*Accidents* Source 2
Brown, Earle	*Times Five* BAM LD 072 CRI SD–330
Cage, John	*Variations II* Columbia MS 7051 *Cartridge Music* DGG 137 009 *Imaginary Landscape No. 1* Avakian 1
Cage, John and Lejaren Hiller	*HPSCHD* Nonesuch H–71224
Carlos, Walter	*Sonic Seasonings* Columbia KG 31234 *Variations for Flute and Electronic Sound* Turnabout 34004
Chadabe, Joel	*Echoes* Folkways FTS 33904
Davidovsky, Mario	*Synchronism No. 1* CRI SD–204 Nonesuch 71289 *Synchronism No. 2* *Synchronism No. 3* CRI SD–204 *Synchronism No. 5* CRI SD–268 *Synchronism No. 6* Turnabout 34487
Druckman, Jacob	*Animus II* CRI SD–255 *Animus III* Nonesuch 71253
Erb, Donald	*Reconnaissance* Nonesuch H–71223
Hendrix, Jimi	*The Jimi Hendrix Experience* Reprise 6261
Lucier, Alvin	*North American Time Capsule* Odyssey 32 16 0155

Luening, Otto and Vladimir Ussachevsky	*Concerted Piece for Tape Recorder and* *Orchestra* CRI S–227 *A Poem in Cycles and Bells* CRI 112 *Rhapsodic Variations for Tape Recorder and* *Orchestra* Louisville 545–5
Moroder, Giorgio	*American Gigolo* (soundtrack) Polydor PD–1–6335
Moss, Lawrence	*Auditions* CRI SD–318
Mumma, Gordon	*Cybersonic Cantilevers* Folkways FTS 33904
Reich, Steve	*Violin Phase* Columbia MS–7265
Riley, Terry	*Rainbow in Curved Air* Columbia MS–7315
Stockhausen, Karlheinz	*Kontakte* Candide 31022 Vox 678011 Wergo 60009 *Mikrophonie I* *Mikrophonie II* Columbia MS–7355 CBS 32–11–044 *Mixtur* DGG 137 012
Subotnik, Morton	*Prelude No. 4* Avant AV–1008
Tangerine Dream	*Rubycon* Virgin VI–2025
Vangelis	*Chariots of Fire* (soundtrack) Polydor PD–1–6335
Varese, Edgar	*Deserts* Columbia MS–6362 Angel S–36786 CRI SD–268
Zappa, Frank	*Lumpy Gravy* Verve 6–8741

Chapter 16
Composition Projects

As the title suggests, this chapter consists entirely of projects designed to develop the individual student's compositional skills. In contrast to the projects and exercises presented up to this point, all of which have focused primarily on the ability to use equipment effectively and the development of studio production skills, the emphasis of the following projects is more on developing an awareness of the practical aspects of composing in this medium and on discovering some of the ways in which esthetic considerations will normally define a piece of music and the techniques used in its production.

In some respects, these composition projects have been left purposefully vague, particularly in comparison to the earlier projects in this book, in order to avoid what might be construed as advocacy for a particular compositional style or studio approach. This neutral stance places the creative burden on the student. We recommend that, time permitting, students be encouraged to work from several different approaches in several different projects, perhaps emulating the approaches the student may have found particularly interesting from some of the listening examples that have been referred to throughout the text. It is also probable that the nature of the performance medium used (e.g., prerecorded tape alone, tape with live performers, live synthesis, or mixed-media) will influence the student's compositional approach. While each of these projects outlines at least a general technical approach to a piece, these are intended to be only suggestions for possible starting points.

Having allowed for and even encouraged so much leeway in conceptual intent and technical approach to these projects, it is difficult to prescribe any absolute criteria for judging the quality of each student's realization of any one project. Naturally, the rigorous technical standards established in the earlier exercises and projects should be scrupulously upheld. Tape recordings should be undistorted, scores clear and self-explanatory, and production techniques efficiently organized. The esthetic goals of both the composer and the work should be expressed as clearly as possible, both before the project is executed and afterward, when it is presented to the class or in a public concert. To a great extent, a particular project is successful if it satisfies the composer's carefully considered and defined esthetic goals, regardless of what those goals might be. As composers, the authors of this book are inclined to believe that a successful electronic music composition has, as its broadest goal, the shaping and organizing of sound in a distinctive and meaningful manner, although one must keep in mind that what is meaningful to one person may not be to another. This is one of the aspects of all contemporary music composition that allows each of us to make a unique esthetic contribution to the art.

Composition Project No. 1

Create a very short (one to four minute) Musique Concrète tape work using only the most minimal sound source material possible—a *single* recorded natural acoustic sound of your choice. This sound source will have to be chosen very carefully, since it will determine every sonic aspect of the entire piece. The technical emphasis of the piece should be on the extensive alteration of the sound source material through tape manipulation and editing techniques, with, perhaps, some very minor usage of electronic processing techniques (filtering, reverberation, electronic switching, etc.). Consider the following works and their sound sources: Iannis Xenakis's *Concret P-H* (the sound of burning charcoal), Hugh LeCaine's *Dripsody* (a single drop of water), and Ilhan Mimaroglu's *Bowery Bum* (a plucked rubber band).

Composition Project No. 2

Produce a tape piece using a variety of recorded natural or acoustic sound sources and employing several tape manipulation and electronic processing techniques (tape editing and manipulation, filtering, frequency shifting/ring modulation, phasing/flanging, etc.—but no voltage-controlled techniques). The full signal processing resources of the electronic music studio should be used, as available. The choice of complementing or contrasting sound sources will determine the esthetic and technical approach to the piece.

Composition Project No. 3

Construct a short tape work from a *single* electronic signal source, using very extensive signal processing and some tape editing, as needed. The signal source may be an oscillator or several oscillators, a harmonic generator, white noise, a frequency shifted or ring modulated electronic sound, etc., and the processing techniques used may include any that are available in your studio. Consider Henri Pousseur's *Scambi* (using only a white noise source).

Composition Project No. 4

Compose a "pure" electronic, non-voltage-controlled tape work using only electronic sound sources (oscillators, harmonic generators, white noise, frequency shifters/ring modulators, etc.) and relying on extensive mixing and signal processing techniques, but only minimal tape editing and manipulation techniques. If possible, attempt to provide a clearly notated "score" for this work, one with enough detail to enable someone else to easily follow the progress of the music.

Composition Project No. 5

Produce a work on tape using any mixture of Musique Concrète and electronic (but non-voltage-controlled) sound sources and any kind of manipulation or processing techniques that are available. In this project, careful thought will have to be given to the timbral and temporal qualities of the sound sources used, and to the kind and amount of manipulation and processing that is to be employed, in order to avoid an aimless montage of unrelated sounds. Consider Stockhausen's *Gesang der Jünglinge* or Halim El Dabh's *Leiyla and the Poet*.

Composition Project No. 6

Produce a tape piece that is intended purely as an accompaniment for some other artistic medium. This might be a score for a television show, play, film, or even a museum showing. In any case, the specific needs and goals of the other medium will have to be fully considered.

Composition Project No. 7

Construct a piece for live performance consisting of only a *single* complex voltage-controlled synthesizer patch that will, with adjustment of the control settings, yield a distinctive, gradually changing work of any suitable duration. This piece will probably require a lot of studio experimentation using a fairly large complement of synthesizer modules. If a score for the work is produced, it will more than likely consist of a timed sequence of module setting changes.

Composition Project No. 8

Produce a live-performance work for voltage-controlled synthesizer (perhaps using some external electronic processing devices as well) in which the sounds produced by the live performer are converted (via envelope followers, pitch followers, Schmitt trigger generators, and sample/hold circuits) into control signals for operating the synthesizer. The final sounds may be a mixture of the performer's sounds and those of the synthesizer, or the synthesizer's resulting sounds alone.

Composition Project No. 9

Produce a live, "improvised" real-time voltage-controlled synthesis piece. Such a work should be of moderate duration (10 to 15 minutes) and should be at least generally "planned" as to its basic patching and manipulation/processing sequence, and its general sonic and textural shape. A further aspect of the work might include the "improvised" interaction of dancers or of a lighting technician. Regardless of the production forces involved, some kind of pre-performance decisions and some amount of actual rehearsal must be assumed.

Composition Project No. 10

Construct a work using a live performer or performers and some form of live tape manipulation and amplification/mixing system (amplification, real-time tape loops, various types of tape delay techniques, etc.). Such a work will normally require extensive rehearsal and some kind of score for the live performer(s) and the tape/mixer technician to work from during the performance.

Composition Project No. 11

Record the performance of a work for solo acoustic instrument (your own work or a work from the chosen instrument's repertoire). Edit, process, and manipulate the parts of this performance (the phrases, the sound gestures, even the individual notes) by tape transformation or any available electronic processing techniques to produce an entirely new "sound sculpture" in which none of the original sounds of the live performer are recognizable as such.

Composition Project No. 12

Compose a work involving the interaction or integration of a live performer or several live performers with taped electronic music, produced by whatever manipulation/ processing techniques are available and desired. This work may require accurate notation to coordinate the performer(s) and the tape, or the tape part may be considered only as a background to a freely flowing instrumental part. The choice of the instrument(s) to be used will be important in determining the type of complementary or contrasting electronic sounds and processings to be employed. If you are not well versed in the intricacies of the pitch control systems used in contemporary music, consider the use of non-pitched percussion instruments for the live performance parts. Consult any of Jacob Druckman's *Animus* works, the entire series of *Synchronisms* by Mario Davidovsky, or Morton Subotnik's *Serenade No. 3*.

Composition Project No. 13

Create a work emphasizing a variety of phasing and variable spatial location techniques and effects (ideally one using a four-channel playback system). This project will require consideration of the performance space to be used (whether it be a standard concert hall or a shopping mall!). All other aspects of the work should be reduced in importance in order to clearly focus upon and emphasize the subtle changes in phasing and spatial location that may be produced. Some tape manipulation techniques (such as multiple tape loops and echo/delay effects) may be effective. Many of the "process music" pieces of Steve Reich may serve as examples.

Composition Project No. 14

Compose a taped electronic music piece to be choreographed. The composing of works (electronic or otherwise) for dance presents some rather unique problems. The composer must consider the specific needs of the choreographer and the dancers (theme or story, rhythmic treatment, synchronization points or pulses, etc.).

Composition Project No. 15

Produce a multi-media work involving several simultaneously integrated art forms (film, dance, live performers, lighting, etc.). Such a work is often designed specifically for the performance space in which it is to be presented. It will involve extreme cooperation and collaboration of all the participants, as well as a good deal of planning and rehearsal. It is often helpful to begin with some kind of conceptual "plot" or theme, unifying the actions and interactions that are to take place.

Composition Project No. 16

Construct an environmental or interactive sound installation in a public space. Either of two general approaches may be adopted: 1) a number of microphones are positioned in a public space, and a continuously changing "piece" is produced in real-time by manipulating and processing the sounds picked up by the microphones and played back in the performance space; or 2) a completely preconceived work is presented in a public space so that the listener hears changes in the work in relation to his movement through the space itself. Alternatively, both of these approaches may be combined in the same work. Obviously, the exact nature of the performance space must be taken into account when devising such a work. Some pieces of this type have been produced that last for hours or even days. Consider some of the works of John Cage, such as *Variations IV*.

Bibliography

Bekesy, G. von. 1960. *Experiments in Hearing*. McGraw-Hill, New York.

Cross, Lowell M., ed., 1967. *A Bibliography of Electronic Music*. University of Toronto Press, Toronto.

———. "Electronic Music, 1948–53," *Perspectives of New Music* VII, No. 1, 32.

Helmholtz, Hermann von. 1863. *On the Sensations of Tone*, 4th ed., 1877. Trans. by A.J. Ellis, 2nd English ed., 1954. Dover, New York.

Roederer, Juan G. 1975. *Introduction to the Physics and Psychophysics of Music*, 2nd ed. Springer-Verlag, New York.

Runstein, Ronald E. 1974. *Modern Recording Techniques*. Howard W. Sams & Co., Inc., Indianapolis.

Stravinsky, Igor. 1974. *Poetics of Music*. Trans. by A. Knodel and I. Dahl. Harvard Univ. Press, Cambridge, Mass.

Woram, John M. 1976. *The Recording Studio Handbook*. Sagamore Publishing Co., Inc., Plainview, New York.

Zwicker, E. G. Flottorp, and S. S. Stevens. 1957. "Critical Bandwidth in Loudness Summation," *F. Acoustical Soc. of America*, Vol. 29, 548.

Index

Joel E. Naumann is an associate professor of music and director of the electronic studio at the University of Wisconsin, Madison. Formerly, he was on the faculties of Catholic University of America and Eastern Illinois University. He was the founder of the Washington Sinfonia and a past member/director of the Washington Contemporary Music Forum. He has been the recipient of Fulbright and NEA grants for composition and has had performances/commissions throughout the U.S., in England, Australia, and Europe.

James D. Wagoner is a composer member of the board of directors, Director of Publications, and a Programming Committee member of the Contemporary Music Forum, Washington, D.C. He has directed the electronic music studio and the Contemporary Music Ensemble at the Catholic Univesity of America as well as the chorus and orchestra at Texas Tech University. His compositions have been performed in many parts of the U.S. and he has lectured extensively on technology in modern music.